ELIZABETH DOROTHEA COLE BOWEN was born in 1899, the only child of Protestant Anglo-Irish parents. She grew up in Dublin and at her family house in Cork, Bowen's Court. When she was seven, her father, a lawyer, had a nervous breakdown, and she and her mother went to live with Anglo-Irish relatives in Kent. Her father recovered in 1911, but in 1912 her mother died of cancer. 'Bitha' was then looked after by her mother's sisters and spent her summers at Bowen's Court. She left school in 1917, went briefly to art school in 1919 and began to write stories when she was nineteen. In 1923 her first volume of stories, *Encounters*, was published, and she married Alan Cameron, who was working for the Ministry of Education in Northampton. In 1925 they moved to Oxford, and ten years later, when Cameron was made Secretary to the BBC School Broadcasting Council, to London, where they lived (with long visits to Bowen's Court) until 1951. Her house was a centre of literary life, and, in addition to her writing, she was involved in war work for the Ministry of Information and, after the war, in lecturing, broadcasting and British Council tours. In 1952 Alan Cameron died. Elizabeth Bowen lived at Bowen's Court until 1959, when, for want of money, the house was sold and soon after demolished. Throughout the fifties and sixties she was writer in residence at several American universities. When in England she lived in Oxford, and, from 1964 until her last illness, in Hythe. She died of lung cancer in 1973.

Between 1923 and 1968 she wrote ten novels and almost eighty short stories. Two of her novels are set in Ireland, *The Last September* (1929) and *A World of Love* (1955). Other fiction includes *The House in Paris* (1935), *The Heat of the Day* (1949), and her brilliant novels of the betrayal of innocence *To the North* (1932) and *The Death of the Heart* (1938). She also wrote a vast amount of literary journalism, and several non-fiction works, including the two published in this volume. Virago will publish a collection of her non-fiction writings, edited by Hermione Lee, in 1985.

D1390590

BOWEN'S COURT

Elizabeth Bowen

With a new Introduction by
Thomas McCarthy

THE COLLINS PRESS

Published by The Collins Press, Carey's Lane, The Huguenot
Quarter, Cork 1998

Bowen's Court first published in Great Britain by Longmans, Green
and Co. Ltd. in 1942

Front cover photograph of Elizabeth Bowen by Angus McBean

Every effort has been made to contact the photgrapher whose picture of Bowen's Court appears on the back cover. The publisher
wishes to apologise for the omission of the name and would be
grateful to be notified with it, so that it can be incorporated into the
next edition of the book.

Printed in Ireland by Colour Books Ltd., Dublin

Jacket design by Upper Case Ltd., Cornmarket Street, Cork

ISBN: 1-898256-44-6

CONTENTS

ILLUSTRATIONS

INTRODUCTION

The Anglo-Irish world has produced many gifted aristocrats but Elizabeth Bowen was one of the most magnetic and attractive of them all. She was a superb novelist and short-story writer, possibly the most gifted of that London group that included such luminaries as Rosamund Lehmann and Cyril Connolly. She was also a brilliant talker, despite her speech impediment, and a faithful friend to many of the disorientated intellectuals of the mid-century.

Her dinner parties were as famous as her literary methods. Personalities as different as Eddie Sackville-West, Molly Keane, Sean O'Faolain and A.L. Rowse were entertained in her County Cork mansion in its declining years. All felt themselves drawn to her as if they were musicians in an orchestral performance. Charles Ritchie, the Canadian diplomat who was based in London during the War, wrote lovingly in *The Siren Years* about Bowen's personality:

'Elizabeth has been going to an Austrian psychoanalyst to be cured of her stammer (which is so much part of her). So far it seems to me that she has told him nothing while he has told her the story of his life. This hardly surprises me ... Of what is her magic made? What is the spell she has cast on me? ... I have been discovering more and more of her generous nature, her wit and funniness, the stammering flow of her enthralling talk.'

It is unlikely that Elizabeth Bowen could ever trust her memory enough to reveal the story of her life. Memory, for a writer, is far too ambivalent, far too useful and impersonal, to be sacrificed whole. Writing changes the nature of one's past. The past is not so much a country as a series of countries, a victim of the changing writerly activity: 'Almost no experience, however much simplified by the distance of time, is to be vouched for as being wholly my own – did I live through that, or was I told that it happened, or did I read it?' ('Out of a Book', 1946)

The reticence of Bowen under psychoanalysis leads us directly to the license that Bowen allows herself as historian and custodian of memory. Part of the attraction of *Bowen's Court* lies in the subjectivity of its remembrance. This book, now published in her native Cork, is beautiful because it often reads like an historical novel. The history is accurate, the heraldry is correct, but the personalitles are fleshed out. Irish history is a room that becomes animated when Elizabeth makes her stylish entrance.

She writes about her distant ancestors as if they were relatives who had just been left on the Mallow train. Dealing with Jane Cole who married the second Henry Bowen in 1716, she writes: 'Perhaps they strolled outdoors in the long white Irish twilights or in steely evenings after the rain – Jane holding the hem of her long stiff skirts clear of the damp ... Henry would tell Jane again about the treasure, and she would, vaguely, reply, what a pity it was not found.'

The Anglo-Irish author of *Bowen's Court* was born in Dublin in 1899. She was the only daughter of Henry Cole Bowen, the reluctant heir to a County Cork estate and Big House and author of *Statutory Land Purchase in Ireland*. She was Dublin-born but her summer-place was Cork: 'I used to believe that winter lived always in Dublin, while summer lived always in County Cork. By taking the train from Kingsbridge to Mallow one passed from one season's kingdom into the other's', she wrote in *Seven Winters*. The idyllic part of childhood did not last long, for when she was seven years old her father suffered a nervous breakdown. She moved to Kent with her mother and waited for her brilliant father to recover. Henry did recover by 1911, but a year later her mother died. Elizabeth's childhood and adolescence were therefore disturbed and fractured. She left school in 1917 and began writing fiction a year later. Her first volume of stories, *Encounters*, was published in 1923. Those stories were precocious, very clever and stylish, and owing a great deal to E.M.

Forster's style. But she quickly developed her own inimitable, dense and yet crisp, writing style in a further ten novels and nearly one hundred stories. Her most perfect and intoxicating works are *The Last September, The House in Paris* and *The Heat of the Day*. The epicurian reader should go straight from *Bowen's Court* to *The Last September* for the sheer pleasure of her sustained narrative and poetic powers.

The Big House, but especially Bowen's Court, became a symbol as well as a setting in the fiction of Elizabeth Bowen. The great houses were a bold social and political gesture built in spite of history; they remain in the Irish landscape as an admirable performance, a pure victory of style over necessity. The irony of Anglo-Irish life is that it seems most beautiful when perceived at some point of decline. Decline was part of its unassailable elegance. The gentry, and Southern Irish Anglicans in general, were born for remembrance. Their children took to autobiography as naturally as they'd taken to horse-riding. What characterises so many of the Anglo-Irish, from Bishop Berkeley to Bowen, is that dramatic self-awareness so conspicuous in poets. Under siege, they developed a deep soul.

The political position of the Ascendancy was always untenable. Ironically, the Penal Laws may have done as much damage to Protestant interests as to the defeated Catholic Irish. As Elizabeth Bowen has observed in this book, the Catholic Irish developed a powerful trading sector, awash with the cash-piles developed through trade. But they were banned from the lending-markets. As well as this, the Ascendancy of the small Protestant nation was based on a series of injustices, from the Cromwellian confiscations to the Acts of Settlement. Even if the Land Acts of the nineteenth century had not happened, the general development of majority Parliamentary politics would have diminished the power of the class into which Elizabeth was born. Yet the Anglo-Irish were in no sense merely a garrison like the English garrisons in India. On the contrary, the gentry in Ireland were absolutely rooted to the localities where they were proprietors. They identified with their own Irish valleys and neighbourhoods, and were as localised in their enthusiasms as the most stay-at-home Irish farmer. The opening chapter in *Bowen's Court* is as good an example as one could hope for to illustrate that deep sense of geography and location within the Anglo-Irish mind:

'In no other direction lies any town or larger village, except Shanballymore, for seven or eight miles. Mallow is thirteen, Fermoy twelve, Mitchelstown eight and Doneraile seven miles from Bowen's Court. Inside and about the house and in the demesne woods you feel transfixed by the surrounding emptiness; it gives depth to the silence, quality to the light ...'

Elizabeth begins, then, acutely conscious of location; and conscious of the power of the house within the landscape. Being a mid-century London intellectual as well as the custodian of an Irish Big House, Elizabeth inherited and embodied the friction of Anglo-Irishness. She embraced the dual loyalties and the inherited contradictions. She writes, 'In the decade following 1760 the Anglo-Irish became aware of themselves as a race. The "Protestant nation" had been born already, it was to be christened at its coming of age. It was growing up with judgement, into the power to place its loyalties where and as it willed. This was the Anglo-Ireland that was to present, for England, an alarming parallel with America.'

But the Anglo-Irish were no sooner defined than they were defied. The fifty years between 1798 and 1848 were politically hectic and turbulent. Bowen's Court was attacked in 1798, but Elizabeth focuses upon the (imagined) feelings of fear and siege within the Farahy household. The whole of that era, a truly momentous one that scorched the edges of Ireland with French revolutionary ideas, is refined by Elizabeth Bowen into a startling image:

'There was a pear tree a few yards down from the southeast corner of Bowen's Court – one surviving shoot of it is in bud as I write. The morning after the raid, the tree was found to bear charnel fruit: a dead man, who must have climbed up to fire, stayed jammed in the fork of two boughs.'

Elizabeth moves quickly past the Act of Union: 'I cannot discuss the Union; it was a bad deal ... Castlereagh finally engineered it; the vast sums laid out in bribes and in buying out boroughs were charged to Ireland's account ... Prominent Anglo-Irish were bought, to their lasting dishonour, by peerages, by advancements in the peerage, and by sums down.'

Her political opinions could be remarkably sharp, and sharply expressed. If she sounds like an Irish Republican in some of her comments, it is not because she has turned against her class, but that she has an overwhelming sense of fair play. Indeed, some of her comments on the collapse of Grattan's Irish dream and the creative enthusiasm of the Patriot Party are rueful. The Bowens may have been too far away from the centre of power to have been offered peerages or sums down.

The Bowens did seem to have a talent for remaining on the edge of things. When the original Colonel Bowen, descended from the insular Gower ap Owens, came over to Ireland with Cromwell he took a pair of hawks with him. During a meeting with Cromwell he is reputed to have paid more attention to his hawks than to the Lord Protector. But Colonel Bowen survived the tiff with Cromwell to inherit nearly eight hundred acres of Farahy land 'in Satisfaction of his arrears' from the Cromwellian settlement. His son, John, married the wealthy heiress, Mary Nicholls of Kilbolane Castle. Kilbolane would feature in many Bowen conversations for the next one hundred and fifty years. Bowen cousins would sue and counter-sue over buried treasure.

Litigation was in their blood. For years, right through the eighteenth century, the Bowens would concentrate on another lawsuit, *Bowen v. Evans*, over Kilbolane bawn and Brandon Castle.

Bowen's Court itself was not built until the 1770s. 1775 was the date cut in the stone. ' At the same time, Henry found himself short of money, and it may have looked, at one heart-sickening moment, as though the roof would never go on at all ... Henry, unwillingly, cut down the original plan: the north-east corner had to be sacrificed. The Italians from Cork were paid off and went their way ...' Elizabeth reports humorously on the whole episode.

But not before she reports with pride the Classical austerity of her family home: 'The great bare block – not a creeper touches it – is broken regularly by windows: in the south facade there are twenty (the hall door takes the place of one of them), in the west side eighteen, in the shorter east side six, in the north back six. All of this expanse of glass, with its different reflections, does much to give Bowen's Court character. When the sun is low, in the early mornings or evenings, the house seems, from the outside, to be riddled with light.'

The Bowens lived on in their Big House for generations, until the fateful marriage of Elizabeth's urbane and very urban parents. With her parents' marriage, and her father's legal obligations in Dublin, 'a break came in the house's continuous human life'. Bowen's Court lay empty for long stretches: 'Fires were lit, but to warm nothing but air.' Elizabeth's father lived the obligatory very social life of a barrister among Dublin friends, many of them companions from St Columba's and Trinity College. Henry Cole Bowen loved Dublin life, the theatres, the Law Library and the new cinemas. But it was not only the Big House that was drained on it's will to survive. Misfortune stalked the Bowens. Elizabeth lost her aunt to consumption and her younger uncle went down with the *Titanic*. 'He had spent the last Sunday with us before he sailed ... So, the *Titanic* disaster was the first black crack across the surface of *exterior* things.'

After her own husband's death in 1952 Elizabeth Bowen returned to County Cork. She stayed on in Bowen's Court for seven years. In the end, lack of money (that great organiser of our lives) forced her to sell out. The house was bought by a local farmer, and, in 1960, was demolished. It was as simple as that. Elizabeth spent the last twelve years of her life as she had spent her childhood; uprooted, wandering, reading and learning. She died in February 1973.

Bowen's Court, the book, is truly the house that has survived. As Hermione Lee pointed out in her 1984 *Virago* Introduction, Elizabeth drew upon many sources for this book, quite apart from the Bowen family papers; Jonah Barrington's *Personal Sketches Of His Own Time* (1827), Dorothea Herbert's *Retrospections 1770-1789* and Maurice Healy's *The Old Munster Circuit* (1939). But it is important to read this book as a filial act of memory, a truly excellent and unparalleled memorial to Anglo-Irish life. It could be seen also as a partial rebuttal of the politics presented in *The Last September*, that extremely clever, Bloomsbury-like treatment of Irish history. Big House contradictions are exposed mercilessly in that early novel.

Writing *Bowen's Court* during the Second World War when 'either everything mattered or nothing mattered', Elizabeth was more loyal and faithful to her people. Even her treatment of Lord Orrery, who was a merciless confiscator of Catholic land and a persecutor of Cork Quakers like Exham, Lowe and William Penn, is far too gentle. 'He had not much with which to reproach himself' she says blandly. But she was writing this family history at a time when generosity was called for. At a time when England faced the might of European Fascism on its own, and when many Anglo-Irish had once more joined in battle against a Continental evil, the Irish Ascendancy recovered a great deal of its moral strength and noble character.

Bowen's Court is one of the most complex and beautiful books produced by Irish memory. It's author was a magnetic person, a truly modern woman, displaced and yet deeply rooted. I'll always remember how Molly Keane spoke about Elizabeth Bowen; with reverence and love and a kind of fearful admiration. Many have fallen under her spell, even in recent years: Hermione Lee, Victoria Glendinning, and the broadcaster and pilgrim Donncha O Dulaing who wrote his M.A. thesis on Elizabeth Bowen.

Through this book one enters the hall door of Anglo-Irish

life, to wander across that prodigious gallery of gestures and misunderstandings, ghosts and litigation. It is part of the triumph of imaginative life that this book now endures. It is Elizabeth Bowen's third Bowen mansion, after old Kilbolane and Bowen's Court. It endures as an act of remembrance, long after the battles and repossessions. The written word has outlasted all the mortar and cut-stone.

THOMAS MCCARTHY

BOWEN'S COURT

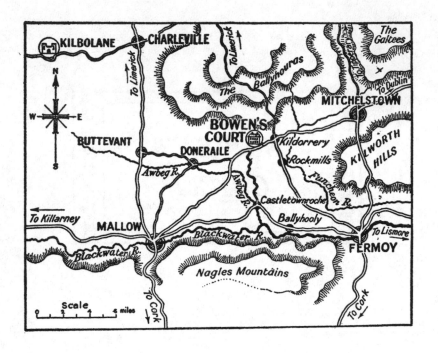

BOWEN'S COURT

UP IN THE NORTH-EAST CORNER OF COUNTY CORK IS A STRETCH
of limestone country — open, airy, not quite flat; it is just perceptibly tilted from north to south, and the fields undulate in
a smooth flowing way. Dark knolls and screens of trees, the
network of hedges, abrupt stony ridges, slate glints from roofs
give the landscape a featured look — but the prevailing impression is, emptiness. This is a part of Ireland with no lakes, but
the sky's movement of clouds reflects itself everywhere as it
might on water, rounding the trees with bloom and giving the
grass a sheen. In the airy silence, any sound travels a long way.
The streams and rivers, sunk in their valleys, are not seen until
you come down to them.

Across the base of this tract of country the river Blackwater
flows west to east, into the County Waterford. South of the
Blackwater, from which they rise up steeply, Nagles Mountains cut off any further view. Behind Fermoy town these
mountains end in a steep bluff: the main road from Cork to
Dublin crosses the bridge at Fermoy, then runs due north over
the Kilworth hills that close in this tract on the east. North of
Kilworth lies Mitchelstown; above Mitchelstown the Galtees
rise to powerful coloured peaks. Galtymore, the third highest
mountain in Ireland, dominates this north-east corner of Cork.
After their climax in Galtymore the Galtees drop into foot-

hills, the Ballyhouras — this range of small shapely mountains borders the County Limerick and slides gently south, in promontories of bogland, into the County Cork fields. The Ballyhouras, forming its northern boundary, face down on Nagles Mountains across the open country of which I speak. The two blue lines, with space and a hidden river between them, run roughly parallel.

To the west extends a long flattish distance, beyond which, though only on very clear days, the Kerry Mountains are to be seen. The country in which Bowen's Court stands is, thus, squared in by hills or mountains on three sides, but melts off into the light and clouds of the west.

This limestone country is pitted with kilns and quarries; the hard white bye-roads run over rock. Our two rivers, the Funcheon and the Awbeg, have hollowed out for themselves, on their courses south to the Blackwater, rocky twisting valleys. Here and there down the valleys the limestone makes cliffs or amphitheatres. In places the rivers flow between steep woods; in places their valleys are open, shallow and lush — there are marshy reaches trodden by cattle, fluttered over by poplars from the embanked lanes. Herons cross these in their leisurely flopping flight; water peppermint grows among the rushes; the orchis and yellow wild iris flower here at the beginning of June. Lonely stone bridges are come on round turns of the stream. and old keeps or watch towers, called castles, command the valleys: some are so broken and weathered that they look like rocks, some have been almost blotted out by the ivy; some are intact shells whose stairs you can still climb.

There are mills on both rivers — one great mill is in ruins — and swans on the Funcheon and the Awbeg. Not far from the Awbeg, under Spenser's castle, there is a marsh where seagulls breed in spring.

The country is not as empty as it appears. Roads and boreens between high hedges, sunk rivers, farms deep in squares of sheltering trees all combine by their disappearance to trick the eye. Only mountainy farmhouses, gleaming white on their fields reclaimed from the bog, and façades of chapels on hills or hillocks, show. The country conceals its pattern of life, which can only wholly be seen from an aeroplane. This is really country to fly over — its apparent empty smoothness is full of dips and creases. From the air you discover unknown reaches of river, chapels, schools, bridges, forlorn graveyards, interknit by a complex of untravelled roads.

On Sundays you get an idea of the population: everybody appears. The roads converging on chapels teem with people going to mass. Horses and traps turn out of impossibly narrow lanes; cyclists freewheel with a whirring rattle down from the mountainy farms. Dark Sundayfied figures balance on stepping-stones, take tracks through plantations, leg it over the stiles. After midday mass the streets of the villages give out a static hum. On holy days and on fair days the scene also becomes living and dark; race days, big matches or *feishes* bring all the hired cars out, and people out on the banks to watch the cars. At funerals the *cortèges* are very long. Early on weekday mornings the roads rattle with ass carts taking milk cans up to the creameries. And from dusk on young men gather at the crossroads and bridges and stay talking, faceless, well into the dark. Sometimes they light fires. On fine summer nights there is dancing, twice a week, on boards put down at crossroads or outside villages. Lights burn late in cottages near the dancing, and the music gives the darkness a pulse. When the music stops, the country rustles with movement of people going home. . . . No, it is not lack of people that makes the country seem empty. It is an inherent emptiness of its own.

At points round the edge of this district are its three principal towns — Mallow, Fermoy, Mitchelstown. And Doneraile, though not larger than a large village, has a comely, set-up and urban air. Mallow and Fermoy are both on the Blackwater; Doneraile lies on the Awbeg some eight miles north-east of

Mallow; Mitchelstown is ten miles north of Fermoy. Fermoy is nineteen miles along the river from Mallow, and Mallow, in the south-west corner of the tract I speak of, is twenty-one miles from Mitchelstown — which, in the north-east corner, is near where County Tipperary begins. So, the Mallow-Mitchelstown main road, crossing this tract transversely, is the major axis of our neighbourhood. The minor axis is the Fermoy-Limerick road, which crosses the other at Kildorrery.

Our road to Doneraile, uneven but pleasant, leaves the Mallow-Mitchelstown road not far from Bowen's Court gates. Doneraile main street, wide, with colour-washed houses, starts uphill (as you enter from our direction) from the Awbeg bridge. The houses are backed by demesne trees; near the bridge stands the urbane Protestant church. In the great days of the Doneraile neighbourhood the line of gentlemen's carriages outside this church on Sundays used (they say) to be a mile long. Doneraile was, till the Union, a parliamentary borough, sending, by right of a charter from Charles II, two burgesses to the Dublin parliament. It was a great place for weavers, and had a marble quarry. . . . Below the bridge the Awbeg curls off through the willowy Doneraile Court demesne. In Charles I's reign Sir William St. Leger — who, as Lord-President of Munster, was to suffer much from his own anxious integrity in the succeeding wars — bought the estate and castle from Edmund Spenser's son. Less anxious St. Legers put up the present Court, whose stucco front looks down a perspective to the Awbeg. In a small alcoved room in Doneraile Court, a Miss St. Leger became the only lady Free Mason. The popular story is that she hid in a clock, her family say she happened to fall asleep on a couch: anyhow, whether by design or accident, she overheard what the Free Masons were saying, so they made her one of their number. In her portrait the lady, who later married an Aldworth, has a dogged, impassible face. I support the idea of the clock.

Lying along the Awbeg, with its rocks and willows, the demesne of Doneraile is a lyrical place. Carriage drives loop about; there are bamboo groves, a soporific lime walk, a clotted lily pond. The demesne was dear to several Elizabethans — Raleigh, Spenser and Sydney all conversed here, strolling along the lime walk or reclining " among the coolly shade of the green alders," Edmund Spenser recalls. To Spenser such hours must have been manna. He liked little in Ireland: his position was sinister and desolating — he was a civil servant, living on granted land. His castle, Kilcolman, lies two miles north-west of Doneraile, on an exposed plateau under the Ballyhouras; the marsh where gulls breed was once his smiling lake — but he never cared for its smile. Kilcolman keep, a torn-open ruin, still stands; winds race round it at every time of the year. The view is of Ireland at its most intimidating — the marsh, the heartless mountains with their occasional black frown. That landscape fulfilled, for Spenser, its conveyed threat: the castle was burnt by the Irish in his absence, and one of his sons, an infant, died in the fire.

Spenser never came back to that unholy countryside full of holy wells and of castles that had fallen before his. He had, however, in his years at Kilcolman, added two cantos to the *Faerie Queene* — the Awbeg is the " gentle Mulla " of that poem, as every Doneraile person knows. And that country at the foot of the Ballyhouras is *Faerie Queene* country — dazzling, for all its woody shadows, and in its openness mysterious. You could not but love the Awbeg itself, even though it might flow through a hated land. It glitters with Spenser's gentler memories, and the flames of Kilcolman were never reflected there. It flows through woods and gardens, through water meadows, under fantastic rocks into the gorge where it joins the Blackwater. Where the two rivers meet stands Bridgetown Abbey, burned and desolated by Cromwell's men.

Along the foot of the mountains near Kilcolman spread the beeches of the Ballyvonare demesne. It was a Harold Barry of Ballyvonare, a Catholic gentleman, who, put in a testing position by the Doneraile Trials, emerged with unstained honour, as I shall show. Canon Sheehan, the parish priest of Doneraile and a beloved humane man, was the novelist of this Ballyhoura region. His *Glenanaar* is about the aftermath of the Doneraile Conspiracy and the subsequent wanderings of Owen Daly, informer and lost soul.

Eight miles south-west of Doneraile lies Mallow. Built along a lip of the Blackwater valley this town turns its back on the river, of which it does not make much. A bridge, of strategic importance in many wars because it commands one principal pass to Cork, spans the river at the foot of the main street: only *faubourgs* of Mallow are at the other side. At the top of the town, on a hill, stands the railway station — an important junction on the Dublin-Cork main line. Mallow was such a pivot in Bowen family history that I shall wait to speak more of it in its place. Its present appearance is congested and dusty: in view of its stylish past it lacks style — though it has town houses built for the Mallow seasons, and the raised pavements, jumbled shop-fronts and hogbacked course of the main street do at least give it character. It features sweetshops, chemists, cinemas, banks; the Protestant church stands back down an avenue, but the Catholic church has an imposing façade and a fine roll of echoing bells. The Spa is in a chalet behind a row of poplars just outside the town. Mallow is generally jammed with traffic, for it marks the convergence of several important roads — to Killarney and through to the rest of Kerry, to Limerick (through Charleville), to Cork and Blarney, to Dublin (through Mitchelstown). And at the station you change for Tralee and Killarney, or for stations along the line to Rosslare — Fermoy, Lismore and Waterford. In fact, Mallow is the key to the South and West, and her future looks likely to lie with tourism. After a phase of decay, then of political burnings, the town is on the ascendent again.

Once, you did not pass through Mallow, you came to stop. From all over the South they came to this Bath of Ireland. The place was the hub of local society, and all Anglo-Irish houses, in a fifteen-mile radius, built their gates as far as possible up the road to Mallow. Gentry swarmed there, the smaller racketty peers and the parasites that went along with the pack. Cosmopolitan visitors did, as I shall show, find Mallow open to criticism; they complained of the poorness of the accommodation and found the fun provincial and rough-house. It was a nerveless, ruthless, sink-or-swim society, no doubt a bit silly — look at the Rakes of Mallow. But the fun, while it lasted, was good enough for my people — till one Henry Bowen fell foul of its limitations and went away to live in Bath, where he died.

Much blood has been shed round Mallow bridge. This was Desmond territory: just inside the present Castle demesne gates stands the magnificent shell of the castle built by the Earl of Desmond, lost in the Earl's rebellion, fortified by the English, granted by Queen Elizabeth, with the manor of Mallow, to a Sir Thomas Norris, burnt by Lord Castlehaven and the Confederates. Sir Thomas Norris's heiress married a Sir John Jephson; the Jephson Norris family put up the present Castle, Jacobean in manner, on a lawn commanding the Desmond shell. The demesne, looking at Nagles Mountains, runs down the river below the bridge.

Fermoy, nineteen miles down the Blackwater from Mallow, has its main square open on to the river. A hill covered with trees and light grey religious buildings makes a pretty backdrop to the square and the town. The road from Cork comes downhill diagonally, crosses the bridge and goes on up a wide perspective to the Protestant church, round which it swerves to the right. These heights north of the river are crowned by villas, the railway station, some acres of burnt-out barracks.

At Fermoy the Blackwater, swelled by the Awbeg waters, is at its most majestic and glassy. There are weirs above and below the bridge, then the river sweeps off round a curve to Lismore. Down the south side, the town side, runs a water-front overhung by windows, shaded by small trees. Though Fermoy in detail looks sometimes brittle and dusty, it has an excellent, open and airy plan. Its projector (for Fermoy owes its unity to being one man's idea) knew how to make the most of his site — the great reach of river, profuse trees, sociable hills. This town was projected, built and began at once to prosper when Mallow was already on the decline: up to the last decade of the eighteenth century there had been nothing here but an inn and a few cabins near the already important bridge. Then in 1791 John Anderson, a Scotsman who had amassed a fortune trading in Cork, bought the site and began to lay out the town. He did more: he soon bid boldly for its prosperity — with the start of the 1798 rebellion the British Government poured its troops into Ireland and let it be known that it meant to maintain them there; a new military station was, accordingly, wanted, and John Anderson, by contracting to build barracks, secured the military for Fermoy. On the plateau on top of the north hill the new stylish barracks went up, on a large scale. The military moved in, liked life and brought in money: Fermoy became a booming garrison town. A line of genteel houses for the officers' ladies ran down the perspective from the church to the bridge; more little houses ran up the Cork hill. Regimental society attracted many new families into the neighbourhood; little gentlemen's places, for entertaining, were terraced over the pretty view. Also, entranced by the military hum and glitter, landowners who had looked only to Mallow now started veering towards Fermoy. So, throughout the nineteenth century and on into the twentieth up to the 1921 Treaty, there was a dashing and sentimental intercourse (best pictured in Russian stories, I think) between officers and the country house families. The steamy softness of the Blackwater valley created a local temperament. Hunting and fishing made Fermoy popular with the Englishmen; there were croquet and tennis, sweet pointless flirtations, balls. Though pleasure may not be very much, so much of the human heart goes into it that its memory can command tears.

When the Treaty brought the removal of the British troops from the South one mode of feeling and living came to an end. The last years of the garrison had been tense, violent and dreadful; the whole position became increasingly false — so the end, when it did come, was for the best. In the Civil War that followed the Treaty the barracks were burnt — they extend now, acres of ruins, over the north heights, along the railway line. They give out a strong feeling of loss and waste; cracked pediments, waving grass in the windows, warped girders frighten the eye. But downhill Fermoy, for which loss was predicted, enjoys quite a new phase of hardy life: the square and the main street show animation, figures group on the bridge, as they always did, and Cork-Dublin traffic streams steadily through.

The road running north from Fermoy to Mitchelstown goes through Kilworth Camp on its glaring hills. Mitchelstown's long, wide main street heads for the Galtees; the town has the coloured background of Galtymore, and, at the foot of the immense mountain, is set in a belt of green, watered plain. Arthur Young, in fact, said of Mitchelstown that it had " a situation worthy of any capital in Europe." The plan is fairly spacious — the Kingstons' taste — there are two squares and some fine perspectives of trees; almost all the houses are painted — pink of all shades, buff, lemon, pistachio green, chalk blue. When sun blazes on to the town and the mountain is in full colour, all this dazzles the eye. Mountain rains, more frequently, blot the whole scene out.

Mitchelstown is a farmers' town: the country people for miles round come in for fairs and shopping. The shops other than chemists' — of which there are many — smell of porter, black bootleather, green bacon, shag and calico. At Mitchelstown, north-east County Cork people feel at the outpost of country that they know — roads go under the mountains or up through the passes into Tipperary and Limerick, but these two counties are another world.

All this once formed part of the extensive possessions of the
White Knight, called Clongibbon. The White Knight enjoyed
more or less absolute power — he hanged a personal enemy on
a demesne tree. He built the original castle, which was lost to
insurgents, occupied by the English, later besieged successfully
by the Lord Castlehaven who burned the castle at Mallow. The
White Knight's only child and heiress, Margaret Fitzgerald,
married Sir William Fenton; the only child of that marriage
was, again, a daughter, who married a Kingston and brought
him the White Knight's lands. A Kingston became a viscount,
a later Kingston an earl. In 1823 the Lord Kingston called Big
George once more rebuilt the Castle, at top speed and on a vast
showy plan: his object was to entertain George IV, but the
King after all never arrived. The new pale cut-stone structure,
modelled on Windsor, posed on a plateau, dazzled the South of
Ireland and was much written up. Inside it was Gothic, with
long waxy galleries and chains of brocade-panelled saloons.
The demesne wall is said to be of greater circumference than
any other demesne wall in Ireland. This Castle, however, lasted
for less than a hundred years; it was occupied and afterward
burnt by Republican forces in 1922. For a year or two longer
the shell stood, then its cut-stone facings were bought and
carted away to build a new wing for Mount Mellary monas-
tery. Stripped, the unseemly inner structure of rubble was left,
then decently taken down: the Castle site is now little
more than a mound; the demesne is in plough or pasture, with
one or two playing fields. One avenue, now little more than
a track, runs downhill to the gates that open on to Kings-
square.

Three sides of Kings-square are occupied by Kingston College — a Kingston foundation for indigent gentlepeople of the
Protestant faith. The twelve gentlemen and eighteen ladies
each receive a dwelling-house and annuity. The dwellings, uni-
fied into one low stone façade and having a chapel and chaplain's house in the middle, look into the square planted with

limes: only ennui appears to trouble this retreat, and ennui, I
fear, has increased since the Castle came to an end. The august
come-and-go from the Castle gates could be, and was, from the
College closely observed. And there used to be tennis tourna-
ments on the Kings-square lawns, brightened by cavalry officers from Kilworth and the Kingstons' young lady visitors.
These days there is silence and lassitude; the square rings only
with voices of children playing in the unkempt grass.

The other, the market, square off the main street is still all
animation, on fair-days. At its foot stands a patriot's statue; this
was the scene of the shooting that started the rally: "*Remember Mitchelstown!*" The handsome Catholic church, built by
Big George Kingston, stands uphill at the opposite side of the
street. On one road out of the town is a ruined barrack, on another a ruined fever hospital. On the Clogheen road is the prosperous creamery, and the factory that sends out Galtee cheese.

So much for the four towns, each at a point round the edge
of our area. Then, there are the villages.

The road I have called our major axis, the through road to
Mallow from Mitchelstown, crosses our two rivers, the Funcheon and the Awbeg. Once over the Funcheon bridge, eight
miles west of Mitchelstown, one goes steeply uphill to pass
through Kildorrery. Kildorrery is so placed as to be a landmark for miles. Cross-shaped, and of some size, it has the characteristics of a hill-village — rather sad weathered houses, sky
seen through arches, draughty streets, an exposed graveyard, a
chapel launched over the distance like a ship. Though its name
means church of the oak grove, one can see no trees: the Ballyhouras are very near, to the north. Only when Kildorrery
stands full in the sunset has it an at all celestial smile. It contains a large white creamery, a dispensary, a Civic Guard barrack, a post office, public houses and shops. Fairs are held twice
a year; between times circuses or travelling cinemas pitch in
the fair field. Its crossroads is not empty of traffic: as I said, the

road from Fermoy into County Limerick here crosses the
Mitchelstown-Mallow road.

Passing straight through Kildorrery (on the road to Mallow)
one drops downhill again into Farahy. Tucked rather deeply
into a crease of trees, this small place is unexpectedly come
upon: here are a bridge over the small Farahy river, two or
three shops, some yellow and pink cottages, the lower avenue
gate-lodge of Bowen's Court, a Protestant rectory and a Protestant church — this last set some distance back among trees.
After Farahy the road goes uphill again, flanked by the Bow-
en's Court demesne wall, past the Bowen's Court upper gates
and through a tunnel of beech.

From this reach of shadow the road emerges into the open
heart of the region of which I spoke at first. Space, then a line
of mountains lie on its either hand; here you feel the tilt of the
country south from the Ballyhouras; this is no longer the road
to somewhere, simply *a road* — something dazzling, abstract
and taut. Here, under the beat of air and light, you see the plas-
tic emptiness of the fields round it, and hear nothing but the
humming telegraph wires.

The turn to Castletownroche, through Shanballymore,
leaves the Mallow road a mile beyond Farahy. This byeway
twists and dips between high hedges, so that for miles you cannot see where you are. Shanballymore chapel, the willow flats
of the Awbeg, the castellated gateway of Anne's Grove are
landmarks on this long, soporific drive. Then the road mounts
above the Awbeg valley: round a turn the view opens out like
a fan and you can see Castletownroche — pale-coloured,
wooded, built up and down a hill, with the Awbeg curling
away round a steep rock. The bloom on the trees, the thin
smoke mounting against them, the light rocky reflection cast in
the river make the village seem to smile in the afternoon.

The main road to Fermoy from Mallow turns through
Castletownroche, dropping down a hill between cottages: it is
here deflected inland from the lip of the Blackwater valley by

the steep transverse gorge in which the two rivers join. This gorge is crossed only, near Bridgetown ruins, by a railway viaduct of alarming height — the Rosslare line from Mallow goes this way. In a heavily wooded last reach of the Awbeg, between Castletownroche and the viaduct, Castle Widenham stands on its almost-island of rock. It is a mansion refaced Gothic, stuck to the flank of an old keep — the keep of the castle of the Roches, once lords of Fermoy. In 1580 the Roches were interfered with by Captain Walter Raleigh, who tried to charge them with treason — the charge was never proved. Then, in the Cromwellian Wars, a fiery Lady Roche, in her husband's absence, defended the castle against Lord Broghill, who bombarded it from the opposite heights. The Roches, refusing to compound with Cromwell, lost the castle, which, having been by Broghill almost completely shattered, was given to some one else. Later, a barrack for a company of soldiers was put in the village: it is now in decay. All round Castletownroche there are limestone quarries, and there are caves in the cliffs below Castle Widenham. . . . Farther down the Fermoy road lies Ballyhooly, a village with a Blackwater bridge.

It will have been seen that this is a country of ruins. Lordly or humble, military or domestic, standing up with furious gauntness, like Kilcolman, or shelving weakly into the soil, ruins feature the landscape — uplands or river valleys — and make a ghostly extra quarter to towns. They give clearings in woods, reaches of mountain or sudden turns of a road a meaning and pre-inhabited air. Ivy grapples them; trees grow inside their doors; enduring ruins, where they emerge from ivy, are the limestone white-grey and look like rocks. Fallen-in farms and cabins take only some years to vanish. Only major or recent ruins keep their human stories; from others the story quickly evaporates. Some ruins show gashes of violence, others simply the dull slant of decline. In this Munster county so often

fought over there has been cruelty even to the stones; military
fury or welling-up human bitterness has vented itself on unknowing walls. Campaigns and " troubles," taking their tolls,
subsiding, each leave a new generation of ruins to be reab-
sorbed slowly into the natural scene.

Not all these are ruins of wars: where there has not been violence there has been abandonment. Mansions, town houses,
farmhouses, cottages have often been left to die — and very few
people know the story of the bitter necessity. That air of waste
and nonchalance about Irish ruins is an irritant to the present-
day English mind. But when fancy loomed larger than eco-
nomics, when fine degrees of melancholy were sought, travel-
lers turned on our ruins a much more complaisant eye. Even
Arthur Young, with his wish for reclamation and order, felt
the merit of bones at Muckross Abbey. He wrote:

Entered the garden and viewed Muckross Abbey, one of the
most interesting scenes I ever saw. It is the ruin of a considerable
abbey, built in Henry the VI's time, and so entire, that if it were
more so, though the building would be more perfect, the ruin
would be less pleasing. It is half obscured in the shade of some ven-
erable ash trees; ivy has given the picturesque circumstance, which
that plant alone can confer, while the broken walls and ruined turrets throw over it " *The last mournful graces of decay*." Heaps of
skulls and bones scattered about, with nettles, briars and weeds
sprouting in tufts from the loose stones, all unite to raise those
melancholy impressions which are the merits of such scenes, and
which can scarcely anywhere be felt more completely.

That was in the late eighteenth-century daylight. Now, we
no longer seek the " picturesque circumstance " — in a crepus-
cular world our nerves have enough to bear. In my childhood
Bridgetown and other abbeys were still in that state of nettles
and bones — raising any impressions you liked to have. Since,
the fine arches and broken lancets have been stripped of ivy and
shored up; on the inside ground, where families still bury, only
wired porcelain flowers rust in the kept grass. Most lay ruins,

however, remain in a state of unchecked decay. No one cares; they are used as shelters for cattle and, at any rate, do not spoil much land. By the roadsides, roofs of abandoned cabins sag in slowly; desolate farms rear chimneys out of the brambles, at the ends of silted-up boreens. Yes, ruins stand for error or failure — but in Ireland we take these as part of life.

When Protestants in a parish decline to a very low number the roof is taken off the Protestant church. Sometimes the church is no more than locked up, sometimes, as in the case of Rockmills (the first village on our road to Fermoy) the building is pared down to the spire. These voluntary ruins go to add to the list. The constabulary barracks or gentlemen's houses burnt before or after the Treaty have almost all been rebuilt — the houses often on a more modest plan. Round us, only Mitchelstown Castle has been erased forever, and only Convamore, on the Blackwater, still looks much as it must have looked the morning after the fire, that bleak spring morning of 1921. Each year a little more stucco drops off the Palladian front; rust eats a little further into the girders. The window-sockets continue to stare blindly at the superb view.

Arthur Young's host at Muckross, Mr. Herbert, was especially happy in having an abbey in his demesne. I know few demesnes, however, that do not contain *some* ruin — chapel, watch tower or massive keep. Set on lawns, these frowning derelict "castles" overtop the façades of Georgian homes. Strictly, they are antiques rather than ruins; their structures and stairs are sound; to them have often been added leaded roofs from which one looks at the view. They could play more part as annexes to family life if they were not so dark inside, and so intensely cold. As it is, they are used to house electric light plants, to store unused furniture, apples, bicycles, rabbit hutches, collections of assegais. Sometimes the castles stand some way from the houses, in which case they are less useful but make romantic objectives for strolls. . . . We north-east County Cork gentry began rather roughly, as settlers, as I

shall show. Few of us have been wealthy enough to expand
expensive fancies — perspectives, obelisks, grottos, constructed
waterfalls, temples — over our demesnes. We planted trees effectively, but beyond that have had to rely on nature and on
antiquity. Contours of valleys, reflecting rivers, near mountains have given us something better than the most notable
planner could devise. And the monuments of the greater Ireland stand in place of the follies we did not need to build.

Castles were almost always built on rivers, and the settlers'
houses have followed them. Well-to-do life, in this part of
County Cork, has almost all run into the creases of river valleys
— or, rather, to the lips of the valleys: here one enjoys sun, the
shelter of winding uplands, rich soil for gardens, the river view.
Along the Awbeg and Blackwater you find an almost unin-
terrupted succession of gentlemen's residences. The Awbeg
strings together the neighbourhoods of Doneraile and Castletownroche; for miles up and down river from Fermoy and
Mallow Blackwater sites, or prospects, have been in demand.
The Funcheon is less populous — the Kingstons owned the
upper reaches of it; its flats are marshy, its gorges narrow and
steep.

Gentlemen's houses round here are all a little alike. Some
stone, some plastered and painted, they stand in crescents, or
broken crescents, of trees, their front steps rising from gravel
sweeps. Where possible, they face south. Few are modern, still
fewer are very old; most of them were built throughout the
eighteenth or in the early nineteenth century. Few demesnes
are quite flat, so that the lawns round houses run either up or
down. Ornamental planting of trees makes a pleasant pattern;
the demesnes are outlined by " screens " (or narrow ribbons of
wood). The walled gardens are often some way away: sun and
shelter are always objects, in this country — in some cases shelter was rated higher than sun, and houses and gardens were too
closely planted about or sunk too deep in hollows. Though

views — if only of lawns up to the skyline — were allowed to the main rooms of a house, trees often press closely upon its other sides. In some cases, backs are turned to the river, whose glint can only be seen from top back rooms. This is a country for wet weather: the steady sough of rain in demesne trees induces by day a timeless and rather soothing melancholy, by night an obliterating, exhaustive sleep.

Handsome stables are seldom quite out of view; the home farm buildings are generally planted out. Rich soil, clement softness and Anglo-Irish genius in this direction have produced some great gardens — inside or outside walls, down rock-faces, on river flats. Indoors, the alteration of sun and damp makes stuffs fade quickly; fluctuations in temperature, where there is no heating, make polish mist over and plaster sweat. Interiors take on a weathered bloom; there are few new things and nothing stays looking new. The not long past of these houses has been very intense: no Irish people — Irish or Anglo-Irish — live a day unconsciously. Lives in these houses, for generations, have been lived at high pitch, only muted down by the weather, in psychological closeness to one another and under the strong rule of the family myth. Lack of means, concentration of interests, love of their own sphere of power keeps most Anglo-Irish people from often going away. I know of no house (no house that has not changed hands) in which, while the present seems to be there forever, the past is not pervadingly felt.

Each of these family homes, with its stables and farm and gardens deep in trees at the end of long avenues, is an island — and, like an island, a world. Sometimes for days together a family may not happen to leave its own demesne. English people, or people from cities, ask what such families " do " all day — and the question, exceedingly superficial, cannot be answered in superficial terms. The preoccupation of Irish country people with their own affairs may be found either mystic or irritating. Each member of each of these isolated households is bound up not only in the sensation and business of living but

in the exact sensation of living *here*. The upkeep of the place
takes its tax not only of physical energy but of psychic ener-
gies people hardly know that they give. Each of these houses,
with its intense, centripetal life, is isolated by something very
much more lasting than the physical fact of space: the isolation
is innate; it is an affair of origin. It is possible that Anglo-Irish
people, like only children, do not know how much they miss.
Their existences, like those of only children, are singular, independent and secretive.

Life in these house-islands has a frame of its own. Character
is printed on every hour, as on the houses and demesne features
themselves. With buildings, as with faces, there are moments
when the forceful mystery of the inner being appears. This
may be a matter of mood or light. Come on round the last turn
of its avenue, or unexpectedly seen down a stretch of lawn, any
one of these houses — with its rows of dark windows set in the
light facade against dark trees — has the startling, meaning and
abstract clearness of a house in a print, a house in which something important occurred once, and seems, from all evidence,
to be occurring still.

Bowen's Court is not built on a river; it has no castle and belongs to no neighbourhood, being much lonelier in its situation
than any other big house in the country round. It is built at the
foot of the Ballyhouras; the bog starts a mile north of its garden
wall. From the mountain, you see the dark mat of the Bowen's
Court demesne trees at the edge of the endless dissolving plain
— in some lights you catch a glint from the roof. The house and
the lands round it are carefully sheltered, at their exposed back,
by plantations: the house itself is set in a shallow hollow, so that
you only see mountains from upper windows, and only realize
how near the whole range lies by walking up to the top of the
front lawn. Up this very long lawn, set halfway with a grove of
trees, Bowen's Court faces: its aspect is south-south-east. (It
must be said that in Ireland a " lawn " does not mean turf sub-

jected to fine mowing; it means that grass expanse that in England is called a park. English people also say " park " where we say " demesne.") From each side of the house run out belts of wood; these throw the structure's staring plainness and the smooth grassy slopes into relief. Two avenues, the Upper and the Lower, meet in a bow of gravel under the front steps. The Upper (which for some time was the only) Avenue is shaded on its uphill course by large lime, ash and beech trees. The Lower Avenue sets out fairly shadeless, but runs under trees on its course downhill.

Our post town, Kildorrery, on the top of its hill, lies about a mile east of the Lower, or Farahy, gates. The Farahy glebe lands, with the church and rectory, are carved out of the demesne. In no other direction lies any town or larger village, except Shanballymore, for seven or eight miles. Mallow is thirteen, Fermoy twelve, Mitchelstown eight and Doneraile seven miles from Bowen's Court. Inside and about the house and in the demesne woods you feel transfixed by the surrounding emptiness; it gives depth to the silence, quality to the light. The land round Bowen's Court, even under its windows, has an unhumanized air the house does nothing to change. Here are, even, no natural features, view or valley, to which the house may be felt to relate itself. It has set, simply, its pattern of trees and avenues on the virgin, anonymous countryside. Like Flaubert's ideal book about nothing, it sustains itself on itself by the inner force of its style.

Bowen's Court, finished in 1776, is a high bare Italianate house. It was intended to form a complete square, but the north-east corner is missing. Indoors, the plan is simple; the rooms are large, lofty and few. The house stands three stories high, with, below, a basement sunk in an area. Outside the front door a terrace, supported on an unseen arch, bridges the area: from this terrace the steps descend to the gravel sweep. The house is built of limestone from a nearby quarry; the south front and long west side are faced with cut stone — the mould-

ings and corners are marble-sharp. The east side and north back
are more roughly finished — the rest of the cut stone was kept
for the stables' front. Inside the angle where the north-east
corner is missing, ghostly outlines of what should have been
doors appear — in the builder's view the house was still incomplete.

Bowen's Court shows almost living changes of colour. In
fine weather the limestone takes on a warm whitish powdery
bloom — with its parapet cut out against a bright blue sky this
might almost be a building in Italy. After persistent rain the
stone stains a dark slate and comes out in irregular black streaks
— till the house blots into its dark rainy background of trees.
In cold or warm dusks it goes either steel or lavender; in full
moonlight it glitters like silvered chalk.

The great bare block — not a creeper touches it — is broken
regularly by windows: in the south façade there are twenty
(the hall door takes the place of one of them), in the west side
eighteen, in the shorter east side six, in the north back six —
and I exclude from this count all the basement windows which,
heavily barred, look into the area. In the south façade the windows have mouldings, on the other sides they are set in plain.
All this expanse of glass, with its different reflections, does
much to give Bowen's Court character. When the sun is low,
in the early mornings or evenings, the house seems, from the
outside, to be riddled with light.

Indoors, the rooms with these big windows not only reflect
the changes of weather but seem to contain the weather itself.
The high Venetian window on the staircase, looking north to
the mountains through a plantation of spruce, sends in, if never
direct sunshine, sun-colours that are almost as bright — this is
most of all so in winter. And on winter mornings, when the
late-rising sun throws the shadows of the circle of elms in a fan
down the frosty lawn in front of the house until their tip
touches the steps, the plaster and marble indoors, even the
white woodwork, looks also frosty and hard. When rain moves

in vague grey curtains across the country, or stands in a sounding pillar over the roof and trees, grey quivers steadily on the indoor air, giving the rooms, whichever room you go into, the resigned look of being exposed to rain. The metal of autumn sharpens and burnishes everything in the house. And summer's drone and spring's yellow-green rustle penetrate everywhere. The front and corner rooms get so much sun, when there *is* sun, that mahogany doors and tables bleach to a pale tan. On summer afternoons the rooms at the south-west corner become as dazzling as lakes.

Bowen's Court is severely classical and, outside and inside, is very bare. The four high downstairs rooms — hall, drawing-room, dining-room, library — are decorated with friezes of Italian plaster-work, and moulded patterns appear on the hall and the staircase ceilings. A plaster design of three pillared temples rests, over the staircase window, on a pair of pilasters with acanthus tops. In the Hall, the four doorways, the inner frame of the front door and the mantelpiece are on the Roman pattern. Upstairs, the rooms are only beautified by their proportions, their outlook and the severe mouldings round the windows and doors. Wall-spaces and, as in the case of the staircase, almost extravagant height have been used by the builder boldly, so that they are not negative. There has been no attempt to break any space up.

In the five-windowed Drawing-room, vast Victorian mirrors now occupy the two windowless walls; in the Hall hang the Bowen portraits; in the Library glass-fronted bookcases stand between or opposite the windows. But the walls could look as well without any of these. In the Hall and all the upstairs rooms the mantelpieces are of a local marble — dark slate-grey with whitish veins and flecks. From the three other downstairs living-rooms the original mantelpieces are, unhappily, gone; their successors date from about 1860 — glossy Victorian marbles, not trivial but tame.

The front door itself stands open all day on to the steps. Inside it, obtruding into the Hall, is a Victorian glass porch with a glass inner door. This, put up by my grandfather, was designed to admit daylight without draughts — a function it fulfills so perfectly well that I cannot, though I should like to, take it away. The Hall occupies the centre front of the house; it is, like the rest of the ground floor rooms, lofty, and runs a long way back. At the far end, facing the front door, is the fireplace, flanked by two classical doorways — of these, one leads through to the Back Hall and the stairs.

As you enter the Hall from the front steps, the Library door is immediately on your right, the Drawing-room door immediately on your left. The Dining-room, whose three windows look out west and are darkened by trees, is set back behind the Drawing-room, with which it connects direct by a high mahogany door. The service door to the Dining-room opens off the Back Hall, at the foot of the staircase.

From the Back Hall, also, a swing door gives on the working part of the house — the back stairs, pantry, bootroom, stairs down to the basement and north wing.

The staircase is lighted by the Venetian window of which I spoke. The steps are shallow, the oak banisters heavy and beautiful. At the first floor this main staircase stops in a gallery — had the house been built as it was projected there should have been flights to the floor above. As things had to be left, the top floor can only be reached by a humble continuation of the back stairs.

From the gallery, a door leads through to the Lobby, over the Hall: here, three south-facing curtainless windows reflect themselves into the bare floor. Off the Lobby open two large corner bedrooms — over the Drawing-room and Library respectively — and the dressingrooms behind them. The third large bedroom on this floor is at the head of the stairs; it is over the Dining-room and has, with its dressingroom, the same west outlook into trees. That is all, on the first floor.

The Long Room, at the top, was to have been the ballroom.

Its length is startling, as you come up into it from the last bare flight of the back stairs — it runs right through the house, dead centre, from back to front. It has a well ceiling, and at each end three windows, set rather low near the floor. Shortage of money, the hurry in which the house was finished, have left the Long Room rather frigid and rough. Its emptiness keeps it full of echoes. Two imposing fireplaces with brasswork do, it is true, exist, but I imagine few fires have ever burnt in them. The walls were hastily plastered — they flake easily. The Italian decorators in plaster had been paid off, and had left, before this floor was reached, so the blue-white concave ceiling is left bare — but for two wavering ovals traced by some inexpert hand. Some one, having watched the Italians at work downstairs, must have come up on his own to this *manqué* ballroom to try what he could do in the same line. So, these two rather touching oval medallions show good will, ardour, but no kind of symmetry in their naive design. As for the floor — it was found out almost at once that this floor would never stand the vibration of dancing. Balls have, therefore, been always held in the Drawing-room. The Long Room has been used, instead, as a promenade deck, as a wet-day playroom for people of all ages, for solitary reflections and for theatricals. Though right at the top, and empty, it remains the core of the house: when one returns to Bowen's Court after an absence one never feels one has really come home again until one has been up to the Long Room.

Six doors open off it — bedrooms and dressingrooms of which, these days, few are in use.

Four floors down the back stairs, the stone-flagged basement with its green area light is on much the same plan as the floors above. Off the axis passage are the kitchen and larder, the wool room, the game room, the servants' hall, the laundry, the wine and the coal cellars. Running out to the north, and overlooking the yard, is the wing of offices built by my grandfather.

In the main block of Bowen's Court there are no small rooms

— the dressingrooms are narrow, but they are long. One must accustom oneself, wherever one settles down, to much space behind one's back, much height over one's head. There are no nooks. Oddly, perhaps, enough, the effect of this is not restless; it is compelling and calm. Steady behaviour of *some* sort, even formality, is enjoined by every line of the house. Even going in and out has its formalities: from the ground floor (which is in fact slightly raised) you have access to the outdoor world only through the front door, opening on to the steps, or through the back glass door leading down to the yard. So, whimsical entrances and exits are impossible — you cannot, for instance, step in and out of the ground floor windows: their sills are three feet high and they overhang the area. The few large living-rooms at Bowen's Court are, thus, a curious paradox — a great part of their walls being window-glass, they are charged with the light, smell and colour of the prevailing weather; at the same time they are very indoor, urbane, hypnotic, not easily left. . . . Any casual life goes on on the front steps: in summer, when there is sunshine, when there are visitors, these, strewn with cushions, deck chairs, papers and books, take on a *villeggiatura* air. The lawns round the house, with their banks and moving tree-shadows, are, like the rooms indoors, nookless and plain.

Indoors and outdoors the house's character, with its inherent beauty, is in its proportions and its sureness of style. I have said that its plan is simple — and shown how simple it is.

On the ground floor, at present, only the Library and the Hall are used for everyday life. The Drawing-room is now quite empty, but for a grand piano; it is hung with a white, grey and gold scrolled wallpaper, put up when my grandmother was a bride, and its five windows, in their blistered embrasures, reflect the green of the lawn into two Victorian mirrors reaching up to the frieze. All alone, the room continues to dazzle in late afternoon suns. Myself, I feel that one suffers from not being in the Drawing-room more. The latch of its door through to the Hall is weak, and the door often swings open in a commanding way. The rational, shabby comfort of the Library gives much to one's life, but that was not meant to be all.

The Dining-room is as crowded — with massive reddish mid-Victorian furniture, put in by my grandfather, who admired it — as the Drawing-room is empty. As I said, its outlook is on to trees, and the backgrounds of the few pictures seem to exude more dusk. So we no longer eat in the Dining-room, but in the Hall — which is sunny till past midday and has a Pompeian red wallpaper fading to apricot. Here, the family portraits keep one company, there is much of the Sheraton dining-room furniture made for the house and expelled by my grandfather, and a grandfather clock keeps up a rather halting tick. In the evenings, in spring, summer and autumn, the four points of candle-light from the dinner-table reflect themselves in the glass door, against the metallic dusk of the green lawn.

The Library, with its bookcases and four windows, is an airy, everyday sort of room, only sombre in the worst weather. The arrangement of its tables, armchairs and sofas conforms, more or less, to the modern pattern of living — the only unexpected factor is, height. At the south-east corner the room receives morning, often still misty, sun. The Library is pleasant, too, in the evenings, when an afterglow comes in from the country round and the log fire, newly made up, blazes away. This is a room so familiar that one is only conscious of its character when one comes back after some time away. It smells of dry calf bindings, humid Victorian bindings, polish, plaster, worn carpet and wood smoke.

Upstairs, the bedrooms are all very much alike. They take character chiefly from the views from their windows, and are called by the colours of their wallpapers — the Green Room,

Yellow Room, Blue Room and so on. Their wardrobes and scrolled mahogany bed-ends are, like the furniture downstairs, bleached by the strong sun. Their cretonne curtains fade quickly. Their open windows let in a smell of woods and country and, often, of mown grass: this, and the penetrating surrounding silence, makes them good rooms to sleep and wake up in. In summer they are invaded by butterflies, and in winter birds fly in to seek warmth, then batter wildly against the windowpanes. On summer nights bats are a trouble to many, and once or twice we have had a white owl in. There is no ghost in this house.

The stables, with their long cut-stone frontage, heavy doors and slatted loft windows, run down one side of the yard, northeast of the house. The harness room and a row of offices, the coach house, the now disused dairy, the wood-stack and cart-sheds also stand round the yard, which is large and shaded by trees. A lane leads from it down to the Farahy stream. Out north of the stables there is a quadrangle of ruined stone farm buildings, and beyond that the haggart.

The lay-out of the grounds round Bowen's Court is simple, rather irregular. Under the west windows lies the great mown square that was once the tennis and croquet lawn, levelled out of a slope and set round with plushy, moist banks. Above this is another, uncut, lawn, planted with clumps of pampas, conifers, flowering cherry; this fades off into an angle of woods and is shaded, also, by the large lime and beech of the Upper Avenue. The front of the house is quite open; the east side looks downhill at a meadow swept round by a belt of trees. On these three sides of Bowen's Court, under the ground floor windows, a clipped box hedge masks the area parapet. All the way from the house to the walled garden, laurels run through the high, shallow woods. On the whole, the effect is at once romantic and bland. There are few flowers, however, around the house.

The flowers are all in the garden — three walled-in-acres lying some distance away, on the mountain side of the woods. One approaches it by walks between laurels and rockeries. Inside its walls, this far-off garden is a world in itself. The continuous rustle of trees round it only makes its own silence more intense. A box-edged path runs all the way round, and two paths cross at the sundial in the middle; inside the flower borders, backed by espaliers, are the plots of fruit trees and vegetables, and the glasshouse backs on the sunniest wall. From the L-shaped rose pergola in one top corner one has a view of the mountains. Inside the bottom wall runs a nursery for conifers, to be drafted to the plantations as they grow up. The silence is now and again broken by the jangle of the bell on the public door — this means, " Shop! ": in this garden planned to feed twenty people or more we raise more fruit and vegetables than we can eat, so we sell to any one who will come and buy. The flowers are, on the whole, old-fashioned — jonquils, polyanthus, parrot tulips, lily o' the valley (grown in cindery beds), voluminous white and crimson peonies, moss roses, mauve-pink cabbage roses, white-pink Celestial roses, borage, sweet pea, snapdragon, sweet william, red and yellow dahlias, Michaelmas daisies of none of your fancy kinds and small dark-bronze and yellow chrysanthemums see the different flowering seasons through. Near the sundial grow two bushes of caroline allspice which, with their clove-smelling brown leathery flowers, are said to be rare. In the early autumn a flag of crimson creeper hangs over one wall. The lavender border grew too bushy and had to be cut down.

Good aspect, shelter and good soil accounted, I think, in the first place for this choice of site for the garden, so far from the house. But also, the wooded, quite lengthy walk there and back has provided, for generations, something to do. To go to the garden, talk to the gardener, cruise round the paths slowly, select flowers, pick them, carry them back, arrange them in many vases fills a Bowen Court lady's morning or afternoon.

There are three heronries at Bowen's Court. The herons — called cranes by the country people — fish in the Funcheon, or in the small Farahy river that flows through the lower woods and bounds the demesne. Back from fishing, a heron skims over the lawns in its flopping flight: its wings move in slow motion. Then, making height in successions of mounting curves, it will gleam and vanish over the trees. After dark, herons utter cries like lost souls. They nest in the circle of elms in the big lawn, above a path called the Bell Walk, and in the high trees over the tennis court — getting this corner known as the Cranes' Wood. In spring their young make a noise like a roomful of typewriters.

In autumn, seagulls blown inland make distracted movements over the lawns.

In the woods round the house there are rookeries. In September, after the harvest, the rooks' existence concentrates feverishly: after sunset they cross the sky over the house in their black thousands, back from the stubblefields. Their swirling, diffused pattern has an intense core; their return has succeeding movements, like a long dance. They pivot on one another in wide whorls, dissolve in the glaring twilight, look like a black snowstorm. Their cries fill the upper silence; for minutes together a tree is charged with them and rustles with them, then they spill out to make their pattern again. Slowly the darkness smoking out of the trees absorbs them; for a long time stragglers continue to cross the sky; it is quite dark before the last cry is heard.

In the early grey of next morning sleepers are wakened by the rooks pouring into the sky again. In the early spring the rooks mate noisily, crashing about in the tops of the bare trees. Later, as the woods mist over with green, there is a furious blue-black come and go round their nests. Their mortality can be counted, for their first sheeny then dulling corpses lie on the wood paths. After rain, when everything steams, the smell of their droppings is rank round the house, in laurels and woods.

This is Bowen's Court as the past has left it — an isolated, partly unfinished house, grandly conceived and plainly and strongly built. Near the foot of mountains, it has little between it and the bare fields that run up the mountainside. Larger in manner than in actual size, it stands up in Roman urbane strongness in a land on which the Romans never set foot. It is the negation of mystical Ireland: its bald walls rebut the surrounding, disturbing light. Imposed on seized land, built in the rulers' ruling tradition, the house is, all the same, of the local rock, and sheds the same grey gleam you see over the countryside. So far, it has withstood burnings and wars.

Bowen's Court did not fall short of the grand idea, though it stopped short in its realization of it. The house felt, before it was even finished, the inanitions of poverty. But the imperfections — the missing corner, the halt of the big staircase in full flight — somehow go to make the scale of the first idea more strongly felt. Though much had to be left undone, very little was modified. Had my ancestor and its builder, Henry Bowen III, been a wiser man, he would not have conceived the house on so large a scale. He was not a wise man; he died (as I am to tell) very much in debt. At the same time, I feel that something more serious than extravagance, less heady than *amour propre*, inspired him. In his remote way (for County Cork was very remote then, and Henry Bowen III seldom went outside it) he was a man of his century, esteeming reason, order and light. He believed in elevation, and he designed for his family — a landed County Cork family, still fairly new to Ireland, of far from unlimited means and of few pretensions other than gentle birth — a house that should be certain to elevate. He honoured life as he saw it, honoured life's inherent future. He linked the house he built on his lonely land as closely as possible to society by setting its gate far up on the Mallow road.

A good deal that this Henry Bowen could not foresee was built into Bowen's Court as the walls went up. In building as in writing, something one did not reckon with always waits to add itself to the plan. In fact, if this (sometimes combative) un-expected element be *not* present, the building or book remains academic and without living force. In raising a family house one is raising a theatre: one knows the existing players, guesses at their successors, but cannot tell what plays may be acted there. Henry Bowen III, the builder, could not do more than indicate that life ought to be lived in a certain way. Time, the current of politics, debts, personalities, weather were all mat-ters for which he could not legislate. Rocking gales, limestone sweats, money embarrassments, complex affections, unhappy alienations, phases of emptiness, fashions, lonely obsessions, strictnesses, latitudes, children and soldiers have all, since he built it, left their mark on the house. A Bowen, in the first place, made Bowen's Court. Since then, with a rather alarming sure-ness, Bowen's Court has made all the succeeding Bowens.

I have shown the setting and plan, and described the house, with a thoroughness that may have been wearisome. This has been done at the start because I want Bowen's Court to be taken as existing, and to be seen as clearly as possible. From now on, I do not want to hold up my story with descriptions or expla-nations of any place. The first half of my story precedes, in time, the house. But if I did not show what went to make the Bowens, from the time of their first coming to Ireland, I should fail to show what went to make Bowen's Court.

The house bears its name for two reasons. It was, as we know, intended to be a complete square — therefore, a *court*. Also, it was named reminiscently: these particular Bowens were the descendants of Henry Bowen of Court House, Ilston, in the Gower Peninsula, Glamorganshire, Wales.

COLONEL BOWEN

AND THE HAWK

THE SURNAME " BOWEN " IS DERIVED FROM THE WELSH " AB Owen," or " ap Owen " — by Grimm's law the two consonants are interchangeable. " Ap," or " ab," means " son of." Welsh surnames of an early date were represented by a string of Christian names divided by " ap ": thus, you got a man called " David ap John ap Rees ap Thomas." But when a member of a family amassed money and became important he would take simply, as surname, the Christian name of his father, discarding, as an unnecessary distinction, the names of those who had gone before. Any man whose father was christened Owen *could*, of course, call himself " ap Owen." Alongside, therefore, of the main Glamorganshire family of ap Owens there came to be a number of people who, though using the name, did not, strictly, belong to the main stock. Again, the whole of the brothers of one family did not always choose to take the same surname.

The Bowens of Court House, Ilston, Glamorganshire, became " ap Owen " about 1441. The Bowens of Llangevelach, in the same county, did not take " ap Owen " till 1550. (The Court House and the Llangevelach Bowens trace back to a

common ancestor, Owen Gethyn.) In both branches, " ap
Owen " was changed to " Bowen " early in the reign of Queen
Elizabeth. In the will, proved 1582, of Henry Bowen of Court
House, the testator refers to his two brothers and to his eldest
son as " ap Owen," but to his two younger sons as " Bowen."
The transition from the old form to the new was thus, clearly,
not made all at once: it remained a matter for individual choice.

The coat of arms borne by the various Bowens seems to have
varied slightly from branch to branch: it always, however, featured a stag. The Bowen's Court (originally the Court House)
Bowens' coat of arms, as now entered with the Ulster King of
Arms, is: " *Azure, a stag lodged argent, attired or, vulned in the
back of an arrow gules, feathered of the second,* and for motto
' *Cautus a futero.*' "

Pedigrees tracing back the Bowens of Court House to Bleddin ap Maenerch, last British sovereign of Brecknock, are recorded in *Limbus Patrum Morganiae et Glamorganiae,* by G.
T. Clark, and in *The Golden Grove Book,* by Hugh Thomas,
Deputy Herald, 1703. These pedigrees, however, differ considerably and do not appear to be complete. Covering a space of
three hundred and seventy-nine years — from the death of
Bleddin in 1098 to the death of Morgan ap Owen in 1467 —
they represent only nine generations.

This all — the number of Bowens, the slightly differing stags,
inconsistencies or lacunae in pedigrees — goes to create confusion in the present-day mind, to which at the best all origins
are obscure. Glamorganshire, and the Gower Peninsula in particular, came to be congested with an increasing number of
Bowens — some *bona fide,* others people who made use of the
promising name. Living-room shrank as families multiplied,
and the resulting pressure expelled, from time to time, various
Bowens in search of expansion elsewhere. Two different Bowens went to New England, one went to Ireland, to Queens
County (where his family later built Balle Adam), one settled

in Devonshire, one again went to Ireland, to County Cork —
and he was my ancestor. Stationary Bowens were those of
Llangevelach, Kittlehill, Pennard, Ilston, Llanmadock and
Bishopston — all in Gower.

The founder of the family of Court House Bowens was the
Morgan ap Owen of Swansea who in 1441 purchased Court
House and Mawr House, and lands pertaining thereto in Ilston,
with the lands of Wogan Hill in Pennard, from Geoffrey de la
Mare. Morgan ap Owen died in 1467 and is buried at Swansea,
St. Mary's Church. He left three sons, of whom the eldest,
Richard, for some time Receiver of Gower and Camwyllion,
inherited Court House.

Richard became the father of Harry ap Owen, who married
Elizabeth Hopkin and had by her one son, Thomas. Thomas
inherited Court House and married Jennet, daughter of David
ap Evan of Yehan. Henry, the eldest of their three sons, in time
got Court House. This Henry now shed the ap Owen chrysalis
and called himself Henry Bowen. He married Ellen Franklyn
of Park le Brewys, had three sons, made the will I have mentioned, and died 1582.

This Henry Bowen of Court House seems to have favoured
the third of his sons, Harry. Court House had to go to Thomas,
the eldest son, but Harry, a child at the time of his father's
death, was left substantial property in the Llanellan lands. He
got, also, his father's " best brasen pan, and best crock, with a
couple of round pans, and my pewter platten, my standing bell
and appurtenances, being upon my loft." A paternal uncle John
(still) ap Owen was to be tutor and guardian to the little boy.

We are Harry's descendants, therefore from this point on
the history of what were to be the Bowen's Court Bowens
branches off from that of the Bowens of Court House. The
Court House line continued (through the descendants of
Harry Bowen's eldest brother Thomas) but soon no longer
meant much to us.

The fortunate Harry settled down in his house on his lands

at Llanellan, and married Margaret, daughter of Harry Holland, rector of Cheriton. When he died, in 1641, he left two
sons, Henry and Thomas, and one daughter who married a
Henry Morgan. The elder son, Henry, inherited Llanellan.
He was that Henry Bowen who was to leave Gower, go (as a
lieutenant-colonel in the Cromwellian army) to Ireland and get
the County Cork lands. He was the first of our Bowens to die
in Ireland, he was the founder of the Bowen's Court family, so
from now on I shall call him Henry I.

Henry I married three times: his first wife, Margaret Bassett,
died childless in 1625; by his second wife, Anne Maunsel, he
had one son, John (who went after his father to Ireland), and
two daughters, Mary and Hester. By his third wife, Catherine,
daughter of William Price, he had four more sons — Nehemiah,
Cornelius, Henry and Benjamin, who subsequently all died
without issue, and one daughter, Elizabeth, who died unmarried. Nature must have decided to leave no more of this particular line of Bowens in Wales. John Bowen, the son who
went to Ireland, came in for father's estates there — and was
to add to these by an advantageous marriage. Colonel Bowen
(Henry I), before his death in County Cork, settled his Welsh
lands on his wife, whom he was again leaving, then on to his
Welsh son Nehemiah, whom he afterwards showed no wish to
see. Pressure of natural affections in Colonel Bowen was said by
his enemies to be very low. He loved his hawks and hawking,
doubted God and cared almost nothing for man.

Gowersland, Gower or the Gower Peninsula is the western
extremity of Glamorganshire. Like Ireland it is notable for its
ruins, and like Ireland made complex by an imposed race. The
British, Romans and Normans all left remains behind them —
druidic stones, broken forts, castles and chapels go round the
steep, rocky, " extremely romantic " coast, or overtop the
small area inland. . . . Swansea bay, scooped out south of
the peninsula's neck, is pretty and has been compared to the Bay

of Naples. The peninsula is about six miles across the neck: if you make a coastal circuit of Gower you cover from forty to fifty miles.

In the reign of Henry I (King of England) this virtual island Gower was forcibly colonized by some Flemings, or Normans, who, sponsored by Henry Beaumont Earl of Warwick, assumed the privileges of a conquering race. " Between the new settlers and the native Welsh jealousy and animosity occasioned complete alienation: and the colonists, retaining much of their own national characteristics, adopted the language of the English, by whom they were countenanced and assisted. Rarely intermarrying with the Welsh, and holding comparatively little intercourse with them or with others, they are still peculiar in dialogue and dress. . . . Their language, radically Saxon, includes a number of obsolete English terms." To-day the Gower English continue to charm the traveller with a burly, super-Devonian quaintness of speech. And they are responsible for such place-names as Cheriton, Ilston, Bishopston — names that dot the map oddly among the Welsh. They refer to the Welsh-inhabited Gower districts, I do not know how disparagingly, as " the Welsheries." In fact, their self-conscious apartness is still marked.

This miniature parallel with Ireland holds good only up to a point. For instance, the stress laid on *mutual* jealousy shows that the Flemings, while they established themselves, failed to increase further their holdings or sphere of power. The countenance and assistance they had got from the English were not unlimited: English interest gave out. Disagreeable tenacity, rather than aggression, must have been the Flemings' chief offence, to the Welsh. Indigenous Gower Welsh families — such as the Bowens — continued to exercise power and to acquire and hold land. Again, while the Normans who went with Strongbow to Ireland became absorbed into Ireland and were to espouse her cause — life there on the lordly scale bringing with it lordly affections — the Gower Flemings'

smaller, farmer or burgess interests circumscribed and helped
to isolate them. Wales seems to exclude the stranger; Ireland
seduces him. This up-to-a-point resemblance between Gower
and Ireland does, however, make one thing probable — Colonel
Bowen must have arrived in Ireland taking inter-racial friction, mistrust and envy to be the *sine qua non* of country life.
His Gower had fretted under colonization. In Ireland *he* was
to colonize.

The main Bowen lands in Gower — Ilston, Bishopston, Pennard — lands bought from the Fleming de la Mare, lie along
the south of the peninsula, inland from the coast. The land is
good, well-timbered, with patches of gorsy common. Roads
twist from village to village, passing manors, churches and
farms. Often woods, sometimes ruins top the cliffs; in the
small bays creeps or thunders the sea. Sea winds freshen the
inland country; sea mists sometimes obscure it. On the whole
Colonel Bowen's lot was cast in a pleasant place. But something worked on his temper — all that we know about him
suggests that he felt an oppressed and a baited man. Something
in Gower — perhaps partly the number of Bowens? — got
him down, then finally got him out. The Civil War decided
his life for him — he was to end up in Ireland. America might
have offered a better break: one does not know if he ever
thought of America.

What sort of home did he leave behind? In the seventeenth
century, the Welsh squires' manor farms were two-storied,
stone-built, with thick walls; they were roomy and sufficiently
dignified, in a sturdy rather than elegant style. The furniture
— chairs, chests, tables, four-poster beds — were of the pattern now only too well known to amateurs and copiers of the
Welsh antique. Beams and austere small windows made rooms
dark inside. The estate, unless it were very poorly developed,
furnished almost every commodity needed by the household.
Rough roads and rough weather tended to isolate different
families. Living was patriarchal, I do not know how moral

but on the whole severe. Theology, bargaining and censorious gossip appear to have dominated the talk. The only regional sport I know of — having reason to know of it — was hawking. Henry Bowen I's third wife, *née* Miss Price, kept, from all evidence, a good deal of company, but her company can have been far from gay — it was dominated by visiting ministers. In this circle, Colonel Bowen was not *persona grata* — Mrs. Bowen came in for a good deal of sympathy as being the wife of an impossible man. Puritanism, in its then exact sense, cannot yet, though, have got a footing in Gower, for when the Civil War broke out Gower, in common with the adjoining country, declared for the King.

It was as one of the King's party that Henry Bowen I left home for the wars, and with the King's party he stayed until he fell foul of them. He then took up arms on the opposite side. The Civil War must have swept into both armies numbers of such natural *condottieri* — temperamental fighters, malcontents, firebrands, actuated by love of movement, desire to leave home or hopes of gain. I doubt whether Henry Bowen ever cared much for either King or Parliament: he may hardly have distinguished between the two. He was one of those men of whom it is hard to say whether their ideas breed their passions or their passions breed their ideas. Such men live in a heat or ferment of inner anger; they feel freed and eased by action, but their haughty subjectivity makes for contempt for " ideas " from the outside. Fighting had this over hawking: it took him further from home. We know nothing of his first two marriages — except that the second gave him a son at least some way after his own heart; of the third, we have the ghastly vignette in the tale of the Apparition. The four sons of this third marriage were, I take it, far more their mother's sons, and no doubt were her partisans. At all events, Henry I took only John to Ireland, leaving Nehemiah, Cornelius, Henry and Benjamin to the Gower lands, to their mother, to barren marriages and to early deaths.

We should not know as much as we do about Colonel
Bowen were it not for the affair of the Apparition.

It was Mr. Richard Baxter, deep in psychic research and in
compiling a case book with a didactic bias, who investigated
and wrote up this Gower tale. Lieutenant-Colonel Henry
Bowen of Glamorgan became *Case 2* in *Baxter's Worlds of
Spirits.* This book, printed in London in 1691, has a promising
title: *The Certainty of the Worlds of Spirits.* Sub-titled: *Fully
evinced by the Unquestionable Histories of Apparitions, Operations, Witchcrafts, Voices, etc. Proving the Immortality
of Souls, the Malice and Miseries of the Devils and the
Damned, and the Blessedness of the Justified. Written for the
Conviction of Sadducees and Infidels, By Richard Baxter.*
There seems no doubt that Baxter, though biassed, was fairly
thorough. We do not, of course, know if he sifted his evidence.
His object was, to give factual background to what, avowedly,
should be cautionary tales. In his pursuit of *Malice and Miseries,* Baxter certainly did strike lucky in Colonel Bowen. For
what made the Gower story, already shocking, more shocking was that Colonel Bowen, though absent in Ireland, was
proved to have been *living* when, at his home in Llanellan, the
Apparition was seen, and to have survived for several years
after this. One could only feel that he had projected himself
— here was a clear case of *Malice* on the part of the damned.
At the same time, the violence in Ireland and the nightmare
obsessions reported to Baxter by Captain Foley and others
made it equally clear that the man was in *Misery.*

Baxter may have had connections in Gower from whom
he first heard the likely tale. His check-up on it was methodi-
cal. In 1656 he began by getting in touch with a certain Colonel Rogers, Governor of Hereford, who was known to have
access to, or to have in his possession, a document with a
covering note requesting every discretion. " More there was,"
concludes Colonel Rogers darkly, " but they do not think it

convenient to put in paper. My request is, that you will not
expose it " (the document) " to publick view; it may rather
do harm than good." Colonel Rogers' wish for discretion was
purely moral — the whole story had, clearly, scandalized him
— for the paper *he* sent was unsigned, and mentioned no names
or places, other than the county name of Glamorgan. But Mr.
Samuel Jones, " a Man of known Learning, Piety and Hon-
esty, though a Silenced Minister," had more pressing reasons
for asking Baxter's discretion. Enclosing the narrative of a
Mr. Bedwell, also a minister in Glamorganshire, Mr. Jones
asks that the matter may not be publicized, or that, if Mr.
Baxter were determined to print, " you may conceal my
friend's name and mine own, lest any offence should be taken
by some of the parties Relations in Parliament and Council."
Henry I's relations in Gower were, in fact, about that time,
numerous, touchy and sufficiently powerful, and neither
Jones nor Bedwell, perfectly inoffensive, wanted the pack of
Bowens on to their necks. The fact was that Jones, in his note
with its uplifting comments, and Bedwell in his detailed narrative, had been circumstantial in their references to Llanellan
and free in their use of the Bowen name.

Baxter ignored all requests with an equal impartiality. His
defence was, that *Worlds of Spirits* was not actually published
till 1691, thirty-five years after the date of most of his documents. By this time, the more militant Bowens, if not Mr.
Jones and Mr. Bedwell themselves, might be taken to be either
out of action or dead. At all events, Baxter's *forte* was zeal
rather than tact.

Mr. Jones, in his rider to Mr. Bedwell, writes: " You desired
me to impart what I received by Relation, concerning the Apparitions in one Colonel Bowen's House, and upon my return
to procure you some further intelligence touching that Tremendous Providence. Whether it be by Time, or Familiarity
with the noise hereof, or rather, the (no less to be admired)

Blockishness of the Spirits of Men, that the Horror of that
terrible Dispensation be allay'd, I know not, but surely the
thing itself was very stupendous, and the remembrance of
it carries much Amazement with it still, to them that have
anything of Tenderness or Understanding left them."

Colonel Rogers, of Hereford, had been the first step, Mr.
Jones (and *via* Mr. Jones Mr. Bedwell) the second. Baxter
next approached a Mr. Higgs, Gower resident, who had just
missed being a witness — too late by one night. Mr. Higgs
had, however, succeeded in interviewing Mrs. Bowen's maid,
who *had* been mixed up in the ghostly scandal, was judged
" thoroughly Godly " and was willing to attest. Mr. Higgs
regretted that Mr. Miles, the local minister called in to pray
with Mrs. Bowen " in the time of the disturbance," was now
— by the time the Baxter inquiry started — gone to New England. Mr. Higgs concludes, to Baxter, with a good wish. " I
commit you, and your huge labours to our mighty and merci-
ful Lord. . . . And if you can think of any thing farther for
me . . . vouchsafe to impart it, and imprint me (poor worm)
on your Soul before our Father. I have somewhat trespassed
by Prolixity which becomes me not to such a person, in such
a Sphere: But excuse him who is, Your afflicted poor brother,
Daniel Higgs."

After Gower, Ireland. It was essential that Baxter should
check up on the still blatantly living Colonel Bowen's reputation there. Two brother-officers in the Cromwellian army
willingly gave him the low-down on Colonel Bowen. Captain
Samuel Foley wrote from Clonmel. He also wrote round, on
Baxter's behalf, " to the neighbouring Ministers and Gentlemen " of his acquaintance, who might be still more closely
on Bowen's tracks. " From them I hope to have a more full
account concerning this poor Man." These further reports,
however, were still not to hand when Baxter was getting
Case 2 ready for press. Colonel John Bridges, from somewhere
in County Cork, confirms, rather briefly, Captain Foley's ac-

count of Bowen's manner of living. Baxter gives only a *précis*
of Colonel Bridges' letter — perhaps it was less agreeable than
the rest.

I can give the clearest account of the Apparition by inter-
leaving the two that I have to hand — (*a*) the anonymous
Document sponsored by Colonel Rogers, and (*b*) Mr. Bed-
well's letter, sent on by Mr. Jones and further vouched for by
Mr. Higgs as being the transcript of a verbatim account got
from Mr. Miles (unhappily now in New England), Mrs.
Bowen's minister friend. In quoting from these two accounts,
I shall number them *A* and *B*.

(*A*) " In the beginning of the late War, a gentleman of
that County " (Glamorgan) " being oppressed by the King's
Party, took arms under the Earl of Essex, and by his Valour
obtained a good repute in the Army; so that in a short time he
got the Command of Lieutenant Colonel. But as soon as the
heat of the War was abated, his Ease and Preferment led him
to a careless and sensual Life; insomuch that the Godly Com-
manders judged him unfit where he grew so vain and notional
that he was cashiered the Army; [1] and being then at liberty to
sin without any restraint, he became an absolute Atheist, denying Heaven or Hell, God or Devil (acknowledging only a
Power, as the antient Heathens did Fate), accounting Temporal Pleasures all his expected Heaven. So that at last he
became hateful, and hating all civil Society, and his nearest
Relations."

(*B*) " As to Colonel Bowen's House, I can give you some
brief particulars. . . . The Gentleman, Colonel Bowen,
whose house is called Lanellin in Gowersland, formerly was
famous for Profession of Religion, but this day is the Saddest
Man in his Principles I know living. To me, in particular, he
hath denied the Being of the Spirit of the Lord; his Argument
thus, Either 'tis something or nothing; if something, show me,

[1] I know of no foundation for this statement.

tell me what it is, etc., and I believe he gives as little Credit to other Spirits as the Sadduces."

(*A*) " About December last " (December 1655) " he being in Ireland, and his Wife (a Godly Gentlewoman of a good Family, and concluded by all the Godly People that knew her to be one of the most sincere and upright Christians in those parts, as being for many years under great afflictions, and always bearing them with Christian-like Patience) living in his House in Glamorgan, was very much troubled one Night with a great Noise, much like the sound of Whirl-wind, and a violent beating of the Doors or Walls, as if the whole House were falling to pieces: and being in her Chamber, with most of her Family, after praying to the Lord (accounting it sinful Incredulity to yield to Fear) she went to bed; and suddenly after, there appeared unto her something like her Husband, and asked her whether he should come to bed. She, sitting up, and praying to the Lord, told him, he was not her Husband, and that he should not. He urged more earnestly: What! not the Husband of thy Bosom? What! not the Husband of thy Bosom? "

(*B*) " She refusing, he gave this answer, What, refuse the Husband of thy Bosom? And after some time, she alledging Christ was her Husband, it disappeared: Strange miserable Howlings and Cries were heard about the House."

(*A*) " Yet had no power to hurt her. And she, together with some Godly people, spent that Night in Prayer, being very often interrupted by this Apparition. The next Night, Mr. Miles (A Godly Minister) with four other Godly Men, came to watch and pray in the House for that Night, and so continued in Prayer . . . without any interruption or noise at all that Night. But the Night following — "

(*B*) " His Tread, his Posture, Sighing, Humming, were heard frequently in the Parlour, in the day time often the Shadow of one walking would appear upon the Wall. One night was very remarkable, and had not the Lord stood by the poor Gentlewoman and her two Maids, that night they had been undone. As she was going to Bed, she perceived by the impression on the Bed, as if some Body had been lying there, and opening the Bed, she smelt the smell of a Carcase some-while dead; and being in Bed (for the Gentlewoman was somewhat Courageous) upon the Tester, which was of Cloth, she perceived something rolling from side to side, and by and by, being forc'd out of her Bed, she had not time to dress herself, such Cries and other things almost amazing her, but she (hardly any of her clothes being on) with her two Maids, got upon their knees by the bedside to seek the Lord, but extreamly assaulted, oftentimes she would by somewhat which felt like a Dog under her knees, be lifted a Foot or more high from the Ground: some were heard to talk on the other side of the Bed, which, one of the Maids hearkening to, she had a blow upon the Back: Divers Assaults would be made by fits; it would come with a cold breath of Wind, the Candles burn Blew and almost out. . . ."

(*A*) " – the Night following, the Gentlewoman, with several other Godly women, being in the House, the noise of Whirl-wind began again, with more violence than formerly, and the Apparition walked in the Chamber, having an insufferable Stench, like that of a putrified Carcase, filling the Room with a thick Smoak, smelling like Sulphur, darkening the Light of the Fire and Candle, but not quite extinguishing it; sometimes going down the stairs, and coming up again with a fearful Noise, disturbing them in their Prayers, one while with the sound of Words which they could not discern, other while striking them so that the next Morning their faces were black with the Smoak, and their Bodies swollen with Bruises."

(*B*) " And this continued from some nine at Night to some three the next Morning, so that the poor Gentlewoman and her servants were in a sad case; the next Morning, smelling of Brimstone and Powder, and as I remember, Black with it, but the Lord was good. Fires have been seen upon the House, and in the fields; his Voice hath been heard luring his Haukes, a Game he delights in, as also the Bills of the Haukes. . . . I could wish, that they, who question the Existancy of Spirits had been but one Night at Lannelin. . . . This continued so violent that the Gentlewoman was fain to withdraw to her Mothers House."

(*A*) "Thereupon they left the House, lest they should tempt the Lord by their over-bold staying in such Danger, and sent this Atheist the sad news of this Apparition; who coming to England about May last" (May 1656) "expressed more Love and Respect to his Wife than formerly; yet telling her, that he could not believe her Relation of what she had seen, as not having a power to believe anything but what himself saw, and yet would not hitherto go to his House to make trial, but probably will e'er long, for that he is naturally of an exceeding rash and desperate Spirit."

A — the Document — leaves the matter at that: that was probably all the writer knew. But Mr. Bedwell — *B* — dating his account two months later, has kept himself more closely informed. He concludes: "Her Husband coming about some four Months since his Confidence did not serve him to lodge at Lannelin, although we have heard nothing of trouble to the House since his coming over. . . . He is as Atheistical as ever, all his religion, if I may call it so, being comprised in the acknowledging a Power, which we, as he saith, may call God, and wanting for some infallible miraculous Business to verifie to him all the rest we own as our Religion. Sure, Sir, if ever a Blasphemer was unworthy to live, this is the Man; and certainly his sin will find him out. He is now gone to Ireland. . . . At first we concluded, the Wretch had been dead, but 'twas otherwise, and therefore the more remarkable."

To sum up: these occurrences happened over three nights. On the fourth night Mr. Higgs (whose first appearance this was), Mr. Miles and two other ministers hurried to Llanellan, ready to join in prayer, and also willing, no doubt, to see whether Mrs. Bowen's black face and bruises were all that report said. Disappointingly, they found the house empty: Mrs. Bowen had fled to her mother's — black face, bruises and all. Her intrepidity had been astonishing. Mr. Higgs only succeeded in interviewing the maid. That was in December 1655. In May 1656 Colonel Bowen returned on a visit from Ireland, but soon went back. One can see why he might not care to stay long. It was in August of that year that Captain Foley, of Clonmel, wrote of him to Mr. Baxter in these terms: " He is little sensible of his sad condition. He lives in the County of Cork, in a beggarly way, though he hath a fair Estate. Some months since, he turned his Wife and Children from him, in that sad unkind manner, that they were forced to seek relief from some friends in Youghall, to help them in their return to Wales, where they continue. Not long since, in Discourse with Baronet Ingolsby, and Mr. Gilbert, Minister of Limerick . . . he said he would give ten thousand Pounds to know the truth about God. 'Tis reported he is haunted with ghastly Ghosts and Apparitions, which frequent him."

" After this " (Baxter says) " Colonel John Bridges wrote to me out of Ireland, that Bowen immured himself in a small Castle, with one Boy; who said, he oft rose in the Night, and talked as if some were talking with him."

The third Mrs. Bowen, then — if these reports be correct — followed her husband to Ireland in the early summer after the Apparition, taking with her all or some of her four sons, Nehemiah, Cornelius, Henry and Benjamin. Did she hope to establish herself permanently with him on the Irish side of the water, on the " fair Estate," or did she mean to induce him to return to Wales? Whichever her object was, she failed: the expedition, clearly, was a fiasco. Colonel Bowen would not see her; he had become " hateful, hating all civil Society, and his

nearest Relations." So back they all went, *via* Youghal, to
Llanellan. The Welsh children cannot have kept at all a happy
impression of their one Irish trip. And how many shocks had
these children sustained already? Where were they at the time
of the Apparition? We have one vague reference to " her
Family " as being present in the Llanellan house.

The Llanellan Apparition would make a likely study for
the psychiatrist. I have preferred to give this tale of my ancestor as it was told, without uninformed comment. The hallucination must have been bred of two tormented, tormenting
natures — his and hers. *Could* he have sent that terrible *Dop-*
pelgänger had she not been awaiting it? Did he really haunt
her, or did she haunt him? Who sent those " ghastly ghosts "
that, in Ireland, troubled *his* bed? In Wales, then in Ireland,
he fought every inch against his wife's God. Enough that was
shocking must have darkened that married life in the dark
little Gower manor before the Apparition ever appeared at
all. I cannot but be glad that we County Cork Bowens descend from the second marriage, not from the haunted third.
When Henry, near Limerick, told the minister and the baronet
that it would be worth ten thousand pounds to him to know
the truth about God, was he an obsessed person, a really tormented mocker, or just a retired colonel, through with the
Godly Army, having his bit of fun? The Llanellan affair just
misses being a smoking-room story: it was a sort of ghastly
harlequinade. Was Colonel Bowen a bit of a *farceur*? Even
the historic dead, and the unhistoric dead certainly, live to
puzzle us with some ultimate mystery.

Colonel Bowen, who loved hawking, whose happiest times
at Llanellan must have been in those fields where they heard
him luring his hawks, and who either liked or could not help
shocking his fellow men, took, then, with him to Ireland his
black soul (coals to Newcastle) and at least one pair of hawks.
From these last, a much prettier story hangs.

With the seventeenth century, the situation in Ireland, already painful and dangerous, became more complicated. New elements came in. In Ireland as well as in England the new English middle-class policy began to make itself felt. Solicitude for investments and dread of Rome now plainly dictated the English attitude. The Stuarts gestured, faltered and double-crossed. In both countries a gallant era was at an end — in England with the death of Queen Elizabeth, in Ireland with the Flight of the Earls. In Ireland, Elizabeth's courtier-soldiers had shown some regard for an enemy fighting for its own land; the fairly new Elizabethan aristocrats did at least salute, while they struggled to circumvent, the older Catholic lords of Ireland. Mountjoy had shown ruthless ability, not spite. But now any chivalric element disappeared from the struggle. The complete subjugation and the exploitation of Ireland became the object of the English burgess class. The Sword of the Lord was drawn for the *rentier*.

Lord Mountjoy's defeat of O'Neill had been definitive. When, in 1607, the dispossessed Earls of the North took ship for Rome, forever, they headed an exodus of Ireland's hereditary leaders to Catholic courts abroad. In the North, the seized lands became the Ulster Plantation. From Munster, the last Desmond was gone; his lands were divided up and settled by Englishmen. New titles were to stand for profitable aggression, or for wealth with English power behind. Ireland, already dense with her own sorrows, reflected English changes as a cloud reflects distant changing light.

In Munster, some of the " old English " — descendants of the original Norman stock, such people as the Roches and the Fitzgeralds — still held land and exercised power. But the new regime increasingly threatened them. Richard Boyle, the first Earl of Cork, was the outstanding success-boy of this new regime.

With regard to Ireland, James I had been, in the first place, well-meaning. Cork city did not give him a good start: the

Mayor, Thomas Sarsfield, chose to regard the Scottish king's
accession to the English throne as fishy. On these grounds,
he held up the Proclamation, in spite of express orders, for
several days, and when told that James I had already been
proclaimed in Dublin, replied, rather smartly, that so had
Perkin Warbeck. The delay, whether frivolous or malevolent,
gave time for a small rebellion to break out. The rebellion —
muddled, pointless and possibly almost inadvertent — was confined to the city districts. Violent anti-Protestant demonstra-
tions took place. Sarsfield, alarmed and knowing Mountjoy's
firmness, wrote the Lord Deputy a tactful letter, admitting
" they had received the King's proclamation on the 11th of
April, but had put off the ceremony till the 16th, that it might
be done with more solemnity." It *had*, in fact, been done, but
outside the city walls. Mountjoy, having dealt with what he
regarded as a similar piece of nonsense on the part of Waterford, marched on Cork and entered the city peacefully. Idle
ploughshares, symbolic, lined his route through the streets,
and Mountjoy (the last, for Ireland, of the Elizabethans) did
not ignore the damage done to the countryside.

He did not ignore, either, the unwisdom of the Elizabethan
policy of setting up the cities against the country by granting
the cities charters of privilege. This capricious and purely urban rebellion showed the danger of over-pampering towns.
Privilege, concentric interest, tamer notions of living had up
to now kept the Irish burgesses circumspect. But Cork was
ardently Catholic and, as this affair showed, not loyal past
the point where its interests stopped.

Mountjoy dealt with Cork with almost insulting mildness,
and James, one may imagine, took no note of the matter.
James, still with Mountjoy as his strong hand, could continue
to be well-meaning. He indicated, if he did not express, a wish
for religious tolerance. Unhappily, his Irish good intentions
went down in the storm of anti-Popish feeling that, in England, followed the Gunpowder Plot. He could do no more

than attempt to temper the severities of his Parliament when, by the legislation of 1606, they anticipated the later Penal Laws. His tact in attempting to institute a modified Oath of Allegiance for loyal Catholics got snubbed by papal intransigeance. In the end, James I could do little more for Ireland than watch the troubles of this new era in.

Charles I as a king of Ireland did not promise badly. He had the High Church objection to extreme Protestantism, a Catholic wife and a general pacific wish that things should run as smoothly, and as fairly, as his own egotism allowed. His vain or timid mistakes came back to him all too soon: an abler man could have got away with much more. For poor Charles, the deluge came in his own time. I feel sure that a man with such a sense of his own myth, with Celtic blood and with such kingly looks could have held Ireland: " This race did ever love great personages." In England, he was up against the ideal that has made of some parts of England a Metroland. In Ireland, such an ideal does not exist. But as it was, he muddled his cause away.

Charles did attempt to compute with the Irish on matters of religion and land. Lord Falkland was instructed to offer " Graces," and in 1627 the Romanist peers and bishops sent over agents to England to bargain with the King. The agreed sum — £120,000 — was paid over, but Parliament, owing to furious Puritan counter-pressure, was not called to confirm the Graces: the King kept the money; the Graces were *not* confirmed. The position of Catholics in Ireland remained equivocal: they were left dependent, from day to day, on Charles's Tolerance by Prerogative. His slightly guilty good will and anti-Puritan bias continued to keep life possible till the Cromwellians came. In Dublin there were, for some time, thirty " Masshouses."

When Strafford, the King's man, came to Ireland to become Lord Lieutenant, his single purpose and " thorough " policy got him straight across the new Protestant monied class. He

found these people not only more disagreeable than the native
Irish but infinitely more dangerous both to the King's power
and to the health of the land. They showed, with a sour disloyalty to the King's person, suspicious opposition to Strafford's reforms. They had, in fact, feathered their nests nicely,
and were far from anxious to give account of themselves. This
Strafford determined they were to do. His first object, when
he arrived in Ireland, was to account for, and cause to be made
up, an annual deficit of £20,000 in the revenue due from that
country to the King. He planned also to establish the Church
of Ireland (on whom, with Laud behind him, he imposed the
Thirty-nine Articles) and to raise and ensure the maintenance
of a standing army in the name of the King. These projects
(the second involving the reclamation of Church lands
wrongly annexed by laymen) made him a pack of enemies.
The London City Companies who had put up money for the
exploitation of Ireland saw their returns threatened. And a
far more personal enemy was the Earl of Cork, who had
smelled trouble when he heard Strafford was due. Cork (then
Boyle) had been in trouble already, in Elizabeth's reign: the
speed with which, having come to the country penniless, he
had built up an imposing fortune by traffic in forfeited lands
had appeared more than suspicious to Sir Henry Wallop, and
Boyle had been called to London to account for himself. No
one of any nice conscience had been satisfied: at the same
time, it had not been possible to pin anything on him. Safe
back in Ireland, Boyle continued to flourish. He had a great
way of breaking his enemies. He got the unfortunate Raleigh's
Munster possessions, including the Youghal Church lands, for
a song.

The first brush between Boyle and Strafford was about a
tomb — a large egregious affair in black marble that Boyle had
had put up in the chancel of St. Patrick's cathedral, to the
sacred memory of his second wife. Its position — where the
altar ought to have been — was obnoxious to High Church

feeling; its self-importance was obnoxious to all. Strafford lost his point over this: the tomb stayed where it was. But then Strafford had Boyle on the mat for illegal possession of the Youghal Church lands and their revenues. Things once more looked ugly for Boyle, who on the whole got off lightly with a fine of £15,000. The reverse annoyed him as much as the loss of money. Laud, at the other side of the Irish Channel, rubbed his hands: one more " church cormorant " coughing up. But Strafford had made a finally fatal enemy, who ran with tales to England when Strafford fell.

Strafford proceeded with " thoroughness." He set up a Commission for Defective Titles, to examine tenures of land. In all matters, his impartiality was ruthless: he overruled all factions, serving only the King. Policy, and regard for the revenue, made him aim at keeping a balance between Catholics and Protestants. The insecurity of the (cheated) Catholics resigned them to further expense: they paid up — but so, and still more unwillingly, did rich Protestants not anxious for inquisition. Land values, threatened by the Commission, began to drop, and investors in England quailed. In both houses of the Dublin Parliament that Strafford summoned in 1633, Catholics were represented, though by a minority.

No appeals to England got past the Court of Castle Chamber Strafford had set up. Thus, grievances were kept smothered, till he fell. Taking Mountjoy's view of the pampered and heady cities, he docked city charters. At the same time, he promoted shipping and encouraged industries; by a large investment of his own money he put the new linen industry on its feet. His purpose, throughout, was quite alarmingly single, and this made for consistency in his plan. In his own manner, and in the King's interest purely, he was on his way to do more for Ireland than any Englishman had. His fall came too soon. The English Parliamentarians, who destroyed him and his work, thought highly of sharks like the first Earl of Cork.

When Strafford fell, a figurehead was appointed to succeed

him as Lord Lieutenant. The King's overlooking of Lord
Ormond — a leading royalist Protestant, with Catholic connections, and a man of honour who could have kept the peace
— for this position was fatal. Lord Ormond stayed in command of the army Strafford had raised, but administrative
power, from Dublin outwards, fell into the hands of two
Puritan Lords Justices. To add to the King's troubles by
fomenting trouble in Ireland appears to have been the Puritan
policy. To this end, the two Lords Justices left no stone un-
turned. Fresh persecution and penalization of Catholics set
in all over the country; to all classes, the position became intolerable — the Irish rose. In Ulster, the Catholic Irish fell on
the Protestant settlers: there ensued a massacre, bad enough
in reality but greatly exaggerated by propaganda. This Ulster
massacre gave the name of reprisals to the succeeding Cromwellian atrocities. Tough men seemed to be needed to beat
the Irish, and when it became possible Cromwell brought them
over. It has already appeared that Colonel Bowen's unruly and
desperate spirit was felt to fit him for the Irish campaign.

The rising in Ireland preceded the outbreak of the Civil
War in England by one year. It did, as had been hoped, add
to the King's troubles. But it complicated the issue for his foes.

The war in Ireland to which Colonel Bowen came had been
for some time tripartite. The Catholic Confederates (also
known as " The Irish " or " the rebels "), the Royalists under
Lord Ormond, and the Parliamentarians were all up in arms.
Behind the Catholic Confederates a fourth party, the Ultramontane, exerted an often intransigent influence. Led by the
old Anglo-Norman, as well as by the purely Irish lords and
gentry, the Confederates, while fighting for their religion, had
at the same time sworn allegiance to the King: they were
pledged, by the terms of the same Oath, to make no peace that
ran contrary to their faith.

Munster, largely, was the scene of this war. One evening in

the October of 1641 the Earl of Cork, at dinner with his son-in-law the Earl of Barrymore, his son Lord Broghill and the Lord Muskerry, received ("coolly") the news that the Irish were in arms from Leinster to Clonmel, and were perpetrating horrible outrages on the English. Though Lord Cork's sympathies, since the affair Strafford, had been pro-Parliamentarian, he was not disposed to commit himself till he saw how things went. Lord Broghill, not his father's son for nothing, foresaw further openings for Boyles with the Parliamentarian cause. Lord Muskerry, a Confederate Catholic, conscious of having in his pocket a commission from Charles I to raise 4,000 men, made light of the rumour but left the table quietly. Lord Barrymore was to claim, later, that the Irish had offered him the chief command, but that he had turned down their offer owing to principles. Lord Cork, still non-committal, returned to Lismore Castle, but saw to it that Sir William St. Leger, at Doneraile, was notified. Sir William was Lord President of Munster; it was for him to act and, if necessary, take the blame.

The next thing Sir William St. Leger heard was that Lord Muskerry was up in arms, at the head of some thousands of Irish rebels. To Sir William, a passionate faithful Royalist, this looked like one more blow to the King. He raised a force, marched, confronted Lord Muskerry at Redchair, a pass in the Ballyhouras near Kildorrery, and drew up for battle. Lord Muskerry, however, sounded a trumpet, sent out and offered to show St. Leger the King's commission. The King's commission, produced and closely examined, reversed for St. Leger the entire matter. His own position now looked ambiguous. To the three Boyles in his party — the Lords Dungarvan, Broghill and Kinalmeaky, he said: " I would rather die than be a rebel." He disbanded his forces and rode home, though still in trouble of mind. The Boyles, audibly, sniffed. Lord Broghill, to whom the King already meant little, felt certain Lord Muskerry was putting something across.

The Irish, or Catholic Confederates, now under Lord Mountgarret, marched down from the Ballyhouras to Buttevant, then on to Mallow, where General Barry, who had served in the Spanish army, assumed entire command. Mallow, with its two castles, was held by Parliamentarians. (It was a Sir William Jephson, of Mallow, who was to move later that Cromwell be offered the Crown.) The Confederates took one castle and invested the other: they established themselves in Mallow and did, or are said to have done, considerable damage in the country round. Some Protestants were slaughtered, others annoyed. While the Confederate army remained in Mallow, it is said to have consumed 50,000 cattle and 100,000 sheep. At all events, a number of claims came in. General Barry moved some of his forces towards Cork; others passed down the Blackwater into the County Waterford, threatening Lord Broghill's Lismore garrison. Skirmishes, of rather uncertain outcome, occurred in the river valley between Ballyduff and Lismore.

Cork, Youghal, Kinsale and Bandon were the only towns in the county in the hands of the Parliament party. The outlying English fled to Bandon, a walled town whose protection had been intrusted to Lord Kinalmeaky, third of the Boyle sons. Lord Muskerry marched on Bandon, but was repulsed, with more than a hundred slain. The Lords Justices had sent down from Dublin commissions for the executions of martial law on the loyal Catholic Confederates — called " the rebels." Under the supervision of Kinalmeaky prisoners were, accordingly, killed at the town gates. " And now the boy had blooded himself," wrote his father, jubilant. But this was to be poor Kinalmeaky's only success: he fell at the battle of Liscarrol.

There had been a winter of fighting. February 1642 had seen Lord Muskerry's repulse at Bandon, but in April he marched the Confederates on to Cork: they invested the city. Sir William St. Leger, once more shaken by doubts of Lord Muskerry, lay sick inside the city, unable to command. Lord Inchiquin and Colonel Vavasour got his permission to sally, and chased

Muskerry's Irish out of the neighbourhood. Three months later Sir William, worn by distress and tension, overwrought by the doubtfulness of his own position, by ambiguous loyalties everywhere, died at Doneraile. "Sorrow," he wrote to Lord Ormond, "for these unhappy variances would crack a much stronger heart than your servant hath now left in him." His death left his office empty: it is said that the King, on a belated right impulse, appointed Lord Muskerry — if so, the gesture went for nothing; the Lords Justices made, from Dublin, an overruling appointment and Lord Inchiquin became Munster's Lord President. Inchiquin had married St. Leger's daughter: he was a useful man who had not yet thrown in his lot with either of the English parties definitively, and it was important to tie him to the Parliamentarian side. He was, also, at loggerheads with Lord Cork, who, called upon to provision the town of Youghal, was already grumbling at the cost of war.

Lord Muskerry, after his two misfires, rejoined the main body of the Catholic Confederate force. The entire force, now 7,000 foot and 5,000 horse strong, and with a good train of artillery, now swung round again into the Blackwater country and, under General Barry, besieged Liscarrol Castle, which they took on September 2nd after thirteen days. However, Inchiquin, *parti pris* after his appointment, arrived on the ground at the head of the Parliamentary troops. He was supported by the four Boyle sons — Dungarvan, Broghill, Kinalmeaky and Master Francis, who was to become Lord Shannon, also by Captain Jephson, Lord Barrymore and Sir Charles Vavasour. In the Confederate army were the Lords Muskerry, Ikerrin, Dunboyne, Castleconnel, Brittas, also Colonel Richard Butler and a number of other Irish gentlemen.

This was one of the biggest battles of the Munster campaign. In spite of the Confederates' advantageous position, and in spite of Barry's fine generalship, Inchiquin gained a decided victory. On the Confederate side, losses were heavy; quarter had been given to none. The Boyles lost Lord Kinalmeaky. Inchiquin was prevented, by lack of supplies, from following up his victory: he marched back to Mallow and dispersed his troops in garrisons. The Confederates withdrew from Liscarrol and took up other positions.

The next June (1643) the Confederates avenged that September defeat at Liscarrol. Lord Castlehaven, in command of a body of Irish, surprised a troop of Parliamentarian horse in the early morning mists of the Funcheon valley. The Parliamentarians, flying through a defile in the Fermoy hills, brought Castlehaven after them; he fell without warning, heavily, on their main body camped by the Blackwater. Hemmed in by the valley, the English stood to give battle; they lost their colours and had five or six hundred slain. Their commander, Colonel Vavasour, was taken. Castlehaven, as victor, gave quarter — as Inchiquin had not done at Liscarrol. He attributed his victory to the enemy's cannon being on the other side (from the enemy) of the river, to God's blessing and to a great shower of rain.

Lord Ormond intimated to Castlehaven (already his personal friend) that the Royalist and the Confederate forces might, at this juncture, effectively combine. Negotiations, however, broke down — Ormond fearing to prejudice the King's position in England by granting pro-Catholic concessions the Confederates asked; they being bound not to ask less by the terms of their Oath. Inchiquin, uncertain Parliamentarian, meanwhile made a *démarche* towards the King: he took a part of his forces over to England and placed them under the royal standard there. Not, however, getting what he expected, he once more withdrew his forces, returned to Ireland and fought with redoubled vigour on the Parliamentarian side. He sank his differences with the Boyle family and worked for some time with Broghill, on cordial terms.

Inchiquin and Broghill decided to make a purge of the Irish in Cork city. On the claim of having discovered a Popish plot (which they faked) they succeeded in shutting the Catholic townspeople, of all classes, outside the city walls; at the same time, they suspended the civil authority and the military took entire command. The enactment of this extraordinary farce in Cork so fully occupied the English that Castlehaven, re-entering County Cork at the head of 5,000 foot and 1,000 horse, was able to take Liscarrol, Mallow, Doneraile, Mitchelstown, and burn several castles, with almost no opposition. And the military history of the succeeding year (1645-46) was to consist of little more than the taking and retaking of castles and small towns.

It was in the summer of 1645 that Rinuccini, the Papal Nuncio, landed in Ireland, at considerable risk. In Lord Castlehaven's opinion, it would have been better had he not landed at all. Rinuccini did little good to the Confederate cause; Smith says " he revived the distinction between the Irish natives and the old English Catholics, which split their party into different factions." The final failure to come to terms with Lord Ormond must be laid at his door. Rinuccini returned to Rome in 1648, to be told by the Pope he had acted rashly, and lose his bishopric. Meanwhile Ormond, cut off and profoundly discouraged, patched up some sort of terms with the English Parliament and left the country for France.

Inchiquin, however, was still incalculable. At the head of the Parliamentarian forces, he gained a signal victory over the Confederates, under Lord Taafe, at Knockinoss, west of Mallow. Parliament, hearing of his achievement, voted £10,000 for the service of Munster, and £1,000 for Lord Inchiquin. Either piqued by the smallness of the bonus or feeling that he would like a change again, Lord Inchiquin almost at once made overtures to Lord Taafe: why should they not both fight the English side by side? As a proof of good faith, he declared openly for the King. He followed this up by messages to Lord Ormond, suggesting that he should return from France and re-enter the war. Lord Ormond, only too pleased, landed in Cork in September 1648, to be received warmly by Lord Inchiquin.

The poor King, however, from his prison in England, begged
Ormond to desist from further activities — these could do no
good. Nothing could do Charles any good now: he was executed in January 1649.

Lord Ormond at once had Charles II proclaimed in Youghal,
Carrick, Cork, Kinsale and other towns in the province. Prince
Rupert, the late King's nephew, in deep mourning, entered
Kinsale harbour with sixteen black-draped ships. Having come
to prepare the way for Charles II, he was received by Lord
Ormond with deep respect. His fleet, having made prizes of
several corn vessels, looked like wintering in the Kinsale
waters. Unhappily, the English Parliament sent two admirals to
blockade Kinsale harbour and either dislodge Prince Rupert or
starve him out. As something between a funeral and regatta the
Prince had been locally popular, but he could get no ships from
Cork or Waterford when he applied for aid. He had lost most
of his fleet before he could slip the English and make a dash for
Lisbon. And there (where we are concerned) was the end of
him.

On land, Lord Ormond was no more fortunate. He had assembled, at Carlow, a force of 8,000 foot and 2,000 horse. His
lieutenant, Lord Inchiquin, taking with him part of this army,
branched off and made a successful march through Drogheda,
Dundalk and Newry to Trim Castle, which all surrendered.
He then rejoined Lord Ormond, waiting just north of Dublin,
at Finglass. From Finglass the army made its fatal move to
Rathmines.

Ormond may not have reckoned on Colonel Michael Jones.
Colonel Jones, preceding Cromwell to Ireland, had brought
with him reinforcements for the Cromwellians there. The reinforcements were fresh, and eager for Irish blood. The unhappy
Ormond marched into the teeth of the Jones army, waiting at
the Dublin edge of Rathmines. When he did realize the weakness of his position, it was already too late to retreat. He remained alert through a night, but the alert was in vain —

towards daybreak, the Cromwellians fell on him. Ormond sustained vast losses in men, artillery, baggage and provender, and was, finally, put to entire rout.

In recognition of the Rathmines victory, Jones later received £500 a year from Irish forfeited lands. But Cromwell had had to teach Ireland her lesson before his men could be paid. His campaign was a speculation as well as a holy war.

Up to the time of Cromwell's coming to Ireland, one sort of temper and tempo had ruled this three-sided war — a war that had damaged fortunes and cities, laid waste tracts of country, distracted consciences and broken hearts. There had been *voltes-faces* and betrayals. But on the whole the three parties, even Broghill's and Inchiquin's " English," had fought with a sort of high-spirited dash. The feelings involved could hardly have been more violent, the interests at stake more vital. But it had been a war between three parties of people who fought, felt and acted in one another's terms, people all dyed with the temperament of a country — for even the " English " who fought before Cromwell's coming had been in Ireland, owned Ireland, felt Ireland for some years, and however much remaining distinct in interest, were already temperamentally modified. And it had been, to an extent, a barons' war — the integrity of Castlehaven and Ormond, the foxiness of Broghill and Inchiquin, were parts of the same aristocratic pattern. The three parties were led by lords who had dined at each other's tables, and who were up to each other's tricks. The war had been fought at once with fierceness and with virtuosity. But it had not, possibly, been very businesslike. When Cromwell came, he meant business. The Irish had yet to learn — and they did — what business meant.

It must be said for Cromwell in Ireland that the methods he used were those *de rigueur*, in his time, for subduing and colonizing a savage country — Spain had built up her wealth and power in just this way. Also, that the Irish extravagant showy

looseness of feeling must have been deeply antipathetic to him.
Equally, the cause to which he had dedicated his life in England
would have been incomprehensible to the Irish mind. In England he had fought for the English conception of "freedom";
in Ireland he fought against the Irish conception of it. The two
different ideas were not to be reconciled.

I do not know whether Colonel Bowen came to Ireland
actually with Cromwell, or with the advance army of Colonel
Michael Jones. From our only other story (the hawk story)
about him, we know he was with or near Cromwell in the Munster campaign.

Cromwell landed in Dublin on the 14th of August, 1649,
with 9,000 foot and 4,000 horse. He found Jones and his fol-
lowers in possession, already flushed from their victory at
Rathmines. In fact, Jones's detachment were in only too good
form; they had been committing violences on the people.
Cromwell called them sharply to order. He thus moved north,
to undo some of the damage done by Inchiquin. At Drogheda
he got going. Drogheda, which had surrendered to Inchiquin,
did not again surrender: it was taken by storm and the defenders, about 3,000 in number, were put to the sword. That was
that. "It hath pleased God," wrote Cromwell, "to bless our
endeavours." Intimidated — as they were intended to be —
Dundalk and Trim gave in.

Cromwell returned to Dublin, then moved south; he took his
route to Cork by Wexford and Ross. Wexford, hearing that
Castlehaven was marching to its relief, attempted to gain time
by negotiation. The wait was too long for Cromwell's pleasure:
the castle surrendered, the town fell — with shockingly heavy
losses, though not a massacre. At Ross the Governor, Lucas
Taafe (brother of the Lord Taafe who lost Knockinoss), tried
to get terms from Cromwell, and got the famous reply. Ross,
remembering Drogheda, had to surrender without the terms
Taafe had asked for — here, as in all the taken towns, the mass

and all Catholic practice were now absolutely suppressed. "*I meddle not with any man's conscience*," Cromwell had said, when Taafe tried to stipulate otherwise. (The thing would not have been simpler — you could not go to mass when there was no mass to go to: the predicament, the factor of decision that calls on conscience to function, no longer, therefore, existed: conscience stayed where it was.)

Lord Broghill, who had applied to the English Treasury for £200 in order to get his wife over — and Cromwell advised they grant it — was meantime busy with the ordering of Munster affairs. In this he was assisted by Sir William Fenton and Colonels Blake, Deane and Phaire. Phaire had begun 1649 well; he had been one of the three colonels appointed to supervise the execution of Charles I. After his coming to Ireland he had garrisoned Youghal, which had declared for Parliament, then marched on Cork and its Royalist governor. Fifteen hundred pounds spent on bribes, and efficient surprise tactics, got him into the city: he was a night alarm. Alike, Catholics and Royalists, without their goods, in some cases wounded and stripped, were forthwith cast outside the walls. That November was very cold.

Cork, purged, awaited Cromwell. Missing a brush with the Irish under Owen Roe O'Neill, reclaiming twelve hundred sick troops threatened by Inchiquin, Cromwell marched on Waterford, which he failed to take. He covered up this hiatus in his programme by writing some magnificent letters home. By mid-December he was in Cork. From here, he exchanged shots on paper with the Ultramontane party who, having convened an assembly at Clonmacnois, issued a manifesto. Cromwell's official reply (thought not to have been written by him) was rabid. In Cork Bishop Bramhall, "that Irish Canterbury," gave Cromwell the slip, and in Cork, at this same time, the city bells were converted into battering ordnance. From Cork, Cromwell made entries into subdued Kinsale and Youghal, believing firmly that the people "rejoiced."

At the end of the January of 1650, Cromwell with his now
sufficiently rested army began to move north again. Crossing
the Blackwater at Mallow, he passed round the last spur of the
Ballyhouras into the County Limerick. Broghill, however, with
a detachment, was left in County Cork to besiege Castletownroche. The Roches — " old English," or Anglo-Norman —
were intractable, refusing to come to terms. Lady Roche now,
in her husband's absence, put up that intrepid defence of the
Castle against Broghill, with his cannon, stationed across the
Awbeg. The castle, as it must, fell. Lord Cork had already annexed some Roche lands; the new Boyles and old Roches had
not been on warm terms; it was fitly left to Broghill to polish
the Roches off.

Colonel Bowen, most likely, stayed with Broghill. Inside the
loop described by Cromwell's march through the counties, this
smaller force in north-east Cork kept to one area. My Lord
Broghill's Horse clattered about the country, splashily crossed
and recrossed Awbeg and Funcheon, jogged down the valleys,
stumbled up limestone tracks. About this time a number of
abbeys fell. Broghill's troops gave the name of Canteen Cross to
the crossroads a mile west of Bowen's Court. It was late winter,
early spring; Broghill was already familiar with this region —
St. Leger's army, in which he had been numbered, had massed
at Kildorrery, back in 1642, on their way to the anti-climax of
Redchair. For two days and nights they had awaited the
" rebels ": the army lay in the sloping fields in the snow, and St.
Leger, lying with no pillow, had refused a folded cloak to put
under his head.

Now, old St. Leger with his scruples and halts was gone.
Kildorrery must have looked better in 1650. Bowen, from the
top of Kildorrery hill, may have watched the light-shifted colours and contours of Garrett Cushin the papist's Farahy lands.
Did he stop to desire this tract of country in pauses of the now
not too arduous campaign?

From Castletown, in County Limerick, Cromwell turned

east to Cahir, in Tipperary. He took Cahir, this time as much by tact as by force. Some intelligence must have made him delay his approach to Clonmel, for though Clonmel lies on the direct road from Cahir to Kilkenny, it was to Kilkenny he went first. Here, the warning of Drogheda still stood him in good stead; moreover, the rich Kilkenny citizens, having surrendered, paid over £2,000 to save themselves from plunder. It was now time to bend back again on Clonmel, mopping up Carrick-on-Suir on the way. Clonmel, sighted, still did not look too good. It was April; more than half the Cromwellian troops were enfeebled by the long late-winter marches and by some sickness of spring. On top of this, news came that the Catholic bishop of Ross was now raising an army for Clonmel's relief. Bishops were bad enough without being militant. Cromwell sent into County Cork, to Broghill, urgent word to locate the bishop and smoke him out.

Broghill wheeled off into west Cork after the bishop. At his approach the bishop, with half his forces, emerged from Macroom castle, burnt it behind him, and gave battle on open ground. Broghill routed the Irish and captured the bishop. But the other half of the Irish force still held Carrigadrohoid: led by Broghill up to these walls the bishop was offered his life on condition he told the garrison to surrender. He shouted, " Hold out to the last! " — and Broghill forthwith hanged him, then took Carrigadrohoid. He then made for Clonmel. Cromwell's exhausted army, passive outside the city, rose up with cries, " A Broghill! a Broghill! " Cromwell, showing emotion, embraced his friend. Morale went up all round; the siege was renewed, Clonmel fell. After that Waterford (sole reverse of last autumn) was again attacked, and was taken this time. Cromwell was satisfied. He returned to Youghal, where, for a short time, he took up once more his quarters. He sailed from Youghal for England on May 29th, leaving General Ireton in command.

In July, Ireton was besieging Limerick when it was heard that Lord Muskerry had raised an army for the city's relief.

Lord Broghill made a sweeping reconnaissance. Posting along
the Blackwater, he gave pursuit to some of Muskerry's horse
that issued from Dromagh castle near the river. He then had an
odd encounter — I give his own words: " In the early morning
I passed the river, near Clonmeen, where I met with ninety
Irish, who were under protection. I asked them what they were
assembled for? They answered, they came out of curiousity to
see the battle. Having asked them how they knew there was to
be a battle? they answered, they had a prophecy that there was
to be one fought on that ground, one time or another, and they
knew none more likely than the present. Upon which I again
asked them, on what side was the victory to fall? They shook
their heads, and said the English are to get the day."

The battle was Knocknaclashy. Muskerry's whole force,
which was considerable, emerged from the woods: the fighting
was in the open, and it was desperate and bitter, every inch contested, and for some time inconclusive — at one time, the English were outflanked. Lord Broghill marvelled at the Irish.
" Their priests, all the way before they came to fight, encouraged them by speeches, but especially by sprinkling holy
water on them. . . . Certainly they are a people given over to
destruction, who, though otherwise understanding enough, let
themselves be still deluded by ridiculous things and by more
ridiculous persons." Lord Broghill's battle-cry was " *Prosperity!* "; the Irish cry was " *St. James!* " The Irish fighting at
Knocknaclashy might well have given the prophecy the lie.
But Prosperity won the day. Among the Irish there were atro-
cious losses; little quarter was given; Mac Donough Mac
Carthy, the Lord of Duhallow, was killed charging at the head
of his horse. Lord Muskerry was soon afterwards apprehended;
he was tried for his life, acquitted, he went to Spain, then to
France, where he petitioned Louis XIV for money to carry on
the war, but failed to get it. He had to stay where he was.

So, this makes a point at which it is convenient to leave history and return to the Bowens. The events of two decades in

Ireland, up to 1650, have been briefly and superficially traced. They make a story that seems to have no moral, and that one cannot believe will ever have any end.

When Colonel Bowen, having come to Ireland, entered into possession of the Farahy lands, he took a hawk as his crest, while keeping the stag as his coat of arms. The tale — it is more than a legend — of the Bowen Hawk has been handed down in our family, always by word of mouth. It gathers force in the telling, and though I cannot find it written down anywhere it is the last story that I would ever doubt — it has a psychological, if not a strictly historical, likeliness. Like all stories retold with gusto, it has its variations: every Bowen tells it as seems to him or her best. I will give the version that most appeals to me.

Colonel Bowen, going to Ireland with the Cromwellian army, took with him from Gower his pair of hawks. In intervals of the Munster fighting he continued to practice his favourite sport. He felt, also, affection for these birds — the only creatures, perhaps, with which he was intimate — and always took one round with him chained to his wrist. The Cromwellians did not look kindly on Bowen's hawking — for one thing, it was ungodly and frivolous, more fitting for Royalists or Confederates; for another, it might, like all kinds of sport in Ireland, lead to fraternization with the country people. Colonel Bowen, both as a Celt and an atheist, was already, although a useful fighter, being sufficiently difficult: the Cromwellian team-spirit meant little to him. In fact, he was like a bad boy at a " good " school. One could not wish to have him hawking over the country, picking up all sorts of Irish friends.

One day, Cromwell sent for Bowen to give him an order — or to know why some order had not been carried out. Bowen strolled into the tent with his hawk on his wrist, and Cromwell cast a bilious glance at the bird. Cromwell gave Bowen his orders, but Bowen gave little attention to what Cromwell was saying, because he was busy toying with his hawk. " Leave that

damned bird alone, sir, and listen to what I'm saying! " yelled
the Protector — or words to that effect. Bowen, however, continued to look nonchalant and to caress his pet. Cromwell had
a rush of blood to the head, started up, fell on Bowen and
wrung the hawk's neck. Bowen left the tent in a black huff.

Here the two versions vary — one has it that Bowen, on
thinking the matter over, considered himself rightly rebuked,
whereupon he fought with such zeal and outstanding courage,
and became in every way such a model, that he became due for
some award. The other (which seems to me the more pleasing)
has it that, Bowen's incalculability and fierce temper making
him more and more a man to be reckoned with, efforts to square
him were set on foot. At all events, Cromwell sent again for
Bowen, said, " You know how these things happen," and said
he was sorry about the hawk. He then proposed to give Bowen
as much Irish land as the second hawk could fly over before it
came down, Bowen to choose the spot from which to let off
the bird.

This story has been a little upset by what I have, later,
learned from the Buchan family about hawks and hawking.
Apparently, a hawk rockets straight up through the air and
hangs where it is until it drops on its prey. In which case, Cromwell was smart in his proposition, for Colonel Bowen would not
have got much land. But we know he did get a very solid
amount. I can only suggest that *his* hawk was a mythological
bird, made free of every power and property; or else, that his
hawk was his familiar (which Mr. Baxter probably might bear
out) and that he murmured something close to its sleek head;
upon which the released hawk, loyal, broke with its usual motion and made off in a long cross-country flight with the hum-
drum, unflagging patience of a carrier pigeon. . . . At all
events, we Bowens are left with this — standing near the foot of
the Ballyhouras, Colonel Bowen released his hawk, which flew
south.

Cromwell's portrait hangs at the top of our front stairs, and the Hawk appears on all family silver not occupied by the Stag, on seals, inside books and in the mosaic pavement of the glass porch built by my grandfather. Had the Bowens continued the sport of hawking they might have moulded the story truer to life, and I should not, as the family story-teller, have been placed in my present predicament.

JOHN BOWEN I

FOR JUST UNDER TWO YEARS AFTER KNOCKNACLASHY A STATE of uneven war dragged on, till, on May 12th, 1652, the Kilkenny surrender of the last Irish army marked the Cromwellians' finishing victory. Ireland was prostrate: the fighting part of the campaign had been successfully wound up. But a new, ticklish business now confronted the conquerors — Ireland must be divided and shared out to the satisfaction of all who felt they had earned their share. And that proved to be just as hard as it sounds.

"After the subduing of Ireland," Ludlow writes, "there was no small consultation how to divide every one's portion, until at a general council of war, Lord Broghill proposed, that the kingdom might be surveyed, and the number of acres taken, with the quality of them, and then all his soldiers to bring in their demands of arrears, and so to give every man by lot, as many acres of ground as might answer the value of their arrears. The kingdom being surveyed, and the value of acres being given, the highest was estimated at four shillings the acre, and some only at a penny. Accordingly, the soldiers drew lots for their several portions, and in that manner all the forfeited lands were divided up among the conquerors and adventurers for money. At the same time, it was agreed that the *Irish* should be transplanted into Connaught, which so shattered them that they never made any head afterwards."

The officers and soldiers of the Cromwellian army had, as we know, been hired on credit: they must not expect pay till they had won the war. But even an unpaid army needs financing — supplies had to be got. This was where the Adventurers had come in; it had been the Adventurers who, largely, financed the expeditionary force. This English company had, as early as 1642, invested (or, as they would say, " adventured ") large sums in the promising enterprise; their interests had been guaranteed by Parliament, under the Adventurers' Acts, and they were now looking for their returns. The Adventurers must have been, to the fighting army, almost more trouble than their money was worth; they were typical shareholders — ignorant, fractious and likely to agitate at the wrong times. They were now due to have Irish estates and manors given them at a specified low rate — a rate fixed before the war in Ireland was over and before it had been possible to compute its cost. One million acres of Ireland had to be set aside to meet the Adventurers' claims, before the army, who would not wait for ever, could even begin to be paid off. (The soldiers were to commute their arrears of money for land.) Some of the officers were, at the same time, Adventurers, but on the whole the " adventure " was a civilian matter, and the army — who had, after all, fought — did not look amiably on this rival claim. Disaffection would have been fatal. So, it was at last agreed that private soldiers, troopers and non-commissioned officers should receive the land due to them for arrears of pay at the same low rate as the Adventurers, that lieutenants, ensigns, cornets and quarter-masters should get it at two thirds, and captains and all officers of above that rank at one half of that rate.

The survey was made. Before distribution could be put in practice, it was desirable to clear the land, as far as possible, of those Irish who still encumbered it. The disbanded Catholic Irish armies were encouraged to go and fight abroad. " Foreign nations were apprised by the Kilkenny Articles that the Irish were to be allowed to engage in the service of any state in

amity with the Commonwealth. The valour of Irish soldiers
was well known abroad." [1] The Kings of Spain and Poland and
the Prince de Condé were now all in the market for Irish troops.
Lord Muskerry led five thousand of his own men to the King of
Poland. Sir Walter Dungan and others got permission to march
their men, pipes playing, to the ports for Spain. But these late
fighters were not the only menace; the country was weighted
down with her vagrant and destitute. For these, too, a market
was found abroad. Very large numbers of young boys, mostly
around the age of twelve, were exported as workers to the
Barbadoes, to the English plantations in America, and, later, to
Jamaica. "Who knows," wrote Henry Cromwell, "but it
might be a means to make them Englishmen — I mean, Christians?" Young widows (or wives bereft of their husbands)
and girls were exported to the Barbadoes, where they were
short of women. Jamaica also put in for a thousand Irish girls.
This traffic was only checked by a scandal — some English
young people were inadvertently seized.

Those Irish whose lands were wanted were to move west
into Connaught. The hardships and scandals of that transplan-
tation are too well known to be chronicled here. "On 26th of
September, 1653, all the ancient estates and farms of the people
of Ireland were declared to belong to the Adventurers and the
army of England; and it was announced that the Parliament
has assigned Connaught (America was not then accessible) for
the habitation of the Irish nation, whither they must transplant
with their wives, and daughters and children, before the 1st of
May following (1654) under penalty of death, if found on this
side of the Shannon after that day." [2]

This order applied, or was applied more closely, to the prop-
ertied Irish. (Those of the common people prepared to work
on the land under new masters were allowed to remain.) The
idea was, to remove the Catholic lords and gentry, with their
dangerously feudal influence. All the same, you cannot shift an

[1] Prendergast.   [2] Prendergast.

entire class. Many remained on the dangerous side of the Shannon. Conspicuous figures had to banish themselves, but there
were numerous dispossessed Catholic gentry to be found on or
near what had lately been their own lands; refuging in their
former tenants' cabins they stayed to watch their English successors, and perhaps sometimes — since everything into Ireland
resolves itself into laughter, though seldom laughter of the happiest kind — to laugh at them. For many of these English must
have been funny, doing the grand inexpertly on their new
estates.

We do not know what became of the dispossessed Garrett
Cushin. But we do know, from the sentence in Colonel Bowen's
will, that for some time at least Garrett Cushin, with his relations, stayed about Farahy.

James I had granted Farahy to the Roches when the greater
part of the Roche lands were annexed by the Crown. In 1640,
however, Garrett Cushin, papist, is shown as being in possession. These Farahy lands over which Bowen's hawk had flown
comprised: " 600 acres profitable land, plantation measure, 55
acres unprofitable, in the eight ploughlands of Pharihy and Bal-
lensmisty, on the south-west side of the River Pharihy; 56 acres
3 roods and 27 perches profitable land in Monegabane, the
south-east part; and in Garrandolan 92 acres profitable land,
plantation measure, all lying and being in the Barony of Fermoy, and County of Corke." (" Unprofitable " means " Mountain and Bogg.") In 1653, " the above mentioned Lands were
sett forth to Lieut. Col. Henry Bowen in Satisfaction of his
Arrears." And in 1662, after Colonel Bowen's death, this grant
was to be confirmed by Letters Patent under the Act of Settlement to the name of his son, John.

This, then, was the " fair Estate " on which Bowen, according to Captain Foley, chose to live " in a beggarly way." I suspect that much of Bowen's bad reputation may have come from
his disregard for *ton*. The Cromwellians settling down round
him were soon to be showing the Irish what was what. Follow-

ing the example of Lord Broghill, they were getting their wives over to make them homes — though they were not able, like Lord Broghill, to import these ladies at the public expense. But when Mrs. Bowen attempted to join her husband, we know that she was fired back again. All he sent her from Farahy was, in 1655, that appalling ghost.

The country round him was desolate after war; its only smile came from the sun and changing colours. Did Colonel Bowen show pity? If he experienced pity, he would not show it: he kept himself to himself. Subtle dissimilarities between Wales and Ireland may have made him feel he was going a little mad. Did he find himself in that nerve-wracking abeyance that afflicts fighters at the end of a war? Keyed up, he was left in the vacuum of that dreadful peace. He must have missed the movement of the campaign. But, unlike some of the settlers round him, he was not new to the possession of land — perhaps he had a physical love of it. He took stock of his new property shrewdly, summing up everything with an experienced eye. He beat his own bounds on horseback, riding with slack reins; or, he pressed through woods, went up out on to bogland, trod the ups and downs of the flowing, then hedgeless, fields at a furious solitary walker's pace. And perhaps he went back to hawking. Business or love of controversy took him at least once to Limerick city, where, to the governor (Ingoldsby) and the minister he said his last recorded outrageous thing about God. In the silence under the Ballyhouras, there was nobody to care what he thought.

He took up his quarters in the small semi-ruinous castle just across the Farahy stream; just *off* — by the width of the water — his own lands. The Bowen hawk cannot have swerved east of the natural boundary, and the Mitchelstown Fentons (then, later, the Kingstons) owned the land up from the east bank of the stream. Farahy castle was crabbed, draughty, rough and built on a ridge of limestone; cold exhalations travelled up through its walls. To this cold shelter only, Henry I would be driven back by the drenching rains, impatiently fording the stream in spate. Into this dark doorway he turned at the close of the long dusks. In these chambers he muttered and walked at nights.

In the May of 1656, Colonel Bowen returned to Gower for a short time. While there, he made a settlement of his Welsh estates, conveying these to certain trustees for the use of himself for life, and after his decease to his wife Katherine Bowen. After *her* decease, the lands were to go to Nehemiah, and next, in default of his having heirs, to Cornelius, and so on through the Welsh sons. Should the Welsh line (as in time it did) expire, the Welsh lands were to return to the Irish Bowens. Colonel Bowen then left Gower for ever — so far as we know, without any regrets.

It was later on in this same summer, when he was back in Ireland, that Mrs. Bowen — or so Captain Foley tells us — attempted to visit him.

When his eldest son John Bowen came to Ireland we do not know. We are told he, also, was fighting in the campaign; if so, he got no grant of lands on his own account. I should like to know how his arrears were made up, for I cannot believe that he fought for nothing. In 1656, John would not have been more than twenty-eight or nine. (His father's first wife, Margaret Bassett, died childless in 1625: John, son of the second marriage, could not have been born much *before* 1627.) At all events, he was still a youngish man when he joined his father at Farahy. There was certainly some delay before he came, for Colonel Bowen's solitude was much commented on. Perhaps, like some of the younger, gayer Cromwellians, John was roystering round the Irish countryside. We know his looks and address were agreeable. When John did join his father he was in excellent spirits, pleased with Ireland, unmarried and with a roving eye. This — perhaps — lit on Elizabeth Cushin.

Father and son made a temperamental contrast. Perhaps John's mother, Anne Maunsel — unlike her austere successor

— had been laughing and pretty. John's go and hilarity countered his father's gloom. John was out for whatever might come along; he had tendencies that his father saw with mistrust.

At Farahy, shortly before his death, Colonel Bowen drew up his will, which ran as follows:

Decembr the 18th 1658
Whereas the livess of All Creaters are in the dispose of the Eternall god and maker of all into whose hand I Committ my Spritt: I Henry Bowen of ffaryby in the County of Corke Being of perfect memory and Remembrance doe make and ordaine this my last will and testament in manner following that is to say:

first I give unto my daughter mary bowen three hundred pounds Sterlin to bee payd to hir twoe hundred pounds one yeare affter my desess and one hundred pounds twoe yeares affter my desess.

secondly I give unto my daughter hester bowen three hundred pounds Sterlin to bee payd to hir twoe hundred pounds twoe yeares affter my desess and one hundred pounds three years affter my desess.

thirdly I give to my sonn John Bowen all my lands in Ireland and all my goods whatsoeever upon Condicion that he shall pay the above legeseys to my daughters and till then to mantaine them with meate drinke and aparrel necessary for them: provided that if my sd Sonn doe marry or Contract or bee already maryed to Elis Cooshin or any of Garrett Cooshins ffammyly then my will is that hee my sd Sonn John Bowen shall not have nor injoy my lands nor goods nor any part thereof save only tenn pounds and that then my Sonn Nehemiah Bowen shall have all my lands and goods above mencioned hee paying the above legeseys: and I make my Sonn John Bowen upon the Condicion above expresst my full executor of this my last will and Testament Revokeing all other wills and testaments in witness whereof I have hearunto sett my hand and seale the day and yeare above writen.

So, the Cushin danger must have loomed large in Colonel Bowen's distraught, darkening mind. Was Elizabeth Cushin, child of the dispossessed Garrett, as lovely as she was unfortunate? Did she walk like a living ghost the lands her father had owned, and was John — in the woods, up the stream, on the side of the mountain — constantly meeting her? Had the two been surprised together? All sorts of romances jump to the fancy — the dashing young soldier and the forlorn girl. The affair may have gone quite a long way, or it may, equally, have existed only in Colonel Bowen's brain. In his solitary Farahy years, before John came, Colonel Bowen may have wanted Elizabeth Cushin himself, and so, wished his tormenting longings on to his son. There are too many possibilities. The unfortunate are not always noble; it is possible that the Cushins may have been designing, or that Garrett made use of his daughter's charm to keep the Bowens in play while he salvaged some few perquisites from his lost estate. Or, John Bowen, as heir to the new landlord, may have felt he had certain rights. I do, however, feel clear in my own mind that John did not intend to marry Elizabeth Cushin, and that Henry I's proviso was unnecessary. To have married a papist, at that time, would have spelled ruin. John had seeds of weakness, and he was a flibbertygibbet, but such a man is the last to contend with fate. He was in every way out for a pleasant life — and the marriage he did make *should* have got it for him. Colonel Bowen no doubt detected in John the weakness out of which Captain Nicholls made capital later on; what the father did not take count of was John's *laissez-faire*. The obsession about Elizabeth Cushin must have overcast those last years at Farahy.

And Mary and Hester — whose sex did not even allow them capital letters in their father's will? The fate of these two colourless girls is uncertain: they are said to have married. Had they not looked likely to stay for some time in Ireland they would not have been commended to John's brotherly care. Perhaps Colonel Bowen had brought them back with him when he

returned from Wales for the last time. They may not have got
on well with their stepmother — it is understood that John did
not care for the lady. Did they share Farahy castle with their
father and brother, and, in their pale way, try to give it a
homely touch? Perhaps it was they who, from spinsterish idle-
ness, stirred up the trouble about Elizabeth Cushin. Oppressed
by the change of scene, scared of their father, they no doubt
led a muted existence, creeping about. Did they minister to
their father's illness and death? After that, they would wish to
share some one's roof — but we know they were not made free
of John's married home. They were not important, and they
left little trace.

Colonel Bowen died at Farahy, in mid-winter. In County
Cork, in mid-winter, mornings come very late and the long
mild white twilights last. Dazzling wintry sun reflects itself on
wet trees, wet rocks, wet roads, the floods in the valleys, the
back of cattle in the pale shorn fields. The Ballyhouras look
pure and, in sunshine, pink. The frosty nights are extra brilliant
with stars. I do not know where my ancestor Colonel Bowen
is buried: no stone marks the place. He had commended his
spirit to the Power he did not know — he had never mocked at
God, he had mocked at human belief. I think he must rest quiet;
at any rate his unhappiness does not haunt the Bowen's Court
land. But from this landscape personal pain evaporates, as history evaporates.

In the spring of 1659, very shortly after his father's death,
John Bowen married Mary, eldest daughter and heiress of Captain John Nicholls of Kilbolane Castle, County Cork.

John Nicholls was a Cromwellian, and a very rich man. As
quartermaster in the Lord Broghill's Troopers he had been on
service since 1649. For this, £159. 19s. 8d. had been owing to
him, and he had, like the others, received land in satisfaction for
his arrears of pay. He had also been able to buy up a great deal
more land (including his present portion of Kilbolane) from

troopers who could not afford or did not wish to plant, or who
were tempted by cash down. His estates were by now substantial, and his rule was iron.

Kilbolane is only just inside County Cork; it very closely
borders on County Limerick. It lies about twenty-six miles
n.n.w. of Farahy, eight miles west of Charleville (then called
Rathgogan) along a dead-straight road across a green windy
plain. The land round is very rich; there are few trees. This is a
landscape without a touch of strangeness — though in some
lights its blandness is tender, in others melancholy. In it are set
the colossal fortifications of Kilbolane Castle — built soon after
Strongbow, later owned by the Desmonds. The Cromwellians
in the course of their campaign had burned the habitable parts
and singed what would not burn. Inside the square of these
high rough walls was — is — the bawn, or fortified enclosure:
a grassy space. At each corner of the walls stood a tower, and
each of these four towers came to be called a castle — which,
indeed, it virtually was. The west tower, known as Brandon
Castle, was to be for generations a cause of strife. In fact, Kilbolane altogether was to be *femme fatale* of the Bowen family
destinies. It is important, therefore, to form some picture of it.

Captain Nicholls lived in the East Castle (or tower), to
which he had added a one-storied dwelling house, inside the
east angle of the Desmond walls. This lean-to dwelling had
windows looking into the bawn, which at this time must have
been heaped with rubble and stones. The Nicholls' quarters,
half grandiose, half modest, may have been snug and even
roomy enough. That they were cheerful I doubt. The South
and West castles were, at the time of John's marriage, empty:
the South Castle (immediately facing Captain Nicholls) found
tenants only too soon. An arch in the wall near the ruinous
North Castle led through to the Nicholls' garden, lying west
of the ruin. Captain Nicholls was a widower; Mary kept house
for him; Kilbolane and the lands were to be hers.

We do not know how or where John Bowen and Mary

Nicholls met. The courtship may have begun before the death of his father (which would show the pathetic foolishness of the Cushin alarm) or it may, on the other hand, have been a lightning affair. As an heiress, Mary must have had other suitors. Or perhaps she had but lately come to Ireland when John Bowen's *beaux yeux* did their work. John Bowen was quite a suitable husband: though he did go to live with the Nicholls at Kilbolane he could not be accused of needing to hang his hat up, for he had that Farahy property of his own.

The marriage settlement was drawn up, and was admirably brief:

Whereas there is a marriage to be concluded between John Bowen of Farahy, and Mary Nicholls Daughter of Captain John Nicholls of Kilbolane, the sd. John Bowen makes over all his right, title and interest in the Lands of Farahy, Garraneadrolane and Carron upon the issue of Male of Mary Nicholls begot by John Bowen and for want of issue Male upon her issue female and for every hundred pounds the said Nicholls shall give as a Marriage portion with his sd. Daughter John Bowen shall make over twenty pound yearly as a Jointure, witness my hand

John Bowen.

John's signature was witnessed by a Doctor Blunt, and by the to-be-famous Alexander Body, Captain Nicholls' servant or steward. John signed, clearly, well inside the Nicholls camp. It is clear, too, that John Nicholls was no fool, and that he saw that young Bowen potentially was. For, John Nicholls got John and Mary Bowen, immediately after their marriage, to sign a much more unusual document:

This bill byndeth me John Bowen of Farryhie, in the county of Corke gent^le, to pay unto John Nicholls of Kilbolane in the county aforesaid gentle, or his Assignes: the Just and full sum of five hundred pounds sterl. upon demaund, to the performance of which I bynde me, my heires, Executors etc.

The condicion of the above obligacion is such, that if the above saide John Bowen and Mary his wife doo continue with the above- sayd John Nicholls, during his life, and doe not go to housekeep- ing elsewhere but doe by his advice, sett and dispose of theire owne Estates to the best advantage of them the sd. John Bowen and Mary his wife, and likewise them both, to be aiding and assist- ing of him the saide John Nicholls, both within doors and without in the Managing of the Estate of the sd. John Nicholls, to the best advantage, then the above obligacion to be voide and of no effect, otherwise, to stand in full force and verture in law. In witness whereof I the sd. John Bowen have hereunto sett my hands and seale this 13th of March 1659.

Sd. & sealed   *John Bowen*
                   Mary Bowen.

In short, by what amounted to a suspended fine of five hun- dred pounds, John Nicholls kept the young Bowens in the palm of his hand. He had not only (to put it sweetly) not lost a daughter, but he had gained a son for all useful purposes. John Bowen, from now on, was Nicholls' man. The administration of the Bowen estates passed, virtually, into John Nicholls' hands; Farahy was entailed to his putative grandchildren. John Nicholls, and he only, henceforth was to decide what was " to the best advantage " of John and Mary Bowen. Should John Bowen fail to comply with a Nicholls plan, he must come across with five hundred pounds *instanter*. Nicholls could also com- mand, to any extent that pleased him, John Bowen's help in the working of Kilbolane. And the young pair must not " goe housekeeping elsewhere ": Mary must stay and see to her father's comforts, John must learn " both within doors and without " to fall in with his father-in-law's little crotchets and whims. One can see that Nicholls was not a successful man for nothing: the scheme does credit to him, the old fox. One would like to know how he got John Bowen to sign. Was the arrange- ment agreed to before the marriage (John Bowen being heed-

lessly in love) or sprung on the young Bowens as they left the
church? Had Nicholls detected John in some peccadillo? For
instance, had John — the idea is tempting — ridden over to see
Elizabeth Cushin again? Or perhaps, did the Captain bully his
daughter Mary till she got her husband John to agree? Had
John been a man of character, would he not have blown the
money and got out at any price? Do we take it that, for all his
" fair estate," John could not, as Captain Nicholls well knew,
easily lay his hand on five hundred pounds?

At all events, here are the Bowens, John and Mary, black-
mailed into sharing a home with Captain Nicholls, unable to
take a step to which he did not agree. How this affected their
marriage we do not know — though how it affected John's feelings for Captain Nicholls we do learn from a string of later
events. Three sons — John, William and Henry — were born to
John and Mary at Kilbolane.

In the sixteen-sixties, the Bowen Nicholls *ménage* gained a
distinguished neighbour. The Earl of Orrery, lately our Lord
Broghill, built a sumptuous mansion and took up his headquarters at Rathgogan, which he had re-christened Charleville to
honour the King.

Between 1657, the year before Colonel Bowen's death, and
1660, the year after John's marriage, the tide of affairs had
turned. In 1657, Lord Broghill made one of the committee who,
in Whitehall Palace, offered Cromwell the Crown. Three years
later he found himself back again in the Palace: this time, he
was here with the Lords Ormond, Muskerry, Roche and
Castlehaven to congratulate Charles II on his happy return.
Lord Broghill had devoted his spare time, during the changes,
to polishing up his oratorical powers — he was now more of a
speaker than he had ever been — and to poetry: his book of
sacred verses was now in the press. Charles II, pleased by his
welcome, washed everything out (if Stuarts remember any-

thing) and made Lord Broghill the Earl of Orrery. He also made him Lord President of Munster.

While Broghill (or Orrery) was still at court, a number of Irish Catholic gentlemen petitioned to be restored to their estates: a commission was set up to deal with their claims. Broghill (who with his Boyle brothers possessed the largest proportion of forfeited estates in Ireland) was a member of the commission, and took it in hand. The King, with the now Duke of Ormond, attended the sittings. Unhappily for their cause, the petitioners were represented by Sir Nicholas Plunket, who had been knit up with the Ultramontanes. Broghill was able to bring out of his sleeve documents with evidence of two popish plots — one against Ormond, one involving an offer of Ireland to the Pope, or, should the Pope refuse it, to almost any other Catholic potentate. These deeply implicated Sir Nicholas, and, by association, the petitioners. "Are these men," asked Broghill, "likely to make good subjects?" The King, having examined the documents, said he was satisfied that they were not. The petitioners were dismissed — this made a bad start.

The fact that the main body of Catholic Confederates had been loyal to Charles I, and had taken a loyal oath, was either overlooked by this first commission or not allowed to come up. If Ormond — close friend of Muskerry and Castlehaven, and once would-be ally of the Confederates — spoke of it, he must have been overruled. He did later, during his term of office as Lord Lieutenant — which lasted from 1661 to 1668 — succeed in getting Muskerry restored to his full honours (in fact, Muskerry was made Earl of Clancarty) and in salvaging much of his lost land from the Boyles.

This first total injustice was not permitted to stand. In 1661 an Irish Parliament met to consider the Act of Settlement — English and Protestant interests seemed again to be threatened. In most cases, alarm was needless: when in 1662 the Act was pushed through by Ormond, in much the same form in which

it had come from England, a number of settlers, including John
Bowen of Farahy, had their original grants confirmed by Letters Patent. Charles II did, however, follow the Act up, and to
an extent attempt to modify it, by the setting up of a Court of
Claims. This Court, consisting of seven honest (disinterested)
Englishmen, restored to a number of Catholic gentry, proved
"innocent papists," their estates, or a portion of their estates.
But the Protestant outcry became so loud, so sustained, that no
one dared go too far; the Court of Claims worked more slowly
and ceased to function in 1667. More than three thousand of the
old proprietors remained dispossessed. On the whole, the
Cromwellian Settlement stayed in force: Charles's friends had
been sacrificed to his enemies. The Protestant-Anglican ascendency was from now on an accomplished fact. Charles tem-
porized, Ormond did what he could for the Catholics, but
Catholics had still no constitutional rights — retaining, rightly,
their sense of outrage they came to look more and more to the
Duke of York.

Lord Orrery, in enjoyment of his new office, returned to
Cork. Here he found what he felt to be yet another menace —
the sect of Quakers was growing. Many of the once furious
Cromwellians had been converted to the pacific faith. There
were conventicles in and around the city, and the Quakers,
through their virtue and sometimes wealth, were becoming
more and more of an influence. By 1667 Lord Orrery had decided that they, too, might be dangerous: in order to justify
persecution he followed his old methods and faked a Quaker
plot. Severe measures were taken against conventicles; leading
Quakers were placed under arrest and William Penn (then in
Cork) and Thomas Lowe were gaoled. John Exham, Cromwellian trooper turned Quaker fanatic prophet, walked Cork
streets with ashes upon his head. After that, he left Cork for
Charleville, where Lord Orrery was in residence.

Drawn up before the new mansion in his sackcloth and ashes,
Exham pronounced a long categoric curse on it. Servants began

to drive the madman away. Was it humanity or superstition that brought Lord Orrery out to intervene? Having saved Exham a clouting he heard the curse modified by: " *The evil shall not be in thy day.*"

So, the mansion was not burnt by the Irish till 1690. But the tip of a black wing had brushed Orrery, and he never forgot. In 1668 (the year after Exham's visit) he was, without explanation, called upon to surrender his commission as Lord President of Munster. Suspecting his credit at court to be on the decline, he hurried over to London to put things right. In London, he was prostrated by an attack of gout. While still prostrate, he learned from the Master-at-arms that articles impeaching him of treason were being laid before the House of Commons. Gout or no gout, Orrery rose to defend himself. A friend, meeting him hobbling up the steps from Westminster Hall to the Court of Requests, remarked on his weakness. " Yes," Orrery flashed out, " my feet are weak, but if my heels will serve to carry me up, my head shall serve to carry me down again." It did: he got off — owing much to the influence of that other perennial, Lord Inchiquin.

Returning to Ireland, more than a little shaken, Lord Orrery withdrew from public affairs in order to prepare his soul for eternity. He had not much with which to reproach himself. As a general, he had shown first-rate hardness and head. He had wasted less force and made fewer muddles than any other leader in the Irish campaign. During and since his days as a fighter there had been no nonsense about him, and he had stood no nonsense. Like all enlightened people he had moved with his times. He had been fond of his family. He had served his own interest with that devoted courage that is often denied to a better cause. At the age of fifty-nine he died at Castlemartyr, in the year 1679.

The year of Mary Bowen's — *née* Nicholls' — death at Kilbolane is unknown. Her three sons were not grown up at the time. Her two sisters had married — one was a Mrs. Batwell. Life in that built-up east corner of the Desmond ruin, with John Nicholls growing more domineering and John Bowen more galled by the dominance, must have been full of tensions. She may have died in childbirth, or of a chill caught in one of the great frosts.

Almost immediately after his wife's death, John Bowen cleared out of Kilbolane and moved off into the County Limerick. Whether he paid up the five hundred pounds we do not know — it is likely that after these years of bondage, and with no more poor anxious Mary to hamper him, he saw freedom as cheap at the price. Mobility being his object — and can one wonder? — he left his three young sons with their grandfather at Kilbolane. For a short happy period John Bowen, moving around, made untutored use of his own money, with the natural result that he overspent. Having taken for granted that Captain Nicholls could well afford to maintain his grand-children, John had failed to provide for the three boys — whose futures were, after all, well assured. This brought Captain Nicholls down on him like a ton of bricks: he had no notion of letting John get away with this. Moreover, the two surviving Nicholls daughters — Mrs. Batwell and her unnamed sister — had lately been to their father with demands for money: a portion was wanted for one daughter's daughter Mary, now on the verge of her first marriage, to a Mr. Holmes, and John Nicholls had to pay out two sums of five hundred each. (This young Mary Holmes, later Crofts, is heard of again: she is a figure to watch.) Accordingly:

John Bowen being extravagant, his father in law Capt. Nicholls told him, that if he did not make provision for his three children which he maintained, he would putt 'em away from him. John Bowen then gave a lease to John Nicholls of Farahy for ninety-nine years. Nicholls paying Bowen fourty pounds during his life, fourty pounds to his eldest son, John Bowen, fourty pounds to

*his Second son, Wm. Bowen and twenty pounds to his youngest
son Henry Bowen, the land being then lett for one hundred and
twenty pounds per annum.*

The Bowens seemed fated to live off their own land. Here,
for instance, was John Bowen, free for the first time to enjoy
and direct his Farahy property. But he makes over Farahy to
John Nicholls for the sake of freedom and ease of mind. And,
ironically, the freedom he bought with Farahy he did not use
well. Reacting from the strictness of Kilbolane, he fell into
hopeless company. But what sort of Ireland was this for a man
of no roots, keen senses and unstable character? Towards the
end of this century, in Ireland, the Cromwellians were people
of the ruins. They had as yet no position. To the Catholic gentry, to the workers left on their land, they were still anathema
— they could buy service, they could not buy good regard.
They were confronted everywhere by cryptic faces or dispar-
aging smiles. The vanished old order still held the country people in a thrall of feeling. And the English settlers before them,
Elizabethan gentry who had already made themselves some
position, often looked crooked at these ambiguous newcomers
— townee investors from England or Cromwell's hired toughs.
Cromwellians of character or of good connections were, it is
true, beginning to build themselves up — taking over the houses
of dispossessed lords and gentry they set about living in a becoming style. Their degrees of success in this depended largely
on flair, or on the amount of tradition they had brought from
home. But for some time many Cromwellians remained squat-
ters, busied with the accumulation of wealth but living, like
Captain Nicholls, in patched-up ruins, in the tedium and
squalor of poor whites. They had still no *idea* of living to integrate them: the creation of a new society requires not only
force but taste.

John Bowen should have done better. His Welsh childhood
had had traditional background, and dignity. But he had grown

up to chaos, fought in a rough campaign. He had found his father in Ireland distraught and shunning society. He had fallen in too early with Captain Nicholls — ex-quartermaster, go-getter, graceless, narrow and harsh. Under the exasperations of Kilbolane, John may have been galled into trying to come it over his father-in-law with touches of Glamorganshire county *side*. If so, he got sneers that can have done him no good. Shut up in Kilbolane with the Nicholls, John had had no chance to make friends of his own sort. He was one of those small sad cases — a social figure without access to any society. When he did get free it was too late: he had lost height.

Now virtually landless, John Bowen would have drifted into the towns, to take what he found in the way of company. Susceptible, he no doubt had trouble with women. The normal life of the towns was still dislocated by the disastrous war; the old Catholic burgess families had been evicted from cities and walled towns by a proclamation in 1673. In 1677 a further proclamation had forbidden the holding of markets inside any town walls — for fear the Irish should congregate. Restrictions were being relaxed and Catholics were now filtering back again, but they returned to find their affairs in chaos, and the morale of the cities suffered accordingly: no good comes of turning the decent people out. Footloose Cromwellian soldiers who had sold up their holdings gathered in towns, threw their weight about, blued their money, lost their remaining morals, made a bad element. Cheating, contempt and crossness were in the air. John did not go off the rails in any serious sense, but he ran off the only rails that could have taken him anywhere. Somewhere, perhaps in Limerick city, he met a County Limerick woman called Elizabeth, surname unknown. Out of loneliness, or because he was caught, he married her. He is last heard of in Fort, County Limerick, with his child by that second marriage, Elizabeth Bowen.

JOHN II

JOHN BOWEN II, ELDEST OF THE THREE SONS OF JOHN I AND OF Mary his first wife, had been born in the Nicholls corner of Kilbolane Castle, in or around the year 1661. After their mother's death and their father's departure the boys, as we know, lived on with their grandfather. In spite of the fuss about their maintenance, and in spite of his threat of putting them out, Captain Nicholls took pride in the young Bowens. Age may have mellowed him, for he is said to have made a benevolent grandfather. The children lorded it round the ruins and over the Kilbolane lands. These were the first Bowens to be born in Ireland, and already they felt indigenous. They were given horses and hounds. John, when he had enough head and when he could sit a horse, would have ridden over to Farahy with Captain Nicholls, to learn the workings of this distant estate. The boys' aunt, Mrs. Batwell, and their cousin, the handsome young Mrs. Mary Holmes, frequented Kilbolane. How much John I continued to see of his children we do not know: his affections had drifted a long way from them by the end of his life, when he made that invalid will. John Nicholls and his entourage continued to occupy the East Castle and its unimposing annexe. But John II, who did not ignore, from childhood, his place as a member of the new ruling class, already envisaged a stylish house for the Bowens — it should top the existent garden, be stone, face south. When his time came, he would build.

But his time was not yet. Captain Nicholls, for all his indul-
gence, was not abdicating an inch. John II's youth was a deadlock while his grandfather ruled, and this lasted till John was
going on thirty — to finish with the stampede from Kilbolane.
And, apart from this, the time to build was not now: all over
Ireland the drums and tramplings were to begin again. County
Cork river valleys would once more echo horse-hoofs, and
white roads stream dark with marching men.

When James II came to the throne of England, in 1685, the
Catholics in Ireland at once looked across the Channel to see
what the Catholic king would do. Colonel Richard Talbot,
who had long represented the Anglo-Irish Catholic cause in
England, was created Earl of Tyrconnell and sent over to Ireland to be Lieutenant-General. Tyrconnell had been em-
powered to raise a Catholic standing army, and did — under
Charles II there had only been a Protestant militia. The King's
brother-in-law, Lord Clarendon, a High Church Tory, was to
be Lord Lieutenant — but only civil power was vested in him.
Clarendon came to Dublin in 1686: he did not stay long —
when a clash, which probably was foreseeable, came between
him and Tyrconnell the King took the part of the General and
Clarendon went. Upon which, Tyrconnell was made Lord
Deputy.
    The Lord Deputy's sympathies were confined to co-reli-
gionists of his own class; he ignored, or had little feeling for, the
native Irish themselves. His policy aimed at making Ireland a
Catholic power; he thought in terms of Europe — in which, at
this time, issues were both momentous and involved. Louis XIV
was at war with the League. Equally strong, though conflicting, European interests were to move the Williamite fighters.
And Tyrconnell's patron, Louis XIV, did not intervene in Ireland out of benevolence. The Williamite wars were fought in
a big way, with less narrow passions than the Cromwellian,
though with conclusive thoroughness. Since the sixteen-forties,

every one had grown up a little. Now, Ireland was only one minor theatre of a war of which few Irish knew the motives or plan. Only the native Irish fought for primary reasons — for their survival, for their religion and their land.

King James, as we know, lost England. William, Prince of Orange, " the Whig Deliverer," landed on the 5th November, 1688. In Scotland, the few thousand Highlanders who made a stand for James were routed at Killiecrankie: Scotland declared for William. James, having fled to France, now looked to his third kingdom. He had long been the last hope of Catholic Ireland; now he made Catholic Ireland his last hope.

The time was ripe. Tyrconnell had raised his Catholic army (a new generation had come up since Knocknaclashy) and with it garrisoned Ireland — with the vital exceptions of Enniskillen and Derry. Also, the country was stocked with civil malcontents: successive English laws in the last reign had stopped the cattle export, then crippled Irish shipping. Unrestored Catholics kept their eyes on lost land. Such an Ireland was for King James and his promises — dissentients were silenced almost before they spoke.

Protestants declared for William, but under their breath. The scales now looked like tipping the other way. Seeing what might be coming, large numbers fled to Williamite England, taking what goods they dared and abandoning their estates. Others fled to the cities. Captain Nicholls, however, hung on for some time longer at Kilbolane. In 1689, it was learned that William and Mary had accepted the English Crown.

On the 12th of March of that same year James, still King in the eyes of Ireland, landed at Kinsale. Into Kinsale harbour, escorting him, came a French fleet bringing money, munitions and French officers for Tyrconnell's Irish troops. James was received by the fourth Earl of Clancarty, our Lord Muskerry's grandson. Five thousand French troops, under command of Lauzun and De Lary, followed; they landed at Kinsale the day James left for Cork. To replace these, James sent to France just

over five thousand Irish, under command of General Mac
Carthy — the first instalment of the to be famous Irish Brigade.
Louis XIV, whose object was to embarrass William III, and
with William the League, was prepared to back James, though
not indefinitely — he did, however, send arms for ten thousand men. The transport of the French money from Kinsale
to Dublin was one of James's first facers: having been sent
in small change the money was less imposing in value than in
weight.

James was delayed in Cork by want of transport — horses
and baggage carts. As soon as he had got things more or less in
train, he moved on to Dublin, where he arrived on March 24th.
The entire country, under Tyrconnell, was now up in arms for
him: Ireland looked to James for her freedom, for justice and
for a Catholic regime. James looked to Ireland to help him get
England back. He was loath to commit himself to any measure
in Ireland that might prejudice his surviving English hopes. On
his arrival in Dublin he summoned what came to be known as
" the Patriot Parliament," and this at once went further than he
either foresaw or wished. The Parliament began by declaring
its independence of any parliament in England. It then passed
two bills — one repealing the Act of Settlement (by which
Protestants had possession of forfeited lands), the other, an at-
tainder against those Protestants who had fled the kingdom,
inviting them to return and stand their trials for treason (in
fact, for communication with the King's enemies) and for illegal possession of lands. Three thousand (absentee) Protestants were attainted, and their estates declared forfeit. James
could not but feel that the zeal and courage for which, at the
opening of Parliament, he had thanked the Irish were likely to
prove excessive. And repercussions throughout Williamite Ireland, though they had to be smothered, were furious.

The war opened with the siege of Derry by Tyrconnell's
men. Ulster does not let us forget how this brave little Ulster
city held out from April 17th to July 30th. Its relief, with the

equally valiant defence of Enniskillen, turned the tide in the
North: the Jacobites lost that ground. On August 13th Marshal Schomberg, William's commander, landed, at Bangor,
with twenty thousand men. Throughout the rest of the winter
of 1689, and well on into the spring of 1690, the two armies
faced each other across the river Fane, near Dundalk, but no
battle occurred. In the March of 1690, Louis sent over seven
thousand French regulars. On June 14th King William in person landed at Carrickfergus: there were now two Kings on the
Irish board. William's united forces in Ireland now amounted
to thirty-six thousand men, of whom a large number were mer-
cenaries — Danes, Germans, and Huguenots. Meanwhile, the
English fleet had landed troops in Munster.

July 1st, 1690, saw the never-to-be-forgotten Battle of the
Boyne — at which, as every one knows, King Billy charged on
that white horse that has become the Protestant holy image,
and the Jacobite Irish were defeated conclusively. We owe two
vignettes of this battle to the journal of Dean Davies, a Cork
man who was a chaplain in the Williamite army:

June 30th. At two in the morning we decamped again, and
marched towards Drogheda, where we found King James encamped on the other side of the Boyne. We drew up all our horse
in a line opposite to him, within cannon shot; and as his majesty
[William] passed our line, they fired six shots at him, one whereof
fell and struck off the top of the Duke of Wurtemberg's pistol,
and the whiskers off his horse, and another tore the King's coat on
the shoulder. We stood open during at least twenty shot, until, a
man and two horses being killed among the Dutch guards, we all
retired into a trench behind us, where we lay safe while much
mischief was done to other regiments, and in the evening drew off
and encamped behind the hill.

July 1st. His majesty came up and charged at the head of the
Enniskilling horse, who deserted him at the first charge, and carried off with them a Dutch regiment, but the King's blue troops
of guards soon supplied the place, and with them he charged in
person and routed the enemy.

(Dean Davies marched south with William's army after the
Boyne. On July 13th he preached a Sunday sermon against
swearing to " our whole army . . . by yesterday's pillage full
of beef and mutton "; he saw more action, observed the ways
of the great and, when at Clonmel, had his shoes and pistol
made off with, he supposed by the Danes. Through friends in
Munster he did useful work, checking up on rumours of flying
raids. His journal makes lively reading.)

After the Boyne, James fled to Dublin. He then decamped
to France, leaving the Irish to fight on. In the Boyne slaughter
had been wiped out the remainder of the " Old English " Catholic aristocracy. So much involved and twisted were interests
in Europe, at this time, that the Catholic cathedral in Vienna
pealed with a Thanksgiving *Te Deum* for the defeat of the
Catholic Irish at the Boyne — William III being, with Austria,
for the League, and Louis XIV, who was for the Irish, against it.

King William entered Dublin. Cork, meanwhile, was holding out for King James. On September 22nd, 1690, John
Churchill, later Marlborough, brought a fleet into Cork harbour, having captured a fort at the harbour's mouth. Other of
William's forces, under Scravenmore, invested the city from the
heights. Scravenmore, on his march south towards Cork, had
routed a body of the Irish at Mallow, broken down Mallow
bridge and marched on Castletownroche. This September, during the Cork siege, Irish and English skirmished up and down
the Blackwater. It should be noted that one cannot approach
Cork city by any important route from the north without
crossing this river, and that the Williamite forces (except
those landed by Churchill) were all being moved down from
the north. The Blackwater bridges were, accordingly, vital.
Wurtemberg, on his way to the Cork siege, took his heavy
cannon across the bridge at Fermoy. Wurtemberg did not
get to Cork till September 26th, when, after days of severe
fighting, two more key forts, as well as Shandon castle, were
already in Williamite hands. The belated and fussy German's

claim to be generalissimo annoyed Churchill — who, however, behaved with tact. The cannon went into action, and Cork city suffered a bombardment she was ill fitted to stand. Terms were offered, refused; the bombardment went on again. Inside the walls, Protestants were imprisoned in churches and Quaker conventicles: their sufferings and anxieties were acute. The Irish governor, Mac Gillicuddy, at last found himself forced to surrender the city. He also, however, put into effect his threat of burning the suburbs, in which many wealthy Protestants had lived. Seven Irish regiments now laid down their arms. Churchill secured the city, marched on and took Kinsale.

The rest of the Irish army fell back across the Shannon. It took up two main positions — the head of Athlone bridge and Limerick, which Tyrconnell made his headquarters. Tyrconnell, as Jacobite Lord Lieutenant, represented the government; Lauzun and Brigadier Sarsfield shared the military command. King William tried, and failed, to take Limerick: he returned to England. Athlone also held out. Winter, settling down over Munster, more or less immobilized the campaign — though in the January of 1691 Fermoy was attacked by some Irish under General Carroll and there were skirmishes in West Cork. Flying bodies of Irish, called "Rapparees" or "Tories," continued to menace the countryside.

It was in the October of 1690 that mad Exham's delayed-action curse on the Orrery house took effect. Emerging from the Irish stronghold at Limerick, the young Duke of Berwick (one of James II's irregular sons) set out, with a thousand horse and five regiments of foot, for Macroom. Charleville lies on the main road from Limerick to Mallow — the road through Mallow on into West Cork. The Duke, while on the march, learned that Ginkle, with superior Williamite forces, was coming his way from Cashel, likely to cut him off. He retraced his steps and halted at Charleville: it was now dinner time. Thundering on the doors of shut-up Charleville House — for no Orrery was now in residence — the young Duke clamoured for hospitality. This he got, with much wine. Issuing once more into the autumn night, Berwick found himself hot with Stuart wrongs: he recollected the Broghill Orrery had been. His soldiers received an order and fired the house.

Eight miles away, across the dead-flat plain, they must have seen blood-red reflections fill up the eastern sky. It may well have been this that, at last, determined Captain Nicholls on flight. He was uncomfortably near the Irish at Limerick; he had had already enough of the Rapparees. But it took the Orrery blaze to smoke the old soldier out. Cork, now safe in the hands of the Williamites, offered asylum to Cromwell's men.

A bill from the lawsuit later brought by John Bowen II against his first cousin, Mrs. Mary Crofts (first heard of as Mrs. Mary Holmes), supplies the tale of that flight, and first introduces the dangerous subject of the Kilbolane treasure. Being a legal document it is without stops, and so makes difficult reading: I have therefore, for clearness, punctuated and paragraphed it. I have also cut out one or two repetitions that would seem to be legal prolixities. The excisions are marked by dots . . .

John Nicholls being a very wealthy man, and having very Considerable sums of money and gold lying by him in Cash at his dwelling house of Kilbolane . . . was forced by the iniquity and troubles of the Irish rapparees in the time of the late Rebellion in this Kingdom, some time in the years 1689 or 1690, to quit and relinquish his dwellinghouse in Kilbolane aforesaid and betake himself and family to Corke or to some other place of more security, to avoid the malice and fury of the said rapparees. And having no convenience to carry off his money and gold, or being apprehensive that he should be plundered and robbed thereof in case he attempted to carry the same with him, he buried and hid under the ground severall quantities of his owne gold and silver,

*in severall places in and about the garden, Castle and Castle Bawn
at Kilbolane aforesaid. Having made your orator* [John Bowen II]
*and some of his the said Johns servants privy to the burying of the
said money and gold, and having so hid the said money, he withdrew himselfe and his family to Corke, where he continued till he
died, which happened in or about the month of september or
october Ann. Dom. 1691.*

*The said John Nicholls, before his death, being of sound mind
and perfect sense and disposing memory, did make and publish in
due forme of law under his hand and seale, his last will and
testament, which bears date the 24th day of september Ann.
Dom. 1691. By which last will he nominated your orator* [J. B. II]
*His sole and only executor, and thereby he bequeathed your orator
amongst others all his stock Cattle, money, place, household stuffs,
debts and all his worldly substance not disposed of in his said last
will, except what goods and legacies he bequeathed unto his daughter Mrs. Batwell. And he also devised and bequeathed by the said
last will unto his Grand daughter Mary Holmes, now Mary Crofts,
the sum of 200 pounds sterling for the use of her children, to be
equally divided between them. One hundred pounds to be paid
her within one year, after the said John Nicholls his decease, and
the other hundred pounds to be paid her within two years after his
decease. . . . Your orator, since the Death of the said John
Nicholls, has proved the said will in Common Form in the prerogative Court of this Kingdom, and has taken upon him the burden and execution thereof, and has paid and discharged all or most
of the legacies and bequests therein made and given.*

*But . . . the said Mary Holmes, who is since marryed to Henry
Crofts, gent., being privy to the hiding and burying of the gold
and silver . . . and staying behind the said John Nicholls in the
Irish quarters, where she continued till the surrender of Lymerick,
she dugg up a Considerable quantity of the said hidden treasure,
amounting to £300 or upwards, which she and her new husband,
Henry Crofts, have converted to theire own use and doe absolutely refuse to pay the same or give any account thereof to your*

orator, to whom they very well know it belongs of right; sometimes denying that they or either of them did ever dig or take up any such money or treasure, and at other times alledging and giving out in speeches that the said John Nicholls, before his death, bestowed the money so taken up upon the Deft. Mary for her owne use, which cannot possibly be true. . . . The said John Nicholls never saw or spoke to the said Mary after he took his leave of her at Kilbolane aforesaid. And, your supplyant is able to prove that the said John Nicholls, not long before his death, procured and got together a Considerable squadron of horse and Dragoons, in order to goe from Corke for the said money — which the said John Nicholls then wanted for his owne family and support, being forced to borrow money from the Merchants of Corke for his present subsistence.

Which actings and doings of the said Mary and Henry Crofts are Contrary to Equity and good Conscience, and tend to your Orator's great loss and damage, whereby your Supplyant is rendered unable to pay the Debts which he owes at the receipt of his Maj^{ties} Excheq^r in the right of the said John Nicholls.

Your Orator is remedyless in the premisses at Common Law, he being a stranger to the Number, kind and Value of the money and treasure . . . hid and buried by the said John Nicholls, and taken up by the said Defts., one of them, and for that the witnesses who could prove the digging and taking up of the said hidden money by the Deft. Mary, and the kind and value thereof, are all either dead or dispersed into remote places to your Orator unknown, soe that your Orator Cannot produce them to give theire testimony. . . .

Therefore, your Supplyant conceives his only and proper remedy and release is, in Equity, in the Chancery side of his Honble. Court, before your Lordships, to the end . . . that the said Mary Crofts and Henry Crofts her husband, being touched in theire Consciences, respectively may, in theire severall and respective answers . . . to be made upon oath on the holy Evangelists . . . sett forth, confess and declare the truth, and whole truth of . . .

the matters, alligations and suggestions in this bill contained.
. . . More especially, that they may respectively confesse and
say, doe they know or beleeve that the said John Nicholls
made his last will and testament at the time, or at any other
. . . and bequeathed the specifick legacy of 200¹ to the said
Mary for the use of her children . . . without making mention of
any more to be given to her? Did not the said John Nicholls give
a Considerable portion, and how much, with the said deft. Mary
on her first marriage with Mr. Holmes? And was there not a good
jointure settled upon her in Consideration of the said portion? Do
they, or either, or which of them, know of any, and what sort of,
Treasure, money, gold or silver hid or buried, at any time, and
when, and where, by the said Nicholls? . . . And what was the
value of such treasure so hidden? How much gold or silver was
soe buried, to the best of their knowledge? . . . Was such money
or gold put into a box, Earthen potts or other vessell or Vessells,
and what and how much in each? Who were present at the hideing
and burying thereof? . . . Did the said Mary, or any other person
by her orders . . . at any time, and when, and where, take up any
part, and how much, of the said hidden money and gold? Was
there any, and who by name, present at the taking up of such gold
or silver, besides her selfe? Was the gold or silver so taken up in an
Earthen pott, or what other vessell? And was the same full of
treasure, and what treasure, and what was the measure of such
pott or Vessell, and how much water or liquor would such a pott
contain? What were the severall Species of Coyne therein con-
tayned? How many and what peeces of gold were in it? And how
much silver was there also in it? Why did she meddle with it?
What is the reason why she and her husband refuse to satisfie or
pay the same to your supplt.? Doe they, or either of them, know
Alexander Body? And that the said Mary may set forth and con-
fesse, does she know or believe that the said Alexander Body was
present at, or privy to, the burying of the said gold and silver?
. . . And whether he know how much was in Each Parte?
And to the end, the said Mary may particularly describe and set

*forth the place where she, or some other for her, tooke up the gold
and silver, and the exact sum or value thereof. . . .*

Punctuated, what was a wad of writing springs alive: it ends
on a note of hysteria. In fact, this obsession about the Nicholls
treasure was at the root of that main Kilbolane obsession that,
for generations, continued to rule the Bowens, unbalance their
view of life, and, through lawsuits, lose them so much money.
We do not know — it never has been established — how much
treasure there *was*, in the first place. We do know that the
whole of the treasure — on that scale, at least, on which Bowens
envisaged it — was not ever found. The longer it remained
missing the greater its visionary proportions grew. Bowens
have always been prone to avoid or baulk at facts only to tor-
ment themselves with fantasies — look at Colonel Bowen's obsession against Elizabeth Cushin.

John Nicholls certainly knew where the treasure was: why
was he content to let the secret die with him? Or, did the old
fellow die suddenly — broken up by the flight from his stronghold at Kilbolane, or swept away by that miasma-bred pesti-
lence we hear of after the Cork siege? At all events his executor,
John Bowen, was told nothing. What about those dragoons
Captain Nicholls hired and sent from Cork to bring back some
of the money from Kilbolane? Who gave the dragoons the
money — who then had access to it? Alexander Body? Had
Alexander Body been trusted once too often? Was Body the
crook?

I must say I think it likely that Mary Crofts, a smart girl and
not John Nicholls' grand-daughter for nothing, made at least a
try for the treasure. Mrs. Crofts was intrepid — fearless she
kissed her grandfather goodbye and, standing (more or less) on
the doorstep of the Desmond ruin, waved the family off on its
flight to Cork. The Irish held no terrors for Mary Crofts — in
fact, we are told that she stayed behind ' in the Irish quarters.'
Her bold bad eyes had already made her more her grand-

father's favourite than the young Bowens liked, and no doubt
she felt she could manage the Irish, too. Having seen Captain
Nicholls, her younger Bowen cousins, and, no doubt, her aunt
Batwell safely off the premises, young Mrs. Crofts went for her
spade and dug. She dug, but she dug at random about the castle,
garden and bawn — I do not believe that hard-bitten Captain
Nicholls *had* trusted his pretty Mary with such a secret as this.
I think Mary Crofts got little out of her digging — but she
would be damned rather than let John Bowen know.

We do not know if John Bowen's suit against Mary was ever
actually brought into court. If it was, either Mary cleared her
character or the petitioner failed to get anything proved. Had
she had the treasure she would certainly have spent it — and the
Crofts continued to live quite modestly. This, with some other
unknown circumstance, served in time to divert John Bowen's
suspicions from his cousin Mary to his own brother William.
We hear that John filed several suits against William for the
recovery of the Kilbolane treasure. This created, early on, a
split in the Bowen family. John may have suspected William
of conspiracy with Alexander Body. William Bowen died during the litigation, and John was prevailed upon by a family
friend, Mr. Allen, to settle the matter with his brother's executors. In a declaration signed in 1702 John agreed " *to put a final
end to all matter of suites, variances and controversies.*" But
that was not anything like the end.

The spell of winter broke up. In the late spring of 1691 help,
and new spirit, reached the Irish from France. Lauzun's army
had been recalled, but now the Marshal St. Ruth — gallant,
enthusiastic — came over with arms and stores and with a commission to unite all the Irish in one force. Fifteen thousand men
were raised; hopes ran high. But Ginkle, commanding the Williamite armies, broke down Athlone's resistance, and St. Ruth
with his Irish had to fall back beyond Ballinasloe. On July 12th
at the battle of Aughrim, the Irish made a final and magnificent

stand. St. Ruth, who rallied them, fell; the losses were crushing. Sarsfield marched what was left of the army back to Limerick.

Ginkle drew up on Limerick and besieged it. (Galway and Waterford had surrendered already; Limerick was flying the last flag.) Sarsfield, heroic in looks and legend, conducted in a heroic spirit this final defence. In intense expectation of French aid, hourly watching for ships on the wide Shannon, the city held out from September 4th to October 3rd, 1691. Then Sarsfield's hopes died and he decided to treat. Almost as the Treaty was signed, by Sarsfield and Ginkle, the French ships, in what might have been all their beauty, came up the river — just a day too late. The fleet now served to transport the five thousand defeated Irish who went to fight for France and not to return.

The surrender of Limerick dealt the final blow to an Ireland that had up to now — and Heaven knows how — survived. The actual Treaty of Limerick did not give ruthless terms: Sarsfield — loser at the end of a two years' war — asked for fairness, and got it. Ginkle, who had behind him William's authority, was a foreigner — so, disinterested — and a gentleman: he made a soldier's, not an oppressor's, peace. The defenders were not to be disarmed completely, and were to lose no more than they had already lost. In the main, the aim of the Treaty, with its thirteen clauses, was not retaliation but settlement. Ginkle gave guarantees, on behalf of his royal master, that Catholics should be protected and to some extent restored. Though in effect the Treaty confirmed the Act of Settlement, it was capable of a liberal interpretation. Such an interpretation William, on his own judgement, might have been glad to give it — he was another foreigner: liberal, well-meaning, still unversed in many of England's ways. But his ideas on any subject could be countered by those of his parliament: one is not a constitutional monarch for nothing, and he had not been asked over to do as he liked.

So, what might be called the Williamite Settlement became, virtually, a return to the *status quo*.

In 1697 the Irish parliament ratified the Treaty of Limerick.

The surrender of Limerick restored the Bowens' security; the Treaty of Limerick kept them where they had stood. By the time the alarums of war were over John Nicholls was, as we know, buried, but John Bowen returned as master to Kilbolane. He wound up his grandfather's affairs, and took possession. That lease of Farahy given by John I to Captain Nicholls now reverted to John II, as his grandfather's heir. If the notion of building and living at Farahy ever entered John's head, he must have at once dismissed it. All his plans for the future centred round Kilbolane. So, in May 1697, John Bowen II gave a lease of the Farahy lands, in all six hundred acres, to Mr. Andrew Nash.

The Nashes are said to have come to Ireland with Raleigh; Nashes bearing their coat of arms are heard of in 1400 at Almon Hall, Gloucester. In 1679 Andrew Nash had had, from the Earl of Orrery, the lease of a house and lands near Charleville; this made the Nashes neighbours of the Kilbolane Bowens, and a close and lasting family friendship was formed. Unhappily, in 1688 Mr. Nash's house had been burnt by the Rapparees, and he had been constrained to leave that part of the world. In 1690–91 we hear of him in Galway, where he was once again annoyed by the Irish. Restored, by the fall of Galway, to his calm way of life, he returned to County Cork to become agent to the Hon. Colonel Henry Boyle's Castlemartyr property. Colonel Boyle's death in Flanders having ended the agency, Mr. Nash was once more, 1697, looking round for a home. He had married a Miss Pett, and had one son, Llewellin, born in 1680.

The Nashes were " nice " people in every possible sense; they made ideal tenants, and the Bowens were lucky to get them for Farahy. They appear to have been that rather rare thing in Ireland, gentry content to live as gentry and nothing more — a sort of Versailles fantasy came, as I shall be showing, to dominate too many Anglo-Irish people, to cripple their bank accounts and endanger their private lives. The Nashes aimed at

genteel contentment only. On the Farahy land they built the
house that was the predecessor of Bowen's Court — occupying,
in the sunny shallow hollow, almost though not exactly the
same site. This Nash house was convenient, comely and trim,
and at least one Mrs. Bowen coveted it: it stood till the Bowens,
on their return to Farahy, pulled it down to make place for
something rather more grand. (Its shell, or the heaps into
which it had fallen, was said to provide the stones from which
my grandfather Robert later built our coach-house and servants' wing.) Round their house the Nashes laid out and fenced
a garden; they planted an orchard and they improved the
woods. In fact, the quiet and order of their existence contrasts
with the rather *detraqué* manner in which Bowens went on
living at Kilbolane.

John Bowen I's movements, about this time, are obscure. He
is said to have visited, and even for some time to have occupied,
Kilbolane. But with John II there, married and in possession,
the father's position would have been ambiguous — and my
own feeling is, he would hate the sight of the place. He preferred to keep his headquarters at Fort, County Limerick,
where the child of his second marriage, the mischief-making
Elizabeth, was now rapidly growing up.

At a date unknown — some time before he was thirty — John
Bowen II had married his first wife: Deborah, daughter of
Arthur Hyde. Her home, Castle Hyde, is about a mile up the
Blackwater from Fermoy: here a cliff, jutted with ancient towers, overlooks a lovely reach of the river and the woods that
rise gently up beyond. (A handsome Georgian house now
stands at the edge of the river, its back to the cliff.) These
Hydes were well-connected, and might have made, had their
daughter Deborah lived, a useful connection for the Bowens —
James II's first wife, Clarendon's sister, had been a Hyde; she
became the mother of Queens Mary and Anne. This Hyde
marriage of John II's accounts for the story that King William
III, while in the south of Ireland, paid a visit to the Bowens at

Kilbolane — they being his wife's people — and presented them with a set of communion plate. The only communion plate now in our possession is, however, in Victorian style. But King William's portrait, framed to match Oliver Cromwell's, hangs beside Cromwell's at the top of Bowen's Court stairs. If he never did stay with us, he no doubt wished that he could.

Deborah Bowen (*née* Hyde) unhappily died childless, and in 1696 John II (now Captain Bowen, he being in the Militia) married again. His second and less romantic choice was Catherine, daughter of Richard Stephens of Newcastle, County Limerick. (William Bowen, that next brother of John's with whom there had been the trouble about the treasure, had also been married; he left descendants somewhere in County Limerick. The third brother, Henry, died unmarried.)

Catherine Stephens, that woman of character, was heiress to some Devonshire property. By the terms of his marriage settlement John Bowen II had to make over in trust to Catherine's father land of enough value to ensure Catherine a jointure of one hundred pounds a year should she be left a widow. (As, in time, she was.) Pending the land's being placed in trust, John was to hold himself Richard Stephens' debtor to the extent of sixteen hundred pounds capital.

It may have been this Catherine Bowen who, as a bride, cast the final vote for Kilbolane against Farahy. At Kilbolane she was almost in her own county, nearer her people. It may, again, have been Catherine who urged John Bowen into the lawsuits about the treasure. The idea of that muddle about the Nicholls fortune would have been maddening to her exact mind. She had no doubt taken against bold Mary Crofts at sight, and may have had some objection we do not know of to William Bowen's County Limerick wife. I am certain John took no step of which Catherine did not approve. From girlhood, Catherine had been a person of force; she grew up to be the intimidating old woman who left her mark on our family. She must, also, have shared John's early views about Bowens no longer squatting but living in proper style. For, not a long time after his second marriage, John II built the present Kilbolane House. To get stones for this he pulled down the Nicholls lean-to and demolished two of the Desmond Castle towers.

Kilbolane House stands where John had envisaged it — at the top of the former Nicholls garden, now a long pleasant lawn. It faces south; its façade is sunny, smiling and strong. Its front door, with a simple fanlight, stands at the head of high steps with curved balustrades. The front windows have now lost a little of their first character from having mid-eighteenth-century sashes put into their William and Mary or early Queen Anne frames. A sundial with a voluted pillar stands on a grass plot just east of the house, and the belt of beech trees that flanks the castle ruin stops near the east windows. The avenue curves up to the front door between the lawn and the castle trees. (The pen-and-ink map of the castle bawn and the house, drawn for Henry III's lawsuit, is a little misleading: in fact the house stands further back from, or north of, the ruin than is shown in the map, and not the front of the house but its east flank is towards the ruin.)

Inside, Kilbolane House is a little Dutch in feeling — partly perhaps because of the pensive flatness of the landscape seen from the windows, partly from its proportions — lucid, modest and dignified. It is a more intimate house than Bowen's Court. The entrance is into an oblong hall, lit by the staircase window whose light falls through a doorway with a second fanlight above. There are four parlours: the two in front have strong, very lovely plaster ceiling designs, and in one the mantelpiece is the original. The sweetest parlour, however, is at the back: north light fills it kindly and not coldly. Here the fireplace is across a corner. The windows, like others at the back of the house, are the originals — small square panes in very heavy white wooden settings — one window goes right down to the floor, and from it a flight of stone steps with heavy white balus-

trade descends to the garden. I should like to think that this
parlour became Jane Bowen's.

The foreground of this garden behind the house is set with a
pattern of box-edged beds. Above the hedge that backs this
appear the twisted tops of elderly apple trees. The garden is not
walled in — down one side runs a beech hedge, cut low now but
so strong at the base that it must be very old — so the windows
of the north parlours and bedrooms look beyond it over a sea
of land.

The staircase ends at the lobby above the hall. This lobby
owns the wide window over the front door, and in its ceiling
appears the same plaster sunflower that centres the two parlour
ceilings below. The present occupier of Kilbolane keeps in the
lobby, in a juxtaposition that I find beautiful, a billiard table
(with appropriate lights), a rocking horse and a full-length
rococo mirror. From here open the two main bedrooms — one
would have been John II's and Catherine's, the other, after
Henry II's marriage, Henry's and Jane's. The smaller north
bedrooms are off a corridor, and a second shut-away staircase
leads to very low attics in the pitch of the roof.

The basement is no more than a half-basement — the
" ground " floor is reared to some distance above the ground.
Catherine Bowen's south-facing, white-washed kitchen is,
therefore, extremely light. It is, like the rest of the basement,
paved with small, irregular flags; hooks for hams and bacon-
sides stud the ceiling, and an oak dresser-cupboard that from its
style and blackness must date from Catherine faces the fireplace.

Kilbolane House put a dangerous spell on me from the moment I walked into it — only some days ago. I could feel ves-
tigial stirrings of the Bowen obsession — though what the
Bowens ate themselves over, and broke themselves and me by
litigating about, was not the house but the land and the hypo-
thetical treasure, and I should be happy to have only the house.
I drove back that April evening to Bowen's Court — leaving

the bald Charleville main road for that *Faerie Queene* area of
trees and rivers that begins round Kilcolman and stretches
round Farahy — with the seeds of an infidelity in my heart. I
know there are many houses in Ireland, England and Holland
in form, if not in feeling, like Kilbolane. There is no house like
Bowen's Court, with its great pale Renaissance plainness set
under near mountains among showering trees. Kilbolane is no
more than pensive; Bowen's Court can be ecstatic. Bowen's
Court, though at least seventy-five years younger than Kilbolane, stands in very much stranger and more timeless air. It
is on our first Bowen land. But —

I should like to live in both houses at the same time.

Into Kilbolane House, then, when it was finished, John II
and Catherine moved with their four children — Henry, John,
Stephens and Thomasine. The change to these new quarters
must have been pleasant after the cramp and darkness of the
Nicholls set-up. The calmness with which the expense of building was, apparently, met suggests that the Bowens were not
doing too badly, even without the lost Kilbolane treasure.
Young Henry II, John's heir, had now a fine home to offer a
bride. He should make a good match — and he did.

Queen Anne reigned. Summers droned and winters whistled
round Kilbolane. One by one the four young Bowens grew up.
In 1716, the year of young Henry's marriage to Jane Cole, there
were adult male Bowens of three generations living — old John
I, aged about ninety, over at Fort, John II, ruling at Kilbolane.
and John II's son, Henry II. It was in this year, however, that
poor old John I made his terrible gaffe.

John I, now sickening for death, was in the charge, and the
power, of his second wife — that Elizabeth of obscure origin.
Their unmarried daughter Elizabeth came and went; she had
her headquarters at Charleville where she may have chosen to
settle with the object first of getting to know, then, after a
snub, of annoying, her half-brother's Kilbolane family. These

two grim designing Elizabeths, mother and daughter, stood over poor old John Bowen I with his darkening mind. Some mixture of pride, shame, perversity and secretiveness may have kept the old man from letting his wife and daughter know exactly how his affairs stood — that he had, in fact, nothing that he *could* leave. If he ever had tried to tell them about those previous settlements, they had been too pig-headed or greedy to understand — or else, they took the womanish view that there is nothing that you cannot get round. As for him, as he grew sicker and more senile, he may have lived in a half-dream, a regained world of power. However it happened — "*on his deathbed, when senseless, there was a will brought him,*" and John Bowen, shaky and witless, signed, in the presence of witnesses. The two Elizabeths had had this Will drawn up: "*Whereas it is Incumbent on all persons to make such a disposition of their worldly substance as may prevent contention and strife among their posterity,*" it begins, ironically — and by it John I left his Farahy lands, *and* the lands in Gower, to his "*beloved daughter Elizabeth Bowen and her heirs forever.*" A jointure of thirty pounds a year was to be raised from Farahy and paid to his dear wife Elizabeth, who also was to enjoy, during her life-time, one third of the profits from the Gower lands. The will is dated September 12th, 1716.

The beloved daughter Elizabeth needed money immediately. Not waiting for her father to die — which he did not actually do till 1718 — she posted off, with the signed will, and sold her interest in Farahy to George Evans, Esq., of Caherassy in the County of Limerick. For this she was to receive a hundred pounds down and "*diverse other goods and valuable considerations.*"

But Elizabeth realized no more than thirty pounds. When he had paid over that sum (and we fear that he lost it) George Evans got wind of those earlier settlements. He "*filed a bill against John Bowen*" (John II, of Kilbolane) "*to discover his title, but as soon as John Bowen sent him a copy, and show'd*

him the Settlements, he desisted and never enquired more."
What George Evans, so badly stung, said to Elizabeth Bowen
is not on record. I imagine that she replied that there must have
been some mistake. She hung on to the will, lay low, and, some
time later, attempted to sell the Farahy lands again. She also
entertained offers for the lands in Gower. That next time, it
was Llewellin Nash and the warrior Catherine Bowen who had
to contend with her.

The too-near presence, in Charleville, of the seedy and
crooked spinster Elizabeth Bowen must have been trying for
the Kilbolane family. No doubt they kept her dark, for as long
as possible, from young Jane Cole, the pretty, fastidious heiress,
when Jane brought into the family her toy spaniel, her trousseau and her extensive Ballymackey lands. John II must have
been alarmed as well as angry when, through George Evans'
demand to see the Farahy title, he learned what his half-sister
had been up to now. There was no knowing what Elizabeth
would be up to *next* — so in 1718, as soon as poor John was
dead, John II prudently got in touch with Welsh lawyers,
ejected tenants from the Llanellan property and " *gott possession of sd. lands by virtue of the Settlement.*" Shortly after,
Henry II was sent to Wales " *to prove himself the right heir to
Colonel Bowen.*" This done, the Gower lands were re-let: the
rents from them were bequeathed by John II to his second and
third sons, John and Stephens Bowen.

HENRY II AND
HENRY III

WHEN THE BOWENS MOVED OUT TO KILBOLANE BAWN TO THEIR
new mansion north-west of the ruin, they did not leave the
affairs of the bawn behind. They kept access to it through the
arch or " passage " near the destroyed north tower. Near that
they continued to stack their peat. But uncertainty — dating
back to the time of Captain Nicholls — as to the actual *ownership* of the bawn, and of the west tower known as Brandon
Castle, lasted: it made for friction and was to blow up, later,
into an ugly case.

One strong inducement to Captain Bowen to build the new
house and move in may have been, that from the early seven-
teen-hundreds the Bowens no longer had the bawn to themselves. The Weekes family had, from the days of Nicholls, kept
their ownership of the South Castle (or tower). And contiguous to this South Castle, inside the walls, it now pleased William Weekes to put up a house. This Weekes home, preceding
in date the new Bowen mansion, came to be known as " Kilbolane Old House." It had exactly faced, down the grassy
length of the bawn, the Bowen dwelling dating from Captain
Nicholls, and its superiority, both in size and pretention, must
have chagrined the Bowens till they went one better. Till they

moved from the Nicholls quarters they were overlooked by neighbours, and had to share the bawn. We know of nothing, however, against this William Weekes until, being short of money, he sold the South Castle, the new building adjoining and his share of rights in the bawn to that very George Evans of Caherassey to whom Elizabeth Bowen had tried to sell Farahy. The Elizabeth Bowen affair must have left a residuum of awkwardness, and the Bowens may well have felt that Mr. Evans lacked delicacy in making himself their near neighbour. Happily, this Mr. Evans (who had for some time been M.P. for Charleville) died shortly after the purchase, and his son Thomas leased the South Castle and house to a Mr. Allen.

If the Bowens, now safely outside the bawn, *had* to have a neighbour, they could not have had a better than Mr. Henry Allen. (He was that same good Mr. Henry Allen who, in 1702, succeeded in patching up the trouble between John II and his late brother William's executors in the matter of the lost Kilbolane treasure.) Mr. Allen made no sort of trouble about the Bowens' continued access to the bawn, or to their and their servants' frequent comings and goings. A lover of peace, he would have been the last to combat Mrs. Catherine Bowen, who continued to look on the bawn and on Brandon Castle as hers. On the ground floor of Brandon she was keeping fowls to fatten; in the room above she bred black-and-white rabbits; also, she used the castle for storing gooseberry wine. Servants of hers, as deponents in the *Bowen v. Evans* lawsuit of 1759, recalled daily trips to this castle, as part of their duties, with cabbage for rabbits or to draw off wine. Mrs. Bowen got her one reverse, in the affair of the bawn, from Thomas Evans, a narrow-spirited man.

During a two-year interim in the Allen tenancy, Thomas Evans elected to occupy Kilbolane Old House himself, and, while there, to interfere in the running of things. The tale of the well, and of what then happened, comes from one James Grady, who became a deponent in the 1759 case:

*During the said two years that the said Thomas Evans lived at
Kilbolane, he employed the Deponant and some other men to open
the well in the Bawn in Dispute. . . . While this Deponant and
said other men were at work clearing the said well, Mrs. Bowen
. . . came to the Deponant and said men, about 10 o'clock in the
morning, and complained that her Servants had Droped into the
well Severall Particulars such as a Pott lid, a saucepan, a spoon and
other Kitchen furniture, and sayed she expected this Deponant
and said other man to be Accountable for them if they were not
found. Upon which, the said Thomas Evans came out and lett Mrs.
Bowen know that she had made her Servants pay Double they
were worth for them before, and that she had no right to expect
them. Whereupon the said Thomas Evans took the said Mrs.
Bowen by the arm and led her away, and desired her not to Inter-
rupt his workmen. And thereupon the said Thomas Evans sent for
a mason and made up the Passage, to prevent her coming to disturb
the workmen again.*

Mrs. Bowen lay low till the odious Evans was gone and the
nice Allens resumed their tenancy. She then, we understand,
had the passage unblocked again, Mr. Allen looking the other
way. Access to Brandon and its amenities was once more hers.
When Mr. Henry Allen died he was succeeded by his nephew
Edward, who carried on the tradition of neighbourly kindli-
ness: during her last days, Mrs. Bowen "*when terrified or
frightened of robbers being in the country, used sometimes to
quit Kilbolane mansion and lodge with Mr. Edward Allen at
the old house of Kilbolane.*" In return for this (says her cook,
Elizabeth Murphy) Mrs. Bowen let Mr. Allen keep " plow
tackling " in Brandon Castle. But she later asked him to take his
tackling away, as she wanted to put her fowl back, to fatten.
Her fowls had to go again when her second son John, for some
time a cornet in the 5th Dragoons, commandeered Brandon to
kennel his hounds in.

There also for some time " dyeted and lodged " at Mr. Al-

len's a choleric clergyman, the Rev. Jeremiah King, who was to
become the Bowens' only too zealous friend.

Jane Cole, who in 1716 married Henry Bowen II, had not
only looks and a fortune, she came of a fairly illustrious family.
It has, even, been claimed that the Coles descend from Coel,
that British King who was founder of Colchester and who may
have been the original Old King Cole. When the mists of antiquity clear, Coles are found in the West of England, mainly
in Devonshire: they trace unbroken descent from one William
Cole who was living at Hutensleigh (now, Hittisleigh) in 1243.
In 1380 a John Cole was knighted in France by the Earl of
Buckingham; his grandson, Sir John Cole, fought at Agincourt,
receiving his spurs for conduct on that glorious field. Sir John
(of Agincourt's) second son, John, married Jane, daughter of
Robert Meryon in Devon, and *their* second son, William, married Elizabeth, daughter of Sir Richard Weston of Wiltshire.
Their grandson, Thomas, died in London 1571, and his grandson, William, married Elizabeth, daughter and heiress of Na-
thaniel Deards, of London, " silkman." It was the seventh son
of this marriage, Robert, who, in the seventeenth century, went
to Ireland, and acquired (perhaps bought) the Ballymackey estate in County Tipperary. This Robert Cole was M.P. for
Enniskillen in 1661, at that first Dublin Parliament after the
Restoration — the Parliament that rushed the Act of Settlement
through. He was knighted at Whitehall ten years later. He was,
in 1689, one of the Protestant absentees attainted by James II's
" Patriot Parliament." Sir Robert Cole had one son, Robert,
who had one daughter, Jane.

This was the Jane Cole, heiress of Ballymackey, who came as
a bride to Kilbolane. The Bowens absorbed her lands and her
Cole name — ever since Jane's day each and every one of her
Bowen descendants have been christened " Cole " at the font.
(So much so, that the Bowen's Court Bowens have got to be
known as " Cole Bowen," as though they had a double surname

— but this is incorrect: " Cole " is no more than a family Christian name.) Jane also brought to the Bowens the name Robert — there had been no Robert Bowens before her day. Her grandson, my great-great-grandfather, was the first: since then, there has been one in each generation. I should have been christened Robert, had I been born a man.

It must have been a love match. Jane Cole was young and pretty and rich; she had important connections in several worlds; she certainly could have done better than Henry Bowen. She was unlike that first heiress a Bowen married — poor downtrodden Mary Nicholls of the ruins. Henry II was, to judge from his portrait, no beauty: he was tall, though, and had the bony stylishness of his race and type. He had a high-bridged nose, ruddy fair skin, light-blue, alive eyes; his forehead shows an expectant intelligence. He had a mobile, fairly expressive mouth. Above all I do see something merry about him. Perhaps his merriness won her, perhaps he touched her senses, perhaps she knew she held, and felt the beat of, his heart.

In her Bowen's Court portrait Jane looks lovely — instinct with poise and grace and unconscious mystery. Her hair is combed back from her softly-moulded face, with the wide apart sloe-dark eyes and short firm drawn-in chin. Her throat and her breast, above the fall of lace, and her rounded forearms are ivory. Her toy spaniel sits on her knee, in the supple folds of her dress of an indescribable, light-shot blue. There is a background of fulminous woods, clouds and a colonnaded mansion not ever built. She must have been an adorable wife in all senses: to the world well-mannered and to her husband tender. Her air, in the portrait, is of faint surprise and detachment, but of complete control.

Surprise and detachment may well have been Jane's reaction to Kilbolane. She had been used, I think, to more gracious living, and to households more in touch with the world. From every evidence Jane was an orphan — her step-grandmother Lady Cole, an Oxfordshire lady who only died, in Ireland, in

the year of Jane's marriage, may have had some hand in her
bringing up. At Kilbolane, about this time, sport, quarrels, estate management, family feeling and dreams of more litigation
seem to have occupied the Bowens almost exclusively. And the
isolation of Kilbolane — as real as the isolation of Bowen's
Court, though less romantically visual — would tend to rule
social life out, even had old Mrs. Bowen had time or temper for
it. The Bowens had, perhaps brought with them from Wales, a
haughty disregard for amenities. One cannot baulk at the fact
that they were a bleak family. Though serenity is in each line
of Kilbolane House itself, I cannot help feeling that something
in Catherine Bowen's children ran counter to this. And the
house was not large — its very compactness would tend to
throw people upon each other. All Jane's husband's relatives
were at home — John, Stephens and Thomasine (pronounced
" Tamsine ") were not yet married, and their father and
mother, John and Catherine, ruled. Poor old John I, dying over
at Fort in the hands of his two unpleasant Elizabeths, would be
a daily subject of speculation and fret. Mrs. Bowen, Jane's
mother-in-law, continued to bear down on every detail, to
exact, to comment, to let nothing pass. I suspect that she no
more than suffered the bride. Even if withdrawals — into, I
hope, that north parlour with the corner fireplace and steps
down to the garden — were possible for Jane and Henry, Mrs.
Bowen would not like to have anybody out of her eye for too
long — she was the sort of woman who would remark, these
days, that she did like people to be *about*. In the family parlours
there must have been restless chaos — the gentle descendant of
Old King Cole, rare bird in this nest of half-fledged hawks,
would have sat a little apart with Bowens constantly bumping
against the back of her chair. I hope Thomasine Bowen, now a
girl in her 'teens, had a *schwärm* for Jane, studied style from
her, tried to copy her clothes. We know how good Thomasine
was, later, to Jane's son. Young John, Henry's brother, would
be much away with his regiment: when at home, he would be

too busy intriguing to dislodge the rabbits from Brandon and
get his hounds in to have interest for his pretty sister-in-law.
Stephens Bowen was still a hobbledehoy.

What a placeless place, this small country house packed with
people, for a young pair of married lovers — and how idyllic
they could have found it if they had been alone! One can imagine their glances across the candles, their regretful smiles at
one another through windows, their snatched minutes alone by
some parlour fire, Jane's *moues* when some one came between
her and Henry, Henry's pettish frowns, her dropped eyelids,
their slipping-off early to bed. Perhaps they strolled outdoors in
the long white Irish twilights or in steely evenings after the rain
— Jane holding the hem of her long stiff skirts clear of the damp.
The orchards, garden and woods would be theirs once the
senior Bowens had finished their days' rounds. Perhaps they
crept through the arch in the wall of the Desmond ruin and
round the bawn in the dark — steering clear of the peat stacks,
avoiding the old well. They would smell the night smell of
stone and of tired refreshed grass; the smell of shut-up rabbits
would come through the Brandon chinks. Kind Mr. Allen,
burning his candles late in Kilbolane Old House, would ignore
their muted voices and steps. Henry would tell Jane again
about the treasure, and she would, vaguely, reply, what a pity
it was not found.

When, after John I's death, Henry was sent off to Wales to
establish the Kilbolane Bowen's right to the Gower lands, it
must have been cruel having to leave Jane. She may, too, have
been with child at the time: she had had two children before
her husband died. In view of the shortness of their married life,
this tedious journey to Wales seems a tragedy. In Gower this
Irish Henry must have been homesick; he would have raced
through his business with Swansea lawyers, dealt abruptly with
tenants, and viewed with the un-emotion of one whose heart is
elsewhere the Llanellan fields, in which his great-grandfather
hawked. After Kilbolane, Llanellan House — if it stood —

would have seemed to him dark and runty. Though, axiomatically, all Bowens want all land, I doubt Henry felt any itch to regain Gower. He wanted County Cork and the breast of his darling wife. To these he returned — but not for long.

I have said that in 1716 three generations of male Bowens were living — John I, the grandfather, John II, the father, and Henry II, the son. Within the next six years there had been a holocaust: the two Johns and young Henry were dead, and, even, a fourth generation had come and gone — Henry's and Jane's first son had been born only to die. John I died in 1718, John II in 1720, and Henry II in 1722, some few years after his infant son. John I had been for a long time due to die, and the poor baby may have been delicate — but what swept off, within two years of each other, John II, at the end of his 'fifties, and Henry II in the prime of his youth? Did some fatality hang over Kilbolane? Did miasmas come out of the old well? Did Kilbolane simply not suit Bowens? I have heard of *no* fate on the house since; it is inhabited now by another family, and the air round is palpably healthy and pure. Perhaps, between 1720 and '22, some slow malignant fever crept through the Bowens. If so, it took only the two men. Possibly John, Stephens and Thomasine were sent away. Mrs. Catherine Bowen, grim and I think tearless, buried her husband, watched her son through his brief reign, buried her son, then offered her old widowed resigned bosom to Jane's young widowed hopeless tears.

The start of the pattern of Henry II's existence has suffered from being abruptly torn across — this happens to patterns of torn stuffs — so that one cannot even gather what kind of man he was on his way to be. He was not designed to die young — but who outside fiction is? He began to consume love while still waiting for life: one can see him only in terms of senses and scenes.

In 1722, when young Henry II was dying, he had made his will. Jane was to have the Farahy lands for her lifetime — the

lease to the Nashes being due to expire in 1728. Generous provision was made for the little daughter Catherine, the only child
living at the date of the will. But there was another factor: the
dying Henry knew that Jane was *enceinte*. So, there might still
be a male heir. If Jane's child yet to be born should be a son, he
was to inherit the whole property — Farahy (after his mother's
death), the Kilbolane lands in Cork and Limerick, and the
Ballymackey estates brought in from the Coles. Three friends
— Robert Oliver of Castle Oliver (five miles north-west of
Farahy in the Ballyhouras), Henry Rose and Llewellin Nash
(son of Andrew) of Farahy — were Henry's executors, and
were due to be guardians to the unborn child.

At Kilbolane, aching with the final absence of Henry, Jane
awaited the birth. One cannot doubt that Mrs. Catherine
Bowen, who waited with her, was at this juncture kind. Just
before her time was due, poor Jane went down with measles
and was grievously ill. " In measles " her son, Henry III, was
born — doubly crimson and momentously delicate. Following
Irish custom in such crises, they sent out and had a sheep killed
and tore the skin off and wrapped the half-living child in the
life-heat of the skin. So, this third Henry was saved, to build
Bowen's Court. He was christened Henry Cole, and the country people used to call him " Cooleen."

After the birth, emotional anti-climax set in. Innate lack
of sympathy, woman-antagonism between the two Bowen
widows made itself felt. Jane might well feel she had done her
last duty by Kilbolane now she had borne her Henry's young
Henry there. When she was well again, she took her daughter
Catherine and the boy baby Henry III and moved off with
them to Limerick; she also took away with her the spaniel that
had been painted on her blue trousseau dress. Unable to touch
Henry III's inheritance, she realized money she needed by selling part of what had remained her own lands. Solitary, mute
and laborious, Jane made herself and her children a new home.
She need not have troubled — not much more than a year after

Henry II died, his wife Jane Bowen had died too. It is said that
her spaniel fatally bit her. If she died of hydrophobia, one
cannot contemplate that.

The year after Henry III, as an unknowing baby, lost his
mother, the nest of Bowens at Kilbolane began to break up.
John, Stephens and Thomasine, perhaps by their mother's influence, showed a disposition to marry into the County Limerick. John and Stephens were quite well off; not only did they
inherit, from John II, the rents from the Gower lands, but their
mother, Catherine Bowen *née* Stephens, divided between them
her Devonshire property, from which they were also able to
draw rents. Catherine Bowen did not do this for nothing; she
took the £1,000 that was John's bride's dowry, and later collected £100 from Stephens, in consideration of his rather
smaller share.

When, in 1724, John Bowen, the ex-dragoon, married Elizabeth Chidley Coote, he removed himself, his bride, his hounds
and his interests from Kilbolane and settled at Carrigadrohid
— where Broghill had hanged the bishop. His son John acquired
Carrigadrohid Castle and Oak Grove; his granddaughter Jane
Bowen married, in 1777, John Colthurst of Dripsey Castle; his
great-grandson, Robert Bowen, inherited Oak Grove, acquired
Dripsey Castle and, having added by Royal Licence the Colthurst arms and name to his own, founded the Bowen-Colthurst
family.

So much for Henry III's elder uncle, John Bowen. His
younger uncle Stephens married Elizabeth Sprigg, lived for
some time at Farahy and, when he died in 1762, left three
daughters.

In 1729, when Henry III was six, his aunt Thomasine left
Kilbolane as the bride of Ralph Warter Wilson, of Bilbo,
County Limerick. Thomasine, who is said to have made an excellent mother, raised at Bilbo her family of five Wilson children, but this did not make her forget her nephew: Bilbo was

always open to Henry and gave him the most cheerful home
that he knew.

After their mother's death in Limerick, Henry III and his
little sister Catherine had been sent back to Kilbolane. The
second great phase of Mrs. Bowen's existence, that of guardian
and grandmother, now set in. She was not, it is true, in law
Henry's guardian, but she chivvied those who were. She not
only ran the house and estate like a dragon; she plunged deep
into business. This remarkable woman appears to have had all
documents at her fingers' ends; also, she knew the family's
legal history by heart. Henry Rose, Robert Oliver and Dr.
Llewellin Nash were no longer able to call their souls their
own. Mrs. Bowen was quick on her pen: letters containing in-
junctions, reminders, reproaches — and, often, pretty sharp
raps — came fairly whizzing over from Kilbolane. (Much of the
current business, in these big landed families, consisted in the
letting and re-letting of farms and land to the Irish.) Mrs.
Bowen's letters were circulated among the three gentlemen.
" *Another letter from Madam!* " begins Llewellin Nash, in a
covering-note sent over to Castle Oliver. Llewellin Nash — as,
I take it, a doctor of law — got the brunt of the fuss. This long-
suffering, genial, fairly distinguished man continued for some
time to live at Farahy — when the Nash lease expired, in 1728,
he must have taken the place on from year to year. He had interests in Cork City, was a J.P. for Cork in 1735, and in 1763,
two years before his death, received the freedom of the city in
a silver box. When he took over the guardianship of young
Henry Bowen he was about forty-two; he was married and had
three sons. One feels that his middle years must have been made
really hideous by Mrs. Bowen. All the same, Nash enjoyed and
developed his relationship with the boy himself. We hear that
he kept a pack of hounds at Farahy for young Henry's pleasure
— and at young Henry's expense. He seems to have encouraged,
guided and, to a degree, flattered his promising ward. Happy
days spent with the Nashes at Farahy may have given Henry III

the bent he, as a man, followed, back to these original Bowen lands.

As a grandmother, Mrs. Bowen was more energetic than cosy. There can have been little to mitigate, for young Henry, that sadness of death that still hung over Kilbolane. Quite early, he lost his sister Catherine, of whom we only know that she " died young " — no copy of Jane was to survive. With his uncles and aunt all gone to their married homes, the boy and his grandmother would be left *tete-à-tete*. Those rooms so restlessly crowded for his young father and mother would now be restlessly empty. The new house felt forgotten. When Henry was sent out to play, I expect that he took his little spade and, as hopefully as others before him, dug for Nicholls treasure about the castle and bawn. We know that he had that obsession, and that he transmitted it. At nights, when the trees creaked and wind whistled round the neighbouring ruin, Mrs. Bowen's one standing fear — of robbers — would become dominant. No, Kilbolane was not cheerful for Jane's son: we know that Henry took against the place and never spent much time there once he ruled his own life. In his childhood, a much dearer home was Bilbo, with its warm welcome and pack of Wilson cousins. Aunt Thomasine no doubt talked gently to Henry about his mother, said how lovely Jane was, what a pity her death had been. Whatever she said or did, Thomasine riveted Henry's heart to herself and her family. There must have been something about the people at Bilbo that was most anti-ghostish and reassuring. One knows this magnetism of family life for the rather solitary and nervous child. Henry III had a grand time when he grew up, but he was never able to get on without Wilsons. As we shall hear, he eventually married one.

Henry also, when visiting Farahy, spent days with his other guardian at Castle Oliver, in its cold spectacular setting under the mountainside. This was the Castle Oliver whose kitchen arrangements were, later, to scandalize Arthur Young.

Mrs. Bowen really had cause to worry when Elizabeth Bowen, of Charleville, became active again. Mrs. Bowen sent post haste, with a wad of other writing, this (undated) letter to Farahy:

Dr. Llewellin.

I can't but acquaint you with what I hear, which I am sure is not true. Mr. Bryan was the other day at my cousin Robin Thomas's, he told him that he had bought the Estate of Farahy and Wales from Betty Bowen, and had pay'd Thom. Clay thirty five pounds of the money, and that he held the deed, which I don't believe. Cousin told him that he and I would oblige him to produce it. On what head he should say this I can't tell, because I gave you the deed of settlement made by my Father Bowen on his wife Mary Nicholls and her issue male, and for want of other issue on her issue female: Dr. Blunt and Alexander Body subscribing witnesses. You told me you did carry the deed to Corke, and showed it to Alexander Body that liv'd there, who was a servant to Captain Nicholls. He told you it was his father and not him. As I ever found you and believe you are, that you would never betray the trust I confided in you to give a Deed of soe great Consequence to any Man, I hope you will produce the Deed that we may have it atested by responsible witnesses. For if anything should happen to you or I, the Deed may be mislay'd, and then my Grand Child and family lose the best part of their fortunes. I desire you will send me a Copy of the Deed and your answer to my letter.

In the wad of writing this note covered Mrs. Bowen recapitulates, absolutely correctly, the history of all the Bowen settlements. The deed — which no doubt Llewellin had by him the whole time, in the Bowen box, for he was an orderly man — must have been produced, for Betty Bowen subsided and Mrs. Bowen calmed down. Of course, at the outset the whole rumour may have been greatly exaggerated by Cousin Robin

Thomas — in Ireland we love to post over with upsetting news.
If Mr. Bryan did pay over that thirty-five pounds, I should like
to know if he ever got it back. If not, Betty Bowen had raked
in, in all, sixty-five pounds, quite a sum in those days, on property to which — as we know and as I feel sure she knew — she
had not the ghost of a valid claim. She must have had a nerve:
one should take off one's hat to her. From this on we hear no
more of her, which I regret.

As to the education of Henry III no details seem to be forthcoming. One can only assume he was ever taught anything
from the fact that he wrote a fine flowing hand. He did not, I
am sure, go away to school or college: Dr. Nash may have
found a tutor for him. It seems possible that the Rev. Jeremiah
King, who lodged with Mr. Allen, may have acted as Henry's
tutor at Kilbolane. As a clergyman, Mr. King would have had
some Latin. But Mr. King's chief feeling was for horses, dinners
and quarrelling. He kept Henry up to his interest in the family
treasure. He and Henry, over a pile of grammars, may have
pleasantly droned some few daily hours away. I imagine that
Mrs. Bowen would not support education, as being liable to
give Henry ideas. *Her* own only reading must have been documents. Henry may have been conscious, as he grew older, not
so much of lack of learning as of lack of experience. Auto-
cratic, effulgent, lordly as he continued to be, he may, at times,
have suspected that he was a provincial. He sent his eldest son,
Henry IV, to Oxford: nothing was to be good enough for
Bowen of Bowen's Court.

Education is not so important as people think. Nothing he
learned, certainly, but at the same time nothing he did not learn,
impaired Henry's flair for living, his innate stylishness and his
love of the grand. Had he had the education of a Renaissance
prince he would, I think, in a few years have discarded everything that he could not reduce to his own terms. The pleasures
of the mind, the arts, discourse were all denied to Henry III —

one can hardly say denied, for he never demanded them. His destiny was, to be a *beau* in Mallow society, a liberal landowner, the builder of Bowen's Court. Did he miss much? He lived his life to the full. In the society of Mallow, during the hospitalities of Henry III's Bowen's Court, many of my readers would wince and droop. Henry, a pre-eminently social figure, lived in a Philistine, snobbish, limited and on the whole pretty graceless society. But he got somewhere, and lived to die in his drawing-room surrounded by hosts of children and the esteem of what looked like a lasting order. And to what did our fine feelings, our regard for the arts, our intimacies, our inspiring conversations, our wish to be clear of the bonds of sex and class and nationality, our wish to try to be fair to every one bring us? To 1939.

Henry Cole Bowen was very much Jane Cole's son. A sort of bloom and richness appear to him. The elements of Jane's mysterious charm come out in Henry as a shy virtuosity. Every one seems to have liked him. In spite of his ancestry, he got from the country people the feeling they used to keep for their natural lords. His baby nickname " Cooleen " was still used, with affectionate irony, when he was a great smiling lusty grown man. In Ireland, one endears oneself by palpably having a good time. And Henry, for all his Protestant politics, by now *felt* as Irish as Lord Muskerry.

The Irish and the English squire are very differently placed: the first is imposed and the second indigenous. The English squire considers God gave him a function, the Irish considers himself his own end, put where he is by some sport of the Divine will — in fact, an aristocrat. The English squire can, or could till quite lately, combine with the parson in dragooning the lower classes into healthy activities; exceedingly conscientious, he feels he is where he is to teach the poor what is what. Clubs, institutes, patrols and associations are promoted by him, and the men, women and children of the less fortunate classes urged into them, to this end. The Irish landowner, partly from

laziness but also from an indifferent delicacy, does not interfere
in the lives of the people round. Sport and death are the two
great socializing factors in Ireland, but these cannot operate the
whole time: on the whole, the landowner leaves his tenants and
work-people to make their own mistakes, while he makes his.
The greater part of them being Catholics, and he in most cases
being a Protestant, they are kept from him by the barrier of a
different faith. He does not feel the English urge to improve
morally: he improves his property; if he acts rightly he repairs
his cottages, but he makes no attempts on the outlook of those
inside. He came down (till lately) on tenants when he wanted
more money; he comes down on work-people when he wants
more work. Otherwise, he pursues, inside his demesne and mansion, his centripetal and rather cut-off life. This may or may not
be a pity, but it is so. There exists between classes, at least in the
country in Ireland, a good-mannered, faintly cynical tolerance,
largely founded on classes letting each other alone. There does
also, in many cases, exist a lively and simple spontaneous human
affection between the landed families and the Irish people
round them – this is said to have roots in the foster-system,
which until quite lately prevailed. In a crisis, there may always
be an alliance – against outsiders, in money troubles, against
the law.

On the whole, I think it is English rather than Irish country
life that is singular and phenomenal. Irish country life, in
Henry III's day and to an extent now, is more on the general
pattern of that in France, Italy, Poland and pre-revolution Russia – the outstanding difference is the religious split, and also,
the fact that the Ascendency classes came, in the first place,
from a different land.

I have tried to make this clear, to show that Henry III had no
analogies in the England of his day, and, in his modern form,
would have no analogies now. He was no absentee; he kept an
eye on his lands and spent his rents no further away than Mallow. But he was a free lance: there was no hereditary system,

as there would be in England, to condition his interests and bind his heart.

By the terms of his father's will, Henry's minority was to last until he was twenty-four. (Did Henry II, looking back at the Bowens, wish to prevent his possible unborn son from, too young, entering into settlements?) However, the three guardians were amenable; they gave Henry the run of a good allowance, and with this he took himself off to Mallow, to see the world. Having outgrown his early delicacy, he was now a tall, broad-shouldered, volatile young man. In the Bowen's Court portrait, painted in later life, his face is ruddy and open, his air is easy and disengaged. He shows a touch of obtuseness, more than a touch of arrogance, a shade of mistrust (for Henry did not like facts), enough heart and immense geniality. He has, also, the *entêté* look of the dreamer — his dreams were not heroic, they were no more than grand. All his life he liked and wore, with good effect, good clothes. His infant — in fact, infantile — nervousness stayed, I feel certain, at the core of his being: under the superstructure of looks and manner moved currents of self-distrust and a sort of dread of the dark. He was not only Jane Cole's quite elegant son, he was the great-great-grandson of tormented Colonel Bowen. He was one of those big, rather showy, get-away-with-it men who quite often, fundamentally, need a good cry. He needed a mother — and knew where to look for one.

I do not know the date of Henry's grandmother's death. There is a silence about her, from the time of his early manhood, that she would neither have liked nor allowed — so I take it that she was dead. Her death would have made his whole existence easier, for he could square his guardians where he could not square his grandmother. He may have mourned her with a quick rush of sentiment, with a self-reproach made sharper by his relief — but with no more, I think. I do not know, either — and this is still more annoying — exactly what Henry did with Kilbolane House: he may first have shut it up, then let it to another family, possibly to the Evans. At some date, it was sold: we do know that Kilbolane House had been out of the family for some time before the Bowens finally lost the lands. In the space between Henry's departure from Kilbolane and his occupation of the new Bowen's Court, he still sometimes describes himself as " of Kilbolane " — but also as " of Kilcumer," " of Farahy " and " of Annabella."

It must have been from Kilcumer — or Kilcomer, or Kilcummer — the new Wilson base, that Henry made his first descent on Mallow society. He is " of Kilcumer " when he is twenty-six.

The cheerful Wilsons were growing up and marrying — their names were Ralph, Edward, William, Catherine and Margaret. The eldest of them would have been Henry's junior by seven or eight years, but they were his generation, so his life moved with theirs away from Bilbo into their married homes. I do not know whether Catherine actually *was* the eldest Wilson (daughters are only listed after the sons are finished), but evidently it was Catherine who married first. Her husband was John Grove of Kilcumer — a not large but pleasant old house above the Awbeg valley, not far from the Bridgetown abbey ruins, below the steep Castletownroche woods. When Catherine's brother William got married, the William Wilsons joined the Groves at Kilcumer. This made, in the pretty Awbeg surroundings, an amiable family quartette. Margaret, the youngest of the family, must have been about also, as a very young girl. This re-nesting of Wilsons not far from Mallow would strengthen Henry's new fondness for the neighbourhood. Mallow is eight or nine miles from Kilcumer; the road runs along the north lip of the Blackwater valley — a pleasant, not difficult, ride or drive. So, Henry stayed on and on at Kilcumer. There was room enough.

The age that saw the heyday of Mallow, and with it the heyday of Henry III, has been stigmatized as selfish and corrupt.

The Protestant newcomers' liveliness and well-being was wholly at the native Catholic expense. The new ascendency lacked feeling: in fact, feeling would have been fatal to it. At the same time, I do honestly think this ascendency identified God with its good luck. The Cromwellian justification was deep in family fibre; innate conviction was at the root of their zest. And, in their three or four generations of life in Ireland, something had worked on their temperaments: they were now Irish in being, if not in interest.

In Queen Anne's reign, anti-popishness in England had been exacerbated by Louis XIV's support of James II's son's claim. During the years of the War of the Spanish Succession it had looked as though the French King might land Prince James Edward in Ireland to raise the Catholics and threaten England's west flank. So, further laws, effectively restrictive and disabling, were passed against Irish Catholics. By the end of Anne's reign, Catholics had been debarred from holding office in the State or army, forbidden to act as grand jurors and finally disenfranchised. Laws forbidding Catholics to inherit land except from each other, to buy more land or to obtain leases of more than thirty-one years stopped any growth (or rather, recovery) of territorial power. A law compelling the estate of any deceased Catholic to be shared out equally between all his sons — unless the eldest " conformed " before he came of age — aimed at the shredding up of remaining Catholic estates, and at the reduction of Catholic landowning families by bringing them to the small-holder way of life. Catholics were not permitted to carry arms, and, for a short time, as the final humiliation, were not allowed to ride. The same system that denied the Catholic gentry their status pushed the poor right under — they suffered atrociously. The settlers had built their houses out of the stones from ruins; their descendants now built a society out of another ruin.

Immediate expediency had made High Church Tories in England lend themselves to these measures: in the main, as we know, they were not virulent anti-Catholics. The Queen's childlessness — or, rather the vainness of the poor woman's fecundity — caused a predicament: leading Tories looked darkly on the Hanoverian prospect, and Bolingbroke openly was for Prince James Edward, after Anne. In Ireland the second Duke of Ormond, as Lord Lieutenant, was avowedly Jacobite. And, already, a certain amount of anti-English feeling, and anti-Whig feeling in particular, had sprung up among those Anglo-Irish hit by restrictive English trading laws; the more Anglo-Ireland flourished and integrated, the more she became a critic of English policy. The moral, and finally patriotic, stand taken by Anglo-Ireland did not come till later on in the century; Swift started it and Berkeley carried it on; Flood and Grattan were to make it felt in politics.

So, not only Catholic but Tory Irish hopes continued to rivet on Prince James Edward, till the Whig imposition of George I dealt a bitter blow to Bolingbroke, warped Swift and forced Ormond's flight to France, where he later died. The new Germanic monarch — uncomely, dull, fiddling and middle-class — left Anglo-Ireland slightly aghast: he did not, somehow, seem to be quite the thing. George I's intentions towards Ireland, if any, were perfectly nebulous — and, anyhow, were quite immaterial: his Whig parliament would settle matters for him. The Jacobite rising in Scotland, in 1715, just after George's accession, was watched from across the water. As we know, it failed.

So the Ascendency settled down to their King. He was part of the system that was their frame, and they could forget him, except when drinking the toast. Young Anglo-Irishmen such as Henry Cole Bowen now fairly fell on life. The society of which Henry made a part was, in these middle decades of the eighteenth century, at the vital, growing, magnetic stage: it enjoyed not only material but real psychological dominance. Each of its microcosms, such as Mallow, shed excitement and vigour. Such a society had its roughnesses, but it had not that vulgarity of assertion only necessary when there is decline. (That is why to detect a vulgarity, in ourselves, in a friend or associate, worries us: it is the morbid symptom we recognize.) Provincial Irish society, round the seventeen-fifties, took itself for granted; there was no need, yet, to say, " We are the people! " There was not a ripple of intellectual doubt — perhaps not much intellect for doubt to ripple in. They *were* the people, and others fell in with them — which is why I call this society magnetic. Remaining Catholic gentry were drawn, by class interests, by this new reign of old pleasures, to the new-comers' new big houses, the entertaining, the grand manner acquired in Irish air. Many Catholic gentry conformed — and who dare criticize them? As for the poor, they had to flatter to live — and, even so, most of them barely lived at all.

There was, in these decades, not much more persecution. Enough, for Catholics all over the country, was the dulling pressure of circumstance. And, in the coma of these eupeptic days, zeal ebbed from the Protestant faith. Laud's and Straf-ford's work, the established Church of Ireland, now had a phase of prosperous apathy. Continuing to draw tithes from the Catholics, it left spiritual upheavals to the Dissenters, in return for tithes that it also drew from them. In the gentlemen's churches, as in England, the Ten Commandments, graven on sorts of tombstones, reared up over communion tables bare of suspicious objects. Jehovahism sometimes broke from the pul-pits, but one allowed for choler in clergymen. Rational thought from Paris — with delays, lacunae and misunderstandings, like a long-distance telephone call — travelled *via* London and Dub-lin to County Cork, and the Age of Reason did just this for Mallow: one assumed that God was not after one the *whole* time. Few clergymen and still fewer baronets would, these days, have taken umbrage at Colonel Bowen's remarks: the Welshman had distressed himself unnecessarily. All the same, observance remained *de rigueur* — there was that Sunday mile of gentlemen's carriages.

Books, in Mallow, were heard of and even owned; they were
the proper fittings of a gentleman's house. That their contents
did much to aliment talk, I doubt. Opinion gave statements
variety, colour, character; in a life lived at Mallow pace there
was not much context for knowledge. Our self-consciousness
asks for literature: Mallow was not self-conscious at this time.
And what need to diversify hours that clattered past, like
coaches over the stone roads from gate to gate? The Mallow
gentry had no nostalgia, no wish to escape. . . . Meanwhile
the Gaelic culture ran underground, with its ceaseless poetry
of lament. (Gaelic was spoken in the kitchens and fields and in
untouched country the settlers did not know.) It has taken the
decline of the Anglo-Irish to open to them the poetry of regret:
only dispossessed people know their land in the dark. These
boon companions of Henry III's were strangers to the culture they were to breed. But they did build, and their houses
are monuments.

Events, at almost the height of the century, gave Mallow one
more agreeable shake. It is to the Jacobite rising of '45, in Scotland, that we owe the inception of the *Moyallow*[1] *Loyal
Protestant Society*. To fail, in the winter of '45 to '46, to be one
of the Loyal Protestants clearly was to be nobody in that
world. Young Henry III, having taken a general look round,
must have perceived this immediately; it became, I feel certain,
his first ambition to make this club. This he succeeded in doing
at the third meeting — possibly through the good offices of
Philip Oliver, a foundation member and a relative of Henry's
Castle Oliver guardian. Henry was only twenty-two, so this
was not bad. On the other hand, without being too cynical, one
must keep in mind that Henry was pretty rich, willing to please
and with no liabilities; he must have looked like putting up
quite his share of the drinks without which the Society's proceedings did not proceed far. Once in, he worked himself in
so deeply that he was able to carry away the Society's minute

---

[1] Moyallow was the old name for Mallow.

book, which is now at Bowen's Court, having come down to me. It is handsomely bound in tooled and gilded black leather, and bears the name and date of the club outside. Inside, the good-quality paper, now rather brown, shows entries in various handwritings.

At, or within two days after, their first meeting on November 4th, 1745, thirty Loyal Protestants signed this Manifesto:

We whose Names are hereunto Subscribed, being met together to celebrate the Remembrance of the late Happy Revolution, achieved under God by the Late King William of Glorious and Immortal Memory, Under a Deep Sense of our Duty and Loyalty to our most Gracious and Rightful Sovereign Lord King George and regard for our most Holy Religion, together with our Liberties and Properties, at this time, when a horrid and most unnatural Rebellion is entered upon, and now actually carrying on, by Papists and other Disaffected Persons, against his Aforesaid Majesty's Person and Government in Scotland, in favour of a Popish Pretender long ago and solemnly abjured, to the entire Subversion of our Most Happy Constitution both in Church and State; do, by these Presents, engage to Meet at the House of the Widow Callaghan at Moyallow aforesaid, on each and every Friday from the Date of these presents during the Continuance of the said abominable and Detestable Rebellion, until a Victory, by God's Blessing on his Majesty's arms, shall be obtained over the Trayterous and Perjured Authors thereof; there to concert such measures as we shall from Time to Time think most proper for the Defence of his Most Sacred Majesty aforesaid his Government and our Mutual Security, against all Persons that may Presume to disturb the same in this Kingdom. And in case any of us whose Names are Hereunto subscribed, shall neglect or omit to meet at the Time and place aforesaid, We do hereby promise to pay unto such person as the Majority of the Subscribers hereunto shall appoint, the sum of one British Shilling, for each and Every day that we shall be absent, to be disposed of as the Majority of the said Subscribers

shall appoint. Given our hand the Day and year above mentioned.
(November 4th, 1745.)

Among the thirty signatures that follow are family names still
known, or fairly freshly remembered, in a twelve-mile radius
of Mallow — Longfield, Lysaght, St. Leger Aldworth, Welstead, Stawel, Oliver, Newman, Lombard. There are, equally,
names that have died out in the nearly two hundred years since
then. In the second, the '55 phase of the club, we find two Jeph-
sons and an Evans — no doubt the Doneraile branch. Doneraile
and Castletownroche, as two Mallow outposts, contributed
members, to my certain knowledge. The Robert Grove on the
first list is no doubt a connection of the John Grove Catherine
Wilson had married. The only non-locals, the floating members, were cavalry officers stationed at Mallow.

In addition to signing the Manifesto, each Member took the
Oath: this, too lengthily worded to be transcribed here, was
in effect brief — he swore whole-hearted allegiance to King
George II and to the House of Hanover, he declared abhor-
rence of all popish practice and plots, he denounced the Pretender's claims to the throne and he pledged himself to oppose,
outwit and defeat any further " attempts " or conspiracies. To
the Oath was appended this Declaration:

I, A. B., do solemnly and Sincerely, in the Presence of God, Pro-
fess, testify and declare, that I do believe, that in the Sacrament of
the Lord's Supper, there is not any Transubstantiation of the Ele-
ments of Bread and Wine into the Body and Blood of Christ, at
or after the Consecration thereof by any Person whatsoever; and
that the Invocation or Adoration of the Virgin Mary, or any other
Saint, and the Sacrifice of the Mass, as they are now used in the
Church of Rome, are Superstitious and Idolatrous: And I do sol-
emnly, in the presence of God, profess, testify and declare, that I
do make this Declaration, and every Part thereof, in the plain and
ordinary Sense of the Words read unto me, as they are commonly
understood by Protestants, without any Evasion, Equivocation, or

*any mental Reservation whatsoever; and without any Dispensation
already granted me for this Purpose by the Pope, or any other
Authority whatsover; or without believing that I am or can be
acquitted before God or Man, or absolved of this Declaration, or
any part thereof, although the Pope, or any other Person or Persons, or Power whatsoever, should dispence with, or annull the
same, or declare that it was null and void from the Beginning.*

The Loyal Protestants — country gentlemen, officers, clergymen — were a dining club. Impeccably Protestant, they went
on to have a high old time together — except when, as apparently often happened, they were dining elsewhere on club
nights. Fines were to be collected by the Treasurer, the Rev.
Thomas Meule, and sent to the Protestant Poor of Mallow.
Fines for absence, however, were to be drunk — and throughout the minute book of the Society we find no mention of any
others. The orange cockade regulation, introduced later,
brought in some sixpences which the poor may have got.

From the Society's second meeting, November 15th, fourteen Members are missing; these are noted as fined — or rather,
as due to *be* fined; about the collection there was often a hitch.
At the third meeting, November 22nd, one new member,
Henry Cole Bowen, is voted in. Henry missed his next meeting,
the one on the 29th, at which the decision about the orange
cockades to be worn in all Members' hats was reached. From
this same meeting a circular letter, a whip-up, was sent out, requesting Members' attendance, the following Friday, to deal
with " affairs of consequence." Response to this was still not
quite satisfactory: Henry was absent next time; also the Treasurer, the Rev. Thomas Meule, continued to show himself a
confirmed absentee. In fact that week's President, Mr. Longfield, had himself to find the five shillings due to the messenger
(or Champion) who had taken the letter round. That same evening, the defection of Mr. Meule also obliged Mr. Longfield to
pay out eight-and-eight. Therefore: " *Agreed that the absence*

of the Treasurer at Meetings of this Society is highly to the Detriment of the P. Society."

Twenty-three Members, including Henry Cole Bowen, were absent on December 13th: the fines mounted up nicely and, except for the appointment of Arthur Lysaght to act as next week's President, not much business got done. Henry, however, was present when, on December 20th, it was unanimously resolved that Richard Newman, Esq., be recommended to the Lord Lieutenant for an Independent Troop of Dragoons. But Mr. Meule, in spite of every reproof, continued not to turn up — was this lack of keenness, or clerical busyness? (They bore with him until July 12th, when they appointed another Treasurer.) On January 8th, 1746, twenty-two Members being absent, it was decided to make the meetings fortnightly. On January 31st young Henry Cole Bowen — no doubt a little rattled — was President. At the next meeting, on St. Valentine's Day, we find simply, " *All the Members Absent* " — and wonder why.

On May 9th it was agreed the Society should, from now on, meet only once a month; also, that Members really *must* pay their fines. It was voted that a reward of £2. 5s. 6d. be offered to any person who should, within three calendar months, apprehend James Quinlan of Mallow, indicted at the last Quarter Sessions for assaulting the wife of John Dory, the gunsmith. This marked the first assumption, by the Loyal Protestants, of definite civic responsibility; up to now, there had been no more than the understanding that if anything threatened they should call out the troops. A smaller reward was, at the same meeting, offered for the apprehension of George Hasset Butcher, deserted from General Whitchet Roe Bligh's Dragoons. Eight members, including St. Leger Aldworth, were dropped on for not wearing orange cockades. And, thanks were voted to Captain Owen Wynne for " *drawing out his troops and ordering them to fire on the joyful news of his Grace the Duke of Cum-*

berland obtaining a Glorious Victory over the Rebels in Scotland."

Perhaps Culloden took wind from the Loyal Protestant sails, perhaps steamy summer slackness along the Blackwater valley or the rival gaieties of the Mallow season were too much. On June 11th they celebrated the anniversary of the happy accession of George II, and on July 12th the still more happy defeat of the Irish and French at Aughrim: on neither occasion did any business get done. October 11th found no one there but the President, Nehemiah Donnellan: he censured every one else and imposed fines. At the end of October, this being also the end of the Loyal Protestants' first financial year, " the Champion " was sent round from door to door to stand on the Members' steps till he got the arrears of fines. After that, the Loyal Protestants went into abeyance for ten years.

In December 1755 the Society, *" after a long recess "* reassembled in excellent form and agreed to continue meetings. Henry Cole Bowen, Philip Oliver, John Longfield, John Welstead, St. Leger Aldworth, Nehemiah Donnellan and many more of the original '45 Members were still there. Jonas Stawell brought in his son Henry. Nicholas Evans and Ruby McCarthy are also on the initial '55 list. A number of new Members — including three clergymen, the Rev. Robert Nettle, the Rev. William Mockler and the Rev. Norris Jephson (of the Mallow Castle family), another Jephson, Robert, and two cornets, Pennyfeather and Walker — were soon added to the revived club. And one change was agreed to: there must be fewer thick nights:

Agreed that all Meetings of this Society, no member shall pay more for his Ordinary and Wine or other Liquer than three shillings and ninepence halfpenny, nor shall more than one bottle of Wine or a Like Proportion of other liquer be allowed each member. . . . Agreed that Henry Cole Bowen be our next President.

. . . Agreed . . . that all Succeeding Meetings be Monthly and held alternately at the Respective Houses of James Magrath, and William Cooly. [The Widow Callaghan's had, evidently, lapsed.]

The '55 and '56 Loyal Protestants *began* by putting up a pretty steady attendance; unhappily, they did not keep to this. One or two, though elected, never showed up at all, and were warned that, if they did not come, " *or send a Sufficient Apology,*" their names would be struck off the list. In May 1756 the Society once more concerned itself with the peace of the countryside:

Whereas at the Last general Assizes held for the County of Cork John Lott of Carrigoon near Mallow, Taylor was capitally convicted for Robbery and Burglary, and ordered for Execution on Saturday the first day of the Instant., and whereas the said Lott was not hanged till he was dead, according to his Sentence, but is now alive, hath been seen by numbers of Persons, and is lurking about in Neighbourhood of Carrigoon aforesaid, this Society doth agree to give a Reward of Five Pounds Sterling to any person or Persons who shall within three Calendar Months from the Date hereof, apprehend and Lodge the said Lott in any of his Majesty's gaols in this Kingdom.

And the Treasurer is desired to have an Advertisement to this purpose inserted in Bagnell's Corke Newspaper.

On June 8th the President, Thomas Smyth, fined himself for not wearing his cockade. Also:

Agreed that for the time to come No Raffling, Wagering or any kind of Hazardous Gaming to be on any account whatsoever admitted at any meeting of this Society; and that any Person who shall hereafter propose any such Raffling, Wagering or Hazardous Gaming shall forfeit one Dozen of Wine.

In July, August, September attendance dropped off again — once more the steamy summer, or the lure of the town. In

October the Treasurer, Mr. Hingston, was "*admonished for his neglect of duty*" — the fines list had got into a thorough mess. The Society's year closed, on December 14th, 1756, with all Members absent except four: Christmas was coming and there was much in hand. And attendance was not lively early in '57. At the February meeting:

Agreed that the Members of the Club do meet at the House of Jas. Magrath on thursday the seventeenth day of March, being St. Patrick's Day, to have a merry Day and to spend the fines, or Such Part of them as shall be thought necessary by the majority, then and there. . . . Whereas a great Number of Fines remain uncollected, agreed that the Champion be employed to collect the same.

On March 17th we find *no* absentees.

In April by reaction, in May I suppose from habit, the absent once more preponderate — among them Henry Cole Bowen. On July 12th, 1757, the Aughrim defeat anniversary clearly carried less weight, for we find only Henry Cole Bowen, Ruby McCarthy and Thomas Smyth at the club. The August lull again ruled out almost every one, including Henry; in September the meeting was put back by a week so as not to conflict with the Assizes. And throughout the rest of the year 1757 Henry, in common with most of his fellow Protestants, was not present at all. On February 14th, 1758:

Agreed that all the said fines hitherto incurred for Absence be applied to the Purchasing of One Silver Medal for each of the Members of this Society, by them respectively to be worn publickly, appendent to an Orange Ribbon, and the Treasurer is hereby desired to get in the said Fines at all Convenient Speed. . . . And the several Members are desired to bring in such Devices and Mottoes, for the said Medals, as they shall think proper, out of which a Choice to be made at the next Meeting.

That next meeting, however, fell on St. Patrick's Day, so the choice of the medal mottoes was adjourned. In fact, the whole good idea was completely dropped.

In the early months of 1759 a definite effort was made at a round-up, and a number of members (not, I am glad to say, Henry) were struck off the list for persistent non-payment of fines, non-attendance and neglect to excuse themselves. Henry hardly showed up at all, that year — perhaps for a reason I shall afterwards show — but his fines were on several occasions paid by his friends, and his explanations must have been quite in order. On August, 1st, 1760, he *was* present; we read:

Mr. Bowen paid one Guinea in full of all Absentee Money to this Day, out of which the Treasurer is to pay Mr. Magrath the Bill drawn on Mr. Bowen the 17th of March last for seventeen shillings and fourpence. [Members failing to notify absence were, quite fairly, bound to reimburse Magrath, the innkeeper, for an uneaten dinner.]

The Moyallow Loyal Protestants met for the last time on December 9th, 1760, at the house of a Mr. Large. There were twenty-four absentees; Norris Jephson was President. Henry Cole Bowen was not there (he had not been there since August) so I should like to know how he closed on the Minute Book. The Society did not die; it faded away: in December the Members, in fact, parted with the declared intention of meeting again:

Agreed that this Club be adjourned to the Seventh Day of April next at the House of Mr. Magrath. In case the King's Coronation be then performed, or if not, then to such Day whereon the said Coronation be held. Robert Grove, Esq., to be President. And that Notice thereof be published in Bagnell's Cork Paper.

The Treasurer paid Mr. Magrath thirteen shillings due to him for the last days when none of the Members attended.

Balance due to the Treasurer Six Shillings and Six Pence.

That is the final word. George III, as we know, was crowned, but the Loyal Protestants never met again. They did not meet again, I feel quite sure, for one of those thousand-and-one conclusive unconcrete reasons for which, in Ireland, things do *not* happen again. They felt that this was a pity, but there it was. Their nights had been merry; they had raised the tone of Mallow and provided one more bulwark for the Protestant faith. The most confirmed absentees no doubt most deeply regretted the lapse of the club they had always meant to attend. And Henry III, as I say, walked away with the Minute Book.

HENRY III AND
BOWEN'S COURT

DR. SMITH, HISTORIAN OF CORK, SAYS OF MALLOW, IN 1750:

It is pleasantly situated on the north bank of the Blackwater, over which there is an excellent stone bridge, whereby it is made a great thoroughfare. Not far from the castle is a fine spring of moderately tepid water, which bursts from the bottom of a great limestone rock, and approaches the nearest, in all its qualities, to the Hot Well waters of Bristol, of any that has been discovered in this kingdom. Here is generally a resort of good company during the summer months, both for pleasure and the benefit of drinking the waters. . . . Near the Spa there are pleasant walks, agreeably planted; and on each side are canals and cascades for the amusement and exercise of the company, who have music on these walks. There is also a long room where assemblies are held for dancing, card playing, etc. Adjoining to the well is a kind of grotto, on which the following lines were written, and printed in the public papers when it was first erected:

> Joint work of judgement, fancy, taste and art,
> Nature's wild wondrous rival's counterpart:
> By avarice oppos'd, by envy blam'd,
> By bounty built, to future ages fam'd.
> Live long; by time or malice undestroy'd;
> By avarice, or by envy unenjoy'd.

The town being well situated, the country about it pleasant, and the company agreeable, it hath obtained the name of the Irish Bath. Here is a well-built church, in which is a gravestone to the memory of Cornet Charles Sybourg, only son to General Sybourg, who died here in the twentieth year of his age; here also is a market house and a barrack for a troop of horse.

The principal seats near Mallow are Anabell, to the north-west of the town, belonging to Courthorp Clayton, esq., and Quarter-town, to John Dillon, esq., with good plantations on the south side of the Blackwater, near which a chalybeate spa has been lately discovered.

English Arthur Young, twenty-six years later, takes a more disenchanted view. He notes:

September 13th. Left Doneraile and went to Colonel Jephson's at Mallow. . . . I walked to the spring in the town to drink the water, to which so many people have long resorted; it resembles that of Bristol, prescribed for the same cases, and with great success. In the season there are two assemblies a week. Lodgings are 5s. a week each room, and those seemed to be miserably bad. Board 13s. a week. These prices, in so cheap a country, amazed me, and, I fear, should prevent Mallow being so considerable, as more reasonable rates might make it, unless accommodations proportionable were provided. There is a small canal, with walks on each side, leading to the spring, under cover of some very noble poplars. If a double row of good lodgings were erected here, with public rooms, in an elegant style, Mallow would probably become a place of amusement, as well as health.

Young, who praised only the Mallow poplars, did really ask too much. On his Irish tour he had been chiefly staying in the houses of the enlightened great who had one foot in London. His technical interests lay outside Mallow; in the town he found " but little manufacturing; even spinning is not general " — in fact, parasitism on visitors. Provincial gaieties were right off his beat, and the *élan* of Mallow left him cold. Given proper amenities (he said) Mallow " *would probably become a place of*

amusement." And this with Mallow in full swing! Did not
"fancy, taste and art" already combine? What about the
grotto and the cascades? No, he saw the scum on the canals
under the poplars, perhaps the drowned bird slowly losing its
wings; he smelled the reek in the lodgings; he saw the rubbish
blowing into the grotto, the greasy thumbmarks on the Spa
drinking cups. The long room for cards and dancing seemed to
him poky — but it held enough illusion to float Bath.

There were no colonnades, no aerial terraces; the main street
down to the bridge was humped and crabbed, with coach
wheels bouncing from rock to rock. The irregular roof-line
jagged on the placid sky. There was one double line of passable
town houses, two or three single façades: in the main, the lodgings were over shops. But, throw up a back window south of
the street and freshness from the Blackwater water meadows,
a distant peaty chill from the hills stole in on the indoor air —
indoor air rancid with candles, with drinky breath, sweated-
into brocades. In the summer season long yellow dusks from
the country burnished housefronts and windows and fought
with the candle light. Below, the river swept east in its noble
curve. And all night, while the parties were going on, Mallow
was locked in unknowing silence of fields.

Every summer morning there was the promenade to the Spa,
along dust-whitened causeways over the Dublin road, or between puddled road and rain-swollen canal. In town, cavalry
tittupped between the coaches that blocked the street; elbows
polished the flymarks off windowsills. The air was salty with
horses: the Loyal Protestants, country dust in their tricornes,
came clattering in from their outlying estates, and their ladies
were there before them, buying up ribbons, chatting in shops
and quizzing the visitors. Magrath's, Cooly's and Callaghan's
inns brimmed over into the gutters: the gutters, no doubt, stank.
The place was slapdash, seedy, jumbled and full of swank, but
at the height of one of those summer seasons pleasure did dignify Mallow town.

Henry III, with his youth, fortune and prospects, present-able person and Cole connections all over the other kingdom might have looked beyond Mallow, but he did not. Not only did he not make the grand tour, but we do not hear of him crossing the water at all. I detect in his nature a mixture of pride and timidity. He had not the temperament of an absentee: he was Henry Cole Bowen of Kilbolane, Ballymackey and Farahy, and he chose to live, yes, and *se faire valoir*, in a world that knew what these properties meant. No man ever was more con-scious of his position; at the same time, from some inborn right-ness of nature, I think he was conscious of limitations too. He was too proud to spend his rents being just less showy than the gentlemen of Dublin, London or Bath. He would not stand as a stranger at any one's — no, not at King George's — door. He posed himself here in Mallow, in the rich positiveness of a pro-vincial society. This first Irish Bowen to come to full bloom held always, for all his *dégagés* manners, a metaphorical fistful of Kilbolane, Ballymackey or Farahy earth, and was prepared to flatten his hand and say, " This is mine." I have, for clearness, numbered my ancestors as though they were kings — and, in a sense, every man's life *is* a reign, a reign over his own powers. Henry III, for all his misjudgements, reigned well. And is there anything ignoble, or is there something gifted, in being able to find the adumbrations, the passions, the architecture of that great abstract, Society, in a miniature spa?

Entering an assembly, Henry was quite a figure. He was tall; his coat had the best cut Cork could give; he would know how to look round with that genial challenging calmness that only the nervously conscious man commands. Perhaps his hair was unevenly dashed with powder, perhaps his ruffles had speckled tips. But he would look what he felt — and what in his world he was — a grandee.

These appearances that he made in Mallow could only be from time to time: the management of his three estates kept him busy. And in Mallow I cannot tell myself that he was never

bored. That much-advertised raffishness, in fact, the Rakes —
squireen playboys, or cadets of the greater families — made a
noisy element that would soon pall. If the Rakes did not ride
down Mallow street letting off pairs of pistols, like cowboys in
a Wild Western into town on a spree, that was about all they
did not do.

> *Bowing, belling, dancing, drinking,*
> *Breaking windows, cursing, sinking,*
> *Always talking, never thinking —*
> *Live the Rakes of Mallow!* Etc., etc.

They sound unthinkably dreary. And one can gather, from
Henry's non-attendances, how quickly the Loyal Protestants
must have palled. In the first place they had made Henry a few
useful connections, and got him, while still on his probation
with Mallow, the *entrée* into what might be going on. Over the
door of any still unknown group or clique or society there
seems, to the eye of ambitious youth, to be written: " *You want
the Best: We have it.*" But, once in, one finds there is not really
so much there. The awful boringness of the Loyal Protestants
— gentlemen buttonholing each other with long wheezy stories,
tipsy mutual good esteem, clergy with their jowls sagging into
their neckcloths, pink-in-the-face cornets blowing off *ad lib.*
— must have entered deep into Henry's soul. Once he got the
Loyal Protestants taped, he was through with them. Besides, I
take him to be one of those men who soon have enough of
purely male society. A sort of fastidiousness got from his
mother, the romanticism of the orphan brought up on the
mother-myth, the only-childish love of the cosy feminine smile
would all go to make Henry prefer mixed company — or,
probably, that of women alone.

I know nothing of his sentimental affairs. I believe that vanity
made, and caution kept him, a flirt. He was an excellent match,
and not only neighbouring daughters but the cream of the

young lady visitors to Mallow must have been deployed for him. He did not marry till he was thirty-seven, and, as when he did marry the zest of his married life produced twenty-one children, I cannot think that up to thirty-seven Henry remained a lily: he was a man of his age. I must say that in his portrait he does not look like a lily. He may have had loves about Mallow town; he may have liked married women — if so, their husbands were unaware or complaisant, for he was involved in no scandal, that I have ever heard. He may have met no women as nice as the Wilsons, but must have met many gayer. It would be pretty to say — and it may be true — that Henry's heart remained tied to his cousin Margaret. Quite likely, whenever he thought of some other bride, he found he could not envisage actually keeping house with any woman other than Margaret. I suspect he had some idea that Margaret would wait for him, and meanwhile, was willing to have his fling.

The floating existence to and fro from Kilcumer became less satisfactory as Henry formed more ties. He desired to entertain, and to this end he looked for a base in Mallow. Some time between 1749 and '52, he leased Annabella from Courthorp Clayton, Esq., and took up residence there. Annabella — commended by Dr. Smith as " Anabell " — was in that lovely position, at the top of a hill at the north-west end of the town, now occupied by Mallow railway station and by the adjoining Royal Hotel. The house has, since Henry III's day, unhappily been burnt down; nothing remains of it but its name, on a terrace of gritty villas, *circa* 1880, and its gardens, which are now the hotel's. It faced south across the Blackwater valley, and had behind it the blue-green plain. Annabella, in its groved gardens, was in fact a villa in the Italian sense: it existed for gaiety, ease, retreat. Through its ilexes one looks down on town, plain, river and hills: about not only the prospect itself but one's sense of commanding it there is something generous and urbane. When Henry took possession of Annabella he was between twenty-seven and twenty-eight; his wish was to live *en prince*, and no doubt he did.

But business worries were many. Henry's early happy relation with Dr. Llewellin Nash ended, I am sorry to say, in a bad quarrel. When Henry's minority ended, Dr. Llewellin turned over to him the Bowen affairs, with a detailed account and expense sheet which, in the first place, Henry did not challenge. But that was not the end of Dr. Llewellin's claims: some time after everything seemed to be wound up more bills came in, for expenses hitherto overlooked. These expenses were more than legal; there was an awkwardness about a Farahy visit — it appears that Henry, after he came of age, had spent a year and a half at the Nashes', and that the maintenance of the number of servants and horses Henry Cole Bowen found suitable to his station in life put that household to considerable expense. Dr. Nash (as Henry thought, rather gracelessly) weighed in with a bill for the servants' and horses' keep. Henry, who like many extravagant people did not like paying out money for which he got no fun, contested all the belated Nash claims with spirit. And he charged Dr. Llewellin with keeping back, or at least failing to pass over, " Deedes and other papers " relating to the estate. The quarrel was kept out of court; by the consent of both parties it was submitted to the arbitration of Mr. Robert Grove (Henry's co-Loyal Protestant) and Mr. William Freeman, also of County Cork. Their pronouncement was, that Henry should pay over (or rather, remit from the rents for Farahy due to him from Dr. Nash) " Four Hundred and Fifty pounds Sterling and no more " — these being for *bona fide* legal expenses, as shown. They did, however, find Dr. Nash's concern for the keep of the horses and servants to be excessive, since Henry Cole Bowen had, as all his acquaintances knew, been coming and going (and rather going than coming) throughout that year and a half.

The Nash quarrel was settled in 1749. The signature, as a witness, of the Rev. Jeremiah King appears on one of the documents, and I must say I suspect that turbulent Kilbolane clergyman of having done much to aggravate any trouble between Henry and the well-disposed Dr. Nash. To call Mr. King Henry's evil genius might be too much; my having even named him as Henry's tutor is pure supposition. But Mr. King (who stood well with Mrs. Catherine Bowen, who did not like Dr. Nash) does seem to have played a part in Henry's lonely boyhood, to have flattered him and given him fantasies. Mr. King, I fancy, had watched with no great approval Henry's move from the Kilbolane orbit into the Mallow set: the clergyman, meanwhile, lay low at Kilbolane, and it is with a sinking heart that I notice him reappear. I am convinced that Henry engaged in the Kilbolane lawsuit at Mr. King's instigation, and under his influence.

The Kilbolane lawsuit, known as the *Bowen v. Evans Dispute about Brandon Castle*, began in 1759, the year before Henry married, and, dragging on well into 1764, overshadowed years of his married life. The documents — bills, letters, volumes of depositions — would fill a good-sized coffin, and very well might. Henry may have gone into the business fairly light-heartedly, but soon the Bowen obsession had him in hand: he *knew* Brandon contained, or stood over, or was very near to, the still unfound Nicholls treasure. So this handsome sociable man, from the calm of his Annabella, fought like a savage for the shell of a Desmond tower, and for not much more than an acre of ruin-enshadowed land — and it was a cold, long, inky and bitter fight. In full natures there is often this streak of fanaticism: war, religion, a phase of sexual love suddenly takes a man away from society and at once dehumanizes and superhumanizes him. With Henry Cole Bowen, litigation did this.

To recapitulate what we already knew — Kilbolane old castle had had four towers (or "castles"), one at each corner of the bawn. The North Castle, in ruins, went early out of the story: nobody wanted it. The East Castle belonged to, and had been occupied by, the Bowens, as Captain Nicholls' descendants. The South Castle had been bought by the Evans from the Weekes, and leased on and off by the Evans to the Allens. And the West Castle, otherwise Brandon, was to be the cause of all these tears.

Henry, by leaving Kilbolane for Mallow, had left the ground free for further Evans encroachments. The question of rights in the bawn itself had remained a fairly delicate one. Mr. Allen, with his usual tact, had waived the matter and treated old Mrs. Bowen as virtual mistress of the bawn. And to her claims on Brandon he had always deferred — when he kept his " plow tackling " there it was by her good will. But now the Allens were gone and the Evans were back again: Thomas Evans (who had had that brush with Mrs. Bowen about the spoons in the well, and who went so far as to have her private passage through to the bawn blocked up) was now succeeded by his son Eyre. This Eyre Evans treated Brandon Castle as his: he had put his own tenants to live there. The Rev. Jeremiah King, from his house just down the road, watched these proceedings with a fulminous eye.

Brandon Castle, it may be said, had already been the cause of Mr. King's receiving a psychic bruise. In the days when Mr. King lodged at Mr. Allen's, he had obtained permission from Mr. Allen (who no doubt first referred the matter to Mrs. Bowen) to stable his horses in the ground-floor of Brandon. Mr. King, accordingly, had a manger erected, and a handsome paved floor put down at his own expense. But then Mr. King had a quarrel with Mr. Allen, and crashed violently, and forever, out of his house one night. Next morning, he sent round men to Brandon and had the manger torn down and the pavement torn up: Mr. Allen should profit by nothing that had been Mr. King's. From then on, the very mention of Brandon must have sent the blood to Mr. King's head.

The first shot in the Bowen-Evans war was fired on July 10th, 1759. It appears that Mr. Eyre Evans, considering Brandon his, became concerned for the safety of good oak floors and rafters that the castle contained. To keep out possible thieves, he decided to have a strong new door, and door-casing, fitted to Brandon. So, on July 10th, his steward Gerald Guybon arrived, with masons and carpenters, to put the work in hand. To these men appeared the Rev. Jeremiah King, who commanded them, in the name of Mr. Bowen, to cease work and clear off the Bowen property. Both sides afterwards claimed that the other used violence — Mr. King, I do not doubt, was an ugly sight. Mr. King at once got in touch with Henry and told him Brandon, and all it meant, was at stake.

On the 17th of the October following, Mr. Eyre Evans received a summons, bidding him give up the Bowen property. Gerald Guybon and each of his workmen were also served with summons, on the same date. Henry's claim was that he and his family had been in " actual, quiet and peaceable possession " of Brandon and of the bawn adjoining for more than sixty years before the present date, having inherited same from their ancestor Captain Nicholls. The Evans counter-claim, to emerge, was, that no Bowen had, and no Nicholls ever had had, any title to Brandon or to that part of the bawn, Brandon having been the property of the Weekes and sold by the Weekes to the Evans along with the South Tower.

The very day the summons were served, Mr. King behaved with further precipitation. (Had Mr. Eyre Evans ever, for one instant, considered that he might cede to the Bowen claim, Mr. King, I fear, was enough to decide him otherwise.) Brandon Castle was, this October, still lived in by Evans tenants, a quiet peaceable couple, James Grady and wife. This evening, it being just past milking time, Mrs. Grady went out to fetch the milk; her husband went out to pick up firewood with which to cook their supper. They thus left Brandon empty, but for the geese and fowls that they were fattening in an upper room. Recrossing the bawn in the autumn dusk, the Gradys found Mr. King, with stick raised, before their door. He " drove them away."

Mr. King then had a padlock, on stout staples, affixed to Brandon door. He further (according to the Evans) encamped in the bawn a number of his own men, who " offered violence " when the Gradys, or other Evans people, tried to approach Brandon or even enter the bawn. The Gradys, with their fowl shut up in Brandon, went through distress of mind: they had also left in the castle valuable papers belonging to their son Thomas, a cooper in Limerick. When, many days later, they were let back to Brandon, they found their fowl " starved and rotted " — though the papers were safe.

After this, Mr. Evans could only fight — and he did. If the Nicholls treasure ever *had* been dug up it could not, at its best, have amounted to anything like the money Henry spent on *Bowen v. Evans*. I think the loss of the suit — for we did lose it at last — determined and hardened his nature in many ways. In fact, the building of grandiose Bowen's Court may have been a final one-in-the-eye for the Evans — for the Evans added to their offences by growing really unbearably grand: the original George Evans, having been M.P. for Charleville, had been made Lord Carbery. I rather wonder the Wilsons did not try to do more to calm Henry down, for the second Wilson son, Edward, was at the time either married or on the verge of marriage to the Hon. Frances Evans, daughter of the second Lord Carbery and first cousin to Henry's detested Eyre. But by this time probably nothing would bind or hold him; the case rolled on, tried and re-tried, mounting costs up and gaining fierceness from year to year.

The whole question at issue was highly ambiguous: the Evans can only have won by a hair's breadth. Henry produced a deed of sale (of which I hold a copy) of Brandon to Captain Nicholls by one Upton Odell: Henry said this deed had been passed to him by Llewellin Nash with the rest of the Bowen papers on his majority. But the paper must have looked fishy (I am sure Henry did not think so) for the Court refused to accept it. Armies of country people, old employees and servants, children of employees and servants to both families, were brought in as deponents. The Bowen half of them swore that they had heard from their cradles that Brandon had always belonged to the Bowen family; the Evans half swore they had heard, from as early days, that Brandon had always belonged to the Evans. The bawn well, the plow tackling, the gooseberry wine, the poultry, the black-and-white rabbits and Mr. King's manger and paving were all dragged up. In these days, Henry may have thought of his grandmother: the fight — its fury if not its imprudence — would have been after her own heart. Nice Mr. Allen's nephew Mr. John Allen deposed in the Evans favour, I am sorry to say. Henry's uncle John, from Carrigadrohid, said, yes, he had always kept his hounds in Brandon: why not? And Henry's younger uncle Stephens Bowen (whom Henry had already helped out of a money crisis) was more than emphatic about the Bowen claim.

In 1764, the case was to come up, in Cork, for the last time. The Court bade Mr. Evans, and his people about the bawn, give the jurors, on the 14th of August, facilities to view the disputed ground. To this, Henry added impassioned personal letters, urging the gentlemen to come and see for themselves. But, alas, the jurors were either cagey or slack. Mr. Supple, of Supple Court, was indisposed and could not get to Kilbolane with " any degree of safety "; Mr. Norman Uniacke, of Mount Uniacke, was " positively engaged to go to Corke " on the date appointed; Mr. James Smyth's wife was " extreamly unwell "; Mr. John Parker, of Cork, had to go to Dublin " on a sudden affair of importance of Lord Kilburne's," and Mr. Warm St. Leger, of Howard Hill, simply could not make it, and promised to tell Henry why when they met. Letters of excuses rained into Annabella and were by Henry, rather bitterly, kept. Perhaps he came to think the jurors' negligence accounted for the defeating verdict he got. He lost his case — but that was not the end of that: Kilbolane was still to bring Bowens into the House of Lords.

The Kilbolane case, its cold furious bitterness, did Henry's nerves no good. And in '59, or early in '60, he went down with a fever: he was desperately ill. Family saying (which seems to me good enough) connects in the following story his illness and marriage.

Henry, still a bachelor in the latter half of his thirties, had no direct heir to his large estates. Should he die, as he was, his lands, together with his position as head of the Bowens, stood to pass to his Uncle John, of Carrigadrohid, then on to his Uncle John's son, John II of Carrigadrohid. Now, Henry had no use for his cousin John, in fact he disliked him abominably; and the dislike, we understand, was returned. John's claim to the main Bowen succession was one fact that Henry had not faced up to yet. Now, in late '59, early on in the Evans lawsuit, Henry, overtaken by fever at Kilbolane, lay in the dismantled mansion, grievously ill. One night, his worst night, a *coup de trois heures* of worry about the lawsuit had superimposed on it a desperate dread of death: Henry's eyes never closed on the dark of his sick chamber. All at once, he saw on the walls and ceiling a pink then scarlet bold reflection appear. Were the Irish " up " again, or were these the infernal fires? Henry started up and cried out, to know what the thing might be. Then " they " came in and told him, it was his cousin John Bowen, who having heard of Henry's mortal illness, had come from Carriga- drohid and given orders that bonfires, ready for lighting, be laid all over the Kilbolane estate. And here, at this small low hour when death was to come for Henry, was John lighting the first. . . . Whereupon, Henry Cole Bowen leaped from his dying bed, calling on God to witness John should never in- herit. He was on to his horse (more or less) and off to his cousin Margaret before his deserted fever-bed was cold. He asked Margaret to marry him, and she did, and not only gave him his heir, Henry IV, but, to be on the safe side, twenty children more.

(Coldness between the Bowen's Court and the Carrigadrohid

Bowens lasted, I am sorry to say, for some generations more, and was only ended when Robert Bowen-Colthurst, of Oakgrove, dropped in to pay my grandfather, Robert Cole Bowen, a breezy morning call.)

Discounting the bonfire story, Henry's serious illness no doubt gave him rather a shake, and made him think. And the strain of the lawsuit — his first tussle with untoward fact — would send his desires back to childish, sheltering things. Smiling but womanless Annabella could not do much for him during these worried days. He could go out for his distractions, but that meant late night returns, strung-up, to a cold hearth. County Cork gaieties, in this new mood of his, could do no more than increase his nervosity; his nerves craved the ease of marriage, the sweet, unexacting and constant presence of some woman who, now he came to face it, could only be Margaret. He needed some one to lean on, some one to smile with, some one to open worrying letters with, some one who should rejoice when he won his lawsuit, or who, should he (inconceivably) fail to win it, would put her arms round his neck and say, " After all, does it so very much matter, dear? " So, he rode off — was it to Bilbo or Kilcumer? — and asked for, and took, Margaret Wilson's hand.

Henry and Margaret were married in 1760, and lived their first years together at Annabella.

I do not know the date of Margaret's birth. Her mother Thomasine had married, you will remember, when Henry was six years old. Margaret, as the youngest of the five Wilsons, would have been Henry's junior by at least twelve years, and very probably more. Let us put her age at their marriage, when Henry was thirty-seven, at twenty-three, four or five. No portrait of her exists, and one can only judge of her character by her letters, and from the part that she played. She had been, we know, the child of a happy home. She had had, as the second Miss Wilson of Bilbo, her own secure little place in society. She and Henry shared the same Bowen grandparents, but noth-

ing of old Mrs. Bowen's combative, fidgety nature seems to
have come down to tranquil Margaret. Her appearance was, I
should gather, pleasing and graceful: had she been a beauty I
should have heard of it; on the other hand Henry, for all his
pro-Wilson feeling, would not, I think, have married a plain
wife. He would seek, and set store by, good manners and ease
in society — these one may be certain that Margaret had: had
not the Wilsons formed his first view of the world? And restful-
ness would rank very high with him: he may have admired several dashing women, but he would not in the least want to
marry one. He wanted much the same sort of woman his
mother Jane must have been. Warm-hearted but civilized do-
mesticity — the home not as an alternative to society but as
society's strengthening complement — was Henry's object in
marriage. Bowen future demanded Margaret should be a
mother; Henry's future demanded she should be a hostess, too.
She must not only fill but know how to occupy the large house
he intended to build for her.

And Margaret? Had she loved, as a little girl, her tall fine
cousin, then grown up into being in love with him? Had she
learned how she felt by sharp little twinges suffered on hearing
Henry's name coupled with that of some Mallow belle? Had
the Wilsons seen how things were? I do not doubt that they
did. Mrs. Wilson and her married daughter Catherine Grove
must often have said to each other, how much they wished that
if Henry were *not* going to marry Margaret he would at least
set her heart and thoughts free, however painfully, by marrying some one else. Mrs. Wilson and Mrs. Grove must have
often wanted to sound Henry, or even give him a hint. But the
situation was a delicate one: though he was their near relation,
who had lived under their roof, Henry was at the same time
a remarkably good match — they were nice women; they could
not angle for him. Wilson niceness, Margaret's reserve, Henry's
genial evasiveness must all have gone to keep the thing in the
air. Meanwhile here was Henry, again and again dismounting

under the windows of Kilcumer or Bilbo, grandly, from his latest horse, and Margaret going to meet him with her composed smile. He would stroll in as pleased with himself as ever — though not getting any younger, as the Wilsons would note. With the Wilsons Henry would feel that complete ease that elsewhere he could only affect. They would be that ideal audience, without *arrière pensée*, that the successful ingenuous solitary man craves: he could blow off to them without seeming to boast. He would tell them about this last party at Annabella, and also about the famous times he had had with Miss This (so remarkably fetching) and Captain That, Sir Somebody Something and Lady Somebody Else. He would add, with the best faith in the world, how much he wished *all* the Wilsons had been there. And meantime he would be stealing kind-unkind glances at Margaret out of the corners of his blue eyes. I don't doubt that Henry often behaved to Margaret with the tactlessness of the not quite unconscious man.

Ironically, when Henry did turn to Margaret, at the time when he suddenly needed her, he had least to give. Poor Margaret, she had waited a long time, and now she married a man more than half in love with a fight.

In 1760, Henry III married and George III of England came to the throne. There was change everywhere, a sort of spring in politics, a start of new life. Human feeling heightened. The years of the early Georges, the mid-century, had been sluggish and gross: the Ascendency, in Ireland and England, were in spirit locked in the dullness of a success regime. There had been no outlook; Whig rule had shown its less noble side. The littleness of Mallow fitly and truly mirrored the littleness of everywhere else. But George III rose to shine: he was the first fully English Hanoverian monarch in the sense that Henry had been the first fully Irish Bowen. This new King *had* outlook — he had also will, gusto, morality and an effulgence that somehow melted and shifted the inhibiting dullness of the Hanoverian rule. Ireland soon felt the change in the atmosphere. Though he stood for the negation of the Stuart tradition the King showed himself in some contexts a lively Tory, and what was left of the leading Catholics in Ireland prepared to look more warmly towards the English throne.

It was to be seen, and the King and his party saw, that the kingdom of Ireland had to be reckoned with. Exploitation had not wholly succeeded; the aim must now be development. The Irish parliament functioned in name only; Ireland was knit to England, and checked by England, inside a system that, be·cause it impeded growth, had become not only corrupt but damaging, whose abuses were every day manifest. Irish Royalism had had to feed on a stone: the Stuarts had failed the country, William III had been its iron invader, the two German Georges, halting and apathetic, had not so much as looked across the sea. George III designed to remove power in Ireland from not irreproachable English hands. He wished to have with Ireland, and with her parliament, a direct royal relationship that should not be obstructed by English policy. The King's sole intermediary should be his vice-regent — one of George's first commands was, that his Lord Lieutenant should be continuously resident in Ireland. This command carried with it a double implicit promise: that royal presence by proxy was to give prestige, lustre and focus to Dublin society, and that, in high or in any other office, there were to be no more sinecures.

Though the Anglo-Irish I have depicted so far, the landowning gentry around Mallow, had been up to now like children playing in new gardens, now and then slinging pebbles over the fence, by now they were ready to look up. Their good-timing showed latent energy, their little organizations, such as the Moyallow Loyal Protestants, showed at least a *wish* to organize, to better things and to rule. They were prepared, in fact, to be serious. In the decades following 1760 the Anglo-Irish became aware of themselves as a race. The " Protestant nation " had been born already; it was to be christened at its coming of age. This nation must face its responsibilities. It was growing up into judgement, into the power to place its loyalties where and as it willed. This was the Anglo-Ireland that was to present, for England, an alarming parallel with America.

Persecution of Catholics had, as I have said, already been discontinued for some time. Persecution has its roots in fear, and the Protestants were in an already too strong position. Also, a lapse of fervour (at least in the ruling classes) in both religions had made for peace. But Catholics continued to suffer, in all their doings, under the deadening negatives of the penal laws. Something more active than tolerance, more humane and intelligent than mere good humour bred of prosperity now made Protestants face the evil in this — and not only the evil, the inexpediency (for I cannot say that self-interest did not enter in). The disjection of Catholics from economic life had done no good to the country the Anglo-Irish shared. For instance: by the successful practice of two kinds of business left open to them, the grazier system and the provision trade, a new Catholic monied middle class had built itself up. But this Catholic money, which could have been useful (the extravagant needed it for their creditors, the serious for the development of their estates), stayed locked away from land-owning Protestants while laws forbade Catholics to lend money at interest, to take long leases or to purchase land. At the same time, Protestants engaged in commerce were feeling the brunt of English restrictive laws. Again, landlords might bear down on their tenants and still not like to see those tenants borne down on further, till they barely existed, by the Government hearth tax and the exaction of tithes. The outstanding wretchedness of the Irish poor could be ignored no longer: it was a scandal abroad. Agrarian agitations, especially in Munster, began to threaten the Anglo-Irish peace and to oppose the landlords to injustices out of which they got no profit themselves. The Whiteboys were felt to be England's fault.

This new wish in the new Irish to see Ireland autonomous was in more than the head and the conscious will. Ireland had worked on them, through their senses, their nerves, their loves. They had come to share with the people round them sentiments, memories, interests, affinities. The grafting-on had been, at least where *they* were concerned, complete. If Ireland did not accept them, they did not know it — and it is in that unawareness of final rejection, unawareness of being looked out at from some secretive, opposed life, that the Anglo-Irish naive dignity and, even, tragedy seems to me to stand. Themselves, they felt Irish, and acted as Irishmen.

In 1762 George III's first viceroy, Lord Halifax, received from the hands of Lord Trimbleston a petition signed by the leading Catholics: this asked that Catholics should be permitted to hold office in the Irish army and state. As an interim measure, it was agreed that Catholic regiments should again be raised, though only for service with the King's allies abroad. Townshend, succeeding Halifax in '67, made a drive against corruption and jobbery in the government; '68 saw in the Octennial Bill, by which a general election every eight years was secured. And, in the same year, the Augmentation of the Army Bill provided for, and encouraged, military expansion. In '72, Lord Harcourt took over from Townshend a greatly strengthened vice-regal position, and a government at least on the road to reform.

Life was brought into the hitherto sluggish Irish Parliament by a powerful Opposition, first headed by Flood. This new Patriot Party, which Grattan entered in '75, was Irish Whig, and was in touch with the reforming Whigs in England. It aimed at winning for Ireland a Parliament to be under the King only, and an inheritance, at the same time, of English constitutional liberties — in fact, a " free constitution " such as had been secured for England in 1689. Ireland's army was to be under her own control; there was to be a permanent Habeas

Corpus Act; the position of judges was to be established and
Parliament purified of corruption and bribery. The Opposition, also, proposed to end that commercial subjection to England that had, so far, paralysed Irish export trade. And, Englishmen were no longer to enjoy the monopoly of high offices
in the Irish Church and State. Flood brought in a bill to tax
absentee landlords — but that was defeated. When, in '75,
Flood accepted office as Vice-Treasurer he left the leadership
of the Patriot Party to Grattan — then a young man of twenty-
five.

1775 was the date cut into the stone under the parapet of the
completed Bowen's Court. This was Grattan's first great year,
and the year the American War began. Across the Atlantic,
just such colonial gentlemen as Henry Cole Bowen now fought
the England in whose tradition they were. Anglo-Ireland has
no Mount Vernon. The small town of Alexandria in Virginia
is now a neat noble shrine, and Mallow in County Cork is now
a decayed spa. But in 1775, when George Washington faced
George III of England, when Henry Cole Bowen watched the
date cut and saw the last slate set in Bowen's Court roof, Anglo-
Ireland knew her power and felt her spirit move. And England,
shaken by one defection, to be repeatedly shaken by colonists'
victories, noted the power, felt the unstated threat. Grattan
drew his victories from the American War. Before the slates
on Henry's new roof had weathered, the invisible banners of
" the Protestant nation " were already streaming on the air. At
the sunny foot of the Ballyhouras the new house — first Bowen
house on the first Bowen's land — stood in more than the sun:
it was raised in an age of hope. There was warmth in the spirit's
air already when, indoors, Margaret Bowen had her first fires
lit to draw the rawness from the Italian plaster, the native
quarry-cold from the strong walls. Perhaps symbols are dangerous: they tempt one to deflect narrative or misrepresent
facts. But all thought starts in feeling, and all thought is dominated by the symbolism of the dream. Bowen's Court is no

more than itself. But it is a 1775 house, boldly letting in light
and exultantly serious.

At the outbreak of the American War England, by one
more unpopular move — an embargo on Irish exports to the
colonies — strengthened the Patriot Party's hold on the public
mind. Sympathy, in all classes, was more or less overtly towards
America: nevertheless, Parliament was not yet Grattan's; the
loyal tradition bound it to vote war supplies to England and
allow troops to be withdrawn from Ireland for English use.
The parliamentary gesture, though made against real feeling,
may have been telling: certainly England, disheartened by
mounting defeats in America, began to show herself more conciliatory. In '78 Lord North, the Prime Minister, obtained several concessions from the British Parliament in favour of Irish
trade. Further, the same Parliament made a bid for Catholic
favour in Ireland — a favour it became urgent to win away
from the threatening Grattan — by coming down to the matter
of Catholic relief. Edmund Burke acted in London for the
Catholic Committee throughout the negotiations that were to
follow. British fear of the Pope's intentions in Ireland were, at
last, allayed by a declaration that, drawn up by the Munster
bishops and accepted by most of the Irish Catholic clergy,
limited papal authority to the non-temporal sphere. This, as a
modus vivendi, was good enough: in '78, Gardiner's Relief Act
allowed Catholics who took the oath of allegiance indefinite
leases of land, though not freeholds, and allowed them to inherit land under the same conditions — or rather, the same freedom from conditions — as Protestants.

I do not know that these English concessions did much to
wean Catholic Ireland from the Patriot Party. They did serve
to break ice for Grattan, and short-circuit some of his work.

It is now that we hear of the Volunteers — that movement
that armed the Anglo-Irish and placed them solid behind the
Patriot Party, ready for anything. So great a part of the Irish
" augmented " army of '68 had been voted away to England to

fight in America that the country was, as Grattan could point out, now in a dangerously undefended state. There had lately been no militia. Now, by a master stroke, Grattan brought into being, and got armed by the Government, the Irish Volunteers. Protestant, raised by local subscription, officered by the lords and gentry, brilliantly uniformed, humming with ardour, bristling with Government muskets and commanding some cannon, the Volunteers were just undeclared enough in their purpose to send some uneasiness down the English spine. *Loyal* they patently were, but to what, to whom? Grattan said they stood for " the armed property of the nation." (As property generally keeps people quiet, this sounded good enough.) But to this Flood added " that the Volunteers were there to exact Ireland's rights from England, and to remain on foot till these were secured." By 1779, the Volunteers were already forty thousand strong: they had doubled this number when the movement reached its height. They were, in many cases, subscribed for by Catholic gentry, though " common " Catholics did not enlist in them. All new Ireland felt the military thrill; the gentry, superb and serious in their uniforms, swung out to drill in the squares of the little towns. Yes, the Volunteers were the fashion — but they were more than a fashion, they were a force. They did more than adorn occasions, they implemented demands — the day the Free Trade petition went to the Lord Lieutenant, Volunteers from all over Ireland lined the Dublin streets. They did more than enrapture ladies, they could command the future. Volunteers saluted and glittered all over the countryside, and De Burgh said, " England has sown her laws like dragons' teeth, and there have sprung up armed men." For, with dukes at the head and stable boys at the bottom, the Volunteers were, to a man, behind the Patriot Party.

County Cork did well in the matter of Volunteers. Here are some of the cavalry: *The True Blue of Cork, The Mitchelstown Light Dragoons, The Blackpool Horse, The Youghal Cavalry, The Bandon Cavalry, The Muskerry Blues, The*

Duhallow Rangers, The Imokilly Horse, The Imokilly Blue Horse, The Kilworth Light Dragoons, The Doneraile Rangers, The Glanmire Union, The Cork Cavalry, The Mallow Cavalry.

And some of the infantry: *The Cork Boyne, The True Blue of Cork, The Mallow Boyne, The Bandon Boyne, The Carbery Independents, The Aughrim of Cork, The Loyal Newberry Musqueteers, The Roscarbery Volunteers, The Passage Union, The Youghal Independents, The Youghal Independent Blues, The Kinsale Volunteers, The Kanturk Volunteers, The Hawke Union of Cove, The Blackwater Rangers, The Blarney Volunteers, The Newmarket Rangers, The Mallow Independents, The Duhallow Volunteers, The Charleville Volunteers.*

There were also *The Cork Artillery* and *The Imokilly Blue Artillery.*

Henry III, by this time residing at Bowen's Court, plumped for The Mitchelstown Light Dragoons. He must have horses, and his personal tastes bent him to Mitchelstown rather than Doneraile — though Doneraile was a mile or two nearer his gates. Of the Mitchelstown Light Dragoons we read: " Enrolled 1774. Uniform: scarlet, faced black, silver epaulets, yellow helmets, white buttons. Furniture: goat-skin, edged black. Officers in 1782 — Colonel, Viscount Kingsborough; Lieut.-Colonel, Henry Cole Bowen; Major, James Badham Thornhill; Captain, Harmar Spratt; Lieutenant, William Raymond; Cornet, William Alsop; Chaplain, Thomas Bush; Surgeon, David Fitzgerald; Secretary, John Ryan."

The Doneraile Rangers, Henry's alternative, were rather overstocked with St. Legers and Evans — though these Doneraile Evans were no more than cousins of the noxious Charleville branch. We read: " Doneraile Rangers L.D. Enrolled 1779. Uniform: scarlet, faced green, edged white, gold epaulets, yellow buttons and helmets, green jackets faced red. Furniture: goatskin. Officers in 1782 — Colonel, Sentleger Lord Doneraile; Major, Hon. Hayes Sentleger; Captain, Nicholas

Green Evans; Lieutenant, John Watkins; Cornet, Nicholas
Green Evans, Jun.; Chaplain, Hon. James Sentleger; Surgeon,
John Creagh, M.D.; Adjutant, Robert Atkins; Secretary, James
Hennessy."

1782, the date at which the rolls of most corps are taken,
was the year of the great Volunteer Convention at Dungannon. By this time, the movement was at its height: delegates of
a hundred and forty-three corps attended, and there presided
Lord Charlemont (the Commander-in-Chief), Flood and
Grattan. Outstanding among the resolutions passed was this:
" That the claim of any other than the King, Lords and Commons of Ireland to make laws to bind this kingdom is uncon-
stitutional, illegal and a grievance." Also, the ports of Ireland
were declared open " to all ships of countries not at war with
his Majesty." And Grattan, in Volunteer uniform, got accepted
with cheering the motion that " As Irishmen, Christians and
Protestants, we rejoice at the relaxation of the penal laws
against our Roman Catholic fellow subjects."

So far, the benevolent noon was at its height. The question
of Catholic enfranchisement, and of Catholics in Parliament
(Grattan was for it) was, however, shelved by the Volunteers.
Flood was not for looking, at present, beyond a reform of the
Protestant franchise. Only the Englishman Frederick Augustus
Hervey, Earl of Bristol and Bishop of Derry, went further than
Grattan: the exuberant bishop was in favour of going the whole
way. Dissenters and Catholics — why should they not unite,
with Protestants, in the fight for constitutional liberty?

This February convention at Dungannon no more than
opened glorious 1782. America was within sight of her independence; Lord North's Tories (from whom had already been
wrung what was virtually Irish Free Trade) could no longer
sustain the onus of the successive English defeats: Lord North's
government fell. This left the field open to English reforming
Whigs — Fox, Burke, Rockingham — with whom, as we know,
the Patriot Party in Ireland already stood well. In April, the

Duke of Portland arrived in Dublin, a viceroy instructed to
make further concessions. The Viceroy invited Charlemont
and Grattan to take office, but they preferred to stay free in
the Opposition. Time questions the wisdom of their decision,
for this left the actual government with anti-progressives such
as Fitzgibbon and Beresford. But no anti-progressive could
hold up what was to happen this vital spring: the Patriot Party's
objective was in sight. On May 27th, the Irish parliamentary
independence was, by the Parliaments of Britain and Ireland,
formally recognized.

The Duke of Portland made known to the House in Dublin
the Westminster decision — urged in the Lords by Lord Shel-
bourne, in the Commons by Fox — to meet the full Irish claim.
In Dublin, the roar rolled out from the House into College
Green, through the streets and spaces, down the river, into the
countryside. Bells and salvos, if they were not sounded, were
heard inside heads humming with joyous blood. "*Ireland is
now a nation.*" May sun dazzled the noble parts of the city and
filtered into the ignorant slums. The free Parliament, in an access of feeling, voted £100,000 to the British Navy, and gave
England leave to withdraw five thousand more Irish troops.

All great Irish speeches are not made from the dock. It was
on his day of triumph that Grattan rose, to trace the progress
of Ireland from Swift's time, on through its injuries, through its
arms, to the high noon of to-day. "*Ireland is now a nation. In
that character I hail her, and bowing in her august presence I
say, Esto perpetua.*"

Henry III's decision to build Bowen's Court must, like all
great decisions, have come on him gradually. It had two
sources: the wish of the head to set up a monument, the wish
of the heart to live on his own land. His maturity came to him,
with marriage, just when he most felt Anglo-Irish maturity.
His sense of his own consequence as young Henry Bowen
widened to something nobler and more austere. His Mallow

play-days were over; his children were being born; life flowed through him from the past on into the future and he resolved to make a worthy channel for it. He thought more of vocation and less of privilege.

To Henry's decision to live at Farahy Margaret, I feel sure, gave her full assent. I have been told, however, that Margaret would have preferred to take on the former Nash house, at Farahy, as it stood. Its pleasantness would appeal to her Wilson tastes; it had the merit of already existing and its compactness should make it easy to run — the Bowens, as will appear from the Chester letters, had already had servant trouble at Annabella. Continual pregnancies may have made Margaret a little nervous, a little lazy, a little too much in love with the easy course. On the plans for Bowen's Court littering Annabella — curling-up parchment with those vast elevations, four-figure estimates — Margaret Bowen may have looked with a doubtful eye. The story is, that she was so set on the Nash house that Henry, to spare himself the pain of arguing with her, sent her away on a visit — perhaps into County Limerick — and in her absence had the Nash house pulled down. So that, on her next eager visit with Henry to Farahy, Margaret turned the bend of the avenue to see only gaping foundations and heaps of rubble. Upon which she said, " Oh, Henry . . ." Upon which he, with his overbearing, slightly evasive brightness, said, " Well, now, dear, we really must build another house, mustn't we? " So she sighed and said, " Oh, Henry . . ." again.

Not one of those architects' plans that littered up Annabella is to be found to-day. I have searched Bowen's Court for them with a thoroughness that towards the end became almost fanatical. In none of those boxes, drawers and cupboards that gave up so much for this family history have I been able to find so much as a sketch or a note relative to the building of Bowen's Court. Nor are there, among all the family letters, any referring to the going-up of the house. The ground plans, the elevations, the estimates, the builders' notes and receipts, the records of

stone quarried and trees felled, the Italians' designs for the fireplaces and friezes, the alternative drawings, with detail, submitted for the grand staircase are all nowhere. Portfolios of
papers, of such bulk and of so recent a date, do not simply get
lost: they must, together with any pertinent letters, have been
destroyed wholesale. And the destruction seems to me sinister:
anything so pointless could only have been effected, whenever
it *was* effected, by somebody in the grip of a neurosis. One of
my aunts suggests that when Henry IV went away to Bath he
may have taken these papers, and that, with all his other possessions — for only his corpse returned to Farahy — they were dispersed about Bath, or destroyed by ignorant hands. If so, I am
left equally helpless: I have not the time or money to search
Bath. Whatever happened, the Bowen's Court plans are gone —
and I must not let this grow on me, like the Nicholls treasure.

So, one cannot document one's imagination of the actual
building of the house. I am told that this took ten years: the
date was cut in 1775, and the family moved in early in '76.
Work was held up by a builders' strike; the workmen demanded a higher rate of pay and the architect had to revise his
original estimate. At the same time, Henry found himself short
of money, and it may have looked, at one heart-sickening moment, as though the roof would never go on at all. Then Henry
set out to raise money, left and right, in a big way, from every
possible source. Every one put up something, including Margaret's sister Mrs. Catherine Grove. At the same time, Henry,
unwillingly, cut down the original plan: the north-east corner
had to be sacrificed. The Italians from Cork were paid off and
went their way before the well ceiling of the Long Room —
meant to crown the house with an oblong bubble of pattern
— was decorated. That small staircase intended to be no more
than a makeshift was run up from the first floor to the Long
Room. Henry III did not for a moment doubt that his son
Henry IV would put in the missing corner and perfect Bowen's
Court into the intended square.

The architect's name is unknown — lost with his papers.

While Bowen's Court was building, Henry and Margaret lived on at Annabella. What millions of revolutions of Bowen coachwheels, and what an urgent clatter of Henry's horse-hoofs, in those ten years, to and fro on the Mallow-Bowen's Court road! At intervals Henry, to watch the great new shell growing, took lodgings over at Farahy — several of his letters, prior to 1775, are addressed to him there. He must have lived in a state of creative nervosity — remember, he was not a man of diffused interests: this building was the great crowning act of his life. Stepping over the planks and in at the doorless front door, he would look up inside the walls as they rose, stone by stone, still roofed by the sky. He must have known despondency when he first saw rain dark-streak the cut stone — was this to be forever? His heart would expand again as he saw fine weather bring back the white bloom. His decision to save (the bills being what they were) the rest of the cut stone for the façade of the stables must have been momentous. Perhaps for weeks together Henry may have tried to absent himself from the growing house. Perhaps he only brought Margaret over from Mallow when there was something strikingly new to see. Was she with him the night the first full moon struck on the rows of new-glazed windows, giving the house the glitter of a superb maniac? When did she first see the completed west flank take the full glare of the declining sun? Did these years of the building estrange Henry from her and make him, as the Kilbolane fight had made him, withdrawn, exalted, obsessed? Henry the big boy, the naive chatterer, the coaxing, loving and rather childish husband, was not present in the building of Bowen's Court. The stern and cold force of his unconscious nature perpetuated itself in stone as the house went up. But Henry was, at the same time, a man of his time's Renaissance: his sense of what was august in humanity made him make his house an ideal mould for life. He was more than building a home, he was setting a pattern. He is said to have said he would

like to beget a child to look out of every window of Bowen's
Court. If he said so to Margaret, she must have sighed again.

Space was essential to Henry's idea of life. The number of
horses and servants he kept with him, even as a come-and-go
bachelor, had already been a grievance with Dr. Nash. For
servants, the Bowen's Court basement gave ample room: any
overflow could camp in shacks round the yard. The proper
housing of Henry's horses, however, came only second to that
of the young Bowens: the stables were so much the complement of the house that cut stone was properly saved for them.
Henry was in no sense " an original ": his traits of mind, his notions, his ways of living were so much those of his class that I
think I can do no better than quote from Arthur Young's rather
tart note (dated the year the Bowens moved into Bowen's
Court) on the Irish country gentry:

In the country their life has some circumstances which are not
commonly seen in England. Large tracts of land are kept in hand
by everybody to supply the deficiencies of the markets; this gives
such a plenty, that, united with the lowness of taxes and prices, one
would suppose it difficult for them to spend their incomes. . . .
Let it be considered that the prices of meat are much lower than in
England; poultry only a fourth of the price; wild fowl and fish in
vastly greater plenty; rum and brandy not half the price; coffee,
tea and wines far cheaper; labour not above a third; servants' wages
upon an average thirty per cent. cheaper. That taxes are inconsiderable, for there is no land tax, no poor rates, no window tax, no
candle or soap tax, only half a wheel tax, no servants' tax, and a
variety of other articles heavily burdened in England, but not in
Ireland. Considering all this, one would think they could not spend
their incomes; they do contrive it, however. In this business they
are assisted by two customs that have an admirable tendency to it,
great numbers of horses and servants. The excess in the latter are
in the lower sort, owing not only to the general laziness, but also to
the number of attendants every one of a higher class will have. This
is common in great families in England, but in Ireland a man of
£500 a year feels it. The number of horses may also be esteemed a

satire upon common sense. . . . An air of neatness, order, dress and *propreté* is wanting to a surprising degree around the mansion; even new and excellent houses have often nothing of this about them. But the badness of the houses is remedying every hour throughout the whole kingdom, for the number of new ones just built, or building, is surprisingly great.

The tables of people of fortune are very plentifully spread; many elegantly, differing in nothing from those in England. Claret is the common wine of all tables, and so much inferior to what is drunk in England that it does not seem to be the same wine; but their port is incomparable. . . . Drinking and duelling are two charges which have long been alleged against the gentlemen of Ireland, but the change of manners which has taken place in that kingdom is not generally known in England. Drunkenness ought no longer to be a reproach, for at every table I was at in Ireland I saw a perfect freedom reign, every person drank just as little as they pleased, nor have I ever been asked to drink a single glass more than I had an inclination for. . . . Duelling was once carried to an excess, which was a real reproach and scandal in the kingdom; it of course proceeded from excessive drinking; as the cause had disappeared, the effect has nearly followed; not however entirely, for it is yet far more common among people of fashion than in England. Let me, however, conclude what I have to observe on the conduct of the principal people residing in Ireland, that there are great numbers among them who are as liberal in all their ideas as any people in Europe.

The number of Henry Cole Bowen's horses hardly amounted, I think, to a satire on common sense. The stables Henry built held, at the time of my grandfather Robert Cole Bowen, sixteen horses, and were then full to capacity. But *that* included farm horses, kept in the lower stable: hunters and carriage horses, in my grandfather's day, took up not more than two thirds of the loose-boxes. Most likely, Henry kept his farm horses somewhere else: he would need, apart from extravagance, room for mounts for himself and his eight sons, and for the carriage horses for Margaret and the girls.

The general *tenu* of Bowen's Court under Henry and Margaret would probably not have come up to Young's ideas. Raw earth and builders' rubbish may, for those first years, have lain under the windows, and at first there was only one avenue. The obliteration of the Nash house and gardens would make necessary new planting and planning; the new trees were still in their infancy and there had been no time for " improvements " yet. Parasitic vague life of half-employed persons, or of persons living on pickings from the new great house, would not only encumber the yards but straggle on down through the woods to the stream. Henry would lose no time in stocking his fine cellar, but there his indoor liabilities stopped. Upstairs there was not, I daresay, " true elegance " anywhere; but there was space, light, liberality, and these elements go to make their own style. The great bold rooms, the high doors imposed an order on life. Sun blazed in at the windows, fires roared in the grates. There was a sweet, fresh-planed smell from the floors. Life still kept a touch of colonial vigour; at the same time, because of the glory of everything, it was bound up in the quality of a dream. The arched staircase window then looked straight on the mountains; treeless north light fell on the staircase, and Henry Cole Bowen, bringing his friends up, said, " We shall add the next flight, to the ballroom, soon." Jane Cole's portrait was hung, and her supple blue dress flowed down, catching the light on the new wall. And her son Henry had his own portrait painted, then had the two portraits framed to match. Those two, son and mother who hardly met in life, continue — he with that engaging turn of his head, she in her detachment — to king and queen it over the house, over the other Bowens living and on the walls.

Henry had the new mansion furnished and fitted up: the furniture, the glass and the silver were specially made for him in Cork. He could not have placed his orders at a better period: Cork cabinet makers and silversmiths were now at their height: these artist-craftsmen could not do a thing wrong. The furni-

ture was — is — Irish Sheraton and Chippendale, whose slender
strong grace need not be praised here. Oval and circular polished tables made pools of light in the rooms, and were ranged
round by chairs with broad seats and shapely backs. Wine-
coolers, fluted knife-boxes, brass-hooped plate-buckets — not
a detail was missing. The family ate at an — appropriately —
very long table, with curved detachable ends. The glass, of
which a few pieces are still with me, gave out a clear ring and
was of strong design. On the silver — Cork eighteenth-century
silver — on the spoons with their patterned handles and pointed
bowls, the coasters, salvers and ladles, the family Hawk appears
— inside medallions or standing in curved space. Only a set of
ridged candlesticks with square bases, and a coffee pot with the
Stag instead of the Hawk, are of earlier date than Bowen's
Court and must have been brought from Kilbolane. What
Henry did with the rest of the contents of Kilbolane is unknown: the place may not have been furnished up to his tastes.
Certainly there is not, and I do not think there was ever, any
Kilbolane furniture at Bowen's Court. Henry's distaste for his
grandmother's home may have made him dispose of the whole
place as it stood.

I have shown that Henry was a sociable man. But there was,
I think, about his love of society something abstract and contemplative: he did not care deeply for individuals. Country
gentleman life in Mallow and County Cork was not, clearly, a
setting for intimacies. Henry lived — and lived well — among
noisy extroverts. But even had he been born — which I find
hard to imagine — into a quite different world, I feel that some
sort of refusal, some sort of contrary shyness inside his nature,
would have restrained him from friendships in any deep sense.
He was one of those manly men, of entirely manly tastes, who
are bored and depressed by too much of men's company. The
root of the matter was, he had really nothing to *say:* his ideas
grew inward; his introspections, if any, remained a locked

book. You may say he was narcissistic. He was certainly, in his
lack of desire for, in his unformed dread of personal intercourse, anti-Elizabethan. Had Henry, walking the Awbeg
banks with his rod, stepped through time and come on Spenser
and Sydney reclining under the Doneraile willows, deep in
their sweet discourse, he would have thought them either sissy
or mad — and, at the same time, wondered how in the world
there could be so *much* to say about anything. Yet Henry was
not a hearty: he was a touchy dreamer. From the woman's
point of view, I feel that flirtation with Henry would have
ended only in chagrin; the interlude would confer consequence
on one, but in the long run one would be left high and dry.
One part of his nature must, I believe, have spent itself — how,
on whom we do not know — before he married Margaret: at
some time he may have found himself dropped in chaos, appalled, wounded, angry, unbearably dismayed. This would
all go to heighten his *méfiance*. His marriage was a homecoming, a return: I believe his love for his wife to have been from
the first domestic rather than passionate. At the same time, that
love was enduring, noble and happy: Margaret was his cousin,
his mother, his only friend.

Henry's popularity — which is his greatest legend — must
have come from his, very largely physical, charm, from his
easy manner and from the sort of grace with which he knew
how to give what society asked of him. And again, which
ranked high in those days, he was generous in all matters, lordly
and liberal. He dealt nicely with his associates — his associates
in pleasure, in business, in loyalty. In the short space left me before I must leave Henry, I should like to give some idea of the
people with whom he was in touch.

Mr. Richard Chester, Henry's man of business in Dublin,
plays a fairly large part from the seventeen-sixties on. Poor
Henry was seldom clear of the law: when he was not tied up in
his own business affairs he was wrestling with other people's.
It was either his fate or his nature to take on liabilities. Having

grown up under three guardians, he was to become a guardian, twice over, himself.

About four years after Henry's marriage, Margaret's second brother (his first cousin) Edward Warter Wilson died. Edward had made Henry his executor, and also guardian to his only daughter and heiress, Frances Juliana Warter Wilson, at this time a child of about ten. Now Frances Juliana was the child, as Edward Wilson had been the husband, of that rather difficult daughter of the second Lord Carbery, the former Honourable Frances Evans. Henry's relations with Mrs. Wilson cannot have been easy, since the Kilbolane affair. And this Mrs. Wilson, as a widow, did nothing to help her husband's executor: she retreated to England, where she refused steadily to read documents or sign anything. Probate was held up, and Henry found his hands tied in every matter to do with the administration of his young ward's estates. For what he did do, he got nothing but blame. In the thick of all this (which all but overlapped on the Kilbolane lawsuit) Henry took his worries to Mr. Chester in Dublin, who promised, if any one could, to straighten the matter out. Mr. Chester's name appears already on some of the less important Kilbolane documents. In 1762, the Chester letters begin.

Mr. Chester may have been an excellent lawyer; he was a most obliging ally and friend, but he seems to have been a despondent and fussy man, not at all calculated to calm Henry, who was easily driven into a fuss himself. Mr. Chester was deeply suspicious of Mrs. Wilson's lawyer Mr. Bradshaw, in whom the widow reposed a far too absolute trust. Mr. Chester took it, and caused Henry to take it, that Mr. Bradshaw was holding up things for his own ends. The deceased Edward Wilson's business dragged on, for whatever reason, year after year. The brighter side of this was that a warm feeling had time to grow up between the client and lawyer: Mr. Chester bought wine for Henry in Dublin, checked over books Henry ordered and had them despatched, bought horses (he showed a good

deal of knowledge and attended the sales), bought clothes for
the Bowen ladies when he was in London, visited Henry's
daughters at their Dublin school, chose Henry a fishing rod,
saw through some business about some sheep and, last but not
least, tried to find the Bowens a cook. And poor Mr. Chester
owed the fatal "infatuation" that very nearly broke up his
married life to getting mixed up too deeply in Henry's affairs.

Mr. Chester never took a bright view. On January 24th,
1769, he writes:

*I shall send you down the Madeira, as many people here think it
good. . . . I do believe you will have a good Deal of Trouble for
a little Time in Mrs. Wilson's affairs, but please God I will soon get
you rid of the Chief on't. I would not have desired you to take on
this Trust though I were to bee ten Times the Gainer I shall by
it, as I feared it would be too troublesome. Your Motives for doing
so every Body must know, and though you should not be thanked,
which is too ungrateful a Return to expect, your Design is, and
will be, equally well rewarded.*

In 1770, Mr. Chester is cheered by finding he really has got
something on Mr. Bradshaw:

*There goes a report about this city not to Mr. Bradshaw's advan-
tage. I think it is, that Mr. Lloyd, Captain Bunbury and a Mr.
Thomas Bunbury met at his house the other day, that the latter
got Drunk and satt down to play and lost £14,000, that he com-
pounded the Debt on paying ten, and passed Mr. Bradshaw's bond
for £1,700, his brother David's for £400, Mr. Loyd's own for
£700, and other securities to that amount as payment. By these
stories and other Enquiries I have found out that Mr. Bradshaw
owes between five and £6000. . . . This I mention to you as a
hint to make you more peremptory in demanding a settlement.*

In these days the Bowens, entertaining at Annabella, failed to
find any local cook that came up to Henry's ideas. Mr. Chester,
enlisted into the chase, writes from Dublin, January 3rd, 1768:

I mentioned the Cookes to you in my last and assure you I have taken all the pains I could about getting one for you. Such a pack of wretches I never met for Drunkenness etc.

And, January 21st of that year:

Mrs. Fitzgibbon has recommended me for you one of the best Cookes, she says, that can be and an honest Sober Man. He has lived with her a good while, but is now in an indifferent state of health. He is recommended Mallow Water, which he thinks you so convenient to that he would soon be quite restored. I would not, however, agree with him till I knew your Sentiments in the matter. As to Hayes Nephew, I would not have anything to do with him, he is so fond of drink.

Evidently the Fitzgibbons' delicate cook did not go to the Bowens, for Mr. Chester is cast down on February 24th:

I do assure you that my trouble about looking for a Cooke was not equal to the Uneasiness at being disappointed and meeting such a hellish Pack. . . . I hope the Sheep have turned out to your mind.

In January 1772 Mr. Chester made a journey to London, where he succeeded in seeing a lawyer (other than Mr. Bradshaw) who was acting for the widowed Mrs. Wilson, and in straightening out at least some of the Wilson affairs. On February 1st, on his way home, he writes from Holyhead:

I shall give you a full Account, please God, of all our proceedings and plan of operation when I go to Ireland, but for the present have neither life nor spiritts to do so, being much fatigued by a very disagreeable and expensive Journey, owing in a great measure to the severity of the weather and depth of the Snow, which has prevented the Mail that should be here yesterday from being yet arrived, and it blows so violently that, even if it were, no ship would venture out. So I am here confined from my business, which has worn my flesh off with fretting. . . . I have got the Stockings

and gowns as directed; how I shall send them God knows, but I
shall do the best I can.

In February 1773 Mr. Chester reports on the Miss Bowens,
Thomasine and, probably, Jane, now at their Dublin school:

I saw the young ladies this day; they promised to write to-night.
They are both well, had little colds. Tomorrow I intend to give
them an airing. . . . Miss Thomasine has not had any return of
her complaint. . . . I got your fishing rod and have it here.

On June 1st, 1776 (this is among his first letters directed to
Bowen's Court), poor Mr. Chester is in a fever about his health:

I am unable to give you any Account of myself till the intended
Operation be performed, which I have expected every day for
some time, and which I can't help saying so Agitates me that I am
unable to think or do anything whatsoever. . . . I trust in God
you will Escape Cold Travelling about.

Mr. Chester's collapse (which was *not*, as we shall learn later,
entirely due to health) came just at the height of a crisis in
Henry's affairs. Before the Wilson troubles were at an end, he,
Henry, had involved himself in a second guardianship — that
of "the minor Bowerman." In the Bowerman business, the
Nettles family were being extremely active. Henry Bowerman
and Robert Nettles had both been prominent Loyal Protestants. So I suppose the friendship that landed Henry in so much
worry — a worry that must have darkened the early Bowen's
Court days — must have dated from that Mallow dining club.
A Miss Nettles had married a Mr. Bowerman; as the Widow
Bowerman, mother of the minor, she seems to have combined
with her brother "Bob Nettles" to make Henry's days a nightmare. What Henry's own guardian Dr. Llewellin Nash had
been put through by Mrs. Catherine Bowen was nothing to

what Henry suffered from the Bowerman-Nettles. In the course of going through the Bowerman business he seems to have turned up some pretty ugly affairs; objection was taken to the line he took; he was nearly accused of misuse of authority. He became anxious to be quit of the whole thing, which, in addition to its unpleasantness, was involving him in journeys and in expense when he most wished for the peace of his new house. Mr. Chester (I think in this case rightly) took an even gloomier view of Mrs. Bowerman and her faction than he had taken of the Honourable Mrs. Wilson. He was now busy trying to obtain from the Court Henry's release from the legal duties of guardian. This, and the interviews with the Bowermans, took Mr. Chester constantly to Limerick, with, as we shall see, the most unhappy results.

Quite (I imagine) out of the blue Henry one morning received at Bowen's Court the following letter from Dublin, dated June 22nd, 1776, from one Mr. Batt Gibbings, an acquaintance of Henry's and client of Mr. Chester's:

Dear Sir,

I came to Town last Wednesday to see how my Suits are going on, and to inquire into the Cause of Mr. Chester's Affections being estrang'd from his Wife and Children, and find it is owing to Mrs. Halloran, a Mistress of the late John Bowerman. She was brought to Town about a Month ago, under Pretence of attending the Suit about the Guardianship of his eldest Son. Genteel Lodgings were taken for her in the same Street Mr. Chester lives in, and overright him. When she was expected to arrive he was all impatience to have his son Richard, who is in a very bad State of Health, go to the Country, and his Mother to go with him to attend him. Accordingly, they went to Donnybrook. When the Coast was clear, Mrs. Halloran in some Measure became Mistress of his Lodgings, so far as dining with him frequently. When that was taken Notice of, she only visit'd him in the Evenings, and continues to do so all-

most every Afternoon (in Company with her Landlady) for whom high pric'd Wine etc. is prepar'd. She has got variety of Silk Coats, has expensive Lodgings, and goes to publick Places. You may know if her Income can support all that Expence. Some of her Letters from the Country to Mr. Chester, such as ought only to pass between Man and Wife, he intrust'd to a Servant Maid, when he was confin'd to his Bed, to burn. But she, instead of observing his Directions, put them into her Box and entertain'd her Friends by reading them. This reach'd his Wife's Ears, and she hint'd to him that that was faithless Servant. He, in a peremptory Manner, insist'd on knowing what she meant. She was then oblig'd to declare the Truth. He, in the Absence of his Wife, as she sleeps every night at Donnybrook, examined the Maid about it so closely that she was oblig'd to own it. And still he keeps this Maid, I suppose at the Desire of Mrs. Halloran. There is no doubt but Letters of the tenderest Kind has pass'd between them, as I have heard it from one I can depend on, who read some of them.

It is fear'd the unhappy infatuated Man will make a Will and leave all he can to her. The Reason of my giving you this Detail is that I look on you to be the only Person that can serve Mrs. Chester and her Children on this Occasion. I therefore request you will be so good as to write to Mrs. Halloran, to let her know you have heard some Hints thrown out, of a Connection between her and Mr. Chester. You can seem not to credit it, and urge her to return at once to her place of Residence, Limerick, as the only Way to get clear of Censure. When she is remov'd, it is expected his natural Affection for his Family will return — which I understand they have been in a great Measure Strangers to since She came last to Town. If you have not heard of this Affair before, I intreat you will keep it to yourself, as I should be sorry to be instrumental in injuring the unhappy Man, who I look on as being infatuated. His poor Wife is making all the excuses she can for him. I had my Intelligence from different Hands, then I examined her closely, and she was oblig'd to confess I was too well inform'd.

*I am, with the greatest Regards to Mrs. Bowen and all your
Family.*

Your very affec. hum. Servt.

Batt Gibbings.

*I shall be thankful for an Answer direct'd to Mountpelier, near
Blackrock, Dublin.*

Henry's first reaction to this letter would, I am prepared to
swear, be one of extreme annoyance with Mr. Batt Gibbings
for bringing the matter up. He would be sorry for gentle Mrs.
Chester (who always, at the end of her husband's letters, sent
her kindest greetings to Mrs. Bowen): it would be painful to
think of her being " closely examined " by the egregious Mr.
Gibbings on matters of such intimate painfulness. For Mr.
Chester I doubt if he did feel sorry; he had already wasted
much sympathy on Mr. Chester on account of his health, and
put up with much inconvenience on that same score. It was not
Mr. Chester's business to be infatuated; his having an inside was
bad enough. That he could not go to Limerick on a client's
(Henry's) business without getting himself mixed up with a
blowsy Limerick *femme fatale* — not to speak of her being the
late Mr. Bowerman's past — was really more than annoying.
And Henry would have been still further annoyed by Mr.
Gibbings' suggestion that he, Henry, was matey enough with
Mrs. Halloran to be in a position to write her letters of good
advice. I suppose Henry had to reply to Mr. Gibbings; I feel
certain he did not write to Mrs. Halloran, and I think it likely
that he wrote tartly to Mr. Chester, suggesting that since he
was apparently *not* going to have that operation, he should give
his whole mind to settling the Bowerman fight. Henry's anxiety
to be rid of the guardianship was being heightened by the extremely alarmist view that Mr. Chester took of the whole affair.
His warnings became almost hysterical. How much of this,
Henry must now have asked himself, had been due to the
agitations of love?

For, " *Now Sir*," Mr. Chester had written in the February of
1775 —

*I must break through my resolution never to urge any person to
do what may rain an emolument to me, but as you are at present
circumstanced it is absolutely necessary that you shou'd bestir
yourself and stick at no expence to get out of the situation you are
in, beset with three or four of the most notorious perjurers that
ever existed, who by their schemes have put you in such a situation
as, if not attended to, must cost you very dear, besides the Attack
on your Character, which I am sure is much more dear to you than
any other consideration on earth. I served another notice, to get
time for you to attend the Examination here till next Term, and
made an Affidavit of your State of health and desire to have the
truth of the matter to be enquired into known. . . . To encounter
which, the Attorney, whose name is Sherret, concerned against
you, and G——,[1] have also made Affidavits—indeed, the Attorney
is not a bit better than the other—in which they swear that you
were positively served with the Subpoenas, and that you sent your
Servants after G—— and M—— to Murder them for serving you,
and many of the like false and Vilainous charges. I have at length
found out where M—— and G—— were on the day they swear you
were served with the Second Subpoena, that is, on the 21st of
June. Mr. Drew has wrote me a letter in which he informs me that
these fellows were on that day at the fair of Broadford and were
at the tent of one Daniel Fitz Patrick, who is a Publican and lives
at Scarriff. So, if we can get Fitz Patrick to attest all will, I hope,
be well over with you. . . . I hope that you will punish those set
of devils. I wou'd have you write to Mr. Drew, thank him for his
trouble in finding out so important a matter for you, and add that
we hope for his further Assistance in bringing a piece of so great
Vilainy to light. I request you will search for two bundles of papers
Mr. King had here. . . . Etc., etc.*

[1] Illegible.

Can one wonder Henry's health was attacked? Surely life
here was for something better than this? However cheerfully
Henry threw things off, he felt undermined by deep, unad-
mitted worry. These perpetual letters, reproaching him with
passivity, complaisance, *laissez-faire*, disregard for peril, carelessness for his good name, must have drummed iron into his
brain. From a good-natured promise made years ago, sitting
easy over the Loyal Protestants' wine, all this last tormenting
bother had spun itself. The Wilsons, as his relations, were to an
extent his business; the Bowermans emphatically were not.

And he cannot have dismissed, for all his buoyancy, the pile
of debts that grew with his fine house. His rents came in steadily; he could pay creditors interest and still continue to live in
style. But there were his fourteen children to make provision
for, and Henry IV, whose grand ideas had been fostered,
would not look kindly on any cuts. Did Henry III say to himself, " *Après moi le déluge* "? But Margaret might have to live
to see the deluge — she did. No, Henry's health was not good;
he suffered from some complaint for which his doctor ordered
him exercise. So he walked the deck every day in the Long
Room — where he had hoped to see his children dance. Up and
down he paced — the light from the south end windows, the
light from the north end windows making two tides on the bare
floor. When he met a threatening thought he would halt, and
Margaret, attentive somewhere down in the house, would look
up till the walking began again.

The Mitchelstown Light Dragoons were Henry's last social
pleasure. In 1782, when the Volunteer roll was taken, he was
fifty-nine: he had six more years to live. For the first time, he
was a soldier: as a lieutenant-colonel he had sprung fully armed
from Grattan's brain. He was the second Bowen lieutenant-
colonel — Henry I, from Gower, had been the first.

When I first put this uniform on
I said, as I looked in the glass —

What did Henry say, confronting that gorgeous figure in
scarlet with black lapels, squared by the silver epaulets? His
thoughts would be speechless, suffused with feeling and, somehow, maidenly. He braced himself, put his chin up, buttoned
the white buttons across his thrown-out chest. The helmet sat
sternly down on his brow. As he mounted his horse he bit his
lip — but his darlings Henrietta and Belle came out on to the
steps to clap. He still sat his horse like a lord, but not with the
old vigour, not without hostile twinges of pain. Off up his
avenue, under his own windows, " the armed property of the
nation " rode in his old style. On the Mitchelstown road he fell
into a saving jog. With Colonel Viscount Kingsborough and
Major Badham Thornhill he caracoled in the blazing sun in the
square.

Major Badham Thornhill was left in excellent fettle by the
departure of Arthur Young. Young, the English expert on agriculture, had, at the conclusion of his Irish tour, been asked by
the Kingsboroughs to take the Mitchelstown agency. Lord
Kingsborough was Lord Kingston's heir: the Kingston estates
(inherited from the Fitzgeralds) were immense. " His Lordship's vast property extends from Kildorrery to Clogheen, beyond Ballyporeen, a line of more than sixteen Irish miles, and
it spreads in breadth from five to ten miles." The arrangement,
which Young accepted, gave Kingsborough, who was an advanced landlord, the chance to try out some constructive reforms, and gave Young the chance to put his ideas in practice.
In fact, the arrangement had seemed excellent to everybody
but Major Badham Thornhill, who, as a distant cousin of Lady
Kingsborough's, had been drawing profit from the connection
in a steady and as it seemed to him innocent way. Major Thornhill was a " middleman." By the middleman system, one leased
farms from the large landlord and re-let them at very considerably more than the rent one paid. Young was right up against
this system from the start — in his *Tour* he points out all the

evils of it, and in his best manner denounces middlemen (who were generally of the petty-gentry, or squireen, class). Now, as the leases of Kingston farms fell in, Young used all his influence to persuade Lord Kingsborough to give new leases *direct* to the occupiers — who would, by the cutting out of the middleman's profits, gain, while the original landlord stood to lose nothing. Major Thornhill, when Young appeared on the scene, was already rack-renting one farm, and had been on the point of acquiring others to re-let at the same advantageous terms. One cannot wonder he did not like Mr. Young.

Major and Mrs. Thornhill were, it appears, all over the Kingsborough mansion — the mansion preceding the Castle run up for George IV. Young lived (this was in 1777) in a house built for him inside the demesne. Her ladyship's cousin and the new agent took stock of each other without pleasure — much as the first Boyle and Strafford had once done.

" I was placed," Young says, " in an awkward situation. It was impossible for me, consistently with the interests of Lord K., in any measure whatever to promote the success of designs which struck at the root of all my plans, as the Major had his eye upon several of the more considerable farms. Lady K. had a high opinion of the Major, who was a lively, pleasant, handsome man, and an ignorant, openhearted duellist. She had of course favoured his plans, and I as carefully avoided saying anything against them. Thus from the beginning it was not difficult to see an underground plot to frustrate things commencing early, but things in the meantime carried a fair outward appearance. I dined very often at the Castle, and generally played at chess with Lady Kingsborough for an hour or more after dinner, and I learned by report that her Ladyship was highly pleased with me, saying I was one of the most lively, agreeable fellows. Lord Kingsborough was of a character not so easily ascertained. . . . His manner and carriage were remarkably easy, agreeable and polite, having the finish of a perfect gentleman; he wanted, however, steadiness and perseverance even in his best designs, and was easily wrought upon by persons of inferior abilities."

Mrs. Thornhill, "an artful, designing woman," looked further, for her husband, than a few more farms to rack-rent: she
had her eye on the Mitchelstown agency. A French governess,
that traditional source of trouble, was part of the leverage used
to get Young out: Lord Kingsborough, I am sorry to say, had
been either having or trying to have an affair with the governess, and Mrs. Thornhill, after some careful spying, found
much to make known to her ladyship. She also drummed into
her upset patroness that Mr. Young was in league with the governess, and might even be furthering the intrigue. Lord Kingsborough, confronted with his (perhaps quite mild) iniquity
had not a leg to stand on: the Thornhills and Lady Kingsborough had him back in their power — first the governess had
to go, and then Young went.

So here was Major Thornhill, by 1782, with the field to himself. No doubt he had got his farms. Lively, pleasant, handsome and well-connected, he would be *persona grata* in that
Mitchelstown neighbourhood. Too few would jib at his source
of income. No doubt he was often at Bowen's Court.

Six miles from Bowen's Court, in the Castletownroche direction, Henry had neighbours of whom Arthur Young approved.
But the Aldworths' ideas were so noble, their way of life so
much moulded on better things, that I fear they may not have
thought much of the contented Bowens. Mr. and Mrs. Richard
Aldworth had taken a lease of Anne's Grove — the house, with
its now famous lovely gardens, stands above the Awbeg, not
far from Kilcumer — and Arthur Young, who often visited
there, found the Aldworths rare birds in County Cork. They
had, he discovered, elegant manners and cultivated minds.

He had made the grand tour, and she had been educated in that
style which may be imagined in a person nearly related to a Lord
Chief Justice and an Archbishop. It was evident that patriotic motives only made them resident in Ireland. A sigh would often escape them when circumstances of English manners were named,

and they felt the dismal vacuity of living in a country where people of equal ideas were scarce. Mrs. Aldworth had in her possession one original manuscript letter of Dean Swift, entrusted to her under a solemn promise that she would permit no copy of it to be taken, nor ever read it twice to the same person. It was without exception the wittiest and severest satire upon Ireland that was ever written, and it was easy to perceive by the manner in which it was read that the sentiments were not a little in unison with that of the reader. This letter was equally hostile to the nobility, the gentry, the people, nay, the very rivers and mountains.

Nothing could be more flattering than the Aldworths' sighs. Arthur Young, uneasy at Mitchelstown, drank them up. He was due back, some day, in England, and how they envied him! He concludes:

I was inclined to think that that degree of a polished and cultivated education, which suits well enough for London or Paris, or a country residence in a good neighbourhood in England, was ill-framed for a province in Ireland. Persons of equal attainments may now and then come across them, but they are compelled to associate with so many who are the very reverse that a more certain provision of misery can scarcely be laid.

Mr. Aldworth did so far participate in the neighbouring life as to be the Colonel of the Blackwater Rangers in 1782. He was a well-informed man, who had already supplied Young with a good many facts he wanted (about local spinning, and the clothier industry) and certainly would not have got from Henry Bowen. He had, also, erected a bolting mill which would grind five thousand barrels of wheat, and improved the breed of his sheep by importing some English ewes. He had planted several acres with hops which, when Young was there, were doing very well. One must honour the Aldworths' (I think perfectly genuine) patriotic motives for remaining in this unsympathetic countryside. It seems a pity that culture made them sigh so much. Repining, among the Anglo-Irish, did not in general start till the following century. In my own day, I hear a good deal too much of it.

Lord Doneraile's conversation, in 1776, did not in itself impress Mr. Young, but he was improving his sheep and importing the long-horned English cow. English waggons Lord Doneraile had tried but abandoned; he was obliged to tell Arthur Young frankly that he found them inferior to the Irish cart. He had also erected a granary " upon a new construction," in which one could dry the corn.

The Right Hon. Silver Oliver, of Castle Oliver, was " assiduous to the last degree to have me completely informed." He also roused Young's admiration by the way in which he had reclaimed, and had had planted with turnips, much " unprofitable " mountain land. Castle Oliver, right up under the Ballyhouras, " is a place almost entirely of Mr. Oliver's creation; from a house surrounded with cabins and rubbish he has fixed it in a fine lawn, surrounded by good wood." Mr. Oliver showed Young two bulls and gave him an excellent dinner. The following year, from Mitchelstown, Young again made his way over to Castle Oliver: finding the owner absent and the house open for an auction, he permitted himself a thorough inspection of it. The state of the kitchens gave him a very severe shock: he devoted a passage to them in his *Autobiography*.

These, then, were a few of Henry III's neighbours. In this social landscape he set up his new house. The smaller gentry, not noted by Arthur Young, shaded in the spaces between the big families. When Henry's health failed and he had to begin to secede from society, his son Henry took all these people on. But with Henry IV we feel the first breath of discontent: perhaps it began at Oxford; it finished him up at Bath.

HENRY IV
AND ROBERT

HENRY IV HAD BEEN BORN AT ANNABELLA IN 1762. HE WAS
followed into the world by seven brothers — John, Ralph,
Robert, Nicholls, William, Stephens and Edward — and by six
sisters — Jane, Thomasine, Catherine, Margaret, Henrietta and
Isabella ("Belle"). Seven infants stillborn or dead soon after
birth helped to space out the fourteen Bowens who lived — one
may have come before Henry (there had been time) but at any
rate from his birth he was the heir. The precedence given, in
lists, to sons makes us not know how the brothers and sisters
alternated. Jane, the eldest daughter, was, we do know, born in
1764, and Robert, the fourth son, in 1769; Nicholls the fifth and
Stephens the seventh son were baptized together at Farahy in
1773, and Henrietta, the fifth daughter, was baptized at Farahy
in 1774 — those are the only dates I can trace. Henry III, while
his house was still in the building, must have set out to inculcate
early love of Bowen's Court by taking his infants over to the
Farahy font.

If it is true that Bowen's Court took ten years to build, Henry
IV was four when it was begun, and fourteen when, in 1776,
the family took up residence there. He must have been fre-

quently taken by his father from Mallow over to Farahy, to
watch the house that was to be his go up. Perhaps Henry III
worked too much on his young son's feelings: there is about
Henry IV's expression, in his grown-up portrait, something
more than faintly resistant, impatient and saturnine. He had
been born, also, while the Kilbolane case was in progress, and
possibly his father's preoccupation, and the strain it may have
reflected on to Margaret, cast some sort of shadow over his
birth. Henry IV was a proud, offhand little boy; I do not think
he ever took very much stock of Mallow; when he grew up he
asked more than Mallow could give. He was good-looking, and
he walked down the street with his rather long, well-shaped
nose in the air. He was brought up to think only of Bowen's
Court. And he grew up seeing money spent lavishly.

So did his seven brothers — and this did them no good. The
tragedy of Henry III, with his innate dignity and wish for the
best, and of Margaret, with her warm heart and high principles,
was that their sons, on the whole, did not turn out well. In fact,
two of them turned out very badly indeed: the graceless worth-
lessness of both John and Ralph was one of the facts Henry
could not avoid confronting in those years when he used to
pace the Long Room. This lay deeper than worry; it was a perpetual wound. And, though I do not think Henry once flinched
in his loyal pride in his heir Henry IV, it was on his fourth son
Robert, his one *solid* promising good boy, that he unadmittedly
came to fix his hopes. Nicholls, the fifth son, became a clergyman, and may not have done so badly. William, Stephens and
Edward all went into the Army: their extravagance was remarkable.

The girls were very much better; they were on Margaret's
pattern and some of them may have shown a touch of their
grandmother Jane. They were probably not spoiled. They
must have loved their father — his fine figure, his optimism, his
kindness — and must have been sorry to see him wounded
though trying to smile it off. One can gather they were good

daughters — handsome, home-loving, pleasant — from the fact
that they must have promised to make good wives: all six of
them married " respectably," and one or two of them married
well. That Henry spoiled his sons and that Margaret failed to
cope with them is, I am afraid, evident. I feel sure there was not
a touch, in this family life, of either cynicism or laxity. But
Henry was in love with everything he had made — also, having
had a rather unhappy childhood, he probably cared too much
to see happiness. He made a magnificent abstract of behaviour,
but his shyness — here, fatally — kept him from other souls.
Let us call him an over-indulgent, too hopeful father, and leave
it at that. As for Margaret — she had become from the day she
married the mother of one grand, exacting, absorbing son:
Henry III remained the only man in her life; he kept her hands
full and her thoughts busy; her perception, her powers, her
moral wisdom were all used up by him. To her real sons she
was a loyal devoted mother, but also, alas, a distracted one. Was
there any effort to rule? The sons grew up unruly. Henry and
Margaret set examples, but the examples were ignored. Two
downright bad and several indifferent Bowens sprang from this
happy marriage, this good home. Trustworthy Robert, lively
sensible Jane, graceful Thomasine and darling Belle, the baby,
were bright spots in this discouraging brood.

There are bills for Henry IV's tuition and board, together
with that of his brothers John, Ralph and Robert, from a Mr.
Ross — of which Irish school is not stated: Mr. Ross adds notes
of various books supplied. The younger Bowen boys went to
Midleton School; I have one or two of the Midleton bills, also,
by me: the boys learned dancing; less costly extras were shoe-
buckles, haircuts and glaziers' charges for mending windows
broken by Bowens. Jane and Thomasine, as we gather from
Mr. Chester, were sent to " finish " in Dublin for a term or two,
and some of their younger sisters went to a school in Waterford.

At home the children could always read, if they wished:

their father had already laid the foundations of what was to be a substantial library. The (now) more or less complete works of Pope, Gay, Dryden, an eight-volume set of *The Spectator, The Guardian, Addison's Poems, Young's Works* (the Young of the *Night Thoughts*) dedicated to Mr. Voltaire, *The Faerie Queene, written by Edmund Spenser, with a Glossary explaining Old and Obscure Words, Lord Chesterfield's Letters to his Son*, translations of *Madame de Sévigné's Letters* and of *Sully's Memoirs, Johnson's Dictionary, A Description of England* (in eight volumes, with plates of religious ruins and notable country seats), *A Tour Through France* (Anon.), *Goldsmith's Animated Nature*, a *Nouveau Traité de Vénerie, Smollett's History of England, Robertson's History of Scotland*, six volumes of *Dodsley's Collections* (*Poems by Several Hands*), *Manners in Portugal, Vertot's Revolution in Sweden, Crevier's Roman Emperors, Memoirs of the Portuguese Inquisition, with Reflections on Ancient and Modern Popery, Essex's Letters* (from Ireland), *Observations on the Turks, Tissot on Health*, a *Life of Gustavus Adolphus*, Arthur Young's *Tour Through the North of England, Collins' Peerage* (eight volumes, 1779), and a *Peerage of Ireland* (1768) are among the books that bear Henry III's autograph, and that testify to a taste not less pious for being orthodox. The greater part of them are in Dublin editions, very finely produced. Some of the sets of poetry and the histories have Margaret's initials, M.B., stamped in gilt on their backs: they must have been gifts to her. Henry III sent his orders directly to the Dublin booksellers; Mr. Chester used to call in to check over the lists, supervise the packing and see that the books were sent off to County Cork.

Henry IV went to Balliol College, Oxford: he matriculated in 1780. Of his time at Oxford I know nothing whatever; I could touch in suppositious pictures, but what would be the point? His going to Oxford has one interesting aspect: it is the first occasion (at least, the first on record) that any Bowen, since the remove to Ireland, had crossed the sea except on visits to Wales. Henry IV must have been conscious, on his arrival at Oxford, of provincial roughnesses that he must shell off. The hardness of some extinct resolution shows in every line of his saturnine, narrow face. I doubt that he was ever naive. I am sure his tastes were expensive, and that Oxford made them more so — on the other hand, in this as in other matters I do not think he was ever quite a fool. He would speak with the intonation of County Cork. (It used to annoy me to hear Sir Lucius O'Trigger played with a roaring brogue; I used to think this was one more piece of the English silliness, for I had been so often afflicted by the English remark: " Oh, but you can't be Irish, you haven't got a brogue." To speak with a brogue, in my childhood, was to be underbred, so I used to find myself tempted into the smart retort: " Oh, but you can't be English, you don't drop your h's." But I know now that the Irish provincial gentry of Henry III's and Henry IV's day did speak with an intonation and rhythm that, in upper-class England, would be remarkable.) I imagine that Henry IV, at Oxford, would at once be at pains to correct this — he would be divided between reluctance to admit that there *could* be anything wrong with him and the wish to make the grade, even to shine, at all costs, wherever he found himself. Whether he was at as much pains in this matter as Mr. Edward Tighe I do not know. Mr. Tighe comes a little later in time than Henry — we meet him in the *Irish Varieties* of Mr. J. D. Herbert, Dublin portrait painter, clubman and gossip — but he comes in so well in this context that I shall introduce him here:

" Mr. Edward Tighe, of the County of Wicklow," says Mr. Herbert, " a gentleman of high family, had imbibed an early taste for reading and speaking *free from the Irish accent;* this taste he cultivated so highly as to become the best English reader of his day. Shakespeare and Milton were his favourite authors: with a volume in either hand he has entertained auditors in the first circle of fashion; wherever he visited he became the arbiter elegantarium; cards and gaming vanished at his approach, and no party, however select, could be considered perfect without Mr. E. Tighe.

". . . Mr. Tighe then gave us a memoir of his life during his study, and explained the manner he adopted to acquire the desirable object: 'When I was young, I became attached to Shakespeare and Milton, and practised aloud, but my ears accustomed to the accent of Dublin, I was not aware of the pernicious habit I had acquired until I went to Eton school; there I found myself out, and laboured to gain the prize in examinations. The youths at that College were chiefly English, and of high family, untainted with provincial or cockney accent; I selected a few of the young men whose accent I approved of, and intreated of them to watch me in my speech and reading, and take notes, which they would oblige me by occasionally giving me. I then prevailed on them to read the passages, that I might profit thereby: they were flattered by the deference I paid to their superious endowments, and were very attentive to my requests. I by this got rid of my native accent, by the time I had finished my studies at Eton; but I am sorry to observe, that had I not adopted that or some other scheme of improvement *myself*, there was no *English* tuition that could have improved me, for many of my colleagues left Eton with the same accent they had brought to it.' "

Henry lacked Mr. Tighe's incentive, elocution, and Mr. Tighe's patience. I feel he would have felt touchy about his own way of speaking, not inclined to invite comment or to receive it well. His years at Oxford probably had the exhilaration of a battle, or an ascent, for him. Any fun he got out of watching the English he would most likely keep to himself: wariness would be making him taciturn. I do not know what school he read, or what class he finally took. He may have felt, at his studies, some unexpected quickening, eagerness or start-awake of the intellect. Or, on the other hand, he may have desired only so much learning as might adorn talk. Of one thing I do feel sure — he would wish to distinguish himself in some field: though heart was not his strong point he was not, like some of his brothers, an unnatural son; he knew his father's pride was vested in him and that he was Bowen's Court's emissary to the large English world. Whatever else Oxford did or did not do to Henry, it inculcated in him a taste for English society and a pressing desire to fall in with its ways. It made Henry, in the latter part of his life, the only Bowen who was an absentee.

Henry IV's being at Oxford did mean much to Henry III. *" My son, who is home from Oxford, desires his best regards to you,"* he happily writes in 1782. And, in another letter that same year, far from happily: *" My son Henry is a student at Oxford, and I do not wish him to meet his brother John."* And, elsewhere: *" I am obliged to have John at home."* Three weeks later: *" My son "* (John) *" came here from Bristol last Saturday, somewhat abashed lest he should not meet with a favourable reception from me. His figure and his promise of a total reformation in his conduct for the future has Determined me to Purchase a Lieutenancy for him in one of the Regiments now in the East Indies or going there. The Colonel assures me he will do everything to aid in the disposal of his Commission and paying his debts. . . ."*

John did not leave Ireland immediately, for in 1787 he peevishly writes: *" My father had not eat a bit of animal food above three times in these last four months. I beg you will (when in town) send me some account of my debts, for I really cannot recollect them."* He did get his commission, though in a *West* Indian regiment. He died, I am glad to say, in 1800, married but leaving no children behind.

Henry III lived to see his two eldest daughters married. Jane Bowen married the Rev. William Berkeley, rector of Ballyhooly, on the Blackwater, and nephew of Bishop Berkeley. There being " no glebe-house " at Ballyhooly, Jane and her husband lived at Woodville, a small country house some miles along the river. The Rev. William Berkeley was not overworked; the Protestant population of Ballyhooly amounted, in his time, to sixty souls. He held another living, Ahinagh, twenty-five miles distant, for which he retained a curate, the

Rev. Basil Orpin, at the moderate cost of fifty pounds a year. Of Ahinagh, in 1775, we read " church in ruins " — but possibly Mr. Berkeley had it patched up. In 1785 the Protestant population of Ahinagh amounted to twenty-one souls. Jane had only one child, a daughter called Arabella, who subsequently married Arthur Riall, Esq., of Westgrove, Clonmel. Jane was left a widow in 1814: she buried her husband at Farahy.

Thomasine Bowen married, at Mallow, the Honourable George Jocelyn, the second son of the first Lord Roden. In time she had six daughters — Harriet, Georgina, Louisa, Sophia, Anne and Thomasine. All these six Miss Jocelyns married. Harriet's marriage made her the ancestress of the Elizabeth Clarke who was my grandmother — Robert Cole Bowen's wife. Louisa married first a Wingfield — the name reappears in my mother's family — and secondly Richard Tighe, a connection of our Mr. E. Tighe.

Henry IV must have left Oxford in 1783. Perhaps he made the grandish tour, perhaps he paid visits. Henry III must have been divided between his wish to have his heir near him in his declining days and his wish that the young man should see the best of the world. From wherever he was in the early spring of 1788, Henry IV was recalled to Bowen's Court, for now his father was dying. Henry III, they tell me, chose to lie in the Drawing-room. The bright March light would have struck at the five windows: they drew the shutters to. This was the grandest, and the most feminine, room: Henry could look up cloudedly at the Italian frieze in which sweet plaster roses trailed from tapering basket-work. Anxious whispers round him faded up into the ceiling, pale faces blurred on the shuttered-up elegance. Outdoors, sap ran up in the trees, mating rooks tore through the branches, beat their blue-black wings. A scratch or cut in Henry's arm had mortified, due to his low state of health; they took the arm off, but this was done too late. Blood-poisoning, with the shock of the amputation, killed him. As he lay in pain and fever, chains of images must have passed through his mind — Kilbolane, Bilbo, Kilcumer, the Mallow parties, the now darkening stone dream of his house. Pray God he died happy — but probably he did not know how he died. When he was in his coffin they brought back his arm (I hear) and laid it beside him, where it should be. Perhaps they fitted it up the sleeve of his latest fine coat. The thought must have been Margaret's: she knew him so well.

Henry IV, at twenty-six, was now the master of Bowen's Court. His shoulders were less broad than his father's, not broad enough for all that they had to bear.

For the confusion was terrible. Henry III's affairs were in a state of disorder that so appalled the trustees under his will — Silver Oliver of Castle Oliver, Arthur Hyde of Castle Hyde, the indefatigable Rev. Jeremiah King and the Rev. William Maunsel — that they refused to act. Finally Margaret Bowen, the widow, proved the will alone. Henry had left his Estate to his eldest son, Henry, and on to *his* sons, if any. Should Henry IV have no sons, Bowen's Court, its lands and the other Bowen properties were to go to Robert (Henry III's fourth son) and on to Robert's sons. The Estate was charged with portions for Henry III's thirteen living children other than Henry IV. The Estates devised by the Testator were of an annual value of about £3,700. The charges created on them by the will amounted to between £12,000 and £13,000. In addition there was a Jointure (for Margaret) of £500 per annuum, charged by deed. The Testator's debts, at the time of his death, amounted to nearly £40,000: most of these bore interest at 6 per cent. This interest was left a charge on the Estate. The Testator's Personal Estate was " inconsiderable."

Henry IV, upon Henry III's death, " entered into the receipt of the rents and profits devised to him by the Will." The place must be kept going, and Henry was soon to marry. But what of the charges? What of the creditors? Something had to be done. So, three months after his father's death, Henry IV " became desirous that a portion of the devised Estates should be sold by the Trustees, under the powers of sale contained in his father's will, for the payment of the debts of the Testator and the other charges thereon." Henry, in fact, decided Kilbolane was to go. If he *did* ever think of the Nicholls treasure, he took a pretty disabused view of it: if the treasure were in the bawn or Brandon, those had been lost already — and anyhow, what were some flower-pots full of gold and silver against the present overwhelming demands? So, the Kilbolane lands — other than that part of the Castle and ground round it already lost to the Evans — were put up for sale. In June 1788, advertisements to this effect were inserted in the public newspapers: intending purchasers were to apply to William Galwey, of Mallow, Henry's agent, to Richard Martin, Henry's attorney, or direct to Henry Cole Bowen himself.

Nothing whatever came of these advertisements: there had not been so much as a nibble, and things looked bad for Henry, when a Mr. George Evans Bruce, a friend of the family, came out with an offer to buy the Kilbolane lands. It was agreed that he was to have them for a sum amounting to twenty-one years' rental, and £100 over. This sum, it is believed, was either £18,000 18s. 8d. or £19,025. Which of these exactly it *was*, no one, later, was able to ascertain. For, later — when, in fact, the Bowens once more dragged the whole matter up — no contract was found to be forthcoming. This was what took us to the House of Lords.

Owing to the confused state of the Bowen affairs, the charges on the Estate and the persistent refusal of the trustees under the will to act in any capacity whatsoever, Mr. Evans Bruce found that some time must elapse before the sale to him of the Kilbolane lands could be completed. He was, naturally, anxious to take possession. And, by this time, many of Henry III's creditors were pressing for payment. Mr. Bruce was, accordingly, persuaded by the Bowen family — in consideration of his being allowed to use the Kilbolane lands before the final deed of Sale was drawn up — to make the Bowens a number of payments on account. He agreed to make payments to several of Henry III's younger children on account of their legacies, also to pay off the more pressing of the debts charged on the Estate. " Taking assignment of them either to himself or to the Reverend Jonathan Bruce or John Boles Reeves as Trustees for himself."

The vagueness of the arrangement could not have been more fatal. For years the incomplete purchase hung in the air. Mr. Evans Bruce, during this period, stayed uncertain as to the extent of his powers and liabilities over Kilbolane. As for the distracted Bowens, Margaret and her children, they came to regard Mr. Bruce as a permanent nest egg. Several times he jibbed and tried to withdraw from the purchase, but Henry's lawyers made this difficult for him — also, he seems to have had an incurably kind heart. Not for nothing was he a family friend. Poor Margaret Bowen leaned on him more and more. In July 1789 we find her writing to him:

Sir,

By a very great blunder of mine in my hurry going twice to Mr. Shannon, I forgot to desire Mr. Jocelyn [Thomasine's husband] *to draw on you for his money; this delay consequently gave you reason to suppose he did not want it, and I find the money had been applied elsewhere. However, I hope you will be so kind as to remedy my mistake, and let him have his money as soon as you conveniently can, as he writes to me in some distress about it. There is another matter which I beg leave to mention to you; the simple contract debts are a charge on the Estate, and are to be paid out of the purchase of Kilbolane — they amount to £2,600, and if your law agent satisfies you in this business, I hope you will have no objection to letting us have the money at the time you are providing for Mr. Jocelyn. Mr. Prittie* [Henry IV's prospective father-in-law] *wishes to sell the entire estate of Bowenscourt to pay off the remaining Judgements, and to prepare Henry for the Payment of the younger children's fortunes as they come of age;*

whatever he desires will be done no doubt; and indeed, Sir, the simple contract debts have been so long due, and the poor people are through necessity become so troublesome to me, I am anxious to have them paid as soon as we can. I am almost ashamed to beg a favour of you for myself; one of the legacies bequeathed by Mr. Bowen was £300 to me. I have Henry's bond for it, and signed by his father also, and as I have taken a house here [Mallow] *which was greatly out of repair, and has cost me a great deal to put into order, I want money to furnish it, if you will be so kind as to let me have the entire or half of that sum, as I have no demand on Henry for jointure till the end of September, you will confer a very great obligation on me, and I am sure he will give you any security for the short time I hope it will remain unpaid.*

> *I am Sir,*
>> *your obedient and very humble Servant*
>> *M. Bowen.*

In October 1794 Margaret again writes to Mr. Bruce:

Dear Sir,

My son Stephens, who was of age the 12th of last month, which gives him a power over his own fortune, acquainted me some time since of his determination to get into the Artillery, if you would be so kind to give him £159 or £200, to enable him to raise ten men for a Lieutenancy. As I have so many sons unprovided for, I thought it an eligible plan, and relying on your goodness I have procured letters of service, which I believe he has received by this time. The men have engaged themselves to him, and nothing is wanting but your assistance. I have therefore only to hope you will comply.

> *And am, dear Sir, etc.*

A month later in that year, Mr. Richard Martin, the Bowen attorney, is writing to Mr. Bruce:

Dear Sir,

Ralph Bowen was with me this day, and has requested I might write to you to inform you that Sir John Carden has offered him

*a Lieutenancy in his new Regiment of Cavalry for £250, which
I think too advantageous an offer to decline. . . . If you can advance what he wants, which possibly may amount to something
more than the actual sum to be paid to Sir John Carden for uniform, etc., etc., you will be good enough to say whether you can
let him have the sum he wants, and address the answer to him at
Kilcumer, Castletownroche, as I set out tomorrow morning for
Dublin.*

In December, Margaret takes up the pen once more:

*This takes the last request I shall make to you; I am really too
troublesome, but when you consider how many sons I have unprovided for, and the opportunities that now offer to get them out
on the world on easy terms (a great object to them) I hope you
will forgive me. Mr. Jocelyn has been so kind as to procure an
Ensigncy from Government for my son Robert, whose wish is to
get a lieutenancy in Sir John Carden's Regiment of Cavalry, we
rely on your consideration and kindness in giving him £400, and
as there is no time to be lost hope for a favourable answer by return of the Post. . . .*

Alas, in October 1796 Margaret was obliged to write again:

*Once more I am under the necessity of requesting your assist-
ance for my Son Stephens, who has been arrested at Blaris Camp
for £50. Lord Drogheda's orders are that if any of the Artillery
officers are confined for debt he shall be informed of it, and they
are superseded immediately.*

*The losses he sustained in raising men have reduced his small
capital to a trifle, and his Commission will inevitably be lost unless
you are good enough to preserve it for him (for it is really not in
my power to do it). . . .*

In fact, Mr. Evans Bruce might not close his purse without
being made to feel he stood in the way of some young Bowen's
vital development. How long can pity for Margaret, optimistic
mother, have kept him patient with Margaret's graceless

brood? And what of Henry IV? Exacerbations and worries
must have borne in on him: this was a bleak Monday morning
to come so early in life. He had quite likely had, and had still
more likely given his Oxford friends, the impression that life on
his Irish estates was to be leisurely, dashing, lordly, spacious
and gay. One has to commend, though one may not love, in
Henry a sort of disabused realism: he now took what arms he
could against this sea of troubles, and one does not hear that he
made any complaint. All this did not sweeten, improve his
temper or soften his temperament. He found himself quite disengaged from the Bowen's Court myth — of which, from his
father, he had had more than enough. All the same, he did dig
his heels in when Mr. Prittie urged the extreme measure of selling Bowen's Court. To be placeless would have connoted for
Henry III's heir not only nullity but disgrace. Dare one blame
Henry IV for the path he afterwards chose? If all life's promise
is hollow then let us turn to pleasure, so patently hollow that it
cannot hurt.

How Henry IV in 1789, at the height of all these embarrassments, managed to bring off his marriage to Catherine, daughter of Henry Prittie, Esq., of Kilboy, Nenagh, County Tipperary, is a mystery. Henry had all the cut of an eligible, but
how, on closer examination, could any father be satisfied? Mr.
Prittie was, at this time, on the verge of becoming the first Lord
Dunalley: a general sense of well-being may have mollified
him. At any rate, we find him content to drop his extreme suggestion about selling Bowen's Court, and to allow his daughter
to marry Henry Bowen. The settlement brought into sight, in
this same year, by the bringing of the *Grove v. Bowen* suit may
have offered some guarantee for Catherine's security. The
Bowens should, soon, know where they stood.

Grove v. Bowen was brought by the Bowens' wish. It had
been agreed by Margaret, by Henry IV, by the family, the
family lawyers and the most friendly creditors concerned that
the only hope of getting things straightened out, of making the

trustees act, or of, in default of this, finding trustees who *would* act was, that some one to whom Henry III owed money should file a bill at the Court of Exchequer in Ireland for the administration of the real and personal estate of the late Henry Cole Bowen. Margaret's widowed sister Mrs. Catherine Grove was chosen to break the deadlock: she had been Henry III's creditor to the extent of £3,100. Childless, amiable, a true Wilson in feeling (she had already met several of her Bowen nephews' money demands on the side) Mrs. Grove would have been the last to make trouble in anything like the ordinary course of things. It was, however, felt that *her* bringing the suit would keep the whole affair "in the family." Mrs. Grove, accordingly, filed her bill against Henry IV, against all the Bowens, Mr. Richard Chester's son John and Henry III's inactive trustees. "The suit, though amicable, was *bona fide*." Mr. Evans Bruce wisely stood outside it. In the course of it, the original trustees were replaced by two Mallow gentlemen, William Galwey and the Rev. William King, "a clergyman of integrity," rector of Mallow and either the son or a close connection of the Rev. Jeremiah King — now, happily, dead. Under the slow even pressure of Court proceedings the knots, if not untied, got gradually ironed out. In 1794 Bowen lands of sufficient value to pay off the debts and charges were put up for auction, by the order of Court. Richard Martin, the Bowen attorney, successfully bid £19,025 for Kilbolane on behalf of Mr. Bruce — whose property, as we know, Kilbolane already morally was. In 1795 Mr. Bruce, by agreement, took formal possession. It was not, however, till 1810 that the conveyance was finally drawn up. *That* might appear, from the point of view of the Bowens, to be at last goodbye to Kilbolane. . . . Wait till *Bowen v. Evans* of 1842.

Grove v. Bowen had the desired outcome: from 1794 on the debts began to be paid off, and the younger Bowens received those parts of their portions that they had not already spent in advance.

How, out of what was so nearly a *débâcle*, Henry IV salvaged enough to live in the manner he did is, again, a mystery. St. John Galwey, son of William Galwey, said years later: "I was intimately acquainted for many years with the late Henry Cole Bowen. . . . While residing at Bowen's Court he usually drove with four horses, and kept up a corresponding establishment, and I always considered him a gentleman of affluent circumstances." The fashionableness and the high play at cards of Henry IV and his wife the Honourable Catherine Bowen have become a legend. They were constantly dashing over to Kilboy, for Prittie reunions and highspeed Dunalley fun: their coach with the four horses forded Farahy stream at the foot of the Bowen's Court woods and pitched up the road that is now a rutted, brambled boreen. ("That," said a very old man to me, pointing into the brambles, "is the road Mr. and Mrs. Bowen took when they would be driving to Lord Dunalley's.") Reciprocal parties were given at Bowen's Court — in those days, parties lasted two or three days; many candles were burnt, the cellar was drawn on steadily. Poor Dorothea Herbert, in her *Retrospections*, gives us some idea of the sort of thing, round Clonmel and at the Waterfords'. (She was a clergyman's daughter, fatally well-connected; she broke her own heart, failed to marry and writes through a mist of queerness: she could not stay the course.) These Bowen-Dunalley parties were of a tempo Henry III's would not have tried to approach; they were the nearest one got to the *beau monde*. Henry IV was "worldly" in the sense that his father had never been. The Berkeleys from Woodville, the Robert Bowens from Mallow looked on, not knowing what to think. Henry IV and his wife have, to my eye, the slight opaqueness of stock figures; they seem to belong more to Maria Edgeworth's fashionable-moral fiction than to the Bowen past. As a child, I used to be told that fashionable people are never truly happy — I never could see why not: such people are busy, they have a ruling idea, an object in life. The family love, which I share, for

Henry III has led, I fear, to a tendency to exalt him at the expense of his son Henry IV. I have even, in spite of proof to the contrary, heard Henry IV accused of having sold Kilbolane in order to pay off gambling debts. In the face of all poor Henry had had to cope with, this does seem to me unfair. He did, it is true, lose our part of a mountain (Quitrent) at cards; his marriage was childless and broke up; he deserted Bowen's Court. But it was his father, dear Henry III, who bequeathed us our lasting embarrassments.

Henry IV and his wife, because they were childless, had her little niece Miss Prittie to live with them. This little girl — " Miss Pretty," we always called her — has left behind her at Bowen's Court not only her legend but the garden she made. Up in a clearing near the Cranes' Wood she tied two young, tender beech saplings together with a bit of twine: now two lordly beech trees stand grown into each other, Siamese twins. A child can just creep through the arch their boles form. Some one under Miss Pretty's direction carried great big stones, almost rocks, and made a ring round the trees — about fourteen feet in diameter, with a gap left to walk in, facing the arch. The bluebells that carpet these woods in May change, round Miss Pretty's Garden, to a delicate mauve-pink: they may be her hyacinths run wild. As a child, I thought a good deal about Miss Pretty: no one could ever tell me enough about her, and no amount of living young company ever quite uprooted her from my heart. Did she have a pony to ride? Did she lie awake upstairs while parties were going on? Was she pretty? — for my pleasure she had to be. Was she lonely? — I must say, I never was. I was only told that she loved her uncle and aunt. Some one heightened my interest by saying she died young. Some one said that, while still a bride, she was killed in the hunting field. What did really become of her I do not know.

And, was Miss Pretty there when Bowen's Court was attacked? If so, was she frightened? What did she say? . . . The attack on Bowen's Court happened in 1798. For the first time, Ireland clashed with the house.

The '98 rising dealt the final blow to the Ireland Grattan had hoped to see, that Ireland he had already saluted on the May day of 1782. The reign of Anglo-Irish high confidence was to be, after all, for less than two decades. For eighteen years Grattan's Patriot Party, with good will throughout the country behind them, fought to integrate Ireland. They failed — why? Why did the promise of 1782 never realize itself? What kept a lacuna between the idea and the fact?

The irony, and the disabling weakness of " Grattan's Parliament " was that it was never Grattan's. His passion for keeping his hands free made him refuse office: he headed the Opposition, but the Opposition was outnumbered enormously. Grattan and Flood were both out to be " thorough " in Strafford's sense, but, as ever, interest stood in their way. The new Constitution was made ineffective by jammed and rotten machinery: Grattan and Flood pressed for the cure of two radical evils; their aims, which were many, had two primary headings — Catholic emancipation, parliamentary reform. These two leaders, who could have been complementary had their joint programme worked out, were unlike in method and temperament: Grattan was aristocratic in outlook, generous, optimistic; from 1782 on he was ready to make to England the gestures of the free equal. Flood, the democrat, took the more stern, disabused, realistic view; he had native suspiciousness deeply inbred in him and was, early, to speak of the " fatal infatuation " of 1782. Events proved him right: Grattan's hopes had been premature.

The representation of Ireland in this new Parliament, as in its predecessors, was no more than travestied. Two thirds of the seats in the House — as Grattan was to throw out in 1790 — were private property. Limited franchise, bought votes and rotten pocket boroughs kept power where interest lay — in reactionary hands. The idea of rival parties was not admitted. The deadening conservatism of Fitzgibbon and Beresford opposed its weight to every Patriot measure. Behind this appeared the unenlightened self-interest of those in office, the Dublin Castle clique. These men in power had much to lose and nothing to gain from change; their assent to the new Constitution had been in form only. Fitzgibbon and Beresford kept in jealous touch with Pitt: removable only by reform, they were in the position to make reform impossible.

And, Ireland's independence was limited: flaws in the new Constitution more and more appeared. The English cabinet could still urge the King to veto bills sent to him through both Irish Houses. The Lord Lieutenant continued to be appointed by England, to be controlled by the English Prime Minister and to receive his instructions from the Home Secretary. If he seemed to exceed his powers in the Patriot interest he could, as in the case of Lord Fitzwilliam, be summarily withdrawn. Thus, Pitt's conservative dominance in England could cement Irish conservatives firmly into their places.

With 1782, things had started grandly enough. The vigour of youth and their first definitive triumph was in the Patriot Party. The horizon was brilliant with possibilities — it is for its possibilities, not for its achievements, that we Anglo-Irish still mourn Grattan's Parliament. There set in a period of prosperity apparent enough to build up a great morale. Revenues increased and were under control of Parliament; the surplus was put to the encouragement of trades and industries, and to public works. The beautification of cities gave the new order visual dignity. And the importance of agriculture was recognized: large areas were put into tillage; Foster's Corn Law of 1784 made this a great corn-growing country; surplus corn found its market in England — already going industrial. Land-value rose, and with it the landlords' rents — which must do much to account for the recuperation of the Bowen finances after the chaos of 1788. In all articulate classes satisfaction was felt.

But this prosperity had its inverse. Money made by trade and industries in the towns did not circulate widely. Slums with their suffering gave the cities' grandness a rotten underlay. Among the peasants and small farmers there were passing sops but no cure for agrarian discontent. The tithe system, the Hearth Tax with their grotesque exactions made decent living impossible; the lack of check on landlord and rack-renter forbade any hope of security for the poor man. Not enfranchised, the mass of Ireland must await any redress the Patriot Party could get for it. The Hearth Tax was remitted in 1783. Generosity was to be hoped for; anything like justice was not even in view.

The Patriot Party was a gentleman's party: it showed all the vision and the *élan* but also the limitations of its class. And its backing — the thousands of Anglo-Irish like the Bowens, who had cheered it in, who continued to wish it well? I fear that here we find a fatal lack of connection between enthusiasm and resolution, between the heart and the guts. We could envisage general reform, but not face the details of sacrifice. We were already committed to a way of living that the old order (whether or not we faced this) did do much to support. Had we truly come up to scratch, perhaps Grattan might not have failed. We did believe we did something: we lived well, we circulated our money, we, consciously or unconsciously, set out to give life an ideal mould. And we were building away: Arthur Young must have voiced the sincere view of his hosts when he wrote, in 1776:

In a country changing from licentious barbarity into civilized order, building is an object of perhaps greater consequence than may at first be apparent. In a wild, or but half cultivated tract, with no better edifice than a mud cabin, what are the objects that can impress a love of order on the mind of a man? He must be wild as the roaming herds; savage as his rocky mountains; confusion, disorder, riot, have nothing better than himself to damage or destroy; but when edifices of a different solidity and character arise; when

Bowen's Court, with Elizabeth Bowen walking across the front lawn

The Approach

The Front Steps. Carson McCullers, in the foreground, plays at driving the veteran racing car belonging to Elizabeth Bowen's cousin Dudley Colley

Dining Room in the big hall, wherein the Bowen portraits hang. Around the table, starting from the left: Ursula Vernon, James Egan, Mary Delamere, Elizabeth Bowen, Stephen Vernon, Iris Murdoch

The Long Room, the core of the house: used as a promenade deck, as a wet-day playroom for people of all ages, and for solitary reflections

Bedroom

Kilbolane House, built by John II nearby the ruined Desmond castle of the same name

Jane Cole, young wife of Henry II, sitting with a toy spaniel on her knee

Henry II, tall with a bony stylishness and something merry about him, who died in the prime of life

Henry III, the builder of Bowen's Court

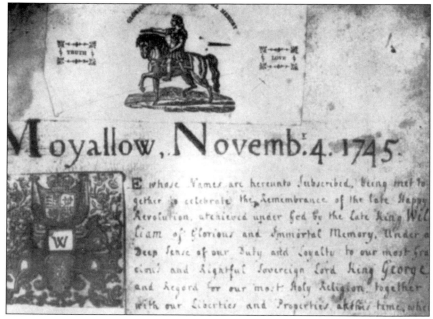

Page from the Moyallow Loyal Protestants' Minute Book, 1745

Page from the Moyallow Loyal Protestants' Minute Book, 1755

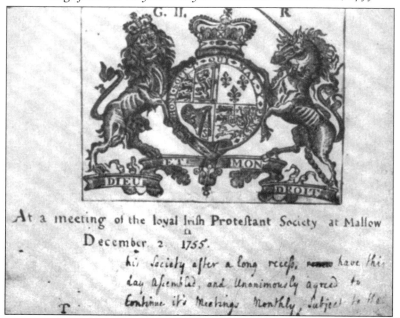

Henry IV, who sold Kilbolane to pay his father's creditors

Elizabeth Clarke, the wife of Robert Cole Bowen

Robert Cole Bowen, who made numerous alterations and improvements in the plantations and Bowen's Court, his nearly revolutionary work being the erection of the "Tower"

Florence Colley Bowen, wife of Henry VI: Elizabeth Bowen's mother

Henry VI, Elizabeth Bowen's father, who broke with tradition to become a barrister

Victorian picture. In the chaise, the widowed Mrs. Henry Bowen (neé Eliza Galwey) and her sister Miss Galwey. Holding the pony, Miss Annie Bowen, unmarried daughter of the old lady. The two children in the nurses' arms are Henry Bowen VI (later Elizabeth Bowen's father) and his sister Sarah.

Aerial view of Bowen's Court

Bowen's Court

great sums are expended, and numbers employed to rear more expressive monuments of industry and order, it is impossible but that new ideas must arise, even in the uncultivated mind; it must feel something first to respect, and afterward to love. . . .

One would like to think so. But what had gone to keep the Irish " uncultivated," savage as their own mountains, brutalized by the very sight of the cabins in which they must, notwithstanding, live? This question was, before the end of the century, to be borne in by rumours of two freed countries, France and America. To the semi-mystic idea of Irish survival, democratic urgency was to be joined.

And, under England's aegis, everything was being done to keep the Anglo-Irish tied to the *status quo*. The more prosperous Anglo-Ireland became, the more it became worth while to flatter her. Crumbs from the English august table were only too eagerly snapped up. I should like to say that the Bowens refused such crumbs, but I fear that, plainly, they were not in the way of any: they were very remote gentry, inactive in public life, not in a big way, not, in short, worth buying. But offices, sinecures, pensions and, above all, peerages did shower on those who were more important, more active or nearer the capital. Thus were mouths that might have spoken for Grattan and progress stopped; eupepsia lulled any dreams of reform. At any possible crisis English far-seeingness authorized, through the Lord Lieutenant, what Professor Curtis has called " an occasional gush of peerages." Arthur Young had said that the number of horses in Ireland was a satire upon common sense: the same came to be true of the number of peers. And after the Union this was even more so.

The Volunteers, the *chevalerie* of Anglo-Ireland, were, by the way, disbanded. Optimistic Grattan saw no more purpose for them after 1782, though Flood, not nearly so certain that Ireland's rights *had* now, in fact, been secured, was all for their continuance. They held a second Convention in '83, and Flood made a bad impression by going on straight from this to the

House in his Volunteer uniform, to introduce his Reform Bill:
intimidation was felt to be in the air. The Bill was, of course,
thrown out. The anti-progressives liked the smell of the Volunteers less and less; the movement clouded over and, together
with Flood's hopes for a Protestant democracy, went into
steady decline: the death-blow came with the Arms Act of
1793. The Volunteers were, in 1796, succeeded by the Yeomanry — aggressively Protestant, officered by gentry holding
the King's commission. Not only musical-comedy brilliance
but idealistic fervour was lacking in this new Yeomanry: their
lack of discipline was notorious, and in '98 they played a. de-
meaning part. The Catholics, excluded, formed that Militia of
which Wolfe Tone was to entertain hopes.

Two crises, two kicks of the heels on the part of Patriot Ireland, went to feed Pitt's apprehensions and tighten the jealous
English hold. In 1784–5 the breakdown of trade talks between
Ireland and England, introduced by Pitt's wishes under the title
of Orde's Commercial Resolutions, put every one out of temper. The original English propositions had been generous
enough: as such, they had been accepted at the Irish end. Then
English commercial interest got several points retracted, and
Ireland, in this case solid behind Grattan, refused to accept the
amended form. Pitt, having sponsored the gesture in an excellent spirit, could only regard this as a rebuff. Then came the
affair of the Regency: in 1788, the year Henry Bowen III died,
George III of England went mad for the first time, and the
question of a Regent had to be faced. Prince George (to be
George IV) commended himself to Ireland in temper, politics,
sympathies; he was young, he was a declared Whig, he looked
like being the Patriot Party's man. While the English Tories,
who did not care for the outlook, were still humming and haw-
ing over formalities, the Patriot Party, led by the Duke of Leinster, chose to use that right of direct approach to the Throne
that the new Constitution had given them: they got passed in
the House, by two votes to one, an address to the Prince urging

him to assume forthwith full royal powers in Ireland. This address reached the Prince (though not through the orthodox
channels, these having been blocked by Pitt) and was received
very graciously. As it turned out, the King's recovery deferred
the Regency question for some time, but this *démarche*, coming on top of the Orde reverse, stamped the idea of Irish menace on Pitt's mind: from then on, the Union came into view.
It would be too grave a charge to bring against Pitt's government to say that, like the English Parliamentarians before 1641,
they fomented trouble in Ireland for their own ends. But certainly, through his agents Fitzgibbon and Beresford, Pitt did
check every reform that could make for Irish peace, or that
could make Grattan's position more tenable.

Even without this unstated intrigue for Union, the French
Revolution set up a conservative panic that, in the ruling classes
in Ireland and England, could only militate against reform. In
Ireland, the old order felt the shock and the threat: the French
King's execution, in 1793, was the signal for several repressive
acts. Simultaneously, though, there was felt a need for concession — to the Roman Catholic church in particular: she was an
influence dead against godless France. One bogy had come to
succeed another; Red France was the terror now, not Rome.
What could stabilize ought to be bolstered up: the Catholic
Relief Act came in 1793.

But concession must be only up to a point. Lord Fitzwilliam,
the Irish landowner and friend of Grattan who became Lord
Lieutenant in 1795, did not clearly enough keep this in view
when he proposed to dislodge Fitzgibbon and Beresford, to
persuade Grattan into office, then to bring full Catholic emancipation into effect. For Grattan, after his struggles, this was
the now or never — and it was to be never. The Dublin irre-
movables kept their close touch with Pitt, and poor George III,
unhappier sane than insane, lent an anxious, addled ear to Pitt's
voice when he was told that to grant further concessions to
Catholics would be a breach of his Coronation oath. There-

upon, he recalled Fitzwilliam. The day Fitzwilliam's carriage
was drawn through her streets to the ship, Dublin black-draped
herself, and she well might — there went the last real hope of
1782.

And the people of Ireland? The crash of the fall of the Bas-
tille, the song on the march to Versailles had not been unheard
in these hearts. Liberty, Equality, Fraternity — the priests
might stand solid in their denunciations, but the people's soul,
between God and the human idea, did not now know which
way to turn. Democratic feeling slowly raised up its head. The
Catholic Committee, for these last years lethargic under the
polite leadership of the Lords Kenmare and Trimbleston, now
ousted the lords and put in their place a Dublin tradesman, the
active Keogh — and this was symptomatic of the new Dublin
spirit. In the North, the Presbyterian democrats were at once
restless and rational. The times were ripe for Wolfe Tone,
child in spirit of the French Revolution, and for his United
Irishmen.

Grattan's programme, even in its intention, seemed to Wolfe
Tone feeble and limited. Tone, watching Grattan's hopes and
his Parliament play themselves out, saw Ireland no more than
mocked by her incomplete liberty. Grattan's civil predisposition towards England had been already called an "infatuation"; Tone saw it as worse, a disloyalty — the coach-builder's
son mistrusted the flourish, disliked the inbred good will. Tone
was a man of the coming century; his hopes belonged to the
new world; his heart already blazed at social injustice, he had
no need to feed on laments and myths. His plan was, simply,
that Catholics and Presbyterians should bury their differences
and stand shoulder to shoulder for freedom as Irishmen. To
oust England, and dislodge the pro-English junta, they should
call in Republican French aid. Revolution was to succeed ineffective reform campaigns. This young Protestant revolutionary turned Deist saw religion as the affair of the private man —
and no more. The setting up of an Irish republic, to be built

on new wide human principles, was Tone's objective. He did not live to compromise, to have his heart broken slowly, to lose height.

With unflagging determination, the United Irishmen continued to plan and arm. Their executive worked in a vital secrecy. The start and head of the movement had been in Belfast; its heart now began to be everywhere. Wolfe Tone went to America to seek help and arms, then from America to France. Rumours, and a sense of tightening intention throughout the country alarmed the government: at the same time, it was felt that it would be well to force things to a head before they could go further — prematurity should be fatal to the United Irishmen. So, a campaign of provocation was entered upon: soldiers whose lack of discipline was an accepted scandal dragooned and ravaged the countryside, North and South. Incidents multiplied; the sense of outrage grew. In May '97, under the dead black of the coming storm, Grattan pressed for the last time for reform of the vote, for proper representation, for Catholic equality. Ponsonby's motion, to which Grattan had spoken, was rejected: Grattan, with his party, formally withdrew from the House. At the general election of 1789 Grattan refused to stand. In March '98 martial law was declared. The United Irishmen timed their rising for May.

May of '98 came. Then, the rising planned to articulate in its every detail was at the last moment shorn of its heads. Government espionage had, it appears, been thorough, and now took deadly effect. Lord Edward Fitzgerald, Arthur O'Connor and others were arrested on the eve of the day. Tone was still in Paris: two French expeditions, raised by Hoche at his instance, having already failed he was now desperately trying to raise a third, but Hoche was dead and Napoleon indifferent. In Ireland, the revolutionaries found themselves new leaders, but exposures, gaps, dislocations were hampering everything. The actual area of the rising, when it did open, was not large: in Ulster and Leinster heroic poorly-armed forces streamed into

the field, to be ridden down, with great losses, by mounted government troops or by Yeomanry. And England, only too glad
to emphasize both the alarm and the Irish government's weakness when it came to the point, poured her soldiers into the
country. Ulster fought on hardily, flying her democrat principles, her all-Ireland hopes. In the South, the fighting finally
concentrated itself in County Wexford: here the peasants,
stocky with Norman and Saxon blood, were urged on and
sometimes led by their priests. Not by the actual fighters but
by their hangers-on there were a number of Protestants massa-
cred. Now it came to actual battle, the new-world rational
principles went to the winds, and Presbyterian Ulster, disenchanted, saw the Catholic South seem to be making '98 only
another religious war.

To this break-up in its initial principle, as well as to military
insufficiency, the '98 rising owed its collapse. The end was to
be foreseen. That the government's victory was not, in the
long run, more inhumanely signalized was largely owing to
Lord Cornwallis, who, in the double office of Lord Lieutenant
and Commander-in-Chief, showed a soldier's good sense in the
matter of peace. His object was settlement, not revenge:
enough damage to Ireland had already been done. It was at his
instance that, after two months of fighting, an Act of Amnesty
was, on July 17th, carried in the Irish Parliament. In Leinster
the last submissions were made. But this was not quite the end:
on August 22nd the third French expedition landed a thousand
Republican soldiers in Killala Bay. This force, joined by bands
of unarmed peasants, routed some Yeomanry and marched on
into the country until they were, by Cornwallis, stopped. That
October Wolfe Tone, in his uniform of adjutant-general in
the French army, was aboard another French ship of the line,
the *Hoche*, that fell prey to an English squadron in Lough
Swilly. Tone was recognized, arrested, taken to Dublin. His
end is known.

In Munster not very much happened. Tone, in the confer-
ences he had had in France, had voiced confidence in the good
will of the priests. Munster alone could have proved him wrong
— here the Catholic clergy, and especially those in the diocese
of the Bishop of Cork, stood out strongly, denouncing associations, suspecting influences from France. In Cork city the two
Sheares brothers were taken and executed for the part they had
played and were ready to play. The North Cork Militia fought
the Wexford rebels. When in June, the second month of the
rising, an alarm that French ships were again in Bantry Bay
led to the calling out, along with a Highland regiment, of the
" armed companies " (Yeomanry) led by the Protestants, we
are told that " a large number of Roman Catholic gentlemen
immediately offered themselves as volunteers to join their Protestant fellow-citizens, and were well received." In fact, class
feeling, or what could be more prettily called a feeling for law
and order, continued, in Munster, to rule the day. (The ships
turned out to be English: everybody went home.) Meanwhile,
the people's own feeling stayed underground: there *was* some
Munster plot but it never became organic. It was Father Barry,
the parish priest of Mallow, particularly active opponent of
" all kinds of United Irishmen," who informed the government
of a plan to capture the town and set some prisoners free.

Such was the rapidity of the organization [says Sir Richard
Musgrave] that in all the countryside contiguous to Mallow,
Doncraile, Charleville, the mass of·the people were sworn, and
all the Protestants were disarmed, within a few nights. . . . An
immense quantity of pikes were fabricated in Cork. Measures
were concerted for taking the magazines, and so sure were the
conspirators of succeeding that poles were prepared, exactly fitting to the socket of the bayonet.

It is possible that the attack on Bowen's Court was a raid for
arms in connection with this abortive plan. But it may have

been — we are left with this impression — a purely free-lance
attempt to loot. Disaffection was in the air of those poisoned
days; there were a dozen reasons to strike at the big house. And
there may have been a drop in the Bowen credit — Henry III,
with his easy good nature and his ruddy good looks, had been
the countryside's man, but his son Henry IV would endear
himself very much less: his Englishified airs, his fine wife, his
unsmiling concentration on pleasure would all tend to keep him
apart and to, to some extent, make a bogy landlord of him. On
top of this, Henry IV held a commission in the Doneraile Yeomanry Cavalry, and the Yeomanry were, as we know, in bad
repute. If loot were the object, one can well understand — rumours of those big showy Bowen's Court parties must have
made the house sound like a sort of Aladdin's Cave.

What happened was this. In 1798 the incumbent of Farahy
was the Rev. Martin Armstrong, an amiable, diligent clergyman who was on warm terms with the Bowen's Court family.
Mr. Armstrong kept a manservant who, I suppose with discretion, frequented the Farahy public house. One evening, I do
not know in what month, Mr. Armstrong's servant learned,
from whispers over the drinks, that Bowen's Court was to be
attacked that night. Going back to the Glebe, he told his master of this. Mr. Armstrong determined to warn the Bowens: it
was by now very dark, very late; unaccountable horse-hoofs
had already passed the Glebe and anything might happen at any
time. The Lower Avenue (down from Bowen's Court door to
Farahy) did not in those days exist: Mr. Armstrong therefore
took a cut through the churchyard and, swift as a rabbit but
very much more intrepid, crossed the Bowen's Court fields by
the track still taken by Bowens late for church. He found the
house standing up black in the dark — every one had, apparently, gone to bed. Mr. Armstrong flung gravel up at the master's window: Henry slept in the East Room (now, Green
Room) over the library. Henry himself (I imagine) impatient,
a few clothes pulled on, came down with a candle, unbarred

the front door, let Mr. Armstrong in. The clergyman, with what breath he had left, would pant out what he had come to say.

Henry was on the whole a sceptical man — but in those days one could disregard no rumour. It was no doubt with angry efficiency that, having roused any other sleepers, he set about preparing the defence of the house. I do not know with whom he manned his defence: the courageous clergyman stayed on to play his part; there would be menservants, and, quite possibly, guests, or one or two visiting Bowen brothers. Bowen's Court — rough and sheer as a fortress on its east and north sides, protected by areas on its two others — is as strong as a fortress, though never meant to be one. The bars on the heavy doors and the shutters would, almost, withstand a battering-ram. And Henry's household was armed. On every floor but the top bars and bolts must now have clattered into their places; inside the unshuttered windows of the top floor the defenders waited, tense, in the pitch dark. Henry kept on his rounds from post to post. It is said that, coming quietly up the stairs to the Long Room, he surprised, at the far end, a maidservant signalling with a candle from one of the windows overlooking the lawn. Whereupon, firing instantly from the top of the stairs, he shot the lighted candle out of the girl's hand.

By 2 a.m. the attackers were round the house: they dismounted, surged up the steps and beat on the big door. Not a sound for a minute — then the shooting began. In the East Room over Henry's some one, flat on the floor, ingeniously drew the attackers' fire by lighting a number of candles as he crawled about, then flashing a board to imitate, on the ceiling, shadows of men moving. Meanwhile, from the pitch-dark windows of other rooms, defenders fired — twice with deadly effect — at spots from which cracks and flashes came. Whether they knew it or not, they got the leader: there was a dragging scuffle down in the dark; the attackers bolted back the way they had come. They took the Fermoy road.

There was a pear tree a few yards down from the south-east corner of Bowen's Court — one surviving shoot of it is in bud as I write. The morning after the raid, this tree was found to bear charnel fruit: a dead man, who must have climbed up to fire, stayed jammed in the fork of two boughs.

The writer of an account of this attack in *The Cork Constitution* of 1863 says:

I remember many years ago an old man living on the Blackwater, some miles from Farahy. He was very lame, and kept secret for some time the cause of his lameness. In latter years he acknowledged that he was one of the party who attacked Bowen's Court, and a ball struck his knee, laming him for life. He said they were unprepared for any defence on the part of the family, and so sure were they of plundering the house, they had come provided with two very large sacks for carrying off plate and other valuables; but when their captain was shot they lost courage and decamped as soon as possible. They carried off the corpse in one of the sacks, and on reaching Rockmills entered the churchyard, dug a grave and buried the leader in his bag.

The old man, who did not seem to mourn very bitterly for the captain, used always, however, to appear much grieved for the afflicting circumstance that in their haste they forgot to take off an elegant pair of boots with which the body was adorned, and in which he considered it " murder " to bury him.

So, the tip, and the very poor shoddy tip, of '98 touched Bowen's Court. In Rockmills churchyard the leader, a farmer of some circumstance, rotted inside the sack, in his fine boots. Up here, they yanked the corpse out of the pear tree; the blooded, ridden-up gravel was raked smooth. Mr. Armstrong's dependable hand was no doubt shaken, and shaken all round again: a memorial with a Latin inscription was to go up to him when he died. Continuous Bowen's Court life resumed its course; after these more than twenty years it would have taken on a sort of unconscious impetus. All the same, something had happened to Bowen's Court — this " edifice of solidity and

character," this " expressive monument of industry and order "
had, now, been the object of an attack. Henry III's house, built
to stand open to friends of all sorts, had had to repel foes. The
memory of that rigid and brutal night has now evaporated: the
house has stood untouched through more dangerous times; that
first attack was the last. But, like the ball left lodged in the old
man's knee, a bitter residuum stayed in Henry IV's heart.

To such hearts the advocates of the Union could now address themselves. I cannot discuss the Union; it was a bad deal:
and it is, or seems to me to be, a tragedy that puts uninformed
comment quite out of countenance. I have tried to suggest some
of the influences, some of the weaknesses that made the descent
to 1800, from 1782, possible. In 1800 the Union became a *fait
accompli:* the facts of it are all known, or to be known, and
must invite an indignation to which I could add nothing by
phrases of mine. This is not a history book, and I am due to
return to my scene now swarming with Bowens. The Union
was against the stated wish of the country; protests against it
came in from every source; meetings to plan resistance were
put down as seditious assemblies; it was forced through an un-
representative parliament. Castlereagh finally engineered it; the
vast sums laid out in bribes and in buying out boroughs were
charged to Ireland's account. Catholic opposition was weakened, in some quarters, by Pitt's promises – which after the
Union were not kept. Prominent Anglo-Irish were bought, to
their lasting dishonour, by peerages, by advancements in the
peerage, and by sums down. (Even in the Unionist society of
my childhood, one spoke with contempt of " a Union peer.")
The main body of Anglo-Irish lords and gentry rallied, too
late, and opposed the Union with passion. But the fundamental
indignity of their position was to be borne in on them by Lord
Clare's speech.
    When " Grattan's Parliament " met for the last time Grat-
tan, in accord with a general wish, was once again in the House.

A seat had been bought for him. He was a sick man. When he rose to speak, he was seen to be wearing Volunteer uniform of 1782. In this, with the force of both a ghost and a man, he spoke as he had never spoken before. But the House had no acoustics; it was already bought, and bought acquiescence deadened it. Then Grattan sat to hear Lord Clare's (Fitzgibbon's) speech on the Bill — a speech of superb detestable realism. On the Anglo-Irish illusion each phrase of Fitzgibbon's fell like a hammer.

What was the situation of Ireland at the revolution? and what is it this day? The whole power and property of the country has been conferred by successive monarchs of England upon an English colony, composed of three sets of English adventurers who poured into the country at the termination of three successive rebellions; confiscation is their common title; and from their first settlement they have been hemmed in on every side by the old inhabitants of the island, brooding over their discontents in sullen indignation. . . . What was the security of the English settlers for their physical existence at the revolution? and what is the security of their descendants at this day? The powerful and commanding protection of Great Britain. If by any fatality it fails, you are at the mercy of the old inhabitants of this island; and I should have hoped that samples of mercy exhibited by them in the course of the late rebellion would have taught the gentlemen who call themselves the Irish nation to reflect with sober attention on the dangers which surround them. . . .

Gentlemen, you cannot have it both ways. . . .

The only Bowen comment, at this juncture, on Ireland, England and France comes from the doubtful Ralph. High and dry in deserted Mallow, on the eve of the Union, in December 1799, he is writing to his brother-in-law John Wight:

My dear Wight,
    I received yours of some time ago, and would have answered it only I was obliged to go to the country, and you know what a

wretched correspondent you have to deal with. It would give me great pleasure to go and visit my friends in Dublin; but my finances are rather confined: though I have many friends that would be happy to lend me money, yet I don't feel comfortable when in debt. You don't mention having heard anything of Mrs. Metge; she has got a young son to their great joy; to be sure she has suffered a good deal, but is getting much better now. There has been as yet very little appearance of anything favourable to this country from the Revolution in France — Buonaparte certainly is a great man; but if he does not endeavour to do something in favour of Royalty, he will not be long for this world, as we all know what a jealous people the French are, and that they will not be fond of having a foreigner at the head of their government. But what do you think of their sending troops from England in such a hurry and in such numbers? When you see the Bishop, remember me to him, as there are few I wish better than him; but he must come and pay a visit and give us his benediction, as our young CLERGY here are going to the DEVIL headlong. It made me happy to find that your young lady had been so fortunate in the lottery — she has begun early and I hope she may continue as lucky through life as she has set out. There is no man in the world would like so much to become a settled married man as your humble servant; but I have been once disappointed (probably for the better), and it is not every moment a man would meet a girl he would like to make his companion for life. We must console ourselves with the idea that there are as good fish in the sea as ever were caught. Mallow was never so stripped as at this season; but I hope by the time you come from Dublin you will find it pleasanter. We have no news in this part of the world. Remember me to Kitty, and believe me,

Yours very sincerely,

R. C. Bowen.

Ralph Bowen wrote from his mother's house. Almost immediately after her husband's death, or, at least, after her eldest son's marriage, Margaret had removed from Bowen's Court to Kilcumer. Here, for a year or two, she and her younger children must have encamped themselves, for I find Henry IV paying rent for Kilcumer on his mother's behalf. But this was to be a no more than temporary home; by July 1789 Margaret had found and taken a house in Mallow; she was only waiting for money from Mr. Evans Bruce to have the house put in repair, furnish it and move in. A saddened and gentle love of society, memories of her young happy married years and the wish to do the best she could for her children must have combined to send Margaret back to the town. I do not know which house she took; if it was not in Mallow it must have been just outside, for I doubt whether Margaret could keep a carriage. Her two youngest children, Edward and Belle, lived with her; her wild sons were thankful, from time to time, to take refuge under her roof, and affection, from 1800 onward, kept good steady Robert close to her side. She only left Mallow for any time when she stayed with the Berkeleys at Woodville.

Margaret's two eldest daughters, Jane and Thomasine, were, as we know, married when she left Bowen's Court. By 1799, I am glad to say, she had seen her three next girls happily settled — Catherine (Kitty) married Robert's friend John Wight, of the County Limerick family; Margaret married William Perry, and Henrietta (the " Mrs. Metge " of Ralph's letter) married John Metge, M.P., of Athlumney, Navan, Neath. Margaret's clergyman son Nicholls was, in 1789, vicar of Ballyfeard, County Cork. John, the black sheep, married in 1796. Stephens, of the 39th and 90th Regiment of Foot, was enough out of debt to marry in 1799 — he was to show a tendency Robert deplored, that of walking out on his children at any time. Stephens, Margaret's " foolish boy," had been also her particular darling: at least, he was not worse than the rest.

Margaret, perhaps, continued to see Mallow all rosy in the light of the past; if she did notice any decline she would attribute this to her own heart. But the next generation had a more

ruthless eye: Ralph, in his letter of 1799, seems to be out of
temper with local life. Economy forced his stay, and he beat
up what fun he could — if the young clergy round Mallow *did*
go to the devil, it may well have been with Ralph's indolent
help. He was ready to see them smoked by his friend the
bishop. But Ralph, apart from his lack of money, his wish to
mate and his temper, really did have some reason to kick his
heels. As a country neighbourhood Mallow was good enough,
but as a Spa, as a place of amusement, no: one must face the
fact that Mallow *had* begun to decline. This was no longer the
theatre of Ralph's father's day. The waters gushing from under
the rock still kept, unchallenged, their qualities. But Mallow
town, if not yet a bare ruined choir, was losing much of its
glamour: the *tempo* was slowing down. There were several
reasons for this. At the height of Henry III's day, in the seventeen-fifties, the word " provincial " in Ireland was geographic
only: distant Dublin was no more than another town. The road
to Dublin was rough, and the promise poor at the end. But
since then, and most of all in the two brilliant decades following
Grattan's triumph, Dublin had taken on, with its European
status, the magnetic glitter of the great capital. If one could not
make it, one yearned for it. The provinces became " only "
the provinces. Tastes sophisticated, the standard of life went
up, and those shortcomings of Mallow, clear to Arthur Young,
began, these days, to be felt by all.

Unfairly, Dublin's losing of lustre with and after the Union
only had on Mallow a further adverse affect. The first circles of
Irish fashion followed the Parliament to across the water, and
envious eyes looked after them. The great failure, and the
knockout home truths in Fitzgibbon's speech, were burnt into
every gentleman's consciousness. If we *are*, then, no more than
England's creatures, let us cash in on her smart and her monied
fun. A masochistic attraction towards England — too unwilling
to be love — in the Anglo-Irish began, from now on, to be evident. Anglo-Ireland had suffered, with the Union, a vital shock

to its self-respect. So, the poor " Bath of Ireland " lost its hold on gentry who had the real Bath, the Bath of England, in view. Though the Mallow seasons continued, they began to be admittedly second-rate. . . . December in Mallow had been an off-season at the best of times. In 1799, when Ralph Bowen wrote his letter, the after-effects of the '98 panic and the cold forecast shadow of the Union were, simultaneously, in the air.

Happily, we have not all the same ideas. Dear good Robert Cole Bowen, Henry III's fourth son, returning from foreign service to make an extended stay with his mother, found Mallow everything he could ask. Dissipation was not Robert's object; he wished for sport, mainly hunting, and the congenial society of the small country house. The sweet moist bright-green Blackwater valley, flyblown Mallow main street with its familiar faces, Mallow comings and goings, even the Mallow rain delighted him after the glare abroad. Moreover, his mother had waiting for him a circle of most agreeable friends — he was soon *au mieux* with the Galweys of Bearforest; the young Galweys were just at the merry age. And, Robert had a fine bump of family feeling; his happy relations before and after his marriage with his sister Jane Berkeley and her husband, and his sister Kitty Wight and her husband John, make a nucleus, rather badly needed, to the otherwise scattered Bowen family life.

Robert's chronology, up to 1800, is very obscure. There are wisps of family legend, but no exact dates. For some years *after* 1800, his excellent letters allow us to keep a check on every movement he made. As we noticed, a commission for Robert — in Sir John Carden's Regiment of Cavalry — had been the subject of one of Margaret Bowen's letters to Mr. Bruce in 1794. At the same time, it is on positive record that Robert served in India for several years — but for which years? — with the 52nd Regiment. Then there is the — completely unverifiable — story of the Duel: Robert is said to have taken part, as an ensign, in the last duel fought in the British Army. In the mess, some re-

mark of a slighting nature was made at Robert's expense, and
his Colonel drew his attention to it in such a manner that
Robert could not but take the matter up. He called his man, a
superior officer, out, and very severely wounded him. Duelling
was then on the rocky side of the law, and the officer's relatives
chose to make such a fuss that the incident terminated Robert's
Army career. But this happened — if it did happen — when he
was in his teens. By 1794, when Margaret wrote her letter, he
would have been twenty-five: was he — depressing thought —
on Margaret's hands again, and was she, in applying for the
Carden commission, trying to slip him back into the Army by
a back door? We can, I fear, only leave it that Robert *was* in
India, but that we cannot hope to know when. At all events,
here he is in 1800, aged thirty-one, back in Mallow for good,
out of the Army and showing all possible signs of unblemished
character: nothing, in his own or any one else's opinion, seems
to have impaired his reputation for steadiness. The contempt
with which, later, he speaks of his " military brothers " shows
he did not reproach himself with lack of ambition, and suggests
there had been no shadow on his own Army career. Just now,
on his return there to the neighbourhood, he is fresh from a
duty visit to Bowen's Court. He found life there — as he let out
to the Wights and Berkeleys — a good deal too grand for his
tastes, under Henry IV's and " Her Ladyship's " rule. No, give
Robert, on June 30th, 1800, Mallow, the Galweys and billiards,
any day. He is writing to John Wight:

*We will be glad to see you here, and the sooner the better. There
is famous billiard-playing; there are some of the officers of the
King's County that play very well, and will oblige you with any
bets, and always back the master, as he still excels in the game of
billiards. You must be on your good behaviour before the strange
gentleman. . . . You will make a man of me if you can procure
me a piece or two of hickory to make a couple of cues: it must be
five feet two inches long, straight grained, free from knots, and as*

straight as an arrow. . . . I sent to Cork and could not find a
morsel there.

Robert, though he had the best of hearts, was also, I am sorry
to find, touchy. He was upright, he was in general contented,
he showed considerable will, but he had one of those soft-soiled
natures in which sense of a grievance, real or imaginary,
ploughs its furrow. His ruling and I fear his warping grievance
was on the old subject of Kilbolane — of which much more
later. But he was also rather easily huffed: in a letter to John
Wight about a dog he shows "feeling" about Henrietta
Metge:

Whenever you go to Dublin, give Henrietta a good deal of
abuse for forgetting us all, and particularly me. I always thought
she had good nature and a little sincerity till now: it is the way of
the world in general, out of sight out of mind.

And the relation between Robert and Henry? This could
hardly have been more difficult. Remember Robert's position
under their father's will — Robert was that fourth son named to
succeed to Bowen's Court should Henry IV fail to have heirs.
By 1800, when Robert returned to Mallow, Henry and the
Catherine *née* Miss Prittie had been married for eleven years;
there were no children, and there were to be none. Robert's affection for County Cork was well formed; he looked more and
more like being tied to it by the place. Robert, staying on in
and around Mallow in a state of rather bourgeois content, must
have appeared to the irate and chagrined Henry to be only
waiting to step into Bowen's Court. (I doubt that he was,
really: Robert's ideas were on a smaller, triter and cosier scale.)
Robert's oppression when he came on visits to Bowen's Court,
and the cheeriness with which he skipped back to Mallow,
must have been plain to all. And there were more serious reasons for dissonance: not only had Robert one ruling suspicion
but he considered Henry, in all matters of money, indolent,

cynical, even unscrupulous: he did not think Henry had treated
the rest of the family, especially the excellent Wights, well. He
says as much, in November 1801, in another of his letters to
John Wight:

As to your money matters with Henry, I wish with all my heart
they may be amicably adjusted; at the same time he is very indo-
lent in not giving you every answer necessary; but when he neg-
lects his own affairs it can't be expected — though it is no excuse.
As to consulting him about my own money, or on any occasion
whatsoever, I never did or will, as he never seemed inclined to put
any confidence in me, or, as far as I could observe, in any of his
own family. . . . In my opinion, divisions in a family ought to
be avoided as much as possible — indeed it would be better if we
had not so many as we have already: but you are very differently
circumstanced from me, as neither you nor Kitty have been hand-
somely treated by him.

And here, again from Robert to John Wight, this time in
1803, is really rather an ugly flash: Robert shows no patience
with the Honourable Mrs. Bowen:

Henry was here the other day, and pressed Edward and me to
go to Bowen's Court, which we could not do on account of the
Yeomanry; but I understand her Ladyship, with her usual good
disposition, said we were glad of any excuse not to go; but if I
hear her, I'll tell her our real motive for not wishing to be in her
house.

Decidedly Robert, like Ralph, was beginning to need a wife.
The first flush of pleasure from the return to Mallow was over,
and for all his good nature and his high spirits a nervy celibate
pettiness threatened to close him in. Besides, he had lost his
mother: Margaret, whose health had for some time been failing, died either at Mallow or Woodville in 1802. She took with
her, and most of all from Robert, her great gift, that of making
a home. Her warm, sweet, mannerly and, through all troubles,

tranquil presence, to which Henry III had turned for their married twenty-eight years, must have been bitterly missed by Henry III's fourth son. Robert was, I imagine, now left to keep house with his youngest sister, Belle — Edward, about this time, got a commission in the 40th Regiment of Foot. Belle — I wonder why? — did not settle for many years: she was well into her forties when she married, at St. George's Church, Limerick, Captain Edward Sheffield Casson, late of the 18th Royal Irish Regiment.

The last pre-marital touchiness in Robert — after which we can tell a happier tale — appears in November 1805:

I have had a letter from Edward this day, containing an account of his having lost his pocket-book, which contains his bill and some other money — one word of which, I am sorry to say, I don't credit — and begging we may try and send him another bill and expedite his getting his money from Henry. I am certain it is nothing more than a scheme to endeavour to make out more money. His regiment are stationed at Boxhill Barracks, Sussex. I hope he may do well, but I have my doubts — it would be a lucky circumstance if he were on foreign — he might be out of the way of temptation. Nothing provokes me as much as the unsteadiness of my military brothers; they all go to their regiment for six months, and then they are quite satisfied they have seen service, without being a bit better or more respected, and return home.[1] They have none of them proper pride or spirit, or they'd remain until they became independent. Mrs. Ralph has produced another young lady; she is very well and pretty; Ralph as handsome as ever, and very busy farming.

Ralph Bowen, we must be glad to hear, had by now met a girl that he felt he *would* like to make his companion for life. Early in 1804 he had married Miss Mary Doherty, of Mount Bruis, County Tipperary. From Robert we learn of her good

---

[1] The military brothers did *not*, really, do so badly. Several of them are heard of on foreign fields — one, I think Edward, was wounded at Waterloo.

looks, from Ralph's new prosperity, that she must have had
money. Ralph's charm so gained his father-in-law Mr. Doherty,
an otherwise rather difficult man, that he cut his own sons out
of his will and left Mount Bruis to Ralph and Mary together.
It was there, I imagine, that Robert found Ralph " busy farming." And the young couple were busy founding a line. Marriage seems to have done for Ralph all he had hoped — at least,
in 1805, his shares with Robert stand high.

Robert's courtship of Miss Eliza Galwey must, by this year,
have already begun — the Mount Bruis idyll might stimulate it.
Ardour, succeeding to sociability, now made Robert daily frequent Bearforest. This house (I do not know the origin of its
interesting name) stood, and its successor of the same name
stands, on a hill south of Mallow, across the Blackwater bridge.
At the opposite end of the town to Annabella, it has a site as
beautiful — Nagles Mountains rise on its south side; on the
other opens a wide view; the Blackwater sweeps the base of the
hill. To Bearforest front door from the Mallow road a beech
avenue takes a mounting curve.

The Galweys came from the West. I have been told that
they came from Galway city itself, that they were originally
Burkes (one of the great Galway merchant families) and that
wish for distinction mixed with nostalgic pride made them
change their name to Galway or Galwey when they came to
Mallow. In Mallow they carried on the merchant prince tradition: they were exceedingly capable in business; they enjoyed
good living that they could well afford. William Galwey's
family, at Bearforest, were made more interesting by mixed
blood: Mrs. Galwey's father had been a Limerick Wight (a
connection of Robert's brother-in-law John), her mother had
been Anne Dupont, of a Huguenot family that had settled in
County Cork. Bearforest had been a Dupont House. And the
Dupont strain showed in the two successive Misses Galwey who
became Bowen brides — they were both energetically religious
in the bleak French Calvinistic rather than in the gothic-emo-

tional Irish Protestant sense; they showed business ability and they were *maîtresses femmes*. In fact, they did much to bolster up the by now rather etiolated Bowens. They also introduced into the Bowens two Dupont christian names, St. John and Anne.

(The accretion of christian names, as a family goes on, is interesting. When the Bowens arrived from Wales their three stock names had been Henry, John, Elizabeth. William (the first William Bowen was John I's and Mary Nicholls' second son) may have come in from the Nicholls. Nicholls itself then became a christian name. The great Mrs. Bowen of Kilbolane, *née* Catherine Stephens, introduced Catherine and Stephens — and Thomasine may have come from her family. Jane Cole, the next bride, brought in Robert and Jane. Ralph and Edward both came from the Warter Wilsons; Margaret Wilson added Margaret to the stock. The reason for Henrietta is obvious. The Galwey-Duponts, as I have just shown, were responsible for St. John and Anne. My grandmother, the second Robert Cole Bowen's wife, brought Charles and Otway from her Clarke family.)

William Galwey of Bearforest had been, you may remember, one of the two new trustees appointed, under the *Grove v. Bowen* settlement, to administer Henry III's will. He was, in addition to this, Henry IV's agent. But the Bowen's Court business, though he attended to it with minute care, was small beer for Mr. Galwey, who held agencies to important landlords all over the South. Many of these gentlemen were absentees already — first Dublin claimed them, later London and Bath — and the wholesale remove of grand Ireland after the Union left more and more business on Mr. Galwey's hands. Temperament and ability suited Mr. Galwey exactly for the part that he had to play — alas, though, he came to like the ways of the great too well: in the end he could not subsist without the highest society.

William Galwey is said to have had nine children, though

not all of them grew up. Eliza, at the time of her marriage, was his second living daughter; another daughter married a Mr. Creagh. One of his sons, St. John Galwey, succeeded — it must have been difficult — in being at once the warm friend of Henry *and* Robert Bowen; he was a physician and lived in one of those grey-fronted houses that dignify Mallow street. In time, he had a daughter, Eliza — of whom we hear again. When William Galwey decided to add to his other business that of a banker, he gave up Bearforest and moved into Mallow town, where he took the house next door to his son's.

Robert Cole Bowen and Eliza Galwey married in the early summer of 1806. Robert gave up the house that had been his mother's and moved into another — again I do not know which: Robert never heads his letters anything but " Mallow," being Bowen enough to feel this sufficient address. Everything went excellently: the Wights were delighted; the Berkeleys came to dinner almost at once. In the autumn, the Robert Bowens paid a two months' visit to Woodville; they were allowed to leave Woodville at the end of November only on condition that they returned in January. They were back in time for a quite important event — Bowen's Court, after an interval long enough to be marked, decided to pay its wedding call. Robert appears to have bolted at the sight of the carriage, and to have stayed out till it drove away again:

Mrs. Bowen paid Eliza a visit for the first time since we were married, a great deal too long for my peace of mind, as she kept me from home for above an hour; she made a great many protestations — I am sure without any meaning.

Ten days later, this visit is still rankling with Robert; he tells John Wight about it all over again:

I received a note from the Squire of Tarraby [I take it, Henry IV] requesting I would inform you of his having lodged your money in the Bank of Mallow. . . . Mr. Bowen has been complaining that some of the tenants were backward in their pay-

*ments; if they have begun so early what will they be in some time
hence? They were both here the day he lodged the money, for
the first time since we were married; nor do I think she would
have come now only she had a visit to pay to Mrs. Pigott.*

Nowadays, however, there was always Eliza to calm Robert
down: there is evidence that Eliza liked the Honourable Mrs.
Bowen no better than he did. In the summer of 1807, Eliza, a
little bit out of health, went with her mother to Kinsale for the
sea bathing; in August Robert and her brother St. John Galwey
joined her there. Woodville, though virtually a parsonage,
would have been no place for a quiet rest: not only do Mr.
Berkeley's frequent attacks of gout suggest that, like *Mansfield
Park's* Mr. Grant, he was over fond of good living but, from
another of Robert's letters to John Wight, we gather that
Woodville was the centre of a quite rakish life. (*Note:* is " the
Baron " Henry IV again?)

*The Baron was not a bit displeased at your taking the mare to
Bruff, nor would he, I believe, if you had taken her farther. Some
of his friends, I think his piece, sent a report about the town that
you and I had won 26 guineas of the public money from him at
Woodville; he is bad enough without our assistance, or that of
scandal-makers. . . . God send there may be another election in
County Tipperary; and that the Protestant may be returned.*

The Kinsale bathing set Eliza up for a new important ordeal:
on the 28th of January 1808 Robert is able to write in triumph:

My dear John,

*I have great pleasure in informing you my dear Eliza produced
a young fox this morning, about five o'clock, and though weak
she is, thank God, as well as might reasonably be expected. You
should have heard from me by the coach this morning, only poor
Eliza gave us an alarm: however, with the help of God she has been
mending ever since. I am sure this event will give Kitty joy. I
heard from the Berkeleys a few days ago; he was recovering from*

gout, the rest very well. Mr. Galwey has been in that way, but getting better. Mr. Don is not expected to live a day, and Mr. Flynn (the Physician) thinks he has water on his chest: he looks wretchedly.

When you write to Dublin, let them know what I have told you of Eliza having unkennelled a fox, to use a sportsman's phrase. We have no news, so good night, with best love to Kate.

Believe me, yours very sincerely,

R. G. Bowen.

The young fox was Henry V. In time, his parents were to give him two brothers, Robert and Edward, and one sister, Elizabeth. The news of his birth was received at Bowen's Court with, as far as I know, no comment at all.

These days, Robert felt as right as a bell. What he actually *did* with himself all day in Mallow I am not clear, and I doubt if he was himself. He must, I think, have been one of those characters whose moral and sober self-application to the doing of nothing particular places them on a high plane. Tireless people who never let up a moment are quite often less respected and liked. Robert was not only a good fellow; he knew just how everything should be done. His play days — if one may call them so — were numbered: Bowen's Court was waiting to swallow him. Robert was ever ready to listen to duty's call — did he know how near, round the corner, his duty was?

Meanwhile his years in Mallow rolled by, merry and decorous. Kitty Wight was spared by her husband John to spend part of a winter with the Robert Bowens. Eliza's sister Helen got married to Andrew — and there were great doings. A Mr. Latouche, very rich and a great Methodist, proposed for a Miss Cotter and was accepted. Robert and John Wight shared a try in a lottery. The Berkeleys came to Mallow for Mr. Berkeley's gout; they took Mr. Franks' house and Jane rather tried Robert by not bringing the Berkeley carriage to town. While in Mallow the Berkeleys had a good maid, Anne, tempted away from

them by Mrs. de la Cour. Robert failed to control his attacks
of nerves each time Eliza approached a lying-in, so John Wight
came on visits to cheer him up.

Henry IV was tried by no lyings-in, but he lived at a nervous
tension that wore him down. Like a fever ennui, indolence,
moodiness worked in him. To his house he was not a good master, to his estates not a good landlord — and one may be sure he
felt this: he was not without self-respect. But he could no
longer cope: he left more and more of his business to Mr. Galwey, and what Mr. Galwey did not do was not done. His
tenants fell behind with their rents; his cottages fell into shocking disrepair. He left his farm to his bailiff. He had wrung every
possible pleasure from Bowen's Court, and the house now sat
on top of him like a tomb. Henry was sensitive to any decline
in fashion — since the Union, Ireland was not the place to be in.
The best (in his eyes) of his set were already in Bath or London: if they ever thought of him it was no doubt with pity —
poor old Bowen, stuck there in County Cork. And Henry was
fed up — no other word for it — with the rest of the Bowens
and their ways. The Robert-Wight-Berkeley alliance no doubt
galled him. (This little circle was sadly broken into, in 1814,
by poor Mr. Berkeley's death.) On the other hand, there were
the " military brothers " — *they* were a pretty pack.
     And Henry's personal life had gone bad at the core: he and
his wife were now steadily falling out. I do not know why, and
it is not my affair. Her Ladyship's character is a sealed book to
me. If Henry *is* " the Baron " of Robert's letter, his infidelities
were, apparently, known. One of the reasons given for his
flight to England is that he had an inamorata there. I seem to
remember hearing my father say: " He ran away and lived with
some one in Bath." I have heard other allusions to " a lady in
Bath." My father never said anything more than this — he did
not wish to seem to censure his great-great uncle, and he was
delicate on the subject of private life. I doubt whether, if

Henry *had* this passion, it burned with a very vigorous flame; above all his was a tired nature, and tired natures are not fuel for love. His restlessness was of the nerves more than the heart.

Why, Henry must have increasingly asked himself — making the fagging rounds, hearing the sickening complaints, paying the endless bills — should he rust here, in a shabby depleted society, with a cold wife, by a dull hearth, simply to keep the place on for Robert's son? Could he let the place fall down? Well no, not exactly: after all, it was Bowen's Court. Then, who was to keep it? Why not Robert — Robert the heir-apparent, whose son was heir after him? Let Robert — who set such store by the family — become Henry's tenant, pay rent for the house and demesne and make what he could out of them (that was Robert's affair). Robert's life, so far, had been remarkably easy: let Robert step into the breach now. Let Robert keep up the place for his young fox. Robert had been quick off the mark as a critic; it was now high time that he tried his hand. . . . The idea grew in Henry, and he acted on it.

Negotiations followed. There was a sort of good sense about the proposed arrangement that Robert, as Henry V's father, could not ignore. The negotiations — I do not know after how long — culminated in my one at all authentic piece of Bowen family dialogue. Henry and Robert met in Mallow, at the house of a mutual friend, who took their conversation down:

Conversation in presence of Robert de la Cour, Esq., between Henry C. Bowen and Robert C. Bowen, Esq., relative to letting Bowen's Court to Robert C. Bowen, 25th Oct., 1816.
After the usual salutation,

Hen^y.   You shall have the place for one hundred and fifty pounds per Annum.

Robt.   I consider that too high, and will give you one hundred pounds per Annum.

Hen^y.   The devil is in it, if the House, and demesne of one hundred and fifty acres are not worth one pound per Acre.

Robt. *Certainly, they are worth considerably more, but I am undertaking the protection of the place for you, am interested in doing so on account of my family, and am giving up an establishment much better suited to my income, nor do I know how it may turn out. I will give up the place most cheerfully at the end of one year.*

Hen^y. *You shall have it; I shall not return for three years, perhaps not for seven.*

Robt. *I expect you will not dispossess me for any other person.*

Hen^y. *I will not, I have always kept my word. Except in the case of Mrs. Bowen or I coming to reside here, then you shall have six months notice. You are to commence rent the 25th of March next.*

Robt. *Am I to pay anything until March?*

Hen^y. *No.*

Robt. *I asked him for an old horse, car, plough and harrow, as necessary to carry on the business of the place, which were refused but afterwards consented to.*

  The above Statement is, to the best of my recollection, the purport of the conversation that passed between Mr. Bowen and Mr. Robert Bowen on the subject to which it relates.

                                        (signed) Robt. de la Cour.

  So, it was settled. Mrs. Bowen removed to Dublin, where she took a house — No. 50 Upper Mount Street. Henry made her allowance of £1,500 a year. There is no reason to think that they met again. Henry, no doubt, would be punctilious enough to make her a last bow from the steps as her carriage drove off up the Bowen's Court avenue. Perhaps, as he turned back into the silent house, the thought of Eliza succeeding " her Ladyship " allowed him one satirical smile.

  His own departure took place sometime in the winter of 1816–17. " I shall not return for three years, perhaps not even for seven," he had told Robert. He made the preparations of one who does not mean to return at all. The estate papers were already with Mr. Galwey; he sent more personal papers to Mr. Tydd of Clonmel. Did the drawings of Bowen's Court — Bath might like to see them — go quietly into one of his valises? One could love Henry IV for even one touch of naivety. A query hangs over his state of mind as he supervised that solitary packing-up in the grey of the steadily-falling winter rain — County Cork rain he was to see no more. Henry was now a man of fifty-two: he was going away to Bath to pursue pleasure. Inside himself he was in an empty room.

The last morning, the coach waited at the foot of the steps. From the steps, Henry would give that accustomed look at the sky without which no Bowen ever leaves his door. He looked at nothing else; he immediately nodded for the coach to drive on. The equipage rocked slightly over familiar bumps in the avenue; at expected places branch-tips brushed the top. They turned out of the gates. Henry IV sat well back from the windows, with no thoughts at all and a shut heart.

HENRY V

AT MALLOW, TOO, THEY WERE PACKING UP. THEY MIGHT HAVE been going to move a thousand miles. Henry V, now a child of eight years old, watched the house he had known always being taken to bits. When one is a child, the disposition of objects, tables and chairs and doors, seems part of the natural order: a house-move lets in chaos — as it does for a dog. And the family orchestration, those months when the move was pending, must have been rather queer. At the same time, children like change — for one thing, they never anticipate regret. When I hear of children crying at leaving their old homes, I see the foul work of grown-up sentiment. Henry, at all ages courteous and tactful, no doubt kept out of his parents' way. But I can imagine him, irrepressibly, saying:

" Are we really going to Bowen's Court? "

" Yes — now be a good boy."

" Will Uncle Henry be there? "

" No."

" Then what shall we do there? "

" Live . . ."

Ironically, Henry V could have been a son after the heart Henry IV might have had. He was tall, well-mannered, very good-looking. He seems to have had an inherent sweetness of nature that could have sweetened life for any parent of his. He could have admired the world without being corrupted by it. I have seen one picture of him, a large miniature, in my Aunt Sarah's house — alas, I do not know where the miniature is now. The young man looks more *racé* than, as a Bowen, he was. The narrow face and long features that in Henry IV look forbidding and saturnine, are, in Henry V, informed by a sort of glow. Ardour, dignity, understanding show in his eyes and forehead. Here seems to be a spirit content to reserve itself; at the same time, Henry seems to await some distinction life never allowed him — his life was to be short. He was a young man of the Romantic age; an idealized Paris should have been his home; he would have liked to go to the Opera, to make oblations at impossible shrines. As it was, he was to live rather strictly in County Cork, to become a J.P. and to make roads.

Let us leave it that Henry seems a curious child for dear bumbly Robert and rather severe Eliza to have brought into the world.

Some time in the winter of 1817 — I do not know how many weeks after Henry IV's carriage wheels rolled away — the Robert Bowens, with their four children, moved into Bowen's Court. The house, not unkindly, eyed them. The silence displaced itself, but hung up near the ceilings above the encamped family; the rooms, after Mallow, seemed very, very high. In the evenings, Eliza's allowance of candles was just enough to show the rest of the gloom; her fires flickered some way back in the grates. Metaphorically or actually, the rings left by Henry IV's guests' glasses were still all over the furniture. The lovely circular card tables showed worn, grease-spotted tops — but this did not matter, for they were put away. Eliza Bowen passed from room to room, distastefully sniffing the moral air.

Robert, from now on, becomes rather a sad, because a displaced, figure. The animation of Mallow, where he had gone down so well, was all behind him now. At Bowen's Court he was never truly "the Master"; he was his brother's tenant, his son's regent. Estate management, at which he was a complete novice, was to claim every minute of his waking life: if he ever drove the thirteen miles into Mallow it was to do business or lodge money in banks — and he was lucky if there were any to lodge. (Meanwhile in Bath Henry IV continued to draw, and spend, the Farahy and Ballymackey rents: "*He there kept his carriage,*" St. John Galwey says, "*and lived in a corresponding manner, and apparently in affluent circumstances.*") All over the demesne and the home farm Robert found damage he could not hope to repair. The struggle was most disheartening. Eliza not only practised rigid economy but, also, helped in the super-vision — but even so they could not make ends meet. Poor Robert — "*I asked him for an old horse . . .*"

And, at the end of the first uphill year, a year in which the danger of his commitments and the sweetness of the security he had left behind had both fully dawned on Robert, there was a nightmare crisis: Henry, in order "to increase his income," proposed to turn Robert out of the place instanter if he did not come across with £50 a year more. He also seems to have im-plied that Robert was by now behind with his rent. In February 1818 we find Robert, no doubt with Eliza's collaboration, writing this letter from Bowen's Court:

Dear Henry,

When you offered me Bowen's Court nothing but a considera-tion for the place itself and its preservation could have induced me to accept of it. I had no vanity to indulge, no hopes of profit to realize. Altho' my income was scanty in Mallow, yet so were my taxes, my rent and my expenditure — I was independent and out of debt. I could give no stronger proof of my feelings on the occasion than by expressing to all my friends my fixed resolu-tion not to make the change unless I got Bowen's Court £50 per annum under what you demanded. I can confidently appeal to Mr. de la Cour and many others that those were my sentiments then. What is my situation now? I find myself cruelly involved in pecuni-

ary engagements, contracted certainly some of them with my eyes
open from the construction put by Mr. de la Cour and myself, and
my implicit faith in your words — others of them incurred insensi-
bly, and by the necessary expenses of providing farm implements,
collecting manure, repairs about the place and providing a large
family for the first year from distant markets — after which period
I naturally expected some return for the money spent on coming
here, the inconveniences attending which have been severe indeed,
from my having given up my house which now lets for a higher
rent than I paid, and the wear and tear and carriage of my furniture. The manure you speak of giving me I put out at considerable
expense on your grounds, of which I hoped to derive profit hereafter, but it is obvious I could not as yet have benefited. The sow-
ing of the grounds last year happened to be when Wheat was three
Guineas a bag, and being without Horses I was obliged to pay for
the ploughing and it consequently turned out to be an unprofitable crop. I mention this merely in reply to one of the advantages
attended to in your letter to Mr. de la Cour. To another observa-
tion of yours, " that I proposed to commence rent on the first of
May," I most solemnly protest against my having specified any
Galeday or having ever proposed for a foot of ground in my life,
tho' you yourself particularized the 25th March. In allusion to
your intention of dispossessing me unconditionally — to show the
impression on Mr. D.'s mind and my own I state precisely his
words — " I can and will give my oath that Harry Bowen pledged
himself more than once to Robert not to disturb him unless for
Mrs. Bowen or himself and that the inference was then plain on
my mind that Robert's losing the place depended upon the con-
tingency of Mr. and Mrs. Bowen being reunited." With this conviction of your intention, surely it is not unreasonable for me to
expect such compensation for my losses as shall place me in the
situation which I was invited to abandon? Particularly when I
showed so ready a disposition to give you possession at any time
you wished, on those terms. I did hope that my proposal of sub-
mitting my case to the arbitration of friends was the very one that

you yourself would, in case of difficulty, have suggested, and adopted. As to the manner of your proceeding upon this unfortunate occasion, I shall only make the reflection, that the line of conduct that I have always and, please God, will always continue to pursue must make any unbrotherly or hostile step towards me unmeritted on my part. The fact is you have made me completely in your power, and if you harshly exercise that power by depriving me of Bowen's Court so suddenly it will be my inevitable ruin. But, if your motive is, as you say, only to increase your income, then (as the least injurious mode of dealing by me) name what you think I could in reason hope to make it, and allow me to remain on such terms until I can breathe gradually from under my present difficulties.

Believe me yours very sincerely

Robert C. Bowen.

Henry, after consideration, drew his horns in. We do not know if he blushed — we must remember that among Henry III's eight sons the standard in brotherly conduct was not high; in fact only poor Robert had any notion of it. Robert was, it is true, in Henry's power. But Henry, in so far as convenience went — and convenience was a great object with him — was also to a certain extent in Robert's: should Robert allow himself to be bullied out of the place, Bowen's Court, with all attendant worries, would be back on to Henry's hands again. Henry might even be plucked from Bath, and Bath was all he had hoped; he had nothing against it but its expensiveness — and the lady, if any, was no doubt expensive too. Things could no longer be shelved on to Mr. Galwey, for Mr. Galwey was in Mallow no more. Where was he? He had followed Henry to Bath — last elderly swallow seeking the sun of fashion he had, in 1817, resigned his agencies, wound up his affairs and, leaving his own and his clients' papers in irreproachable order in an office in his son St. John's house, crossed the sea forever. Mr. Galwey's arrival in Bath must have been like the simple notion of arrival in Heaven — there, rank on rank, stood the bless'd, all smiling away; some familiar faces, some known only in fame. He had now every right to enjoy himself; he had worked hard and faithfully, and, unlike Henry IV, he was here at no one else's expense. We must hope that he did, in his four years — Mr. Galwey left Bath for Heaven in 1821.

Accordingly, Henry now did his correspondence with Robert through Mr. Tydd of Clonmel. But even this meant writing to Mr. Tydd. It was all very trying, and simply must not go on.

The end of it was that Henry, in April 1818, offered Robert a lease of Bowen's Court for the term of his, Henry's, life. Robert was to take less land, thus reducing his liabilities and expenses, but was to pay at a higher rate — thirty shillings instead of a pound an acre — for the land he did take. This offer of Henry's had involved a decision that must have been repugnant to him. It meant facing a fact — which, as I have pointed out, few Bowens cared to do — it amounted to saying: " I have gone away forever; I shall never come back." If Robert accepted the lease, Henry signed away Bowen's Court to him, as John I (and for much the same reason) had signed away Farahy to Captain Nicholls. Robert did accept the lease. He asked that there should be as few legal formalities as possible, in order to save expense. He asked also that the plantations — slow returns, heavy upkeep — should not be included in his land. He was being severely put to it, at the moment, by having to re-roof the offices — the slates had all blown off in the last storm.

Henry suggested that Robert should run over to Bath for a day or two, to see him and talk things over. Robert replied that he could not. " Should you come this way," he adds with some dignity, " we will be exceedingly glad to see you here."

We may be sure that Robert, like John II, took no step without consulting his wife. With Eliza, the dominant woman reappears in the Bowens. Though less rough and more sprightly

she is a fit successor to, and could have been a match for, the
great Mrs. Bowen of Kilbolane. Pro-and-con talks with Eliza,
perhaps nocturnal, must have preceded every decision; Eliza's
pointed phrasing seems to appear in that last letter of Robert's.
In consenting to make the move to Bowen's Court I feel sure
that Eliza, also, had " had no vanity to indulge." There is no
reason to think that the house impressed her: as William Galwey's daughter she must have constantly heard of, and no
doubt been often taken to visit, very much larger houses with
very much grander names. If Eliza did not belong to the *beau
monde*, she exactly understood its degrees. She could measure
pretension with a discerning eye. Although she loved Robert,
perhaps because she loved Robert, she saw exactly where the
Bowens got off. She must have watched, with malice and humour, " her Ladyship " queening it, and she had no desire to do
the same. The men of her own family, able and popular, had
given the Galweys status: this was enough for Eliza. She must
have seen clearly that to take on Bowen's Court would mean
worry for Robert, a hard life for herself and a wretched inheritance, should they fail, for her son. But this last would be
still more wretched if they did not try. This, to me, is enough
to explain her acquiescence: Eliza was deeply moral and she
recognized Duty.

Besides this, she had a passion for order — and all passions
need something to work upon. When she arrived at Bowen's
Court the green-grown avenue, the unproductive garden, the
empty fowl-house, the neglected pastures rank with thistle and
dock must at once have shocked and exalted her — and so
would the seedy-grand mess indoors. Here was the field for
her mission. Her reforms were moral as well as practical; she is
said, among other things, to have purged the library — the absence, from among Henry III's fairly representative stock of
eighteenth-century books, of any novel has been traced to her.
And one may be sure that, once the lease gave security, Robert
no longer had the expense of feeding his family from " distant

markets ": everything wanted would, from now on, be raised at home. In the garden, the dairy, the poultry-yard, the larder, the sewingroom Eliza would plan ahead like a totalitarian state. Decidedly, Bowen's Court gave her scope.

In calling Eliza " dominating " I may be using an unfair word. The plan or the wish to dominate is vulgar, especially in a woman, and I feel certain she was guiltless of this. But this, by all accounts, small and not pretty woman was passionate, high-principled and inflexible. She must have exercised force without knowing it. She was a good mother in a positive sense that poor dear Margaret had never been. (One may point out that Eliza had only borne, and had only to bring up, four children; she had not borne twenty-one and had to bring up fourteen.) Her great idea of control would make Eliza aspire to keep all affections within bounds; if her love for her son Henry came near to passion or pride she would no doubt chasten herself for it. In her marriage itself, she could not fail to supply all the steel that Robert's nature lacked; she supported, advised and inspired Robert; I feel that her feeling for him was, above all, protective. Her hatred for Henry IV — it can have been nothing less — when she saw Robert victimized must have been hard to govern. When in the Psalms she came to the Wicked Man — the Enemy, the Heathen, the Oppressor — one may guess *whose* face Eliza saw. And, she received from Robert, not as conscious opinion but almost as night by night she received his body, his abiding, deep sense of wrong about Kilbolane. Years later, this was to bear fruit in her.

And Henry V? He is the first ruling Bowen as to whose character I am quite undocumented. I must rely entirely on his legend, and on the memory of that painting of him. He has left behind, to be quoted, no salient remark. I can find no letter of his, nor can I find any letter that describes or comments on him, or that relates any incident in which his character might appear. It *is* known — again through St. John Galwey — that he was immune on the subject of Kilbolane. As he grew up, his

feeling in the affair was simple: he saw the affair as closed, and
would prefer it to be. He must, during his lifetime, have imposed this feeling with some sternness on his mother and wife,
for the great drag-up happened only after his death. We may
judge that Henry was disabused and lucid, and that he took a
detached view of the past. Young man in a young century, his
face was turned to the future; he wished to make, to achieve —
he did make roads. He may have been on his guard against
something catastrophic that he saw in the family temperament.
His feeling for Bowen's Court was sober, without pride, but
had a sweetness about it. To the gravity that was the note of his
character I would add, also, susceptibility.

Everything made towards this. The Robert Bowens, now,
lived at Bowen's Court with the rather bleak simplicity with
which, a hundred years before this, the earlier Bowens had
lived at Kilbolane. One is near nature in an unluxurious country house. To save candles, the great Bowen's Court windows
would be left uncurtained so long as there was any vestige of
day; one would see changing light on the trees and lawns,
shadows stealing across the rooms. Early rising would get one
up only a little after the birds, which is to say, awake for their
chorus whose most unearthly note is lost as the day hardens.
In Septembers, the Bowen children, sleeping up in the top
rooms, would see the great stream of rooks bound for the cornfields rustle across the barely-alight sky. There would be walks
on errands, perhaps for Henry rides, about and across the country: from the foot of the Ballyhouras the *Faerie Queene*
landscape stretches dazzling, etched with valleys, watched by
ruins, shadow-patched with woods. For the little boy who had
lived in Mallow, each season unfolded its surprise. There would
be freedom to make friends in the farms and cottages — the
Robert Bowens' position was democratic: Henry IV was landlord, he drew the rents. There would be few toys for Robert's
children: imagination would have to make all their games. The
shallow Bowen's Court woods could be a forest, darting Farahy

River could be rapids, Colonel Bowen's old castle, theirs. Henry, Robert, Edward and Elizabeth, happier than Miss Pretty in having one another, played where she played. Indoors, they had recourse to the innocent books. On wet days, like all other Bowen children, they must have slid and racketted in the Long Room. From here, you may see a rainbow over the Ballyhouras, or the sun break out suddenly on the wet trees. The influence of Natural Objects . . .

And there was another influence. Religion, for the first time, had become a living force in the Bowens. It would be putting the matter simply, but I hope not cheaply, to say that Eliza Galwey brought religion into the family. There occurred at Bowen's Court, from 1817 on, a sort of spiritual flooding. There was not the violence of a " revival "; I do not mean that Robert's family were caught up into the rapture of one intense, metamorphosing experience. But they did, in the course of days, weeks, years, alter a good deal from what had been the Bowen type. They acceded to a new exaltation; they lived by a new discipline. This had, indeed, begun in Mallow: into God's world Eliza's children were born. But the isolation of Bowen's Court, the rigid living, the emotional tie to nature all added depth to their continuous religious experience. The children, in this bare house surrounded by light and weather, grew up with a constant sense of nearness to God. The sense of God's love or anger ruled and heightened all their susceptibilities. In their own way, they worshipped: they may not have reached great heights — the nature of each oblation can, after all, only be out of the nature of each heart, and Henry III's grandchildren were still Bowens.

Up to now (as I see it) religion with the Bowens had been, before all, an affair of politics; through politics it had worked on their characters. They were conquering Protestants, whether they knew it or not, before they were Christians. The profoundly religious anti-religious passion of Colonel Bowen had, since his time, run underground: it had found its way out, if at all, in the fanaticism with which, from time to time, Bowens litigated for perfectly futile ends. But their feeling for God was, largely, turned on themselves. They had not been without soul — in their very capacity for self-dereliction the untoward work of the soul most appears. But nothing, during those years of their steady increase in property, gave the soul any chance to stand at its full height. I have said of the Ascendancy of the seventeen-fifties that feeling might have been fatal to it. The structure of the great Anglo-Irish society was raised over a country in martyrdom. To enjoy prosperity one had to exclude feeling, or keep it within the prescribed bounds.

At the same time, though one can be callous in Ireland one cannot be wholly opaque or material. An unearthly disturbance works in the spirit; reason can never reconcile one to life; nothing allays the wants one cannot explain. In whatever direction, the spirit is always steadily moving, or rather steadily being carried as though the country were a ship. The light, the light-consumed distances, that air of intense existence about the empty country, the quick flux to decay in houses, cities and people, the great part played in society by the dead and by the idea of death and, above all, the recurring futilities of hope all work for eternal against temporal things. These work for inspiration against method and make a country of loudly-professing sinners and spoiled saints.

At the climax of the Anglo-Irish eighteenth century prosperity and amenable forms of Reason had combined to attempt to deny sorrow and to make a social figure of God. The attempt failed, and decay was following it.

I do not believe that the builder of Bowen's Court, Henry III, had been party to the attempt: he was an emotional man. But Henry III's weakness, as I have in all love of him tried to show, had lain in a sort of infantilism. Nothing shows him to have been without religion, but I see his religion as that of the lonely night-nursery — dreads quickly followed by solace, contrition by exaltation. This was a religion that, as a grown man, he

might feel but could no longer apply. It was a religion ineffica-
cious for the grown man, and most of all for the father. He built
his children a house, but he gave them no principle. Something
failed in him when it came to relationships; as I have said, his
shyness kept him from knowing other souls. Spiritually tongue-
tied, he let his sons make little gods of themselves for want of
any idea of God, and their characters went weak from the vital
lack. Margaret's piety makes part of her legend of " goodness,"
but it may have been too discreet a piety — or else the sons,
given Henry's reserve in the matter, came to dismiss religion
as a woman's affair. Whatever happened, the sons went into the
world with nothing to shore up their weakness or check their
vanity. Humility, forbearance, self-sacrifice were unknown to
any of them except Robert — and, we must hope, Nicholls (for
whom we know almost nothing) the clergyman son. And
humility was not Robert's strong point. Henry IV had just
enough spirit in him to make a tragedy: there is something per-
verse and *voulu* about his cynicism — he had chosen, and he
stuck to what he had chosen, and I believe he knew just how
little it was all worth. Tenderness or spirituality may, from the
first, have been impossible in his character, but vision and principle, I believe, were not.

   Eliza Galwey had been brought up by her Dupont mother
in the fear and love of God. Back in the Duponts lay the
Huguenot memories — vehement worship and religious wars.
A minority fierceness appears in Eliza, and also — in her otherwise least Gallic of characters — the Frenchwoman's drive. Her
nature, at once passionate and ascetic, was framed for religion,
and at the same time framed by it. Religion not only inspired
but steadied her — she was active; she could have been destruc-
tive. As it was, her apprehension of God ruled every use she
made of her faculties. Her faith seems to have added to her
effectiveness. As a housewife, as a practical mother, as co-
manager with her husband of an estate few women could
approach her, as I have shown. But she made her rounds, gave

her stores out, totted up her accounts, sealed up her preserves with one eye on awful, eternal things. The watch that she kept on the estate symbolized the watch she kept on herself — she rode round the fields on a white donkey, stooping, for she was short-sighted, and looking closely through her gold-rimmed eyeglass for weeds: every weed that she saw she had rooted up. And daily she prayed to, also, detect and root up the tares in her own heart — inordinate hate of Henry IV, inordinate love of Henry V. I do not believe she ever chastened herself completely — Eliza would never be a good woman in the sense that Margaret Bowen had been: forbearing, understanding and mild — but for her defeat we must honour her.

As a woman she had one great merit, the greatest: she did not prey on people. Religion engaged her feelings in the hard grapple she knew as love; outside this, her activities used her to the last inch. To bully she had not the time nor the wish. The rigid rule of life she imposed on her family came from the dread of any lapse from grace — she was as ambitious for grace for her dear ones as some women are for worldly promotion. She seems to have treated her children, when she was with them — as children of busy parents they could not but, also, be left much to themselves — as parents should treat their children, with respect and trust. She brought them up in the fear but not in the dread of God. There is no suggestion that, in any Name whatsoever, Henry was oppressed. He grew up neither warped nor soft. In fact, we may gather that a religious upbringing had on him the ideal effect — it taught him to synthesize; it made feeling a force in him, not so much danger and waste, and, for a Bowen most important of all, it placed him outside the power of the immediate day.

Bowen religion, in these days of Eliza, was of the home as much as the church. But the church was there, east of the house, in its belt of trees, at the end of the field-track Mr. Armstrong had taken that dreadful evening in '98. The glebe lands are, in fact, cut out of the demesne. So far, I have mentioned Farahy church only in connection with a few Bowen christenings and Mr. Armstrong's courage. This seems the place to say more about Farahy.

In 1736 Dean Swift had written to Lady Edward Germaine:

His Grace hath now the opportunity to serve a clergyman of merit, Mr. John Jackson. One Mr. Ward, who died this morning, had a sinecure of small value, it was a *Hedge Deanery;* (my Lord Duke will tell you what I mean); we have many of them in Ireland. As it doth not require being there above a month or two in the year, although it be but of thirty or forty pounds yearly rent, it will be of great ease to him; it is the deanery of Cloyne.

Farahy parish was the " corps " or, in fact *was*, this Deanery of St. Coleman's, Cloyne. The deanery dated from the Establishment and the King was patron: in 1851 it was transferred from Farahy to Killeagh. From then on the deans were succeeded at Farahy by a line of rectors — the first of these was the Rev. William Maziere Brady to whose *Records of Cork* I owe these facts.

Dean Swift's estimation of Farahy was, I fear, correct: the deans of Cloyne never did much. They were non-resident and used to employ curates; the curates seldom enjoyed the use of the manse or glebe-house, which was, whenever possible, let. For instance, in 1669 one George Arnold got a twenty-one-year lease of the Farahy manse from the dean, at a rent of forty shillings a year — in consideration of this same George Arnold's having just finished building the manse, and fencing the glebe land, at a total cost of twelve pounds. In 1690, during the Williamite wars, a Mr. Henry Scardeville, chaplain to William's general the Duke of Schomberg, obtained a patent for the Deanery, but did not put in an appearance, to be instituted, until 1695. There were complaints about this, but Mr. Scardeville was able to plead his duties with the forces in England. Though he should not for so long have ignored Cloyne, the cure of Farahy may not have seemed very pressing, for in 1694 the church was in ruins, " lapsed." The Nashes, as active lay-men during their Farahy tenancy, may have made representa-tions and bettered the state of things: in 1720 the church was rebuilt — the actual date on the tower is 1721 — and in 1721 Llewellin Nash, together with a Mr. William Philpot, had " an acre of glebe land with a slate house thereon " conveyed to him by the dean for a Protestant schoolmaster, elsewhere called " an English schoolmaster to teach the English tongue."

Dean Swift, although he had acted with such promptness, did not get Cloyne for his *protégé:* in 1736, the year of the letter, a Mr. Isaac Goldsmith succeeded Mr. Ward. Mr. Goldsmith or his successor may have shown some astuteness, or else, the rents of the glebe lands went up, for by 1774 the Cloyne deanery is valued at £180 per annum. In 1775 the dean's curate was Mr. Edward Delaney, and the Farahy Protestants numbered twelve. Thus Henry III, by moving himself, his wife and his family into Bowen's Court in 1776, more than doubled Mr. Delaney's parishioners, which is a solemn thought. I do not know what curate, if any, came between Mr. Delaney and Mr. Armstrong, Henry IV's friend. Mr. Armstrong had — somehow, appro-priately — died in the January of the winter Henry IV left Bowen's Court. Perhaps Henry stayed on for the funeral; he was, at least, responsible for the tombstone in Farahy church-yard and its inscription: *Hic jacet Reverendus Martinus Arm-strong, circiter trigenta annos hujus Parochiae Vicarius. Qui miti fide et probitate omnes sibi devinxerat cum quibis ulla con-suetudo erat, Charus vixit, defletus obiit, 3d Die Mensis Januarii Aetatis Anno 62do Domini 1817mo.*

I do not know the name of Mr. Armstrong's successor who now read service to Robert, Eliza and their children ranged in the Bowen pew. The church, though its furniture has been al-tered, keeps the character it must have had in their day. Said to be able to hold a hundred people, it has the extreme plain-ness of a conventicle. The square, three-storied tower, once crowned by a wooden steeple, rises at the west end; the vestry, large and for years used as a school, juts out from the south wall of the church. The font, a black marble oval on a red marble pillar, stands near the vestry door.

I can find no record of the church's having been touched between 1720, when it was built, and 1837, when it was " put in thorough repair." Three round-topped, small-paned windows, set rather high up, slant light into the pews from either side. There is a rounded east end. The walls, plastered and painted a pale colour, were in Eliza's and Robert's day still bare of memorials. The only memorial then was the east window, which, again, was to Mr. Armstrong. I have always considered this window beautiful: it is *grisaille*, with three jewel-coloured medallions and a jewel border; in the text divided between two scrolls — *Glory be to God in the Highest . . . And on Earth Peace, Goodwill towards Men* — one might see Henry IV's ironic choice. The pews and shoulder-high panelling must still, for Eliza and Robert, have been those of 1720, already, from the dampness of the church's position, beginning to crack, warp and send out a musty smell. The communion table, pulpit and curate's desk would have been of boxlike plainness. The Bowen pew is over the Bowen vault.

All through the week the church remained locked up. There is felt to be either a touch of demonstration or else a smack of Popishness — reserved sacrament, " images " — about the wish to pray in a silent church: if the Protestant wants God at irregular hours he has to sanctify his own place. There were no weekday services. Throughout fine weeks of summer the shut-up church would bake in the sun that streams through the south windows, warping the prayerbooks left in the pews. At all other seasons mildew set in, and damp clung to the rope of the one bell. In the first half of the nineteenth century, divine service was celebrated once on Sundays, and on the principal festivals. The sacrament was administered four times a year. . . . Decidedly, one had to look for God in one's heart, and worship him in the fastnesses of the home.

The churchyard is elegiac. Trees surrounding it shadow or drip over the graves and evergreens. Catholics as well as Protestants bury here; their dead lie side by side in indisputable peace. The Nashes continued to bury here long after they had left Farahy, and as we know Jane Berkeley brought her husband home. There are blockish old stones, sunk in the grass, and beautiful old ones, whose shallow-carved urns and garlands are now almost effaced; these all, with the rough Celtic crosses, slant. In Eliza's lifetime that terrible square mound, in the south-east corner, was to go up over the pit of famine and fever dead.

The Bowens enter the churchyard near the top, through a narrow door of their own. The rest of the parishioners, and the funerals, come up an avenue from the Farahy gate.

Eliza and Robert met no other gentry at Farahy church. The country, at that time, teemed with other Protestant churches, none with large congregations but all kept going, and the Bowens' acquaintances, other big house families, each went to their own. I say " acquaintances " advisedly: to begin with, the Bowens had no *neighbours* of their own class — I have stressed in my first chapter, and tried to make felt since, the unusual isolation of Bowen's Court. Time, disposition and money were all needed to bridge the gap between it and the houses round. Disposition in Robert was not lacking — he is the sociable fellow *par excellence* — but time and money certainly were. Post-Union Mallow society had exactly suited not only his tastes but his moderate means. But these Bowen's Court days his means were not even moderate, and he could not afford to go the county pace. He could not go dashing about the country; he had not the horses and he was tied to the farm. Could he have afforded to entertain, Eliza and he were too busy to do the honours. Poor Robert, these days, had hardly even the time to notice that he was dropping out. Eliza, though unregretfully, no doubt did. Henry IV's rather doubtful *beau monde* neither

she nor Robert would have wished to frequent. But they were
equally out of the local genial big world that had been Henry
III's. The Kingstons, for instance, would be quite out of their
ken.

So, Eliza, if not her children, would have heard with indifference that the King was coming to stay at Mitchelstown
Castle — and not even in the castle that now stood but in a new
one to be specially built. If she made any comment she may
have said to Robert: " Too bad that your brother Henry
should miss this."

If the stupendous project failed to impress Eliza, it marked
the emergence of Big George — not the king but the earl. For
some time, a long and *triste* lull at Mitchelstown had been felt
all over the neighbourhood — it may, indeed, have been one of
the final reasons for Henry IV's flight. The lull had followed a
scandal of some size. That Earl of Kingston who as Viscount
Kingsborough was Arthur Young's friend and commanded the
Mitchelstown Light Dragoons had, sometime early in the
seventeen-nineties, found one of his daughters gone from a
Mitchelstown house party. He had given chase, taking with
him the little Viscount Kingsborough who was to be Big
George, picked up tracks, kicked in a door in an inn at Kilworth, found a scene of guilt and shot the betrayer, a married
man, dead. Though it was felt he had taken the proper course,
Lord Kingston had to be tried by the Irish House of Lords.
" The peers," says Aubrey de Vere, " walked processionally
in their robes, and each as he passed the throne, laid his hand
on his breast and pronounced the verdict, ' Not guilty, upon
my honour.' " Little Big George had entered on life young.
Next, as young officer in '98, he was captured, held as a hostage
by the rebels and only just escaped from a massacre. When his
father died, George was for years kept waiting about for
possession of Mitchelstown; his widowed mother lived on
there in aggressive seclusion, allowing George not an inch of
rights in the place. When she died and he did come in, he came

in with a roar. He at once sent for an architect: "Build me," he said, " a castle. I am no judge of architecture; but it must be larger than any house in Ireland, and have an entrance tower named the 'White Knight's Tower.' No delay! It is time for me to enjoy."

Big George's intention to entertain George IV is not stated here, but it rapidly got round. There *was* no delay: the old mansion was demolished and the new castle reared itself on the plateau, its diamond-hard angles, towers and turrets cutting the cutting Galtee winds. It stood ready by 1823. The King, after all, was unable to leave Dublin — he was too well entertained; he drank to the gentlemen of Ireland at the Vice-regal lodge, but got no further to see them. But if the Mitchelstown house-warming lacked the royal lustre, that was the only lustre it did lack. Big George did well when he built this Windsor (which is said to have cost him more than a hundred thousand pounds). It sounded a rally — " Where are you all going? Ireland is good enough for me! " — and made them all look pretty silly in Bath. One may say that for the Kingstons it was all very well: they had vast possessions, they had the White Knight's blood in them (see Chapter I) and they ruled here with an absolutism that had not for years been possible for the English lord. They administered justice as they saw it; the execution of the daughter's betrayer had been only one of their haughty acts, and the late Lord Kingston's brush with the House of Lords had marked the first interference from an outside world. The industrialism that was now ruining England for its Big Georges did once, and while the castle was building, try to rear up its ugly head in Mitchelstown: " A wealthy manufacturer," Aubrey de Vere tells us, " built a huge chimney in the square of the town, which crouched beneath the hill on which the castle stood." Big George put over a big act: he drove round Mitchelstown and bade his people solemn, even tearful farewells. " I am come to wish you goodbye, boys. This place is but a small place, and there is not room in it for me and that

man [pointing to the factory]. He says the law is on his side,
and I daresay it is. Consequently, I go to England to-morrow."
Any possible benefit Mitchelstown might have got from the
factory vanished before the threatened loss of Big George: he
spent thousands locally; he was putting in waterworks for the
town — and, he had them hypnotized. "During the night,"
continues Aubrey de Vere, "the lord of industry received a
visit from uninvited guests; the next morning no smoke went
over the woods and towers, and on the third day he had taken
his departure."

Big George gave his people no cause to regret their choice.
He continued that Kingston tradition of improving and building which, in his father, Arthur Young had extolled. He completed, in 1825, his good work on the town's water system; he
built two churches of equal impressiveness, one for the Catholics, one for the Protestants; he town-planned, widened streets,
paved the market square. And he founded (again see my first
chapter) Kingston College, whose upkeep he left a charge on
his estate. His domains, extending into three counties, were, at
least by the lights of those days, modelly run, and his tenants
suffered no oppression but his. His benevolence grew with his
despotism. But, his people disappointed — to put it mildly —
Big George. His sanity was, it turned out, built into his idea of
his absolutism: both were to crack together. A bye-election
pended in Limerick: some doubt was raised as to the loyalty
of the tenant vote. "That matter is settled," the Earl replied —
his County Limerick tenants had had their orders, in fact. On
the election morning Lord Kingston, with the candidate he had
favoured, sat in the open window of Lord Limerick's town
house, drinking champagne and cracking jokes with the crowd.
Gentlemen surged round the back of his chair. As the church
bells rang the Kingston tenantry, in a mile-long procession,
rode down the long fine Limerick main street. The crowd
cheered them. So far, so good. But news came in the evening
— they did not know how to tell him — that Big George's ten-

ants had, to a man, ratted: they had voted *against* the Kingston candidate. " You are hiding something from me," he said, looking round at his friends. . . . He was on the road back to Mitchelstown all that night.

By next night, his tenants from all three counties had been immediately summoned into his presence. They did not disobey: they came. Big George sat on a dais at the far end of the hundred-foot-long castle gallery. As more and more tenants came pressing in at the door, the front of their crowd was pressed more and more up on him. Big George did not cease to cover the mobbed perspective of gallery with his eye. That eye of his, and his dreadful continued silence, renewed the domination of centuries. But they were here to hear him: he must speak. He did not: he took the alternative and went mad. Leaping out of his seat he threw his arms wide. " *They are come to tear me to pieces; they are come to tear me, to tear me to pieces!* "

Forty-eight hours later he had been taken away.

I have made room for Big George because he epitomizes that rule by force of sheer fantasy that had, in great or small ways, become for his class the only possible one. From the big lord to the small country gentleman we were, about this time, being edged back upon a tract of clouds and of obsessions that could each, from its nature, only be solitary. The sense of dislocation was everywhere. Property was still there, but power was going. It was democracy, facing him in his gallery, that sent Big George mad. In other cases, the line between sanity and insanity was less perceptibly crossed; many gentlemen only became " interesting "; the cult for the glen and the tear made a market for lyrics; the tendency to darken houses began. Anglo-Ireland began to claim and patent the everlasting Irish regret. Society — which can only exist when people are sure of themselves and immune from fears — was no longer, in the Anglo-Ireland I speak of, in what I called the magnetic and growing stage; it was on the decline; it was breaking up. It could exist in detail — comings-and-goings, entertainments, marriages — but the main healthy abstract was gone. And with this break-up of society there set in the dire period we are not yet out of, the dire period of Personal Life. This *can* be lived — the Robert Bowens were making out at Bowen's Court; thinking most of all of grace, serious, lonely, busy — but it needs at the greatest, genius, at the least, discipline.

Gothic feeling was even in the Kildare Street Club. I owe this vignette of Colonel Mansergh St. George, a County Cork gentleman met in Dublin, to the Mr. J. D. Herbert whose *Irish Varieties* have already given us Mr. E. Tighe.

On the day appointed I attended Mr. Tighe to dine with Colonel St. George at the Club House, Kildare St. We found the Colonel sitting in the corner of a large room, at a small table with a feeble light, drawing. He was composing a scene, the subject of a forlorn traveller on a wild heath, a lion prowling in the distance. The light was barely sufficient to enable me to discover the design; so I begged permission to light a large candle. He assented, remarking that for melancholy or horrific subjects, he was assisted by a sparing light, but in lively scenes he preferred a full and clear one. . . . [Later on in the evening Mr. Tighe made a good remark and every one was amused.] . . . Colonel St. George was an exception; he looked gloomy and soon left the room.

[Colonel St. George did actually meet the fate envisaged by Lord Kingston. Some pages further on in the *Varieties* Mr. Herbert, without surprise, records his end] . . . Colonel St. George and his agent Mr. Uniacke were murdered by tenants in Co. Cork, subsequently to having been harangued by Colonel St. George during one of his phases of insanity.

But these were troubles of fantasy. In fact the troubles of Ireland since 1800 had been too real. The Union had *not* been a treaty with the Irish people. " I certainly wish," Lord Cornwallis, one of its four authors, had written while the Union was pending, " that England would now make a union *with the Irish* NATION, *instead of making it with a* PARTY *in Ire-*

land. It has always appeared to me a desperate measure for the English government to make an irrevocable alliance with a small party in Ireland." That small party had been Fitzgibbon's; Protestant Union had, avowedly, been the sole object of Fitzgibbon's policy. That bulk of Ireland that had not wished for the Union was now to suffer from its effects.

(I say " now " — with the advance of the century more mature and responsible English statesmanship was to make a real effort to grapple with Ireland's problems and find some cure for her ills; reports were to follow commissions, and " measures " reconnaissance visits; there came to be sunk in Ireland not only English money but English constructive thought, and Ireland, whether she knew it or not, shared some benefits of English enlightenment. This built up in favour of Union, by 1900, a very serious argument, and adult Irishmen, such as my father, supported it not only from the heart but from the head. Sentimental or class-politic Unionism was one thing, rational Unionism another. My " now " relates to the first decades of the century, when Union could only be seen as a complete annexation, the final blow to Ireland's integrity.)

The aristocratic members of " Grattan's Parliament " had at least known their country, if they chose to ignore her. From 1800, Ireland found herself ruled from across the sea by a Westminster parliament that, even if well-intentioned — and in the main it was pretty cynical — had no sort of knowledge of Irish circumstance. Of the about six hundred and sixty members of the House of Commons only one hundred were Irish — an ineffective minority. The financial effects of Union were wholly bad: Ireland, who had as a Kingdom been solvent and even prosperous, now became committed to her share of the Imperial expenditure, heightened by the cost of the French wars. Two-seventeenths of this became due from her, and she was drained by putting the money up. The " protection " she received in return was enjoyed by only a small class. Then, the promises implied if not made by Pitt to the Catholics were not kept during his lifetime — admitting the justice of one Catholic petition he had replied: "Time must always enter into questions of expediency." And the survival of the '98 spirit, the simmerings, the "sullen indignation" Fitzgibbon had underlined seemed to justify, towards the masses of Ireland, a strongly repressive policy. Property was, as had been promised, supported, and the evils of the land tenure system in Ireland were not recognized, and were in fact increased. Commercial hopes — such as had, for instance, influenced Cork city, with its new harbour, into support of the Union — were disappointed. The abolition, in the eighteen-twenties, of duties on a number of imports removed protection from the new Irish industries, which felt and mostly did not survive the blow. As employment declined, trade slackened and rents rose prosperous cities went down in the world again. But the most acute trouble was on the land.

While the war with France lasted — in fact, until 1815 — this trouble did not become apparent. Ireland felt the benefit of inflation. The steady demand for Irish corn in England and the high wartime prices paid for it kept the country in tillage and the people employed. Men without work or land could and did enlist in the English army for foreign service and not make pressure at home. But after the war wheat prices dropped and demand decreased. There followed a movement among the landlords and strong farmers — a movement copied from England and supported by her — to break up small holdings, evict their tenants and consolidate estates and farms into large tracts for grazing. This change in the entire rural system could only make for chaos — on top of it, returned soldiers and out-of-works from the cities came flocking back to the land, to find no land. The peasants were left with nothing: many of them had never handled money; they had given labour to landlords in lieu of rent for their holdings, working these holdings, from which they fed their families, in any spare time the landlords left to them. Now that their labour was no longer wanted for tillage they could no longer earn their land (which *was* wanted) and were thrown off it. Their best hope was to bid for and to reclaim waste patches for which there had been no use. From this poor land they could not raise sufficient crops (potatoes) to feed their families throughout the year, so at given seasons families took to the roads to beg. Those who could not even get waste land took to the roads for good. There was then no Poor Law, no official relief; these unwilling vagrants had to depend on charity — which, temperamental in Ireland, met the occasion in its free-lance way. (In Ireland, misfortune is not suspect; it carries round with it its own dignity.) In 1821–22 the failure of a potato crop produced a famine which, though since eclipsed by the horrors of '47, was enough to complete the despair. The small farmers did not fare much better: the high bidding for land by the big graziers, the quickness of land-lords to evict ruined them. In fact, in the eighteen-twenties the state of rural Ireland — and Ireland is almost wholly rural — could not have been worse.

It may be said that the whole of this cannot fairly be attributed to the Union, that for the poor in all countries this was a bad age — everywhere, after revolution and war, reactionaries were in power. The poor in England, also unrepresented, were suffering in the course of changes that legislation, under a selfish government, was so far making few attempts to meet. (Indeed, Irish representers of Ireland's woes have been too often stupid *à faire pleurer*: they are inclined to talk as though all classes in England, at all times, like the Williamite army that Sunday after the Boyne, " by yesterday's pillage were full of beef and mutton.") But at least in England industrialism was counteracting the slump in the countryside; the dark satanic mills offered livelihood when the fields failed. In Ireland the Union did, demonstrably, check the progress envisaged by Grattan's party and hold up reforms of which England, in the ignorance of which I have spoken, did not see the vital necessity. And the Union put the last seal on an injustice that had for centuries made the country unsound: that confiscation (or series of confiscations) Fitzgibbon had named as being the English settlers' title was the first cause of this landless distress. England continued to govern Ireland in the interests of the " small party " with which the Union was made. England supported " property " with a ruthlessness that " property," had it itself continued to rule the country from Dublin, would have feared, if not blushed, to make evident. For this support of one class against another there were, clearly, two reasons. First, it was in the English interest to separate the Anglo-Irish from the Irish — the menacing solidarity of 1782, the armed hope and flourishing patriotism of the Volunteers, the sense, in fact, of their Irishness in the upper classes must not occur again. English favour and advantages got from it were to demean the Anglo-Irish into unhappy hybrids known as the Loyal Irish. About a hundred years hence, at the time of the Treaty, the Mrs. Micawber-like attitude of these deluded people, no longer of importance to any one but themselves, was to prove embarrassing, tiresome: England was told that she had deserted the Loyal Irish. As a matter of fact, she had. The second reason for the one-sided English policy was that it was difficult for her to see the native Irish as anything but aliens, and as worse, subhuman — potato-eaters, worshippers of the Pope's toe. The squalor in which the Irish lived was taken to be endemic in their mentality: it would have seemed fantastic to reform their conditions. To distract the English conscience the buffoon Paddy was to come into being — the capering simians of the Cruikshank drawings for Maxwell's *Irish Rebellion in 1798* represent him exactly. At the same time, those Anglo-Irish who had not taken to Gothic were to find in the Lever heroes agreeable prototypes in art. Propaganda was probably at its most powerful before there was any name for it. Both classes in Ireland saw themselves in this mirror: the gentry became more dashing, the lower classes more comic. We are, or can become at any moment, the most undignified race on earth — while there is a gallery we must play to it. Those who complain that the Irish are now becoming " sombre " regret, without knowing it, the decline of a myth that English interest need no longer sustain.

The small number, the hundred only, of Irish members in the English House of Commons needs some comment. Ironically, the Union had effected one reform for which Grattan had worked in vain, for want of which " his " parliament stayed ineffective and he saw his hopes run on the rocks. Pocket and rotten boroughs were now suppressed. (Had this been done prior to 1800, and an overhaul of the franchise accompanied it, the Dublin parliament might have been made representative, in which case the Union would not have taken place. As it was, the suppression of boroughs served chiefly to disembarrass Westminster of a threatening number of garrulous Irishmen, and to ensure that the Irish should be outvoted should they try to assert a national wish.) In our area — I mean the area of this book — Doneraile and Charleville were among the seven County Cork boroughs disenfranchised. Lord Doneraile's heirs got £15,000 for the loss of Doneraile, and the Boyles £7,500 for Charleville. Mallow was shorn of one of its two members — I do not know if any one got anything for that.

I have spoken of propaganda, however frivolous, against the native Irish, and of, if they could sink lower, its debasing effect. '98 and Emmett's forlorn-hope rebellion of 1803 had, at least outwardly, failed. Endless night seemed to have followed Wolfe Tone's visionary morning; hopes for the Irish seemed to be in the dust. The people were down; they were disunified, voiceless and without power to see themselves. Their very laments had been re-rhymed and turned into ballads for well-bred melancholy. Their spirit was dormant, and looked dead. But it was not dead; it could wake to answer a voice, and this voice now came from Daniel O'Connell.

The enormous figure of Daniel O'Connell — human enough, but magnified by the feeling round him as a figure is by some trick of the mist — came, with the eighteen-twenties, into the people's view. His eloquence was to rush through remote and downtrodden Ireland like an incoming tide, filling dead reaches, lifting the people, carrying them. He rallied the people of Ireland and made them the Irish people. Tone's power had dwelt and burnt in the idea — revolutionary (rather than rebel), Deist, man of new or reborn cities and of the new world, he might, had he lived, have proved too much a man of the new world for Ireland, four-fifths of whose being is submerged in the past. O'Connell's power was in direct emotion, which his strong quick brain well knew how to use. Catholic, Kerry democrat-squire from his own lawless Darrynane coast, and above all, lawyer — able, he said, to drive a coach and six through any Act of Parliament — this was the Irishman Ireland wanted now. Anti-revolutionary (he denounced '98; he had been repelled for life by the horrors he saw in France) and Royalist (he gave a demonstrative welcome to George IV in Dublin; he was to show strong sentimental attachment to the young Queen Victoria) O'Connell was, all the same, far more abhorrent to Grattan's kind than had been the more fine-strung, if drastic, Tone. His bull-like physical presence, his voice with stops that could make any speech a fugue, his thunder and tenderness, his grossnesses, his genius for evocation and his furious wit made him the people's man. He has been called a demagogue: he spoke *into* his people. He could call up the whole of a racial past; and he could give hope for the future where there had been none. To my view he is an Old Testament figure. But the Irish, unlike the Jews humbled or in exile, had been sustained by no Promise; they got their first real promise from O'Connell's lips. He has been called an agitator: he was — he produced movement by giving people ideas, and he used emotion to drive these in. The first idea he gave Catholic Ireland was the idea of itself — as a whole, as an entity, as a force. In the past the more lordly Catholic leaders had not cared, or been able, to do this. The people's fight for their faith and for their survival had been instinctive and blind. In the nineteenth century instinct and heroic blindness were no longer enough.

O'Connell's first object was to secure the Catholic Emancipation that had been fought for by Grattan and promised by Pitt. His second was to effect Repeal of the Union. He launched his movement in 1821. In 1823 the Catholic Association came into being and began to be powerful. In the course of his campaign, speaking throughout Ireland, O'Connell got solid behind him not only the people but the new generation of Irish-raised Maynooth priests. In 1826 his riposte to a No-Popery clamour in England (started up by the Duke of York, who claimed in the House of Lords that it was agitation on behalf of the Catholics that had driven his father George III mad) was to get the Beresfords beaten out of the field at the election at Waterford. In 1828 he himself stood at, and won, the Clare election: he then appeared in London, at the bar of the House, to plead against the legal prescription that now denied him, as a Catholic, the right to take his seat. By this time he had the whole of Catholic Ireland " up " — not armed, but more incalculably threatening than if it were. He had created irresistible pressure. Catholic Emancipation had to be, and was, granted by the Duke of Wellington, the Anglo-Irish English Prime Minister, in 1829. Even iron must bend: the only alternative, the Duke said, would be war.

Even where the Liberator had not been, he was felt. The psychological change he brought about in the people remains as important as anything that he did. (This had been the change Big George had felt in the Kingston tenants; it was hostile to his power, *not* to his life.) An altered Ireland came, in the course of the eighteen-twenties, to lie at the big house gates. For the most part it did not declare itself; it could be, and was, ignored by the Anglo-Irish till some incident brought class-temper out in a flash. And even then, I fear, class-temper was largely shown on the gentry's side. This was evident, in our part of the world, in the case of the Doneraile " Conspiracy ": 1829.

The country for some miles round Doneraile is packed with
gentlemen's places. The road between us and Doneraile loops
up and down through country as pretty as you could wish —
glossy with woods, dimpled with valleys, set with really idyllic
cornfields and cottages and watered by the smiling Awbeg. In
fact, is just one of those innocent landscapes over which, in a
fairy tale or a Disney film, the ogre-giant's foot stalks, crushing the church spire, or the dragon's breath smokes as the
dragon snaps up little girls. This was what the Doneraile gentry
saw happening — or thought they were to see happening — in
the years 1828 and '9. The Solicitor-General was to speak
highly of the Doneraile neighbourhood's "Magistrates and
Gentry and natural advantages." The fact was, I am afraid,
that the scene was perfectly set for a particular kind of social
hysteria.

The affair started like this — There were four successive
"attempts" on the lives and safety of Doneraile gentlemen.
Shots were fired at carriages driving home in the dark. The outstanding victims, or all-but victims — were Dr. Norcott and
Mr. George Bond of Lowe, "an active and zealous Protestant
magistrate," but Mr. Creagh of Laurentinum and Admiral
Evans of Carker were also annoyed. Though there is now (and
really was at the time) every reason to think that the shots
were let off by footpads, it was felt immediately by the *élite* of
Doneraile that the entire countryside was in arms and plotting
to slay its betters — that, in fact, '98 was brewing over again.
Twenty-one arrests, from among the country people, were
accordingly made by the magistrates, and informers, chief
among whom were the cousins Patrick and Owen Daly, were
brought forward to justify the arrests. The prisoners went up
for trial at the Summer Assizes in Cork. Chief Baron O'Grady,
conducting the Assizes, was, however, a busy man and a realist;
he did not share Doneraile's grave view of the matter and refused to prolong the Assizes to try the men. Piqued, and with
growing alarm for their safety, the Doneraile magistrates, sup-

ported by friends in the County Cork Grand Jury, made representations in such important quarters that " a Special Commission did come down, and Mr. Dogherty, the Solicitor-General,
with it — and a very pretty affair it turned out."

The special Commission sat in the Courthouse, Cork. It
opened on Thursday, October 21st, 1829; the judges were
Pennefather and Torrens; the prisoners were tried in batches
— there were four in the first batch, three in the second, two in
the third. While the second batch were on trial the proceedings received the dramatic check I shall show, and after the
third batch there were no more tried. This Commission was the
occasion of Daniel O'Connell's most famous breakfast (not
mentioned by my authority Mr. Sheahan) — having posted all
through a night from Kerry the Liberator sent for a bowl of
porridge and ate it in Court. He took over the defence of the
three men in the dock from the two counsels permitted them
by the Crown. I shall now give one or two pictures of the
" pretty affair " from the Despatches of Mr. Thomas Sheahan,
lively Cork journalist, relayed hot from the Courthouse while
the Commission sat. Mr. Sheahan's account makes such excellent reading that I only wish I had space to give it in full. The
" Brunswickers " mentioned by him were the members of the
Cork Brunswick Club — composed of prominent citizens and
neighbouring gentlemen. This club's tendencies may be seen
from its name. It ran its own candidate at the Cork elections
and had led various faction-fights. It had lately censured Sir
Nicholas Colthurst for allowing the Militia band to play in
O'Connell's honour when O'Connell came to Cork city fresh
from his Clare triumph. The Brunswickers' support of the
Doneraile gentry would tend to make feeling even worse than
it was.

Now for Sheahan, on the Commission:

Thursday, 21st October.

Pennefather and Torrens opened the Commission this day. The
Court was crowded with country gentlemen — I never saw any-

thing to equal it. It is curious there was no shew of " the people "
— I did not see a frieze coat or a poor man even in the Courtyard.
It looked as though the people paid no attention to the subject
of the Commission, and considered it a mere bottle of smoke.
There is, however, a great gathering of Aristocrats, as if the country were in a state of actual rebellion. . . . By the by, I like
Dogherty's figure and countenance — the former is tall and not
ill-proportioned, the latter has an agreeable melancholy in-
scribed on it. Some do not like the eye of the man — they think
it cold, and that it betokens no heart; 'tis a fine eye, however.
. . . Bills were found against all the prisoners for conspiring to
murder Admiral Evans, Bond Lowe and Michael Creagh, Esqrs.
Some of the prisoners were very decent-looking men. Whilst we
were waiting for the fate of the bills to-day, I fell into conversation with several of the country gentlemen. They all appeared to
be believers in the " Conspiracy," and to the extent the veriest
enemy of Ireland could wish. I should not like to be depending
on the wisdom or mercy of some of them.

O'Connell is greatly wished for — but does not come.

Friday Night.

I have but now returned from the Courthouse, where I heard
sentence of death pronounced upon four of the men charged with
the Conspiracy. I do not know whether they are all guilty, but
the prosecution certainly assumed an appearance on which I had
not calculated. I cannot say I was satisfied with the manner in
which everything went on to-day. I did not like the constitution
of the Jury; I did not like the conduct of the Solicitor-General;
and it occurs to me that the testimony of several of the witnesses
for the Crown could have been attacked more than it was. . . .

The Solicitor-General stated the case for the prosecution. He
was speaking for nearly four hours. . . . The truth is, his speech
was a very fine and clever thing, but it was by no means of that
cool, unimpassioned, matter-of-fact character which it ought to
be. The Solicitor-General should have recollected that he was ad-
dressing a jury . . . having scarcely one thing in common with
those whom they were about to try — the peers of the prisoners
in name but not in reality. His statement was in fact a lordly

harangue, the tendency of which was to confirm the Irish Magistrate, Landlord and Gentleman in the ultraism of his pretensions, and to render him still more hostile to the serf. . . . Lord Kingston and Lord Carbery were listening to the Solicitor-General, and, I have no doubt, will speak highly of the Hon. and Learned Gentleman in the proper quarter. . . .

The witnesses for the prosecution were — first David Sheehan, an accomplice; next, Patrick Nolan, an approver; third, Patrick Daly, the spy; fourth, Thomas Murphy, another approver — and fifth, Owen Daly, a " clenching one " as the Solicitor-General called him. Then followed Mr. Garvan, Mr. Bond Lowe, a Mr. Roberts and a Mrs. Glover, with two or three Policemen. . . .

The witnesses for the defence were Mr. Harold Barry, Lieutenant Coote, Dr. O'Brien, Parish Priest of Doneraile, Garrett Nagle, Esq., Arthur Creagh, Esq., Charles Daly, the brother of Patrick, and one Roche, alias " Cold Morning." They were produced principally to discredit the evidence for the prosecution. Harold Barry, who swore that he did not consider that David Sheehan and Patrick Daly were entitled to credit upon their oaths, was very rudely handled by the Solicitor-General. Harold Barry is a gentleman of property — has taken a wife from, I believe, a high Brunswick family, is a sufferer from Whiteboyism, has handed over to the authorities fire arms which had been concealed in his haggard — and yet, he was hunted down this evening as though he had been " ipsissimus Rock." It seems that he refused to entrap a Whiteboy " by promising his protection," and for this he was whispered against by some creature in the neighbourhood of the Solicitor-General, and the Solicitor-General gratified the whisperer by dragooning a man he ought to have venerated. " I feel, my Lord," said Mr. Barry . . . " that I could not have acted as the police would have me act." The feeling was most creditable to the man.

'Twas characteristic — the grateful bursts of laughter with which the Court rang on the embarrassment of this witness — the lives of four men in the scale — a man came forward to discharge his duty by his fellow-men in distress — the consideration involved in these circumstances could not repress the emotions of the bad spirit. It looked as though the well-dressed savages who filled the Court . . . anticipated still more gratifying captures. . . .

The case having been closed on both sides, Baron Pennefather charged the jury. You may now see the prisoners clustering towards the bar — all of them attentive, evidently sensible of the importance of the moment, but, as far as I could observe, few of them anxious. The old man, Leary, stood in the centre, his arms folded. He manifested the same firmness now as at an earlier and much less agitating period of the proceedings. . . .

Judge Torrens pronounced the awful sentence of the law. Let me tell you that I did not altogether admire his manner of doing it. His Lordship appeared to look beyond the unfortunate convicts, and to address himself, as it were, to the Harold Barrys. . . . His Lordship lifted his arm at one part of his address and enunciated strongly something about justice. The word was good, but the action I think, might have been spared. One of the Convicts seized upon the word "justice" . . . "Oh my Lord," he said in a low voice, "there is no justice for us; we know nothing but vengeance." . . .

Saturday, One O'Clock.

There are various rumours abroad about disclosures being made by some of the prisoners — additional arrests in Doneraile and its vicinity. The Country Gentlemen are, in fact, all shaking their heads at each other, looking serious and determined. . . .

I must tell you that there is a popular feeling being created in reference to these trials. There was no appearance of its existence on Thursday, or even during the earlier part of yesterday. Many, however, have taken offence at the latitude assumed by the Solicitor-General in his address to the Jury, at his overbearing conduct to Mr. H. Barry, and at some other circumstances for which the Solicitor is not accountable. It is greatly wished that Mr. O'Connell was here.

Five O'Clock.

I have to inform you that an express has just been forwarded to Darrynane for Mr. O'Connell. . . . 'Tis almost a forlorn hope — Mr. O'Connell . . . has been known to have engaged himself

to attend a Meeting of the inhabitants of Kerry, to be held in
Tralee on Tuesday. . . .

Sunday evening.

Opinion is greatly divided as to whether or not Mr. O'Connell
will be with us. Some say, that as he did not come before he will
not come now. Others think he will come even at this moment —
but they are afraid he may have left Darrynane now for some
other place; and time is now everything. The more virulent of the
Brunswickers taunt Mr. O'Connell on his absence — they say it
was he who placed the prisoners in the dock, and now he deserts
them. . . .

Monday Night, 12 O'Clock.

O'Connell has arrived. The witnesses for the Crown have been
shaken. I have just left the Jury closeted, and I scarcely think
they'll agree to a verdict. You perceive that I'm a piece of an epic
poet — I rush " *in medias res.*" . . .

Just as the Jury had been completed, Mr. O'Connell made his
appearance. He bore inwards, describing (as usual) no narrow
circle, habilimented as a night traveller. Agitation preceded, followed and environed him. " The People " without and within the
Court were quickened by his presence. *We* were not *many*, most
especially in the interior; but yet, when we saw the Great Dan
amongst us, we felt as though we were a multitude. Mr. O'Connell
bowed to the Bench — the courtesy was returned by Baron Pennefather; Judge Torrens did not appear to have noticed it . . . I
marked . . . the Solicitor-General as Mr. O'Connell entered. I
have been told . . . that the colour fled the cheek of the Solicitor-
General. This may have been the case, but I must say that I cannot
vouch for it.

The statement of the Solicitor-General was, as on Friday, long
and objectionable. It was admitted, however, that the country had
not as much cause to complain of *official eloquence* this day as on
the former occasion. The Solicitor, indeed, lessened his canvas a
good deal. But if the country was spared, Harold Barry came in
for *his* full share of castigation. The Solicitor-General could not
understand how Doneraile, with all its Magistrates and Gentry

and natural advantages could be disturbed unless the fault lay with the Harold Barrys. . . . And he left no doubt on the subject by reading an extract from the Whiteboy Act, stating that the Magistrates could compel any man, under pain of imprisonment, to declare the number of Whiteboys he may have in his haggard or his stable yard. . . .

These repeated allusions to Harold Barry at length drew up Mr. O'Connell, who . . . requested that the Solicitor-General might not travel into evidence or transactions of other trials but confine himself to the particular case before the Court and the Jury. . . .

Three O'Clock, p.m.

No verdict yet — no expectation of a verdict. The decimators are actually becoming wild — some of them have been heard to say, that the peasants wanted a terrible example, and that they should now have one. You may imagine, therefore, their desolation — several of them it is well known, are but scantily supplied with brains. . . . They fear that a check may be put to what they consider retributive justice, but what really *is* — blind passion, hate of those to whose sweat they owe whatever importance they enjoy, and a reckless disregard of frieze-clad and *mere Irish* humanity.

The end of the business *I* must summarize. O'Connell had, before the Jury retired, effectively discredited the chief witnesses for the prosecution, and especially the two Daly cousins. He had also shaken the Solicitor-General on two of the latter's most important points. The Jury, having been charged by Mr. Justice Torrens, retired, therefore, in an upset state — in fact, they were so much upset that they collapsed, and no verdict ever did come from them. From their retirement they sent into Court a pressing request to be discharged on account of the illness of several of their members, notably of their Foreman — who was likely to die of being further confined. Two physicians sent in to visit the Jury returned to Court to whisper — the whisper became important — a confirmation into the

Judges' ears. The Jury, accordingly, was discharged. The Solicitor-General announced there was to be a re-trial of the three
prisoners still in the dock.

O'Connell, on the following day, came down on this like an
eagle. He insisted " that the Court had committed two fatal
errors in its progress to the discharging of the Jury. First, it had
violated the non-access principle by allowing the physicians to
go into the room where the sick Jurors were closeted; and next,
it had conversed with the physicians respecting the state of the
sick Jurors without taking care that the conversation should be
overheard by the prisoners, who had a deep interest in it."
O'Connell went on to hint — I do not know how broadly —
that, should there be a re-trial of the three prisoners now in the
dock (which would mean a start from scratch, with the possible loss of the ground gained for the prisoners the day before)
he might, as their counsel, bring up these two lapses as a plea
against the validity of the whole Commission. The Commission was, it appears, intimidated. The Court ruled that the three
prisoners in question be held over to await the Spring Assizes.

The next day, a new batch — the third, two in number — of
prisoners was tried: O'Connell remaining overrulingly present.
They were acquitted: the new Jury came to its verdict in five
minutes.

Nothing [says Sheahan] could have equalled the joy of the
people — save and except the mortification of the savages. There
were as marked indications of triumph in Court as could be expected under the circumstances. Their Lordships themselves
seemed to me not to be chagrined at the result. They seemed to
be joyous, if not at the acquittal of the prisoners, certainly at
something emanating from their trial. It may be that they are
heartily tired, or something else, of the Commission, and that they
imagine the prosecutors have now got enough of it.

They had indeed. The Commission lapsed: the "well-
dressed savages " had lost this round. The Brunswickers drank

it off at the Club, and the country gentlemen rolled home. Those prisoners who had not yet come up for trial were let go on bail, and are not, so far as I know, ever heard of again. Of the three men left over to the Spring Assizes, two were acquitted, when it came to the time. Of the death sentences passed on the four men in the first batch two looked like being commuted, when Sheahan last wrote.

Though Thomas Sheahan's account of the Bowens' Doneraile neighbours and their supporters throughout the county is brutally hostile, and may have been biassed, I am afraid we must take it that " bad spirit " was evident in the gentry in this case. The Doneraile " Conspiracy," and the trials that followed have, however, aspects that are interesting as well as regrettable. It is clear, from some parts of Sheahan I have not had room to quote, that the very *mixed* character of the prisoners was felt. Sheahan and his friends among " the people " in Court were indignant against the lumping-together, for trial, of decent and blameless farmers like the old man Leary with one or two blatant rapscallions and rogues. It is quite possible that among the twenty-one prisoners were the bad hats who *had* fired the shots: the Doneraile policemen, who knew their job, no doubt had a shrewd idea who they were. But the magistrates and the gentry had not been interested in mere free-lance attempted murder: *their* whole object was to show " conspiracy " in a big way and with a political cause behind. Rapscallions were therefore pointless; they wanted some leading men — hence their very mixed bag of arrests. The informers found the gentry gullible prey: the decent farmer Leary — to the excellence of whose character Arthur Creagh, father of the very Michael who had been shot at, personally and strongly testified — probably found himself in the dock as the result of bad blood with the two Dalys or somebody of their sort.

Again, the continued attempt by the Solicitor-General, playing to the Brunswickers in the Court, to pillory Mr. Harold Barry is interesting. Mr. Harold Barry throughout had shown a feeling for honour that his fellow gentlemen should have only approved. The Catholic Harold Barrys of Ballyvonare have never stood other than very high in the esteem of their neighbours, Protestant as well as Catholic — this so much so that I can only imagine that the boos in Court must have come from Cork Brunswickers. Clearly, Mr. Dogherty saw something in Mr. Harold Barry that did not make him happy at all. The English-inspired Commission professed to deal with a threat from 1798. In Mr. Harold Barry, the landlord standing beside his people, it saw the renewed promise of 1782.

And one more point — the Brunswickers, who before O'Connell's arrival jeered at his absence from Court, seem to have taken it that O'Connell's business would be to defend conspiracy. Actually, O'Connell posted from Kerry to clear prisoners (who were his " people ") of an unjust charge. In itself, conspiracy was as detestable to O'Connell as to any Brunswicker in the Court. Throughout his campaign he expressly denounced and forbade it. He had said: " The greatest enemy Ireland can have is that man who violates the peace."

One sees all this now. At that time, the " bad spirit " did not permit the gentry to think. This bad spirit was bred of three decades of a Union to which neither country, so far, had given its better side. Vanity, panic and adventitious loyalties in which self-interest loomed large set up a class stampede in which the Doneraile trials were only an incident. The stampede was wide-spread — but it was *not* general: there were numbers of Anglo-Irish who, for differing reasons, stood clear of it.

I may say for the Bowens that they did not let themselves be stampeded. This may have come not so much from firmness of character as from a certain independence and cynicism brought with them from Wales and not quite lost. Colonel Bowen's lack of team-spirit with the other Cromwellians, from the time he landed in Ireland, had been marked. Though the Welsh origin — except as a source of income — had soon ceased to count in the Bowen consciousness, they did remain, underlyingly, a Welsh family who had through England got Irish land. To this *land* (their land) existed their one great tie. Though I do not think they were for a moment bound to the Irish by any bonhomous feeling of all being Celts together, the expediency in their pro-English politics was not at all thickly veiled by sentiment. They were gentry, with the received ideas of their class — among these Protestantism and loyalty to the King's person stood high. But character — ruling passion, innate predisposition — stays a long way below the level of "ideas" — such a long way below that often no connection exists. Where ideas were concerned, the Bowens tended to show themselves fractious and changeable — they did not really care much for them. (My father was an exception to this.) Let us leave it that the Bowen ethic was politeness to England, rather than loyalty. They had been hybrids on from their start in Ireland; they were not even pure Anglo-Irish. They could, should, have pushed more than they did in 1782 — Henry III did his best with the Volunteers, but at that time he was an ailing and worried man, and Henry IV was away being smart in England. After that, Ireland, beyond their property's bounds, offered them no opening or function, and they did not — which I find was a pity — attempt to create one or find the other. Of things British they most favoured the Army. When Margaret, writing to Mr. Bruce, speaks of commissions for sons as " *opportunities that now offer to get them out on the world on easy terms (a great object with them)* " she puts one side of the Bowen feeling perfectly. But also, and better, they liked the virile set-up, the panache, the movement about the world and everything that went with the red coat.

The numerous Bowen lawsuits were outcomes of fights with their own class. I can find no note of trouble with tenants, or any suggestion that Bowens felt themselves persecuted by the Irish. (It had been Captain Nicholls who fled from the Rapparees.) They were persecuted, if at all, by each other. In fact,

with their Irish neighbours Bowens seem to have lived on terms
not only of mutual tolerance but of, even, temperamental
goodwill. The raid on the house in Henry IV's time was the one
break in this — as I have no Bowen letters of that year I cannot
gauge their feeling about the raid, but I think it likely that at
least some of the family considered Henry had brought this
upon himself by bad management, English fancies and showing
off. It would be very presumptuous to say that the Bowens have
been popular round Farahy. I can only say, we could not have
been better treated if we had been popular — our hardnesses
have been pardoned, our vagaries suffered, our dicta accepted
with reservations so tactful that we are not aware of them and
our characters thoroughly understood. (I only realize how
much this is the case when I am in England, and feel lonely.)
And I know I have never heard in this house — why should I?
— any remark about " the Irish " prompted either by panic or
the wish to insult. Not only was there no context for such a remark but my father would never have suffered it — nor, I believe, for all their aberrations, would any ruling Bowen before
him.

It is possible that the post-Union blight on their class — or, at
least, the blight on its morale — brought out the best in the
Bowen character. They do seem as a family to have got slightly
better as the Anglo-Irish in general got slightly worse. From
the pollarded tree they made a shoot of their own. It was
largely moral — but they did keep their heads. Though they
were from now on to call themselves Unionists, to be England's
dependants appealed to them no more than it ever had. Robert
and Eliza, for their parts, had no time in which to be devoutly
grateful to England for keeping Bowen's Court where it stood
— they were too busy keeping it there themselves. The Author
and Giver of all Good Things was, for Eliza, only Divine. She
would have found O'Connell a noisy fellow, and she no doubt
considered that he " upset " the people. Her own knowledge
of the people — both as the land agent's daughter and the

woman raised in the matter-of-fact merchant rather than the
up-in-the-air squire tradition — was in its way fairly thorough.
Her activities were not bounded by the demesne walls. Inside
the area she and the white donkey could travel no case of sickness or of acute want is said to have escaped her attention. She is
said (but this may be legend) to have started a lace-making
school at Shanballymore, three miles from here on the Castletownroche road. And this lace-school — to take one step more
into legend — is said to have made the christening veil for
Queen Victoria's eldest child. Eliza passed on this tradition of
work, with others, to the niece who was to succeed her at
Bowen's Court.

It is not clear how much she and Robert saw of the rest of the
Bowens during this time of arduous tenancy. Eliza was to state,
in a deposition, that she had " often been in the house " with
several of Robert's brothers. So one takes it that there were
family visits, and that Bowen's Court, in its now modest state,
remained the family headquarters. The military brothers, now
rather worn and seedy, must often have blenched under Eliza's
eye, as Robert had wriggled under her Ladyship's. And if
Eliza's son Henry V was lonely (which he shows no signs of
being) it was not for want of first cousins of his own age. He
had fifteen first cousins of Bowen name — among these were
three other Henry Cole Bowens, the eldest sons, respectively,
of his uncles Ralph, Nicholls and Stephens. This multiplicity
of Cole Bowens (inevitable result of Henry III's and Margaret's fecundity) all ringing the changes on quite a few christian names, might well, like the number of original Bowens in
Gower, go to create confusion. . . . For instance, I have over
the library mantelpiece three full-length silhouettes of Cole
Bowens, cut by the great M. Edouart, in Bandon, in 1837,
which have for a long time puzzled me. M. Edouart kept duplicates of all silhouettes he cut, and with these a detailed catalogue: he was shipwrecked with his belongings on a return
journey to France, and the duplicates and the catalogue later

turned up in Jersey. From Jersey some intelligent person traced and wrote round to the living heads of the families of all M. Edouart's subjects mentioned in the list. My father bought these silhouettes in response to an offer: they represent a Henry Cole Bowen, his wife and a Nicholls Cole Bowen. Henry has a rather Hapsburg profile; his wife shows a pretty coiffure and neck, and Nicholls wears a Velasquez or goatee beard. The trio are dressed in the height of fashion, and a sort of importance about their stance always made me feel I ought to know who they were. I have now established that this Henry and Nicholls were sons of the Rev. Nicholls Cole Bowen, fifth son of Henry III. Henry Cole Bowen is " of Dundernon "; his wife was a Miss Landers of Kinsale and Nicholls, a bachelor of apparent charm, died at Sunville, Bandon, aged fifty-four.

It is said that handsome Ralph of Mount Bruis left his pretty Mary under the impression that *he* was the next heir to Bowen's Court. (Ralph being Robert's senior this would have been a fact had it not been for Henry III's will.) As Ralph died before Henry IV the illusion did not during his lifetime have to be dispelled, and Mary, as a devoted widow, brought up her eldest son Henry Cole Bowen to expect his father's inheritance. When Henry IV died Ralph's Henry must have taken an unfair knock: however, he grew up to be an artist — he was an amateur painter of some merit — and art combined with his being his father's son to make him run through every penny; he had to sell up Mount Bruis, and no doubt his chief regret about Bowen's Court was that he had not also that to sell. He was sustained by his wife, a former Miss Ely of Foulkscourt, County Kilkenny, and left behind six children, one of whom emigrated to Canada and started a line there.

Besides Henry V's first cousins of Bowen name there were his Bowen aunts' children — Arabella Berkeley, the six Miss Jocelyns, Peggy Perry and a host of Metges and Wights.

On his *mother's* side I do not know how many first cousins

Henry V had. But there was one outstanding — Eliza Wade, daughter of Dr. St. John Galwey of Mallow.

In 1824, at the age of sixteen, Henry V matriculated at Trinity College, Dublin. As to his schooling before that, I am afraid I must leave one of those blanks by now usual in my narrative. His "formative" years were, I think, passed in this house, under the influences that I have shown. He is said to have had an able and quick brain. His career at Trinity College, Dublin, is outside my power to pursue. Samuel Kyle, D.D., later Bishop of Cork and Ross, was Provost at this time.

To find himself in Dublin was probably as interesting to the young County Cork man as to find himself a member of the University: the capital's streets surround the College buildings and lawns, and Henry V would be enough Henry III's grandson to like the movement of these. Thoughtfully Henry may have eyed the city in which he was to play no part, picturing other cities he was not, as it turned out, ever to see. On the subject of Dublin we Cork people always hold a reserved opinion. To the eye Dublin, on one of its great fresh days, looks good enough, with sun and clouds rolling over the quays, the bridges, the fine façades and the squares, with perspectives of street dazzling or ruled across by blue mountains, and a sort of salt brightness coming in from the Bay. On raw, dank days it is awful, like all cities. Henry's interestedness, good looks and grave good manners probably got him, in and outside College, enough friends. Since the Union Dublin was no longer what it had been: it had been said that grass would grow in the streets, and the great (as Henry IV had been quick to notice) had certainly gone. Assuming — which may not be very likely — that Henry V, as a young student of modest means, had enough "connections" in Dublin to go out, his impressions may, in a smaller way, have been not unlike those of Miss Edgeworth's Lord Colambre — who, as heir to *The Absentee* Lord Clon-

brony, breaks his journey for a few days in Dublin on his way
to the neglected Irish estates. My young ancestor and the
young man in the novel both brought to the city their stocks
of legend, but clear minds.

Lord Colambre did not find that either his father's or his
mother's representations of society in Dublin resembled the reality, which he now beheld. Lady Clonbrony had, in terms of detestation, described Dublin as it appeared to her soon after the Union;
Lord Clonbrony had painted it with convivial enthusiasm, such
as he saw it long before the Union, when *first* he drank claret at
the fashionable clubs. This picture, unchanged in his memory, and
unchanged by his imagination, had remained and ever would remain the same. The hospitality of which the father had boasted,
the son found in all its warmth, but meliorated and refined; less
convivial, more social; the fashion of hospitality had improved.
. . . . The guest now escaped the pomp of grand entertainments;
was allowed to enjoy ease and conversation, and to taste some of
that feast of reason, and that flow of soul, so often talked of, and
so seldom enjoyed. Lord Colambre found a spirit of improvement,
a desire for knowledge, and a taste for science and literature in
most companies, particularly among gentlemen belonging to the
Irish bar. . . ."

Quite likely young Henry V never did dine out, but remained applying himself to his studies, with his romantic forehead turned to a windowpane. I did not really intend to follow
him to Dublin — when Bowens leave Bowen's Court they go
off the edge of the screen. He *was* followed to Trinity College,
Dublin, by his brother Robert, who read law and was called to
the Irish bar in 1834.

At Bowen's Court things had eased up a little. From the Bath
front there was nothing new to report. Henry IV, bowling
round Bath in his carriage, left Robert alone to learn by trial
and error how to run Bowen's Court. And Robert did learn —
so thoroughly that he was able to pass his knowledge on. The
expenses of sending two sons to college could be and were met.

This emergence of efficiency in Robert, at whatever dire pains, is admirable. He begins as a rather *soft* character — lively and very reliable, a little too womanish in his love of gossip — he whittles down to a hard one, showing features and frame. (With characters dynamic, shapely in youth the reverse too often happens: something vital is sacrificed to the reconciliation with life.) Robert ceased to fuss over slights and stood up to real injuries. Nothing turned out as he had quite foreseen. In the genial merchant-prince atmosphere of Bearforest he had courted a trim and lively Miss Galwey: he found himself married to a fiery Dupont. In residence he had sought the small-town cosy: he had had Bowen's Court thrust on him. The sweet but reserved manners of his son Henry may have offered unknowing rebuffs to his sentiment. At the cost of puzzles and disappointments, and perhaps of ordeals in his intimate life, Robert attains to a dignity that does not make him seem out of scale with death. By the end of ten years at Bowen's Court he had come to attach himself to the place; he could lean back and look round — this was his home. But while Henry IV was still driving round Bath, when Henry V had been back from Trinity College for only a year or two — in fact in 1828 — Robert was once more called to face a change and a move. He died.

Henry V was twenty when his father died. Everything was now on his hands. (By a string of chances — one could hardly call it a fatality — all Bowens who have been heads of the family have come into power young. John I inherited Farahy from Colonel Bowen when he was about thirty; John II inherited Kilbolane and, virtually, Farahy from Captain Nicholls when he was not more than thirty. Henry II succeeded his father when he was twenty-three and, dying at twenty-five, left his posthumous son Henry III to be born owner of everything, and to take over everything when he was twenty-four. Henry III's death left Henry IV master of Bowen's Court when he was twenty-six. Henry V (as I have just said) succeeded at twenty to the lease of Bowen's Court which was to last up to his uncle Henry IV's death — after which the place would become his own. It did become his own when he was twenty-nine. To go past this point: Henry V's eldest son Robert, my grandfather, succeeded his father when he was eleven, and my grandfather died when his eldest son Henry VI, my father, was twenty-six. I was thirty when, on my father's death, Bowen's Court became mine.)

Any dreams had now to be put away. Henry V, during his childhood in this house, during the years in Dublin, may have dreamed of travel (the romantic tour, I think, more than the grand), of the distinction for which his growing faculties asked and for which they could have perfectly fitted him, of a true *beau monde*, ardent as it was elegant, and of experience in some territory at once so superb and so mystical that he would have hesitated simply to call it love. *Now*, life contracted round the young man of twenty to one duty — Bowen's Court. The mountains he had known all his life were to close in his horizons. To keep Bowen's Court his father had, in the long run, killed himself. Even had Henry had no feeling for the place, he had a deep feeling for his father's morality. He took up the work where his father had left off, and began to get, and to use, experience of his own.

Henry devoted himself to duty with the resolution, the single-mindedness of one who has turned from everything else — and with, I think, the inevitable romanticness of a nature that has sacrificed its romance. His idea of duty comprehended that of an early marriage, and I believe that, with a serious naiveness lack of any deep feeling made possible, he may have discussed the project with his mother. Eliza, steady in grief as she was in everything, was keeping the house going, but this could not last forever. She was prepared to abdicate — but only for a successor in whom she truly believed. Either a goose or a fine lady would, as a bride for Henry, have been shocking to her. She may have detected in Henry, whom she loved so much, capacities for emotion he did not know of, that must alarm his mother, that might hurt him. Early and wise marriage *should* be his aim. Any range of possible brides he and she ran through together was, I think, limited. Quite possibly Henry knew few girls: he had never been much about the country, and Dublin, apparently, had left his heart free. Did Eliza end by saying, in the controlled voice of a woman with something closely at heart: " Of course, there is always Eliza Galwey . . ."?

Eliza Wade Galwey, daughter of Dr. St. John, had the advantage of already living at Mallow, only those miles away. She knew Bowen's Court, and Bowen's Court knew her well. No doubt she had been a favourite with Robert. She was as lively, as self-possessed and as trim as her Aunt Eliza had been as a Galwey girl. She was good. In addition to this she was a gay pianist: she brought with her to Bowen's Court albums of music in marbled boards, with maroon leather backs and " Miss Galwey " printed in gold on maroon leather labels on their outsides. There was the score of *The Duenna*, also *Six Sonatas for the Pianoforte*, composed by J. L. Dussek for a Miss Shaw, and a very large collection of songs and glees — *The Erl King, Viva Tutte, His Sparkling Eyes, The Death of Crazy Jane, I Can No Longer Stifle, Tink-a-Tink, Rosa and Henry, How Shall We Mortals, Adieu to the Village, Fill the Bowl with Rosy Wine*, and others. She also, though I think there never was any dancing, played *Slow Marches, Quick Steps, Cottilons* and *Troops*. Her singing voice, to judge from the rest of her, would be small but have a true, round note. So whenever Henry thought of the Opera he could listen, instead, to Eliza playing and singing. Her piano, a Broadwood now alas noteless, is now in the Lobby.

Eliza was all I have said — as Henry could see for himself. The two cousins, under Eliza Bowen's aegis, would begin meeting rather more frequently. Even to Henry's delicacy it must have become apparent that Eliza was willing. Every one — including St. John Galwey, who had, as I said, as a man of

unique tact, remained a friend both of Robert's and of Henry
IV's — wished for the match. Henry liked Eliza and was in love
with duty: he married Eliza. As he led her down from the Mallow altar he may have seen the sun, a little below his shoulder,
on her pleased, proud little head. They married in March 1829,
and their first child, Robert, was born the following year.

I have taken this anti-romantic though loving view of Henry
V's marriage: I may be wrong. None of Henry III's reasons for
marrying *his* first cousin existed in the case of Henry V. This
Henry had no only-childish nostalgias; he had no years of
amorous wear and tear behind him to make him want to turn in
to a safe hearth. He had an excellent, able mother already, and
though his nature was finer than Henry III's it had more resistance and could have sustained itself. Every movement of this
nature of his, as I see it, should have been outward, exploratory,
towards the unknown, towards the *foreign* in one or another
sense. He had grown up in expectation, however unconscious
— the ethereal beauty of the country round him, the austere
but ecstatic religion in which he was raised would both
heighten this. And, he was " a great reader," they tell me: his
mother had left, among innocent books in the library, poetry
— and is any poetry innocent? His cousin Eliza Wade, to whom
Henry must now offer his twenty-one-year-old passion, was
as known, and as dear, to him as his sister Elizabeth. . . . I have
said that in the eyes of his portrait I saw a spirit content (or
taught) to reserve itself.

Eliza Bowen seems to have stayed on at Bowen's Court after
her son's marriage — though she has a Dublin address, with her
barrister son Robert, by 1844. Henry, pleased to be married
and still more pleased that every one else should be so, would
see no reason why his mother should go. If she ever said — I
am not sure that it ever was said in those days — " But you two
should be alone," Henry would have responded: " Oh no:
why? We should both miss you very much." So Eliza Bowen
either remained in residence or paid very long visits: the two

Elizas ran their part of the place together, and Eliza the dow-
ager saw her niece and daughter-in-law through her confine-
ments, of which there were five. The children's names were
Robert St. John, Henry St. John, Sarah, Anne and Henrietta.
(Henry V's sister Elizabeth married, I do not know at what
date, a Mr. Mathew Braddell, so left home.)

I imagine that the two successive Galwey brides must have
brought in adequate dowries — I cannot find even notes on the
settlements in the two Bowen-Galwey marriages — otherwise I
cannot see how, up to 1837, this family lived at Bowen's Court.
However well Henry worked the limited number of acres that
had been got from his uncle under the lease, and however
closely the two Elizas economized, there cannot have been
much margin. But in 1837 there was a considerable change —
news came that Henry IV had died in Bath.

The poor body of Henry III's heir made its return journey
to Bowen's Court sealed up in lead. On the 13th of February
Henry V, bareheaded in Farahy churchyard, and holding the
hand of his seven-year-old son Robert, watched Henry IV's
coffin take its place in the open Bowen vault. False springs are
very many in Ireland: quite possibly sun fell on damp tree-
trunks and evergreens and a thrush sang. Just as likely, it rained
steadily — in which case Henry V (who was to die of rain
later) stood with his collar up. Wherever Henry IV went to,
I hope that the simplest of his friends, the Rev. Mr. Armstrong,
was there to hold out a hand and put in a good word. " *Glory
to God in the Highest*," said the pink scrolls in the church
window, " *And on Earth Peace, Goodwill towards Men.*"

Driving back to the house after the funeral, or dismissing the
carriage and taking the foot-track over the lawn, Henry V
would see at the foot of the lawn, in its bare trees, the February
gleam of Bowen's Court — now wholly his and to be wholly his
son's. Possession has its spiritual side.

It would have been from this date on that Henry's public
activities began. Unremitting watch on the place was not now

so necessary; not only were things in order but there was more
money. The Farahy and Ballymackey rents now came in to
Henry, as his uncle's heir. I take it that the Honourable Mrs.
Bowen received an annuity in lieu of the allowance made to her
by Henry IV, but this would be the only charge on the estate.
Henry had now time not only to plan for his children's futures
(the English school to which Robert was later sent had been,
I take it, his father's choice) and to make felt in his household
his gentle but firm rule (most evident in the suppression, at this
period, of the Kilbolane grievance) but also to take his place in
the neighbourhood. The society of the " well-dressed savages "
— perhaps still a little chastened after 1829 — was now open to
him. The rigidity of the two Elizas — yes, they were as rigid in
tenets as they were kind in person; they are said to have
" Plyms " (or Plymouth Sisters) who forbade cards and dancing and discountenanced wine — and a certain reserve in
Henry's own temperament would keep convivialities in check.
Henry drove, mostly, about the country in the course of his
duties as a J.P. He had been at pains, we gather from St. John
Galwey, to make himself familiar with just so much of the law
as these duties involved. Driving home after courts he would
see, with the deepened feelings of manhood, the changing lights
and seasons he had known as a child. These old roads that he
drove he knew very well. He was now about to make new
ones.

Henry obtained from the government — or was it the Grand
Jury? — a grant to make roads round Farahy. Such grants were
being fairly freely made; their object was, relief for the work-
less and landless masses — miles of wall went up, with the same
object, and meaningless obelisks were raised.

A result of these grants has been the present, I think lovely,
complexity of the County Cork road-system. From the air (as I
said in my first chapter) the country seems to be braided over
with white: the roads twist and cross, dip down to one-arched
bridges, loop round mountains, converge on villages like the

rays of an asterisk. From one point to another there are, nearly always, three or four alternative routes, all equally indirect. When, at a crossroads, one takes the wrong turning one says: "Never mind, *this* road will do just as well." The few tarred main roads are for the heavy through traffic, the tourists, the big-house cars. But the twisting by-roads — narrow, glaring white in fine weather, in wet weather strung with puddles, sleek with mud — are the veins of local life. Haystacks in motion, ass carts clanking with milk cans, long happy funerals, young cyclists bound for the dancing, cyclists, walkers and traps on their way to Mass, cattle going to fairs, school children, errant and happy donkeys, pedlars of holy medals and young couples straying out of the priest's eye all use these. They are the people's roads.

The roads Henry made lie east of the Farahy river. They run at the foot of, sometimes into, the Ballyhouras, and at some points bend round, across alternate fields and heather, towards Doneraile. The mapping-out, the negotiations for either rights or goodwill (for Henry was here off his own land), the cutting, metalling, hedging of new thoroughfares, the widening and metalling of old boreens all deeply occupied Henry. There were always questions — how far to work on the old, with its disadvantages (boggy subsoils, floodings), how far to risk the new (chances of striking prejudice, more bog patches or unamenable rocks), how best to lay out the public money, how to get the best work from unused, underfed men, how to link up divergent boreens, how to placate farmers each expecting a royal way to his own door. With the men working Henry stood at one clear advantage — he was not a contractor; he had no profit to make. When he drove the men, he drove them from an excitement that they could tolerate if not share. Roads, roads, roads — not crossing horizons but all going *somewhere*, all meaning flux and energy. He did not spare himself. The work grew in him from an interest to an enthusiasm, from an enthusiasm into a passion. This came to such a point that he could not bear to be away from his roads. The Elizas, first with some humour, later with sinking hearts, saw Henry on to his horse and back to his roads again every day, in all weathers.

In all weathers — in the September of 1841 cold rain blew remorselessly down from the Ballyhouras, blinding Henry as he jogged along prospecting, driving in through his coat. When he came in in the evenings the Bowen's Court women kept big fires burning. Then there was an evening when no fire could warm him, when the Elizas saw his shivers go through his chair and looked at each other silently. His face, never quite familiar to them, must have looked less familiar that last evening he sat downstairs. The fever the chill set up was fought but could not be stopped. They watched, and he died of it, at the age of thirty-three. He is remembered for his goodness. But I do not think that the people round him, except possibly his mother Eliza, had any key to the life of this young man.

ROBERT COLE BOWEN

HENRY V'S ELDER SON ROBERT, MY GRANDFATHER, HAD BEEN
born in the August of 1830, and there was about his temperament something torrid and August-like. He was twice over
Galwey, through his mother and grandmother, and twice over
Bowen, though further back — his great-grandfather Henry
III having, as will be remembered, married the daughter of a
Bowen aunt. This may account for the features of my grandfather's character being pronounced to the point of exaggera-
tion. Nobody's attitude to him seems ever to have been negative. He was in fact a very high-voltage man. He belonged to
an age of locomotion and energy — in his day, the first train on
the Dublin-Cork main line was to steam into Mallow.

This Robert Cole Bowen was the first big Bowen since
Henry III. In many ways the circumstances of the two lives
were alike. Robert, like Henry, began as the boy heir left after
the deaths, within an unnaturally short time, of three ruling
male Bowens. Robert inherited an estate smaller than Henry's
by the loss of Kilbolane, but in as good order and as carefully
watched. (Robert owned, from the time of his father's death,
1,680 acres of County Cork and 5,060 acres of County Tipperary.) Henry had been brought up by a grandmother who
had recently lost both husband and son; Robert was brought up
by a mother and grandmother who had, equally, lost their other

objects in life. And even, two main dates in the lives of Henry and Robert correspond, with the lapse of a century — Henry had married in 1760 and died in 1788; Robert married in 1860 and died in 1888. The number of Robert's children actually born was less than the number of Henry's: against Henry's twenty-one children, of whom fourteen grew up, Robert had only thirteen, of whom nine grew up. Both these big Bowens wore, and with considerable effect, the psychological dress of their period; neither were civilized in the sense that Henry V and my father Henry VI were civilized.

Henry III I find, as must have appeared, very sympathetic indeed. I do not know what to make of my grandfather, and he is not for me to discuss. (I never met him; he died eleven years before I was born.) It is evident that a number of people liked and admired him — or, at least, were compelled by something about him into *behaving* as though they liked or admired him. There must have been something attractive, in the literal sense, about the heat and force of his temperament: he never lacked allies, companions, guests. And evidently he could also command Henry III's immense geniality, with, at the same time, more aplomb than Henry III. Among the country people he was at once admired as a big handsome figure, " the Captain," a hard rider, and dreaded (not without relish) as a hard man. A Fermoy gentleman who remembered him well spoke of him to me as " an old Mussolini." He had inherited all the Galwey ability, and he made a big business out of his estates. On the characters of his children he left an indelible mark.

Those of his children still living, or whom I remember as living, speak or spoke of him with an affectionate pride that is stronger for *not* being pious but being, somehow, unwilling. They relate without comment, though not, I think, without some sense of effect, stories of him as a father that make one think. His living children find, and his dead children, I know, found him open to criticism, but they would not wish to have him criticized to the world. And from a world in which, to-day, so many " nice " people seem to be minor characters, I do feel that he deserves, at least, respect. So anything that I may find to say that would not be in my grandfather's favour, I shall hope to say only by omission. Though I have a number of his letters and papers I do not propose to quote from any of them; their interest is considerable, but their usefulness in this book would not be great enough to justify any pain or annoyance that their publication might cause. This Robert Cole Bowen must remain seen from the outside. If his figure should seem blurred or distorted, it must be taken that I have not quite got him in focus: he stands just a little too near me in time.

As I shall not have space to give his career in detail, I had better begin by summarizing it. You have the date of his birth. He was educated at Cheltenham College and at Trinity College, Dublin (B.A., 1852; M.A., 1856). He was a J.P. for the counties of Tipperary and Cork, and was High Sheriff for County Cork in 1865. He married in 1860 Elizabeth Jane, second daughter of Charles Clarke, Esq., D.L., of Craiguenoe Park, County Tipperary. By her, who died in 1881, he had thirteen children, as I have said. In 1882 he married Georgina Constance Antoinette, fourth daughter of Charles Carden Mansergh, Esq., of Clifford, County Cork. His second wife, who was childless, predeceased him by one year.

Robert was, then, brought up by his mother and grandmother. These two must have made immense efforts, as Christians, to keep their beloved Henry V's death above the level of sheer human disaster. Possibly this continuous effort weakened their natures in other ways — if they did not adore the boy Robert they loved him with an extravagance they had permitted themselves in no other love. He was, in fact, rather spoiled. He filled up the Bowen's Court canvas so completely that his younger brother Henry got crowded out — in fact, I only discovered a very few years ago that I ever *had* a great-uncle Henry at all. A coloured daguerreotype on the library mantelpiece must, I think now, be he — a young officer in blazing uniform, choked by a gold collar, broadened out of the picture by massive epaulets. He is fair-haired, with a faint suggestion of whisker; his features are pleasant, irregular, and he wears a deprecating expression, as though not really expecting much of life. He became a captain in the Royal Artillery and died unmarried in 1874.

The three little sisters — Sarah, Anne, Henrietta — did at least hold their ground: they grew up to be the three old ladies of character whom, as my great-aunts, I remember well.

And that effort on the part of the two Elizas to sublimate Henry V's death had a second, and dynamic, result. I have noticed that love of a dead person brings about, in some natures, a deep obscure feeling that might be called resentment against him for the suffering he has caused. Strength of piety battling with strength of feeling made the two women act strangely towards the dead man. If he wished to continue to rule us, their still unchastened hearts said, he should have lived. So, they not only ignored his one great veto, they moved point-blank against it. They reopened, in the name of his son Robert, the Kilbolane quarrel, and took the matter to Court.

Three Roberts, one dead, two living, were present in *Bowen v. Evans and Others*, the great Kilbolane lawsuit of 1844. The first (the dead) was our friend Robert of Mallow, whose feeling, stored up in his widow Eliza, now bore fruit, and on whose remembered statements the Bowen case was to build up. The second was Robert Cole Bowen, of 36 Leeson Street, Dublin, barrister-at-law: he was the first Robert's second son, Henry V's younger brother and guardian of the little boy, the third Robert, in whose name the case was to be brought. I had better number these Roberts I, II and III.

Robert II, in going through the family papers after his brother Henry V's death had, he said, come on statements that more than supported his father Robert I's original claim to keep Kilbolane. Robert II's knowledge of law gave weight to his pronouncements, which were by the two Elizas eagerly taken up. Robert II is said to have said, also, that he had either received or been informed of a certain confession of forgery. In the interests of Robert III, his ward and nephew, Robert II felt it was his duty to act. So Robert II and the two Elizas went to the Mallow solicitor Edward Galwey — grandson of the dead William of Bearforest, son of Dr. St. John, brother of Eliza Wade — and instructed him to take the necessary steps.

That the elder Eliza, widow of Robert I, inspired *Bowen v. Evans* I do not doubt. The two others in the Bowen triumvirate acted: Eliza provided the driving force. Two feelings burned in her — sense of the injury done to her husband, desire to see a belated restitution made to the grandson who bore his name. To the adored boy Robert Kilbolane had got to come back again. This was not vicarious greed on Eliza's part: her sense of vital right was involved. What became an ugly and disastrous lawsuit was started in the spirit of a crusade. When Eliza took arms and made the others take arms, against a sea of *Evans and Others,* she was in fact out against, up against, the old Enemy, the dead Wicked Man Henry IV. From the fact that, in the course of the case, terrible charges were to be levelled against her own father William Galwey's honour Eliza, apparently, did not shrink. The Bowen case, as presented, was Elizabethan in its sense of conspiracy; it became a *Recherche du Temps Perdu;* it was Proustian in its sinister reconstruction of incident, in its demolition of accepted characters.

Bowen v. Evans and Others opened in this manner:

On the 16th of February, 1843, Robert Cole Bowen, a Minor, by Elizabeth Wade Bowen, his Mother and next Friend, filed a Bill in the Court of Chancery in Ireland against John Evans and Mary his wife, George Evans and Mary his Wife and twenty-four Others — Bruces, Bruce Nasons, Nasons, Farrells, a Mr. Bellis, a Mr. Clayton, a Mr. Shute Fisher, a Mr. Braddell — all either beneficiaries under the will of the late Mr. Evans Bruce (see Chapter VII) or being in enjoyment of profits (through mortgages, legal connection or settlements) from the Kilbolane lands.

This Bill prayed that the sale of Kilbolane and Bowensford (adjoining property) to the late George Evans Bruce be declared fraudulent and void. It prayed that the Appellant (Robert Cole Bowen, Minor) might be entitled to have Kilbolane and Bowensford restored to him, on his paying back, with interest, the sums of money advanced, between 1789 and 1810, by Mr. Evans Bruce to the Bowen family.

Why was the sale of Kilbolane and Bowensford to be declared fraudulent and void? Because in the first place, stated the Bowen Bill, the sale had been the outcome of *Grove v. Bowen*. And *Grove v. Bowen* of 1790 — that " amicable " suit brought by Mrs. Grove, Margaret Bowen's sister, with a view to getting Henry III's Estates administered, the debts paid off and the charges cleared — was entirely to be discredited. Why? Because it had been a good deal too " amicable "; in fact, it had been a put-up job. It had been put up with a view to obtaining (as it had in fact obtained) a Court order for the Kilbolane sale. The putters-up had been none other than Henry IV and Mr. Evans Bruce; their accomplices had been Mr. Richard Martin, Henry's attorney, and Mr. William Galwey, Henry's agent.

Mr. Evans Bruce and Henry IV had in fact (the Bill strongly suggested) been acting " in Collusion and Concert " for longer than any one, then, knew. The Judgement in *Grove v. Bowen* — that Judgement authorizing the Kilbolane sale — had been desired and engineered by these two. The lands, being part of entailed property, could not be sold without an order of Court. The obliging Mrs. Grove had thus been the catspaw, and the acquiescent Margaret and the young Bowens the dupes, of Henry IV, anxious to restore his own immediate finances at the expense of the future of the Estate, and of Mr. Evans Bruce, anxious for Kilbolane and anxious to secure it immediately.

Why was Mr. Evans Bruce anxious for Kilbolane — so anxious that he put up with inconvenience for years, took over liability for a number of Bowen debts and made out-of-pocket advances to many Bowens? Because (the Bill now suggested) Mr. Evans Bruce had been a wolf in sheep's clothing — he had stepped forward in the role of obliging and compassionate family friend; he had been, in fact, a speculator in land. He habitually (or so the Bill said) bought properties due to go up in value. His eye had for years been on Kilbolane. Why? Because he had ascertained that a number of the Kilbolane leases were due, shortly, to fall in: they would after that be able to be renewed at exceedingly advantageous terms. Mr. Evans Bruce had, accordingly, been anxious to establish an unshakeable claim to Kilbolane, and to compute with Henry IV for it, *before* its rising value was taken into account. (The annual rent values of Kilbolane and Bowensford had, in fact, doubled since Mr. Bruce got possession.) Therefore, the cheerfulness with which Mr. Evans Bruce had made advances to Bowens, the patience with which he had waited for the Conveyance (not actually made till 1810) must now be seen, the Bill said, in a sinister light. The more he got the Bowens into his debt, the surer his hold upon Kilbolane became.

Again, the price (the nineteen thousand pounds odd) paid by Mr. Evans Bruce for Kilbolane had been much less than the then value of the land, and was *very* much less than its value subsequently. How had he got Kilbolane at this inadequate price? Mr. Richard Martin, Henry IV's attorney, had, it may be remembered, bidden this sum on Mr. Evans Bruce's behalf when the lands were put up for public auction by the order of Court. There had been no higher bids, so the place was knocked down for that. How had this happened? Why had not bidding gone higher? Because, the Bill now suggested, this so-called public auction had been, in fact, a fake. The only two other bidders had *not* been bidders; they had been employees of Mr. Richard Martin's, acting under instructions received from him. And, the sum successfully bidden by Mr. Richard Martin was now

known to have been, to a penny, the sum agreed upon previously in private negotiation between Henry IV and Mr. Evans
Bruce. It was a matter of knowledge that Henry IV had been
permitted by Mr. Evans Bruce to continue to draw a number
of Kilbolane rents for years after Mr. Bruce had entered into
possession — which had been in 1794. Henry had thus been
recompensed personally for a bargain damaging to the Estate.

And there had been still darker dealings than this. Throughout *Grove v. Bowen* the case of the younger Bowens who were
Defendants — in fact, the case of John, Ralph, Robert, Nicholls
and Catherine Bowen — had been conducted by a Mr. Charles
Martin, in whose hands all their affairs were. (John, Ralph,
Robert and Nicholls had been, at the time of the bringing of
Grove v. Bowen, the only younger sons of Henry III who were
not still minors; Catherine had been the only daughter not still
a minor or yet married. The children who were still minors had
been represented throughout the case by their mother; the married daughters' interests were in their husbands' hands.) This
Mr. Charles Martin had been the brother of Mr. Richard Martin — it was true that they represented different firms, but
surely the connection looked sinister? It had been, the Bill said,
as sinister as it looked. Mr. Charles Martin, purporting to watch
the young Bowens' interests, had, in fact, betrayed them. And
he had done worse. He had drawn up the Defendants' Answer
in *Grove v. Bowen* and had presented this Answer as having
been sworn and signed by John, Ralph, Robert, Nicholls and
Catherine Bowen. It must now be known that Robert had since
declared that he had not so much as seen the Answer in question, and had certainly never sworn or signed it. It would have
been impossible for him to have done this: at the date at which
his signature appeared on the Answer he had been abroad with
his regiment. Then . . . had there been a forgery? Yes, there
had; and this forgery had been procured, if not executed, by
Mr. Charles Martin, in the interests of Henry IV and Mr. Evans
Bruce and with the connivance of Mr. Richard Martin and Mr.

William Galwey. It was, moreover, suggested that the four other Bowen signatures on the Answer had been, equally, forgeries. All now appeared to be in the same hand.

What made the Answer, and the validity of the five signatures on it, of such importance now? Because part of the matter of the Answer had been assent, by these five younger Bowens, to the Kilbolane sale. The order for sale had been given, and only could have been given, in view of their assent. To John, Ralph, Nicholls and Catherine the future of Kilbolane had been immaterial (they stood to receive only, and would receive anyhow, the sums of money left to them in their father's will). But to Robert it had not been immaterial. Why? Because, by the terms of his father Henry III's will, Robert was next heir to the Estate after Henry IV. He had thus a close interest in the future of the Estate. The forging of his name on the Answer would have deprived him, had he outlived Henry IV, and *had* deprived his son Henry V and his grandson the present Robert, the Appellant, of a very great part of the entailed property.

So much for the Bowen Bill. Before facing the Evans Answer let us stop to look, with some pain, at the extraordinary position created in the Galwey family by *Bowen v. Evans*. I have said that three Robert Bowens, one dead, two living, were in the field. In the field were also four Galweys, one dead, three living. There was William of Bearforest, the dead big land agent, founder of Galwey fortunes, Eliza's father, young Robert's great grandfather, lately an honoured name. There was his son St. John, the doctor, Eliza's brother, young Robert's grandfather. There was *his* son, Edward, solicitor, Eliza Wade's brother. The fourth Galwey, one Dr. William, appears in the opposite camp: he represented, throughout, one of the Defendants, an imbecile Miss Jane Nason whose doctor and guardian he was. Another of the Defendants, Mr. Braddell, was St. John Galwey's brother-in-law.

William Galwey, late of Bearforest, land agent, now stood accused by the Bowen Bill of behaviour so irregular and unscrupulous that, if it were proved, it must ruin his memory. He had, the Bill said, connived at a forgery. As one of the two new executors put in under *Grove v. Bowen* to administer Henry III's Estate, he had been guilty of a gross breach of trust. Even had he not known of the Henry IV-Evans Bruce conspiracy, his not having known could convict him of negligence — of, in fact, an incompetence so gross as to have disqualified him from his profession. It could be asked, and was asked as the case proceeded, if he had been fit to handle, as he had handled, large Irish estates whose landlords were absentees. One of those most concerned to prove the charges against him was his own grandson Edward, now solicitor to the two Mrs. Bowens who had been Miss Galweys. Had these charges been proved, had the Bowens won their case, all William Galwey's descendants, in and around Mallow, must have suffered from the blow to his good name. They were professional people — doctors, lawyers: the Galwey good name had been capital, so far. . . . One wonders how Edward, William's solicitor grandson, was induced to take up the case at all.

But the Galwey most to be pitied was, to my mind, St. John. The genial capable popular tactful doctor was in a position no one would like to face. On one side, his fiery sister, his fiery daughter, the interests of his Bowen grandson Robert, the ambitions of his own solicitor son — on the other, his father's honour, and all that attached thereto. There is evidence that poor St. John, now well into his sixties, detested *Bowen v. Evans.* " At the commencement," he said under cross-examination, " I expressed my strongest repugnance to the Filing of the Bill, to which, however, I was subsequently reconciled by the opinions of the most eminent Lawyers." He was in the wretched position of being a key witness; he had to stand up to interrogatories whose legal minutiae were enough to turn any doctor of medicine's brain. He stood up to these interrogatories like a man. His depositions, long and laborious, are overhung by a sort of martyrized tact. Ironically, his equally good friendship with both Henry IV and Robert now let him in for trouble — it was taken that he, alone, would have heard both sides of the case. Also, it will be remembered that when William Galwey, in 1817, left Mallow forever to go to Bath, he had left such papers as he had not returned to their owners in an office in his son St. John's house. Through all those papers that might relate to Bowens the unhappy St. John now had to make a search; he had to go carefully through each one and swear to his knowledge of its contents. He had also to swear — with the burning eyes of the two Elizas upon him — to his father's scrupulousness in all matters of business and to the blameless order in which the papers were left — all suggesting, there could be nothing to hide. St. John Galwey was also closely questioned as to Robert's movements prior to 1800 — *had* Robert really been abroad in the year when the Answer in *Grove v. Bowen* had been drawn up and signed? To this last St. John could reply, with unshakeable firmness, that he had not *met* Robert Bowen till 1800 and knew nothing about him before that.

And the Respondent's Answer, in *Bowen v. Evans and Others*? The prevailing note of it was, We are surprised. One is prepared to believe that they were greatly surprised. The outstanding Respondents — John Evans and his wife Mary, George Evans and *his* wife Mary — were, and I understand had been always, living in England. Kilbolane was no more than a bank-book factor to them. Now, on the well-bred order of Wilton Place, Belgrave Square, and on the lyrical peace of Lympsfield, Surrey, the Bowen offensive burst. Was this hallucination? Yes, the Evans decided, it must be hallucination. But the hallucination was not their own.

The Evans countered the Bowen Bill with an Answer of stodgy rectitude. They had not, they said, had any reason to question the validity of the Title to Kilbolane. Their uncle, the late Mr. Evans Bruce, had had no reason to question the Title either. No question had, till now, ever been raised. Had Mr.

Evans Bruce ever felt unsure of his Title, would he, both by
settlements in his lifetime, then by his will, have made relatives
in whose futures he showed a feeling concern depend for income on the lands in dispute? Evans, Bruce, Bruce Nason and
Nason marriages had been contracted, and families reared, in
untroubled enjoyment of the Kilbolane rents. Their uncle
would not have shown this confidence had his position not been
unassailable. As to his character and his dealings in business —
the Evans invited, demanded, examination of both. As to his
being a speculator in land — to speculate in land one must *buy*
land, and what land (this was open to demonstration) *had* Mr.
Evans Bruce ever bought, other than one small County Limerick property, for his private enjoyment, and the Kilbolane
and Bowensford now in dispute? Mr. Evans Bruce made no
practice of buying land. Their uncle's position, when he had
come forward with his original offer to purchase Kilbolane, had
been exactly as he had then shown it to be: he had capital to
invest; he would wish to invest it wisely; he was prepared to
invest it in Kilbolane. Good nature towards the Bowens, distress at their situation had (as *those* Bowens well knew) actuated him. He had, for the same reasons, hesitated to press for
a settlement. He had been delicate, but *not* endlessly patient. He
had soon found the situation irksome, and said so. What was
this sinister patience he was said to have shown? Correspondence could be produced — it was produced: Mr. Evans Bruce
had very frequently written both to Richard Martin and William Galwey praying that the Conveyance be expedited, expressing dissatisfaction with the state of affairs and reluctantly
threatening to threaten Henry IV, who answered none of his
letters, with the law.

As for *Grove v. Bowen* — Mr. Evans Bruce was shown to
have stayed outside that. He had shown no sort of interest in
Grove v. Bowen.

As for the characters of William Galwey and Richard and
Charles Martin — the Evans' lawyers had sifted the south of

Ireland in the course of a very careful check-up, from which the three gentlemen's reputations and characters emerged without stain. The Bowen charges against these three gentlemen would be laughable if they were not so shocking. Even apart from this there remained the known integrity of the Rev. William King, late rector of Mallow. Mr. King had been made, under *Grove v. Bowen*, co-trustee with William Galwey in the administration of Henry III's estate. Why should, how could, this irreproachable clergyman have connived at any shady affair?

As for the so-called fake auction — what was the matter with it? The auction *had* been public; in accordance with the Court's order it had been advertised in the newspapers — the advertisements still existed and could be viewed. It had been established, to the satisfaction of all, that the two other bidders had *not* been Mr. Richard Martin's employees; they were independent persons, in no way connected with him.

As for the young Bowens' Answer in *Grove v. Bowen*, and Robert's statement that he could not have signed this since he had been, that year, abroad with his regiment — the Evans' lawyers had checked up on every detail both of the 52nd Regiment's movements and of Robert's army career: they were satisfied that if Robert did *not* sign the Answer it was not because he was abroad with his regiment, since the regiment had not, that year, been abroad at all. And had not Robert's behaviour been very odd? If he had reason to know his name had been forged, why had he not taken action at once? *Grove v. Bowen* dated from 1790; in 1810 the Conveyance of Kilbolane to Mr. Evans Bruce had at last been effected, still, apparently, without protest from Robert. Why had Robert, within those twenty years, done no more than rumble round Mallow? — a substantial part of the Bowen case had been built up on depositions by people who had been Robert's friends and who constantly heard him say he was badly used. And why, above all, if Robert *had* had reason, ever since *Grove v. Bowen*, to consider

William Galwey not only his enemy but a crook and a cheat, had Robert not only frequented Bearforest but *married William Galwey's daughter in 1806*?

The Evans' Answer laid stress, laid its main stress, on the time-lag. It was now 1843 — more than fifty years after *Grove v. Bowen*. Why had the Bowens waited for fifty years? Their whole case was now built up on the *reputed* sayings of people now dead, who could not be sworn. Their case had the stigmata of an *idée fixe*, and of a dead man's *idée fixe* at that. Robert, having taken no action, had died in 1828. William Galwey, never challenged by Robert, had died in 1821. Henry IV and Mr. Evans Bruce, neither of them ever challenged by Robert, had both died in 1837. The two Martin brothers were dead. John, Ralph and Nicholls Bowen and Catherine afterwards Wight, co-signatories of the Answer in *Grove v. Bowen* but never called on by Robert to prove the forgery, were dead. How could the Bowens hope to support their case? Why had it not been brought when it had (if it ever did have) hopes of support? The Evans urged that the Bowens had not a case now.

Bowen v. Evans and Others was heard before the Lord High Chancellor of Ireland on the 8th of May, 1844. The arguments occupied four days. His Lordship took time to consider his Judgement, and delivered it on the 22nd of May. His Lordship declared that the Plaintiff was not entitled to impeach the Sale of the Lands of Kilbolane. The subsidiary sale of Bowensford, however, was to be set aside. (This latter sale, as not made under the Order arising from *Grove v. Bowen*, had been an irregular act on the part of Henry IV. Bowensford had *not* been released for sale.)

The four factors in the Bowen loss of the case were, as I understand, as follows: (i) Robert's inactivity onward from 1794, with his subsequent marriage to the daughter of the Trustee whom he held responsible for the sale; (ii) the time-lag: impossibility of upsetting a Sale or Contract after the expiration of so long a time, when all persons connected with it were dead;

(iii) the fact that no case had been made for setting aside the Order (the final Conveyance) of 1810, and (iv) the fact that no real proof of fraud had been brought, and that the sum paid by for Kilbolane by Mr. Evans Bruce was found to be a fair price for the land.

So, Judgement was given for the Defendants, with Costs. The Bowens gave notice of Appeal. The Appeal crossed the sea and went to the House of Lords. The House of Lords dismissed the Appeal, with Costs.

Costs . . .

To meet these, the reclaimed lands of Bowensford, with the exception of one large farm, were sold.

Bowen v. Evans and Others was more than a lawsuit. I have given some space and much thought to it because, in the course of the case, I can see emerging our family Character in a composite and very alarming whole. The story, the Bill, the family Depositions and the Correspondence that was brought into Court compose a Bowen case-book that deserved my attention if this history of mine were to be worth writing at all. I have been at pains to summarize their contents. My work was made easier by the fact that the entire *Bowen v. Evans* was beautifully printed for the House of Lords. The case makes a large last act for the unhappy drama of Bowens and Kilbolane — that drama that started with John Bowen I's subordination to Captain Nicholls, speeded up with the hunt for the Nicholls treasure and precipitated, I think, through Henry III's loss of the Kilbolane bawn and Brandon, the ostentatious building of Bowen's Court. Kilbolane had been no more, in the first place, than property brought in by a marriage. But it was at Kilbolane, not at Farahy, that the Bowens first built a house and struck a root into Ireland. Kilbolane became a hereditary obsession, an obsession that had become an organic part of the Bowen family temperament. While there are any Bowens the obsession, in one form or another, will always remain.

And the case confronts one, long after the Judgement, long after the failure of the Appeal, with a baffling mystery. Why did Robert not act, and, if Robert did not sign the Answer in *Grove v. Bowen*, who did? Robert may have not acted simply because he *was* Robert: he may have been more of a Hamlet than we thought. As for his story — there is no smoke without fire: no, not even in Robert's brain.

The family were in Dublin for the hearing. The elder Eliza stayed with her barrister son at 36 Leeson Street — at this house she had already been spending a part of each year. Where Eliza Wade and young Robert stayed I do not know; very likely Edward Galwey found rooms for them and took charge of them there. St. John Galwey stayed for the first two nights with his nephew and sister at Leeson Street, but I fancy the atmosphere got too tense, for he moved off on his own and took lodgings in Grafton Street. Down long canyon-like Georgian streets polished with May light the small party of County Cork litigants took its way to the Court or shuttled between the family lodgings for conclaves at the end of every exacting day.

Dublin, that May 1844, was humming with capital-city rumours — O'Connell, Young Ireland and the Repeal fight. The Young Ireland party was coming up on O'Connell. Was the Liberator weakening, losing his nerve, losing his grip in the middle of the campaign? For years he had stayed his hand: he had been prepared to give the Union a trial. Now he was once more in the field; he had brought up to back Repeal — but perhaps a little too late? — that all-Ireland threat that had got him Catholic Emancipation. Catholic Emancipation had been granted with bad grace; much had at once been done to restrict its effects — forty-shilling freeholders, for instance, were disenfranchised — and England was not yielding another inch. Just a year ago, at a meeting at Mallow, O'Connell had issued what rang like a challenge to war. But this time England was ready: mass threats were not to succeed again. Wellington had thirty-five thousand soldiers in Ireland. O'Connell's May challenge had been followed, that autumn, by the great anticlimax of Clontarf — where a Repeal mass meeting was cancelled at the last moment, at a rumour of troops. In O'Connell's view this averted a butchery, but Unionists crowed and Young Ireland reproached him with playing the people false. At Clontarf troops patrolled the quite empty scene of Brian Boru's battle — but O'Connell's arrest had followed: with his associates he was indicted for criminal conspiracy. At the close of a twenty-four days' trial, in a glare that made him a world figure, he was, with the rest, convicted. But the Dublin trial had been, demonstrably, corrupt: the panel had been tampered with, the jury were all Protestant. He appealed; the Appeal went to the House of Lords and O'Connell and the others were set free on a writ of error — black reverse for Wellington and for Peel. His triumph was celebrated on his behalf. But if he loomed larger in the eyes of the world, in his own country his shadow lessened a little. The Young Ireland party only did not steal his thunder because they did not want thunder; they did not believe in thunder. Too much thunder, the younger cold minds felt, had been O'Connell's mistake from the first. He had made the people of Ireland believe in O'Connell. Young Ireland meant to make them believe in themselves. He had built up a faith — was his failure to break it down?

In all quarters, all parties, Dublin feeling ran high. May accentuates the temper of cities; the brightness goes through the eyes to the nerves; long daylights keep people late in the streets. O'Connell, still the big figure, but with Young Ireland — Thomas Davis, Mitchel and Meagher — respectful but always harrying him; the Unionists in the quarters south of the river fixing on iron Wellington and his iron army their eye of faith — that was Dublin that spring of 1844. The tensed-up little Bowen party — the two widows, their escort of three gentlemen, the manly little boy — threaded their way unnoticed through the tensed-up city: they made no impact on it, it made no impact on them.

After the Judgement came the return to Bowen's Court, to the unmoved large rooms, the trees blazing with green. Bluebells, at this time of the Judgement, would be all through the woods round Miss Pretty's garden, and the little girls, Sarah, Anne, Henrietta, may have picked these with a view to cheering somebody up. Twenty-six or so miles away, Kilbolane also enjoyed the late spring sun. Back in Mallow poor Dr. St. John Galwey groaned and heaved himself out of his Dublin clothes. Young Robert no doubt went back to Cheltenham. But no one relaxed — there was still to be the Appeal.

For the Appeal, as I understand, Eliza Wade travelled to London, where she was met by Robert and, I hope, supported by Edward Galwey. The Appeal failed: Eliza Wade travelled home. The little woman of about forty must have had an access of woman-tiredness — the journeys, the cities, the stares, the waits, the courts, the grinding voices, the unremitting strain on her nerves and head. Now the pit of reaction awaited her. She dare not even think back to her husband. " Henry would have been grieved; he would have been angry. We knew Henry did not wish this. . . . Have we been wrong? "

Then, perhaps mercifully for Eliza Wade, the focus of everything changed. Personal life stopped dead. The tragedy of the Famine that entered every spirit entered and filled up Eliza Wade's. This was no time to stand pressing one's hands together. The country was dying, dying up to her door. Eliza went down to the basement and, in the big stone room at the door end of the stone passage (the room now the laundry), opened her soup-kitchen. Her battle began in the half-light below-stairs. Her work was exhausting, relentless, impersonal — no sweet-lady dispensation of charity. And it was half hopeless — she could not feed all the people. She would, I think,

gladly have made soup of herself. As it was, some dead bodies
of people too weak to get to her door were found on the grass
track from the Farahy gate.

The Great Famine reached its height in 1847: that is the date
given it, but actually it lasted for great portions of four years
— '46, '47, '48, '49. It had been seen coming: in the autumn of
'45 a potato blight spread over the north of Europe; its effects
in Ireland, where three-fourths of the people were wholly dependent for subsistence on the potato crop, were at once to be
dreaded. Great efforts, urged on by O'Connell, were made to
stop the export of Irish wheat. But these failed: food that could
have fed the people continued, " in the interests of commerce,"
to be shipped abroad. Had the grain and meat stayed in the
country, it may be said that the people had not the money to
pay for it; agricultural wages, over the south of Ireland, aver-
aged eightpence a day. And thousands were not in work at all.
The wholesale catastrophe of the Famine was the climax of a
cumulative distress. Report after report had notified warnings;
danger had been envisaged but not *realized*. Party strife and the
untouchability of ruling interests in Ireland had, together, made
" measures " planless and incomplete. Poor Law had, now, been
introduced and further relief works (like Henry V's roads) instituted, but no one was fully trusted, no one had been effective;
the ills of too-distant government were again manifest; no
party, in either England or Ireland, had the situation in the
necessary grip. The glissade to disaster had set in, and the potato
blight starting in 1845 only changed a steep slope into a cliff.
In 1846, in Ireland, no potatoes were saved. Landlords, at a
meeting in Dublin, pressed action upon the Government, but
this meeting came too late. By 1847 the horror had reached its
height. The people tried to eat the diseased potatoes and a
bowel fever followed starvation's work. Two millions died;
of those who fled to America, thousands died at the ports, or
died in the coffin-ships.

John Mitchel wrote:

A calm, still horror was over all the land. Go where you would, in the heart of the town or in the church, on the mountain side or on the level plain, there was the stillness and heavy pall-like feeling feel of the chamber of death. You stood in the presence of a dread, silent, vast dissolution. An unseen ruin was creeping round you. You saw no war of classes, no open Janissary war of foreigners, no human agency of destruction. You could weep, but the rising curse died unspoken within your heart, like a profanity. Human passion there was none, but inhuman and unearthly quiet. Children met you, toiling heavily on stone-heaps, but their burning eyes were senseless, and their faces cramped and weasened like stunted old men. Gangs worked, but without a murmur, or a whistle, or a laugh, ghostly, like voiceless shadows to the eye. Even womanhood had ceased to be womanly. The birds of the air carolled no more, and the crow and raven dropped dead upon the wing. The very dogs, hairless, with the hair down, and the vertebrae of the back protruding like the saw of a bone, glared at you from the ditchside with a wolfish avid eye, and then slunk away scowling and cowardly. Nay, the sky of heaven, the blue mountains, the still lake stretching far away westward, looked not as their wont. Between them and you rose up a steaming agony, a film of suffering, impervious and dim. It seemed as if the *anima mundi*, the soul of the land, was faint and dying, and that the faintness and the death had crept into all things of earth and heaven. You stood there, too, in the presence of something unseen and terrible.

In this ever-felt presence, the fight to stem the Famine went on. Local Relief Committees functioned in many districts — they were often bitterly suspect, sometimes attacked. Funds were raised in England and in America, and at home free-lance effort did what it could — the gentry were largely crippled: rents had stopped. Indian meal was dealt out. More relief work was put on foot; the half-living gangs Mitchel saw were slowly extending more roads to nowhere and raising, around demesnes and along highroads, miles upon miles of " Famine walls." No

one did not suffer; few who could do so did not fight. Women
in the isolated big houses worked, like Eliza Wade, on their
own: much of the false feeling was stripped away; natural ties
were formed that have lasted since. " Many," Aubrey de Vere
says of such women, " succumbed under the labours of those
years, or under the privations which they endured in silence.
Over others came a change that did not pass away for years.
The eyes which had witnessed what theirs had witnessed never
wholly lost that look which then came into them; and youth
had gone before their voices had recovered their earlier tone."

And here is part of an unpublished pamphlet by Stephen
Spring Rice:

What was the life led by an Irish squire at that time? You might
have seen him leaving home before daylight, that sunrise may find
him within his relief district, into the destitution of which he has
to inquire. Till sunset makes it impossible to continue his work,
he has to pass ceaselessly from house to house, making every possible inquiry, and exerting all his ingenuity to detect the frauds
attempted by those who wish to job. . . . Being well known, the
people troop down from the hill tops to meet him, in their tens
and twenties, threatening or imploring; and he has to use his best
eloquence for soothing, cheering, or for checking and reproving
them. Wearied at last, he returns in the twilight to his home,
doubting whether he is not carrying to it the seeds of the disease
caught in the hovels he has visited. But he does not go home to
rest. His whole night, and far into the next morning, is occupied
in reducing into an available form the rough memoranda of each
case which he has collected in the daytime. The next day, perhaps,
he has to attend presentment sessions. Amidst roars of anger and
cries of suffering he has to attempt to work out a novel and complicated system; sick at heart with seeing the realization of his
worst fears — the famine, fever, and gradual demoralization of the
lower classes, the ruin of the higher. Throughout the day little
notes are showered in scores on the table; these are the petitions
of the poor, materials for his work at night; for when he at last
goes home they must all be deciphered, classified, considered, and

prepared for the next meeting of the Relief Committee. . . .
And what rest does he get by night? Every half-hour he starts
up from an uneasy sleep, haunted by one idea that still recurs.
He dreams he has lost a little scrap of paper on which he had recorded the name of one that had required immediate relief, and
that from his carelessness a family is starving.

And: "What," comments Aubrey de Vere, "was the reward for all this suffering? The most unbounded misrepresen-
tation, both in England and in Ireland, and in the latter country
frequent violence."

Up in the corner of Farahy churchyard the Famine pit was
dug and not slowly filled. The bodies had to be tipped in coffin-
less, earth shovelled loosely over them, to be disturbed again.
The names of many dead were not known; they were mountainy people drawn down to Farahy by hopes of reaching the
Bowen's Court soup-kitchen. This movement towards help
that was not reached created a higher death-rate in Farahy than
in many of the other parishes round. At Bowen's Court, the
desperate pressure of people against Eliza Wade's door at the
end of the kitchen passage made it necessary that the door
should be barred: through a trap she gave out what soup there
was, then she had to shut the trap and hear groaning movement
continuing hopelessly outside. As she turned slowly away
down the stone passage, *Bowen v. Evans and Others* must
have looked like a dream. . . . What was it we said was right,
once?

In the spring of 1847 Daniel O'Connell left London on a pil-
grimage, to pray for Ireland in Rome. He got no further than
Genoa, where he died. His coffin returned to Ireland, into a
crowded harbour, into the heart of his people he had failed to
save. His break with the Young Irelanders had been, by the
time of his death, complete. They were now for the sword. His
death cleared the path for them. And there was now another
figure in Smith O'Brien, County Limerick gentleman, descendant of Brian Boru. O'Brien hoped, for some time, to work with

his own class: he hoped much of new ties formed in the Famine, of the purge effected in the gentry by horror, of the present strong discontent against failures in government. What might have come of the rally O'Brien contemplated one does not know: it was not carried through, for now the emergence of two extremists frightened the gentry off. Fiery deformed Lalor, Queen's County farmer's son, was for non-payment of all rents; John Mitchel was for the exposure of false measures by refusal to pay Poor Rate, at the height of the Famine. And now, in 1848, the second French Revolution repeated the work of the first: wavering liberals hardened into reactionaries. Smith · O'Brien and Meagher made, again, Tone's appeal to new Republican France, but were not even given Tone's grounds for hope: Lamartine would not meddle with Ireland. In England, the Chartist menace once more tightened reactionary policy — that went, also, for Ireland, in which the Government strengthened its garrison, armed its supporters and fortified Trinity College. Prosecutions for sedition were launched: Mitchel was convicted by a packed jury and sentenced to transportation for twenty years.

Though the English Whig government of 1848, was *not*, like earlier governments, aiming at provocation, the repressive acts its position appeared to warrant were enough, in some quarters, to bring things to a head. There was an abortive rising, sponsored and led by O'Brien, Dillon and Meagher. The country, unready, enervated by famine, had not heart or means to give the three leaders support. Kilkenny, which was to be seized, failed them; Carrick-on-Suir was over-garrisoned; Cashel, on which they were moving, did not stir. Those peasants who marched to join them were recalled by their priests. O'Brien's own tenants marched with him: this feudal aspect of the rebellion, with the little area inside which it moved, got it called the Rebellion of the Cabbage-Patch. A skirmish outside a police barrack was both the climax and finish of the campaign. O'Brien and Meagher were captured: the country gentleman

and the intellectual were tried for treason at Clonmel and sentenced to death — a sentence later commuted to transportation
for life. Dillon escaped arrest and made his way to America.

Next year, Queen Victoria visited Ireland. Everything, in
her own words, went off beautifully. Gloriana was in her mind
as she touched at Cove: " Our visit to Cork was very successful; the Mayor was knighted *on deck* (on board the *Fairy*), like
in times of old. We had previously stepped ashore at Cove, a
small place, to enable them to call it Queen's Town; the enthusiasm is immense. . . ." In fact, her genius and intrepidity had
led her to time her visit exactly. Having been too sick to rebel,
the Irish were now sunk in a melancholy that wanted, only,
diversion. Skeletons, they played the Paddy superbly. " A more
good-humoured crowd I never saw," wrote the Queen, " but
noisy beyond belief, talking, jumping and shrieking, instead of
cheering. There were numbers of troops out, and it really was
a wonderful scene."

During the Famine, the master of Bowen's Court was away
at school. Robert's first years of schooling at Cheltenham must
have been much broken into by *Bowen v. Evans and Others.*
There seems no doubt that Robert enjoyed the case — who
would not, at fourteen? He was to tell his own children how
well he remembered sitting in Court: several Eminent Personages came over, said, " So this is the Appellant? " and courteously shook his hand. He was also invited, he said, to sit on the
Judge's Bench. Few schoolboys, on the whole, are Appellants,
and still fewer have Appeals that go to the House of Lords.
One may therefore take it that *Bowen v. Evans* gave Robert a
cachet among his Cheltenham friends. His mid-term departures
to hearings would be impressive, and he would speak with a
marked ease of the Law. At any rate, his character grew with
each year more positive, more satisfied — not so much with itself as with the world it was growing able to rule. At the same
time, the large-scale defeat of the Bowens, when the Appeal

failed, would have to be met and be carried off. Defeat must
either make or unmake a nation or character: in this case, the
loss of *Bowen v. Evans*, the necessity to face the world as a
loser went a long way, I think, to make Robert what he became.
It accounts for his chin-up attitude throughout life, his hardi-
ness, his almost inordinate feeling for success. Everybody who
came into Robert's orbit *must* excel, in one or another field. In
his relationship with his growing children this was, in time, to
become clear. In himself, he worked all capacities to the full;
he made up the ground he had lost at school; he did very well at
Trinity College. As a young landowner in two counties he
early, in both counties, made himself felt. He got on with people — everybody says that. He stood well where he recognized
power; he maintained a relationship with God.

Eliza Wade, with her Robert away at school, must have been
glad he was spared the horrors of Famine. All the same, to
Robert at Cheltenham the idea of the Famine cannot have failed
to get through. He would, as an Irish boy, be avidly asked about
it, and probably, as a landlord, taxed with it — it must be remembered that Robert's class, the Irish landlord, in England
was coming in for a good deal of the odium that, at home, that
class attached to England itself. Blame for the Famine was
being thrown bitterly to and fro, and, as in all cases where *all*
who rule are to blame, each of the rulers a little hated the others.
Robert must, as an adolescent, have not only hated the Famine
but hated his country for suffering. All this was the negation of
his new cult, Success. The *idea* of Famine may have grown
worse to him than the facts he was not allowed to see. I trace
to the action of the repressed idea that inverse of his hardy con-
queringness — his dislike of the " morbid," so mastering as to
become morbid in itself, his resentment of suffering, so far-
reaching that it extended to sufferers. All his life he detested,
and turned from, sickness and death.

The earliest picture I have of my grandfather is a photograph
taken in the year of his marriage — it cannot, I am sorry to say,

for technical reasons be reproduced here. The young man of
thirty has the long Bowen head; almost excessive power and
energy appear in his forehead, the jut of his eyebrows, his eyes
keenly focussed on nothing, the way his eyes are set in. The
bony structure is good. The upper lip, short and thin, is undershot by the under lip, which is strikingly full. The hands are
unfeeling, untactile – not beautiful hands. Robert's attitude,
with unduly contracted shoulders, seems to be queered by the
camera. No line of the face or body, in this photograph, suggests that Robert could even feign repose. And he could not
bear down on the cold machine as he was able to bear down,
twenty-one years later, on Mr. Brenan, the affectable R.A. who
was executing his portrait in oils.

On his return from Trinity College, Robert took over control of his estates. They were handed to him in excellent order,
by his mother Eliza Wade and his Uncle Robert, with the
breach left by *Bowen v. Evans* repaired. They were now,
under the force of Robert, to become, as I said, a business really
superbly run. Later on, in the new wing at the back of the
house, Robert was to construct for himself an office: here rows
of leather-backed ledgers built themselves up; here a safe was
fitted into the wall; here rents were taken in, with a merciless
punctuality, and wages scrupulously paid out. The room,
rather dark, looks sternly over the yard: it is approached from
the yard by stone steps, a glass door, a passage of some length
– many remember trembling as they came this way. To estate
management Robert gave the best of a capable intellect – he
read round his subject widely, revolved new ideas upon it, then
tested, scrapped or adapted them. And his physical energy was
unflagging: he was seldom not on the go, on foot or horseback;
he owned not a yard of land he did not know well.

He was a great planner, and his plans took effect. He left
nothing to be spontaneous or chancey, even in his personal life.
From the fact that he married when he was thirty, I take it he
planned to marry at that age. It is a suitable age, and his mar-

riage was suitable. Like other marriages, it had elements to it
that could not stay locked inside the will and the head.

In fact, the encounter that led to the marriage was romantic
and chancey to a degree. In the course of a late winter or early
spring my grandfather happened to be in Dublin. One afternoon had suddenly turned wet, and Robert, in the Leeson Park
neighbourhood, was walking with his umbrella up. Looking
across the road he saw, on an exposed pavement, a pair of young
ladies with no umbrellas, obviously embarrassed by the rain.
Crossing the road towards them, raising his hat and showing
every sombre sign of correctness, Robert offered the ladies his
umbrella. The older sister (for they were two Miss Clarkes)
showed agitation and refused the umbrella: she was evidently
extremely shy. It was not for Robert to press the matter; he
was ready to bow regretfully and pass on when he caught a
look, at once friendly, determined, wistful, in the younger Miss
Clarke's eye. She did badly want that umbrella — young ladies,
those days, were not rainproof, and these two were dressed for
calling — and, though not less delicate than her sister, could
really see no harm in accepting it. So, to the younger sister
Robert renewed his offer, which was not refused again. Miss
Elizabeth's graceful self-possession, her good sense and the
calmness with which, with a view to returning the umbrella,
she noted the stranger's name and address all impressed Robert.
He saw her take the current with the ease of a swan. He was,
more than he knew, enchanted. In this state, having replaced
his hat on his last bow, he moved off, with manly disregard of
the rain, while the two Miss Clarkes, under the male umbrella,
moved in the opposite direction. Fate had sounded a bell.

Elizabeth Clarke was given leave by her parents to write Mr.
Bowen a note of thanks. This, arriving with his umbrella at his
Dublin address, completed, just by its wording, the captivation
of Robert. Each phrase, to his eye, was instinct with feeling and
grace. It was for her good manners, Robert announced later,
that he had married his wife Elizabeth. It is possible that Eliza-

beth's *manner* was part of her physical personality. As a girl in her early twenties she was (to judge by successive pictures) less nearly beautiful than in her later life. But her way of holding herself and her smiling candid calmness must always have been distinctive and beautiful. In girlhood, the fine open moulding of her face, her eyes set in like eyes in a Holbein portrait, her rather large mobile mouth must have been distinctive and strange. She always moved with deliberation; her voice was low-pitched; she must have been a mixture of aliveness and repose. The set of her head on her rather short, shapely throat and her way of turning her head were characteristic. Her intelligence must have been palpable, and her taste in dress was, or seemed to Robert, as felicitous as her taste in words. And there was more than this — deep character and a steady, noble capacity for devotion appeared in this Miss Clarke's still young face.

Robert was fortunate. He must, almost at once, have spoken of this new turn of his will to his Uncle Robert, with whom he was staying. It then appeared, Uncle Robert had the Clarkes' *dossier;* he had even met them — they were connections, in fact. Mrs. Clarke had been a Miss Bland; the Blands were descended from one of the six daughters of the Thomasine Bowen who had married George Jocelyn. Several Blands lived in Bath, where the Clarkes, to be near them, quite often spent the winter. Uncle Robert, on a visit to Bath, had seen much of the Blands and had met the Clarkes. In fact, Uncle Robert was in the position to put everything into proper train: he must, I think, have suggested that a call on the Clarkes on the part of both Robert Bowens would now come in well. The Clarkes were, for this winter, staying outside Dublin; they had taken one of those pleasant slate-fronted houses at Blackrock, along Dublin bay. They were wealthy and could make their plans as they chose. Their recently-built mansion, Graiguene, near Holy Cross, County Tipperary, was said to be very fine. Mr. Clarke had only one son, Marshall, and the two daughters

Robert had met. His children had had all the advantages —
education, movement about the world. For the son there was a
substantial inheritance; the daughters should be well dowered
with Bland money.

The Blackrock call was paid; the courtship was put on foot.
It is said that Mr. Clarke rather clearly indicated that he would
prefer Robert to take Sarah — who, though shyness made her
look young, was Elizabeth's senior by nearly ten years. But
Robert would not be side-tracked; he not only loved Elizabeth
but admired gumption, which Sarah lacked. Sarah's vacillations
in the matter of the umbrella were typical of her throughout
life. She wore out several suitors by indecision. She was never
certain that she loved quite enough. It is said that Sarah could
have become a duchess — it was not that an actual duke proposed to her, but that the young man who was her most constant suitor did, by some chance of succession, later become a
duke. She was a most individual, lovable creature, to whom
many people — including, later, her Bowen nephews and nieces
— became attached. She remained unmarried, but showed no
signs of regret.

Mr. Clarke resigned himself to Robert's preference and,
while Robert secured Elizabeth's heart, Uncle Robert, acting
as Robert's lawyer, secured a handsome dowry with the bride.
The marriage settlement was drawn up and signed. There had
then to ensue, I take it, one of those pauses, supposed to deny
any gross hurry, between the declaration and the consumma-
tion of love. (Robert found some outlet for feeling, during this
pause, in redecorating Bowen's Court in superb style.) The
Clarkes spent the following winter at Cheltenham, so it was
there, at St. Luke's church, that Robert's and Elizabeth's marriage was solemnized, on December 3rd, 1860. A little later,
still in the mid-winter, the bridal couple returned to Bowen's
Court.

In the alterations Robert made in the house he gave vent, to
my mind, to a subtle antipathy he must always have felt for

Henry III's taste — yes, even when the factor of fashion has been fully taken into account. Those two big Bowens, one dead, one living, were almost bound to be incompatibles. Though Robert liked the solidity of the Bowen's Court structure, its unemotional plainness was not grateful to him. I think he disliked light (he had much of that out of doors), despised space (as a form of vacuity) and had a half-savage feeling, apart from fashion, for the protuberant, the glossy and the ornate. The object of furniture was, in his eye, to betray expensiveness, to denote extreme solidity and to fill up rooms. It must be said, however, that Robert's forceful temperament could not express itself otherwise than in a forceful style. Every curve, every ounce of weight, every colour meant something to Robert, and though his innovations seem, sometimes, appalling, they were not gimcrack or mean. He did, however, work exactly against the first conception its builders had of the house.

His *chef d'oeuvre* was the drawing-room. Complete, this must have been striking — in its own way lovely — and I would give much to see it as it was then. The white, grey and gold scrolled paper (still on the walls) was hung, and run round with a gilt beading. Against the paper the two frieze-high, gilt-framed mirrors were reared — one over the yellow-and-white marble mantelpiece, one over the new grand piano (Eliza Wade's piano had gone upstairs). Round the top of the room continued to run Henry III's Italian rose-basket frieze. Over the five windows went up gilt pelmets; from these hung satin-striped beetle-green curtains, with inner curtains of gushing lace. On the green-black ground of the carpet, colour of pickled olives, scrolls of gold-green leaves with cherry-pink fruit appeared. The cherry-pink was picked up in the satin upholstery of the couches, the " *tête-à-tête* " and the occasional chairs. Other ladies' armchairs, with shell-fluted backs, were upholstered in a chartreuse-green rep. Several massive oval or circular tables in blond walnut filled up any offensive space. On these tables or on the mantelpiece stood objects in alabaster under high glass domes. There was much painted china; there were shells carved with cameos; there were enormous silver and cut-glass lamps. Over the mirror-surface of the tables were disposed Heath's *Books of Beauty*, in gilt-wreathed cobalt covers, and, also, maroon and olive albums of foreign views. . . . In on all this must have blazed, through Henry III's windows, the immense torrid afternoon sun. On all this, from the arched grate with its brass garland and cupids, the firelight must have flung its glare. This seems to be such a drawing-room as only the starved voluptuary could conceive: it is like one of the drawing-rooms in a Brontë novel. Perhaps, under the regime of the two Elizas, Robert had, at one time, been a little starved.

Upstairs preparations went on, too. Robert acquired a four-poster wedding bed, broad, as George Moore would say, as a battlefield, hung with curtains of a reversible oyster-and-claret damask, with a pattern of, appropriately, vines. I well remember this bed when I was a child: I wondered why nobody seemed to care for it — it stood, then, in one of the spare rooms. When one drew the curtains, on their mahogany rings, they made inside the bed a complete world.

Robert's other improvements on Bowen's Court were made in the course of years after his marriage, but I had better summarize them here. He built on, out from the back of the house, the wing that contained his own and some other offices. He divided the present library into two — the smaller back room, a long slit with one window, was first a bedroom for his invalid mother, then his growing children's schoolroom. Inside the void north-east angle of Bowen's Court, left when Henry III found he could not complete the square, Robert raised the unsteady lean-to that provided pantry, bootroom and footman's room. But his great, his most revolutionary work was the erection of the " Tower " that flanks the back of the house: it contains two water closets, is topped by a tank and approached from the back stairs. This masterpiece of Robert's must have been the result of a long dream. I found as many architect's drawings for the Tower as I had hoped to find, and did not find, of the original house. Plumbing, though only in this small area, thus came to Bowen's Court, and I hope that the glory of the inauguration was not too much obscured by prudery. The Tower's unfriendly predecessors — unchanged, I think, since Henry III's day — are at some distance outside, sunk in a hillock, crowned by a grove, approached by passages not unlike roofless catacombs.

In the demesne, Robert improved the plantations and planted screens to protect his fields from the mountain winds. Round the house he levelled lawns, cut banks up the slopes, planted laurels, trimmed the sweep of the woods. He created, for Elizabeth's enjoyment, the Pleasure Ground, south of the garden wall — a sort of outdoor drawing-room clumped with mauve rhododendrons and overlooked by a rustic summerhouse. His great addition to outdoor amenities was, however, the Lower Avenue. Till now, there had been only one avenue — Henry III's, now called the Upper — running uphill from the steps to the big gates placed as far as possible along the Mallow road. Downhill to the village of Farahy there had been, so far, only the grass track that Eliza Wade's Famine people had used. Now, Robert's carriage, first between curves of meadow, could bowl over the new surface, pass between bulwarks of clipped laurel, turn out through new lodge-gates into the village and over the humpbacked bridge towards Mitchelstown, to pick up the Tipperary road. The construction and constant use of the Lower Avenue showed a reorientation of Bowen life. . . . For farm traffic there was a third, the Back, avenue, this running parallel to the Upper and opening not far from the Mallow gates.

Robert's first child, Henry Charles Cole, was born on the 21st of January, 1862. After him came:

Robert Cole,
Sarah Frances Cole,

Elizabeth Harriet Mary Cole (born September, died October 1865),

Anne Marcella Cole,

Charles Otway Cole,

Mary Elizabeth Cole,

Edward Neville Cole (born July, died October 1870),

Elizabeth Constance Cole,

St. John Cole,

Arthur Marshall Cole (born December 1873, died January 1874),

Mervyn William Cole,

William Walter Travers Cole (born February, died May 1877).

My grandmother can have had little time for the contemplative side of maternity. Robert's children crowded into the world. The elder babies' foster-mother was Mrs. Barry, whose cottage stands halfway between the two lodge gates. Their night nursery, as infants, was that top east room whose one window looks into treetops — one of the least airy rooms in an airy house. From here, life overflowed into the Long Room, and, as the nursery filled from the bottom, the elder infants one by one were extruded into other rooms on that floor. One by one, they next made the fateful descent to the schoolroom sliced off the back of the library. My grandfather did not believe in grossening children: he cut the nursery diet down to a minimum — and in fact these children, who grew tall very fast and lived keyed-up, suffered from inanition. Their skins were pale, though pretty, their eyes blue, their hair generally red-gold. Several of them showed Clarke features — short noses, expressive foreheads, rather marked eye-sockets. Charlie and Lizzie were two exceptions: they were dark-haired, and had the longer features of the earlier Bowen type. Bob was dark-haired, but short-featured. Of the sons, Henry was the most studious (and absent-minded), Bob the best horseman, Charlie the most observant, amusing and on-the-spot. Of the daughters, Mary was the most vivacious, Lizzie the most temperamental. Their child life, congested and isolated, their life as Bowens together made a drama from which, as grown-up people, some of them found it hard to emerge. This was Personal Life at its most intense.

The number and handsomeness of my grandfather's children were a source, I am told, of satisfaction to him. As for them, their consciousness of him as a father was something seldom allowed to rest. The very rate at which they grew tall seems a sort of symbol of aspiration: he would not have liked stumpy children. Bob only stopped growing at six foot four, my father, Henry, at six foot two, none of the other brothers at less than six foot, and none of the sisters at less than five foot nine. For those children (or so it appears to me) the personalities of their father and mother had an almost supernatural surround. Robert was a great believer in education — any earlier Bowen vaguenesses in this matter were more than made up for by him — and he felt education ought to be strenuous. He had, as he often told them, provided for his children a mother who was a model of education and manners. It was his habit, at the mellow end of dessert, to have a selection of children in from the schoolroom and put them through the lessons they had learned all day. His cold undivided attention, his handsome torrid presence, pushed back from the table and veering round in his chair, made some wits work desperately, paralysed others. Yes, they were afraid of him. Their mother, magnetically, remained calm. She showed a sweet understanding, but she was hard to reach.

At the same time, life had its idyllic side. People who think of Victorian family life as being all repression, superstition and fear, as being a foetid nursery of complexes, overlook something — that sweet august illusion to which, in their own ways, everybody subscribed. Loves and hopes and habits had a romantic depth they have lost now. Family life at Bowen's Court, in the 'sixties and 'seventies, *had* its idyllic side.

And this was still more felt at Camira. Camira, near Nenagh

in County Tipperary, had become Robert Cole Bowen's second seat: it formed part of the Ballymackey property brought
to the Bowens by Jane Cole. Ballymackey Castle, once the residence of Jane Cole's grandfather Sir Robert, was by now in
irreparable ruin, otherwise Robert Cole Bowen might have reopened that. As things were, Camira, a seventeenth-century
house that had for years been occupied by a tenant, could be,
and was, reclaimed and put into commission. On this house,
which had not been Henry III's, Robert felt free to stamp himself from the start: consequently, he cared for it very much —
it is said that he liked it better than Bowen's Court. He came to
spend two or three days out of every week here, overseeing his
own large farm attached to the place and keeping an eye on
tenants on the rest of the land. (It must be remembered that,
since the Kilbolane loss, Robert's County Tipperary property
was very much more extensive than the property he held in
County Cork.) So, at high speed and with unremitting energy
he, twice a week, drove the fifty miles between Bowen's Court
and Camira. And, twice every year, for some weeks in each
late spring and early autumn, the entire Bowen's Court household — children, servants — moved to Camira. I have never seen
the house: it is in sight of, if not near, mountains, and is spaced
round with large glossy trees. It stands three stories high — and
my grandfather took off the slate roof to replace it by a tarred
canvas one, with a flattened curve like the roof of a railway
carriage. The children loved Camira; as grown-ups they remember it with nostalgia — it has been sold now. I imagine that
those spring and autumn sojourns must have had the charm
of *villegiatura* — and some of the freeness, too. Here the regime
of Bowen's Court would relax. And there are places where life
seems, always, kinder to one. The children found waiting, at
each return to Camira, delightful surprises, delighted friends.

I have brought in Camira partly because it appears in *The
Bowen Diary*, from Volume VI of which I should like to quote.
The Diary was faithfully kept by four of the young Bowens

— Sarah, Annie, Mary and their brother Charlie ("C.O.C.B.") — writing turn abouts. The date of Volume VI is 1876: in this year Sarah, the eldest writer, was twelve. In reading *The Diary* one must keep in view the social distinction and the social cleavage between different age-groups in a large family. Henry and Bob, as big boys, public schoolboys, came and went in a rather *affairé* way; they lived in, and Sarah (as eldest of the four daughters) sometimes impinged on, a more or less grown-up world. At the other end of the scale, "the little children" were Lizzie, St. John and Mervyn, in this year aged, respectively, five, four and one. Miss Flavelle, by the way, was the excellent English governess who controlled the destinies of the middle group. I only have room to give, more or less at random, some of the daily entries: those I do give are not cut. I wish I could print the whole: *The Diary* loses much from breaks I am forced to make in its continuity.

April 9th.

Bob's birthday, he received our presents. Weather showery. We all went to church. Papa went to poor Aunt Mansergh's funeral.

Sarah Bowen.

April 10th.

We went out with Henry and ran races in the pleasure ground. Mr. Moore came to see us and spent the day here, he said Mrs. Moore and the children are well. Weather cold and windy, there were a few snow showers.

Annie Marcella Cole Bowen.

April 11th.

Mama and Aunt Annie went to Clifford. (Clifford had been the late "poor Aunt Mansergh's" home. Aunt Annie was Robert's second sister Anne Bowen: she remained unmarried and subsequently went blind.) *Mary Bowen* (Robert's second cousin: granddaughter of the handsome Ralph) *and Papa went to ride. Weather cold and snowy.*

C.O.C.B.

April 13th.

Aunt Annie went away. Papa went away to Cork. Mary Bowen rode to Doneraile. Weather fine.

               Sarah Bowen.

April 14th. Good Friday.

We all went to Church. Miss Flavelle, Henry and the four of us took a long walk and crossed the river near the mill, where we had great fun placing stepping stones. A very fine day. Mary Bowen rode to Kildorrery with Papa.

               Annie M. C. Bowen.

April 16th. Sunday.

We all went to Church in the morning. Papa read prayers in the evening. (These were now read at the billiard table that had been placed in the hall.)

               Mary.

April 17th.

Papa went to meet Bob at Mallow station. Miss Annesley went there to look for a house. (Miss Annesley was a lady staying at Bowen's Court after a serious quarrel with her brother, to whose house she did not mean to return.) *Bob has a cough. Weather wet.*

               Sarah.

April 18th.

We had a holiday and walked with Miss Annesley in the morning. In the afternoon we drove up the mountain, it rained so heavily that we had to come home, on the way home it cleared and Miss Flavelle, Henry, Sarah, Charlie and Mary walked across Greague and Miss Annesley and I drove round by the road where they met us near the fox covert, then we all drove home together.

               A.M.C.B.

April 20th.

A fine morning, we walked with Miss Annesley. Mama, Henry, Bob and Sarah and Miss Annesley drove to Doneraile. Miss Flavelle, Anne and I went to the Rectory garden, Williams showed us the nest of a thrush in an apple tree.

               Mary.

April 21st.

Weather wet. Papa went to Camira. Bob rode half way to Rock-mills but was obliged to return on account of the rain. Mrs. Oliver (of Rockmills Lodge) *and Dickie came here.*

                                                      S.F.C.B.

April 22nd.

Bessy left. Miss Annesley, Miss Flavelle and the three of us drove her home. Mrs. Jordan, a new maid, arrived here. Weather beautifully fine.

                                    Annie Marcella Cole Bowen.

April 23rd. Sunday.

We went to Church in the morning, and Mama read prayers in the afternoon. Weather wet. Sarah's two pupils did not come.

                                                      C.O.C.B.

April 29th.

My birthday, but I forgot it. Papa came home. Weather wet.
                                              Sarah Bowen.

May 1st.

A holiday for Sarah's birthday. We kept her birthday, Annie and Bob gave her a picture and a box with a perfume bottle inside and Mary gave her another picture. I gave her a book.

                                                      C.O.C.B.

May 2nd.

Papa and Mama, Henry and Bob went to Mallow. Miss Annesley went with them away to her lodgings. Mama went to see Aunt Creagh and the Galweys. (Aunt Creagh was Robert's third sister Henrietta, who had married her cousin Arthur Gethin Creagh. The couple now lived in Mallow.) *We went to walk. Weather fine.*

                                              Mary Bowen.

May 3rd.

We drove to Annesgrove and brought back a bunch of flowers that the gardener gave to Miss Flavelle. Weather fine.
                                              Sarah Bowen.

May 4th.

Mr. Rice, the photographer from Mallow, arrived in the morning, he took several views of the house and of us in groups, and he took Mama and Papa on horseback. Miss Flavelle, Sarah, Lizzie and St. John sat in the wagonette. Henry, Mary, Charlie and I stood on the steps. And last of all he drew one of nearly all the labourers. A fine day.

A. M. C. Bowen.

May 5th.

Bob returned to school. All very busy packing up for Camira.

C.O.C.B.

May 7th.

The luggage went to Camira. We drove to Ballywalter with Miss Flavelle who had an antimacasser for Mrs. Welstead.

S.F.C.B.

May 8th.

Miss Flavelle, Mrs. Devlin, Mary and the little children went to Camira. Mervyn was very much frightened at the rain. We had a paper hunt an hour too soon.

Sarah Bowen.

May 9th.

Papa, Mama, Henry, Annie, Charlie and I drove to Camira. We left Bowen's Court at half-past eight, arrived at Aunt Jane's at eleven (I think this must have been Aunt Jane Gubbins of Kilthrush, a Clarke connection) *and at the Armstrongs' at half-past two. Arrived at Camira half-past seven. We had a pleasant journey. A fine day.*

Sarah Bowen.

May 10th.

Our first day at Camira, and a holiday. We took a long walk with Henry; first we went to the garden, then to Capa (?) Castle, then we walked through and just as we got on the Toomevara road we heard Bowers calling us, then he told us that Mama wanted

us. In the afternoon the Joneses came to see us. We played Pris-
oners Base with Hume and Rickie. A fine day.

Annie Marcella Cole Bowen.

May 11th.

Mama and Sarah went for a drive. Miss Flavelle, Henry, Mary,
Charlie and I went to Ballymackey. We played at Hide and Seek.
A very fine day.

Annie Marcella Cole Bowen.

(Here there is a break in the Diary.)

June 19th.

During the last few weeks we have been so very busy prepar-
ing for the Sunday school examination at Nenagh that we have
not had time to write in the diary. The principal events as well
as I know were that we heard that Nurse was very sick with jaun-
dice, from which she is now recovering, also we heard that Mrs.
Dickey laid four eggs, Mr. Dickey broke two of them. The
weather here has been very fine. We have had many pleasant
drives about the country, sometime to Nenagh. Once we had a
picnic at Knocknagh. Mr. MacCarthy and Hume Jones were
there. Annie got sick. Aunt Robert (widow of Robert's Uncle
Robert, the barrister — he had died in 1874) *came to spend a few*
days with Mrs. Cashel. Mr. Jones was very ill, he was in bed for
three weeks (Mr. Jones was the Rector of Ballymackey); *we had*
no School for two Sundays. Once we went to Nenagh church in
the morning, and once to Toomevara. Mr. Stawel preached twice,
at three O.C. in Ballymackey church. Hume and Rickie have been
here many times.

Papa has had a beautiful haybarn built. Hanlon and Davy Smith
came down here from Bowen's Court to build it. It was finished
on Saturday last, when Papa gave the men a half holiday and got
up great fun for them, consisting of donkey races, sack races, pull-
ing ropes, etc., etc. Then Papa distributed among them ten shil-
lings worth of bread, afterwards they got eight gallons of porter
and had a grand concert in the yard. Hanlon sang the best. Miss

Jones dined here. That evening after dinner the workmen all came before the hall door. Higgins was the leader, he called out three cheers for Cole Bowen and all the men waved their hats and cheered. Then he added, three cheers for the Coles of Bally-mackey; they cheered again and went away.

The Sunday School Examination took place in the church at Nenagh on the fifteenth of this month. I was in the first class, Annie was in the third, Charlie and Mary were in the fourth class. I had to learn the Articles, the 8th of Romans and the 11th of Hebrews by heart, and to be examined in Exodus from the 20th to the 40th chapters, in Leviticus from the 9th to the 24th chapters, in Numbers from the 9th to the 24th chapters, and the whole of Hebrews. Annie had had the proofs to the end of the Creed, Genesis and Mark. Charlie and Mary had first four chapters in Genesis and Luke. My examiners were Mr. Bowles, Mr. Massey and Mr. Stawel. I answered 28¾ out of 36, and got second prize. Annie answered 23 out of 30 and got second prize. (Further details of the Examination follow.) *The 15th was Corpus Christi, a general holiday for the R.C.'s. It was also market day in Nenagh, consequently the town was very full. After my exams I walked down to Coyne's with Henry and round by the courthouse to the church; then we took Charlie up the Wellington Road, where we met Mr. Bowles who wanted us to go to dinner at his house.*

Sarah.

June 20th.

Henry and Charlie rode in the morning. Henry dropped his watch. In the afternoon Mother, Henry and I walked to Bally-mackey.

Sarah Bowen.

June 22nd.

The Joneses came to Camira. Henry's watch found. In the evening Mrs. and Miss Jones came to say goodbye to Mother, who was very busy all day.

Sarah Bowen.

June 23rd.

Mother, Henry, Charlie, Mary and myself drove to Bowen's Court. . . . We had a very pleasant journey.

Sarah Bowen.

June 24th.

Miss Flavelle, Annie and the little children arrived. Mrs. Oliver, Miss Aldworth and Mr. Montgomery came to visit here.

Sarah Bowen.

June 26th.

Aunt Jane came here. Weather fine.

Sarah Bowen.

June 27th.

Weather fine. We played croquet, and got into the summer lesson hours.

Sarah Bowen.

July 1st.

Papa went to Camira. We played croquet. Weather fine.

Sarah Bowen.

July 2nd.

Mother and Bob rode to Rockmills. Weather fine.

Sarah Bowen.

July 4th.

Aunt Jane went away. Mother and the boys drove with her to Kilfinane. Weather fine.

Sarah Bowen.

July 8th.

Weather wet. We all played in the long room. Mother and Bob went to ride.

Sarah Bowen.

July 10th.

Mr. and two Miss Bowens and Miss Hungerford came to visit here. Papa and Mother dined at Ballywalter.

Sarah Bowen.

July 12th.

The first day of Cahirmee fair. Papa and Bob went to it. The weather dry and hot. We fed the hens.

A.C.B.

July 13th.

The second day of Cahirmee fair. Papa went to it alone. The weather very warm. We fed the chickens.

C.O.C.B.

July 15th.

Weather very warm. The boys, Papa and Mama went to a cricket match at Doneraile. In the evening we fed the fowls.

Mary.

July 19th.

Miss Aldworth arrived. Weather still very warm, the grass very much burned. Fed the hens.

C.O.C.B.

July 20th.

Weather very warm. Mama gave a garden party, there were sixty visitors here, they played croquet. There were six clergymen. It was a very nice party.

M.B.

July 25th.

Henry and I played games of croquet against Papa and Bob. We won one of the games and Papa another. Weather very hot.

Sarah.

July 26th.

A very wet day, for which every one was delighted. Mr. Annesley lunched here. In the evening Papa shot a rabbit.

Annie Marcella Cole Bowen.

July 27th.

Papa went to Cork. In the afternoon Mama, Henry and Bob went to a party at Ballywalter. Weather fine.

C.O.C.B.

July 29th.

Papa came home. Uncle James and Aunt Judith (Galweys, from Mallow) *came with him. Weather fine.*

                                                    Sarah Bowen.

August 1st.

Papa *went to Cork. There was a telegram from Mr. Aldworth. Dr. Tuckey came to see Mervyn, and he came yesterday also. Mervyn has thrush. Weather fine.*

                                                    C.O.C.B.

August 3rd.

Uncle James, Aunt Judith, Henry, Bob and I drove to Doneraile. Weather very fine. Henry and Bob rode to the mountains in the morning.

                                                    Sarah F. C. Bowen.

August 7th.

Uncle James, Aunt Judith, Henry and Bob drove to Doneraile. Bob got his hair cut in a stables. Weather fine. We gathered five full baskets of mushrooms.

                                                    S. F. C. Bowen.

August 10th.

Lizzie's birthday, we all gave her presents. We drank out of the little tea things.

                                                    Mary Bowen.

August 11th.

Maud and Tommy Bunbury came, then we all went a grand picnic, we walked up the mountain, we had great fun. Papa brought his Alpine stick.

                                                    Sarah Bowen.

August 16th.

Henry and Bob went back to school. Papa went with them from Kilmallock to Templemore. A fine day.

                                                    Annie Marcella Cole Bowen.

August 21st.

Papa and Mama drove to Oakgrove to spend some days. (With the Robert Bowen-Colthursts, descendants of John Bowen of

Carrigadrohid: the family breach, dating from Henry III's day, has just been healed.) *Weather very hot.*

Sarah Bowen.

August 23rd.

We went down to the river to get some sand.

Mary Bowen.

August 24th.

We made a grand new walk in the cone shrubbery. Mrs. Oliver and Dickey rode here. The chimney caught fire. Mrs. Morrow called here. Weather very fine.

Sarah Bowen.

August 25th.

We made another walk. Mama and Papa came home. We went to see the hens. A very fine day.

Annie M. C. Bowen.

August 26th.

We showed Papa this morning the new walk. A fine day.

C.O.C.B.

September 1st.

Weather fine, we played croquet. Mr. Batwell's horse broke the swing gate.

Sarah Bowen.

September 5th.

We were all very busy packing. Miss Holland and the small children went to Camira.

S.F.C.B.

September 6th.

Mother, Papa, Sarah, Charlie, Mary and I started for Camira at eight o.c. We arrived at Aunt Jane's at about half-past twelve, we arrived at Camira about 9 o.c. A very wet day.

Annie Bowen.

September 7th.

We were very busy unpacking. Weather fine.

C.O.C.B.

September 16th.

Miss Flavelle returned from London. Weather fine.

Mary Bowen.

September 18th.

We recommenced lessons. Weather fine. I went for a drive.

Sarah Bowen.

September 29th. Michaelmas Day.

Mr. Gabbot's harriers met here, we followed them in the wagonette. There were three carriages besides ours. Mrs. Gabbot, Mrs. Smithwick and child and the Miss Smithwicks lunched here.

Annie Marcella Cole Bowen.

October 4th.

The annual Protestant Orphan meeting was held in the Lecture Hall in Nenagh. Mama, Miss Flavelle, Sarah and I went to it. Charlie and Papa rode and we drove in the wagonette. The meeting was very well attended. The High Sheriff was in the chair. The speakers were, the Dean of Cashel, Mr. Head, Mr. Jones, Dr. Bell. Rev. Mr. Bowles read the Report and Archdeacon Robins closed the meeting. Mr. Bassett Holmes collected. We saw a great many of our friends there. We liked the speeches very much.

A. M. C. Bowen.

October 11th. Old Michaelmas Day.

The Harvest Thanksgiving service was held in the church of Ballymackey. The church was decorated with apples, melons, vegetable marrows, potatoes and wreaths of berries. There was a large attendance. . . .

C.O.C.B.

October 17th.

We walked to Ballymackey to say goodbye to the Joneses. Weather fine.

Sarah Bowen.

October 18th.

Mother very busy packing to go to Bowen's Court. All the luggage went about 10 o.c. We walked to Widow Kennedy's and gave her a dress. Then we walked to Ridge Mount to enquire for Mr. Brearton, Grace Hill said he was very sick. Weather rainy.

Annie M. C. Bowen.

October 19th.

We got up very early and had breakfast at 6.30 a.m., and at 7.20 Papa, Mamma, Sarah, Annie, Mary and I started from Camira in the wagonette. It was raining a little when we left. We changed horses near Shallee and afterwards at Mr. James, where I mounted the pony, and rode as far as Aunt Jane's, where we lunched. From there I rode as far as Ballyorgan, where the grey horse met us. When we arrived everything was very comfortable.

C.O.C.B.

October 20th.

We fed the canaries, then Sarah rode the black pony, then we went to our gardens and worked there. Miss Flavelle, Mrs. Devlin and Lizzie, St. John and Mervyn arrived 5.30 p.m.

Mary Cole Bowen.

October 21st.

We said some of our lessons. The Duhallow hounds met here at 11 o.c. The three Miss Aldworths, Mr. Aldworth and Aylmer Martin lunched here. After luncheon Charlie followed the hunt. All the hounds were before the hall door, afterwards they went to Shahana, where Charlie's stirrup leather broke. We showed Miss Flavelle the new walks we made when we were last here. A very fine day.

Annie M. C. Bowen.

October 24th.

Papa and Mama went to a party at Mrs. Creagh's. When they were out a telegram arrived here announcing the death of Mary Bowen's Father. Charlie rode the new pony in the lawn. We walked in the fields. Weather fine.

Sarah Bowen.

October 25th.

Mr. Batwell went away yesterday. We walked down the avenue to see Nurse. Miss Flavelle went into the vault to see it, she said

*that it was very clean. Afterwards we went into the fields behind
the lodge and built rockeries. Papa went to Cork, he brought back
young Mr. Hayes in the evening. A fine day.*

Annie M. C. Bowen.

October 26th.

Mr. Henry Bowen's funeral. (This Henry Bowen was that eld-
est son of Ralph's who had been an artist, failed to inherit Bowen's
Court and had to sell up Mount Bruis. The first two of the mourn-
ers mentioned by the children were, respectively, his third son
and his son-in-law: his elder daughter had married a Metge, of
Sion, Meath; his second daughter, the "Mary Bowen" of the
Diary, remained unmarried.) *The hearse arrived about noon. Mr.
Harry Bowen, Mr. Metge and Mr. Shea accompanied it. Rev. Mr.
Hayes, junior, read the Burial Service. Papa and I were there. . . .*

C.O.C.B.

October 28th.

*Annie Galwey was married to Mr. Batwell. Papa and Mama
went to the wedding. I rode with Charlie in the lawn. Weather
fine.*

Sarah Bowen.

October 30th.

Papa drove to Mallow to see Aunt Bessy's grave. Weather fine.

C.O.C.B.

October 31st.

*Papa went to Dublin. Mama, Aunt Annie and I drove with him
to the station at Mallow. After that we went to Aunt Creagh's
and had lunch there. We left Aunt Annie there and Mama and I
returned home to Bowen's Court. Weather very fine.*

Mary Bowen.

November 1st.

*Last night I came down stairs in my sleep. Annie and Charlie
rode in the afternoon. Miss Flavelle, Mary and I walked as far as
the Canteen Cross.* (Where Broghill had stationed his Cromwellian
troops.) *Coming home we went round the gates. Farahy bridge*

*was covered with people, it being All Saints' Day. Weather fine
and frosty.*

           Sarah Bowen.

November 2nd.

 *Mother, Miss Flavelle, Sarah, Mary, Charlie and I drove to
Doneraile. Mary bought some nice white calico with blue spots
for her doll, I bought some pink calico and some red and white
ribbon, and Miss Flavelle bought two packets. In one she found a
locket, in the other she found a pair of earrings. She gave the earrings and some of the sweets to Lizzie, and the rest to St. John.
A fine day.*

           Annie Bowen.

November 4th.

 *Mama, Miss Flavelle, Sarah and I drove to Killee, to see Mrs.
Montgomery. Sarah and I played with Margaret, who showed us
her little donkey. We heard from St. Columba that Henry has
a cold. Weather fine, there are still a great many leaves on the trees.*

           Mary Bowen.

November 7th.

 *Mama received a letter from Aunt Annie to say that Henry was
better. In the afternoon Mama drove to Buttevant station to meet
Papa, and they arrived home about 5.30. Papa brought some pictures for our Scrap Books. Weather fine. Annie rode in the lawn
with me.*

           C.O.C.B.

November 11th.

 *A very frosty morning. We had a nice play on the avenue. As
there was no news from Henry, Papa sent a telegram to the
Warden to know how he was, he received an answer back to say
that Henry was better. Weather wet in the afternoon, so as we
could not go out we played in the long room and painted in the
Schoolroom.*

           Annie M. C. Bowen.

November 14th.

A very wet day. In the afternoon I rode with Papa. We cut out a great many nice pictures that Papa gave us.

C.O.C.B.

November 15th.

The Duhallow Hounds met at Ballywalter. Papa and Charles rode after the Hunt. In the afternoon Miss Flavelle, Sarah, Annie and I drove on the Mountain road and saw the Hounds from a great distance. We met Mr. Annesley. Weather fine.

Mary Bowen.

November 19th. Sunday.

Weather fine. We all went to church. In the afternoon we went to Mr. Hayes' Sunday-school. Papa read service in the hall.

Sarah Bowen.

November 24th.

Lord Doneraile's hounds met at the Kennels. Papa rode after them. We went out in the morning, but it rained too much to do so in the afternoon. Mr. Creagh came to visit here.

Sarah Bowen.

December 4th.

We played in the long room and cut out pictures for our Scrap Books. Papa went to Dublin. A very wet day.

Annie Bowen.

December 8th.

Papa came home. Lord Doneraile's hounds met here. Henry and Charlie rode after them.

Annie Bowen.

December 11th.

We walked along the mountain road. A fine day.

Annie Bowen.

December 13th.

The Duhallow Hounds met here. Henry and I rode after them with Papa. A very damp day.

C.O.C.B.

December 21st.

Miss Evans was married in Doneraile Church to Capt. Anderson. Papa accompanied Mr. Aldworth and Mrs. Jordan to the wedding. There were six bridesmaids. The dejeuner was at Mrs. Creagh's. There were over 200 guests.

Sarah F. C. Bowen.

December 22nd.

Bob came home from school. Mr. and Miss Aldworth and Mrs. Jordan went away. Miss Flavelle, Bessie, Sarah and I assisted in decorating the church.

A.C.B.

December 24th. Sunday.

We drove to Church, as the ground was covered with snow. When we were returning we were obliged to get out of the car, as the avenue was too slippery for the horse.

Mary.

Christmas Day.

A bright frosty day, and the ground covered with snow. We wished everybody a merry Christmas, then Mama called us all up to the Lobby where we received many pretty presents from our Aunts. We also received cards. We did our usual Christmas pieces for Papa and Mama, also a drawing of Black Rock Castle which we got Handlen to frame. Mama liked it very much. We all went to Church, it was very prettily decorated. The text was Gal. iii. 16, " God was manifested in the flesh." We had late dinner with Papa and Mama and plum pudding. After dinner we had great fun playing consequences and with some crackers Aunt Mary sent us. Nurse had a bad night and did not enjoy her Christmas much.

Sarah Bowen.

December 26th.

A very wet day. We had music and scripture lessons only. We painted texts and played in the long room.

Annie Bowen.

Three months after the close of Part VI of the *Diary* was
born a last little Bowen, William Walter Travers — this poor
baby, who never seems to have flourished, died at Youghal the
following May. At Youghal, that County Cork *plage* at the
mouth of the Blackwater, Robert took for his children, every
second summer, one of those stucco villas facing the sea. In
their little tight black boots they ran on the long wet sands —
in fact, they ran a degree more nearly wild here than they were
allowed to run at Camira. Sad that poor little William's death
should have blotted one seaside holiday! The servants, brought
from inland, viewed the sea with mistrust: one screamed pierc-
ingly when she first beheld it, another spoke of it as " the big
bog."

Before 1876 there had been a good many changes. The elder
of the Elizas had died — I think in Dublin — in 1861, the year
after Robert's marriage, and her niece and ally Eliza Wade did
not long survive her. Eliza Wade stayed at Bowen's Court after
her son's marriage — she occupied, as I said, the rather dusky
back room Robert had carved off the back of the library. With
her attendant, Nurse Fitzgerald, she continued to drive round
the grounds in a phaeton. The old-lady face of Eliza Wade is,
in the last of her photographs, feeling and delicate, hardly at all
austere. Behind the eyes and the smile of the person now quite
disengaged from life stay the memories of her short marriage,
the cousin-husband to whom she played the piano, her long
widowhood, the fight for Kilbolane, the fight with the Famine.
Robert's three eldest children — Henry, Bob and Sarah — were
affected by their grandmother, whom they loved. They were
still small, and their nursery procession used to tail the phaeton
round the grounds. Then, half-way through a May night in
1868 these three children were roused by their nurses and led
or carried down (Sarah, aged four, was carried) to the room
behind the library to say goodbye to their grandmother and be
there while she died. The scene, which they always remembered, seemed to the three of them natural, intimate, mystical —

though, if their grandmother spoke, they remembered nothing she said. Though the partition has now been taken down, and the library is its original whole again, her grandmother's bed-room, with the furniture in it, always kept for my Aunt Sarah a solid existence at that north end of the library. Not long ago, crossing the floor with her at once majestic and dreamy gait, Aunt Sarah paused, to mark with absolute certainty a spot in the carpet with her toe. "*This* is where our grandmother died," she said.

Eliza Wade had seen her eldest daughter Sarah married to the Rev. Brabazon Disney, and her third, and prettiest, daugh-ter Henrietta married to Arthur Gethyn Creagh. Sarah's mar-riage took place in 1859 — the year before Robert's to Elizabeth Clarke. In 1865 the Rev. Brabazon Disney became, most hap-pily, rector of Farahy, so Sarah returned to keep house, across the fields from Bowen's Court, in cream-coloured Farahy Rec-tory. From here, being herself by God's will childless, she also kept a lynx eye on Robert's family. Daily calls, and exacting communication, passed between rectory and big house. Aunt Disney (as I was brought up to call her) was a distinctly plain woman, vigorous, articulate, with an undershot jaw and prom-inent, heavy-lidded (though far from languid) eyes. Her prin-ciples were high, and her Protestantism was of the blackest. What she said and read about Rome I should not like to repeat. Also, she lived on terms of intimacy with the more strapping Old Testament characters, whose opinions she would fre-quently quote and in whose failings she steadily disbelieved.

Uncle Disney was, on the other hand, handsome, sweet-natured and mild — though also extremely good. His marriage to Aunt Disney may, I think, have been part of a programme of reform — for Uncle Disney had formerly been a dashing, susceptible cavalry officer. It is said (by frivolous legend, which I will not confirm) that Uncle Disney left the Army as the re-sult of a romantic episode with a senior officer's wife — after two days of illicit bliss he returned and placed himself under arrest. At all events, he underwent Conversion, resigned his commission, became a clergyman and married my Aunt Disney. They lived at Farahy till 1871, when Uncle Disney obtained a larger cure of souls. He was later, for some years, curate to the Hon. the Rev. Mr. Wingfield at Abbeyleix, and this Abbeyleix connection was to bring about the first meeting between my father and mother — he being Mr. Disney's nephew, she, Mr. Wingfield's granddaughter.

My great-aunt Henrietta, by marrying in 1863 her Creagh second cousin whose mother had been a Galwey, made what was virtually the third Bowen-Galwey marriage in three generations. Aunt Creagh, who had bright blue eyes and a spritely tongue, was volatile and, in some matters, decidedly obstinate. She bore, at Mallow, a number of children, of whom many were delicate and few survived — those who did grow up were handsome and owed a distinctive character to being seldom encouraged to leave home. Aunt Creagh withdrew her sons from any schools they were sent to, saying that they missed her and she missed them — of this disregard for education her brother Robert ironly disapproved. Her daughter Mary married Robert Metge of Athlumney, great-grandson of that Henrietta Bowen who had married John Metge, M.P.

Visitors, as may be seen from the *Diary*, were a great feature of Victorian Bowen's Court. The guest-rooms were seldom empty. Not only did relatives make protracted stays, but friends (such as the Aldworths), touring the neighbourhood, would come for some days, then move on to the next house. When not being entertained by afternoon drives, occasional lunch parties or church-going, the visitors had to fall in into the ways of the family — if they were not fond of children I do not know what happened. My grandfather lived at too high a pressure to give much attention to anyone — ladies who cared to ride were mounted and went with him out riding; otherwise he considered that to be staying at Bowen's Court should be enough pleasure for any one. But my grandmother, too well-mannered to be *affairée*, was always at the disposal of visitors: she sat with them in the drawing-room, strolled with them round demesne walks or the garden, drove them (she drove very well) to pay afternoon calls. Her constant gentle social preoccupation put one more fence between her children and her. The wheels of the large household went round smoothly: there were eight servants, including a Protestant butler. A number of Catholics were among the servants, but I am told by my housekeeper, Mrs. Sarah Barry (who was first brought to Bowen's Court, in those days, from Nenagh as a very young kitchenmaid), that such ideal harmony reigned belowstairs that "you would hardly know who was a Protestant." Sarah felt, from the start, no dread of my grandfather, who himself had driven her over from Nenagh in the dogcart. But in this, she says, she differed from many others, who "were in dread of him, the way he would yowl at them." Robert liked, in fact, to see things done properly, and signalized any lapse by a sharp yell. He detested any break in routine. Meals in the dining-room (if not in the nursery) were liberal, punctual and well served.

Though the *Diary* mentions no Bowen's Court dinner parties, I am told that these fairly often occurred. The dining-room (with Robert's new tomb-like furniture) was illumined by cut-glass lamps on the sideboards and down the table; plate glittered; courses whizzed hot up the chain of hands from the kitchen; the claret was excellent — the effect was correct and massive, if not gay. Society was recruited from country houses round Castletownroche, Doneraile, Mallow and the growing Fermoy. From the absence (from lists I have found) of other than local names, I gather that Robert liked to be second to no man there. Talk would turn, as in any country neighbourhood, on local matters and politics — these an excellent subject, as everybody at Robert's table agreed. The Unionist gentry were, in these days, as one man. Married ladies, emerging from broughams for these evenings, wore their lace and jewels and displayed character — each, as industrious consort of a small kingdom, had authority and a blameless prominence. Ladies in these days were not only flattered but liked: County Cork society remained gallant, though it was now very respectable.

Daytime pleasures were, during the summer, garden and croquet parties (tea-tables spread in the shade round the big lawn) and cricket and archery matches; during the winter, Duhallow meets and lunch gatherings after them. Calls were, at all seasons, received and paid. The stables now held their complement of sixteen horses — hunters, carriage- and farm-horses — and the different carriages in the coachhouse were, as may be imagined, constantly on the road. The coachman, and the footman who sat on the box beside him and whose chief function was to get down and open gates, glittered with silver buttons on which appeared the Hawk. Besides my grandmother's carriage and the late Eliza Wade's little phaeton there were, for Bowen family transport, the dogcart, the wagonette and the inside car. Inside cars are, I think, peculiar to County Cork: they are wet-weather vehicles, roofed like cabs but two-wheeled, balanced on one axle; their two small windows look out ahead, each side of the driver's box, and the door is at the back; it is low but is supplemented by leather or mackintosh curtains that buckle across. The inside of an inside car, with the curtains buckled, is very dark indeed and gives out a musty smell. One cannot look out of the little high-up windows without screwing round one's neck. As in a governess-cart, the passengers face each other, knee-caps grinding together, and the pronounced backward tilt of the vehicle keeps the forward passengers sliding upon the others. To a Bowen's Court child who has (as at one time I often have) driven to and from Mallow in an inside car on a wet day, cramp, claustrophobia and *ennui* can do little more throughout life.

Robert Cole Bowen was a great rider to hounds; so were his second and third sons, Bob and Charlie. The eldest son, Henry, was, in this direction, never quite up to what was expected of him — less nervous than *distrait*, quite often oblivious of the fact that he *was* riding and of his horse, Henry would jog anywhere, stooping above the saddle his long thin body and red head. His apathy chagrined my grandfather. . . . My grandmother and her daughters all rode, but were not allowed to hunt. The younger children, on ponies or in the wagonette, went with Miss Flavelle to the near meets.

The Duhallow Hunt is the oldest in Ireland. At one time the Kildares disputed this claim, but the Duhallows, by producing a very early receipt for rent for a covert, were able to establish their seniority. The Duhallows date, in fact, from those great days of Mallow — 1745. Contemporaries of the Moyallow Loyal Protestants, they began as the private pack of a member of that club — that Mr. Henry Wrixon of Ballygiblin whose name often occurs in the Minute Book annexed by Henry III. Mr. Henry Wrixon left the pack to his son, Colonel William Wrixon, who was succeeded as Master by his son, Sir William Wrixon Becher.

When in 1822 Sir William resigned the Mastership to Mr. Robert de la Cour, the hounds became a subscription pack — they did not, however, quite leave the Wrixon family, for Mr. de la Cour was Sir William's brother-in-law. (This was the Mr. de la Cour who had attempted to arbitrate between Henry IV and his brother Robert in the matter of the Bowen's Court tenancy.) There must have been, prior to 1822, some sort of crisis in the Hunt's affairs, for a large Hunt button at Creagh Castle, Doneraile, bears, round the form of a running fox, the legend: "*Duhallow Hunt Revived, 1800.*" Mr. de la Cour moved the hounds to near Mallow, from Ballygiblin where they had been kept till now.

The Duhallow country, as constituted in 1822, covers some thirty miles north to south, by thirty-six miles east to west, in County Cork. On the north it adjoins the Limerick country, on the south that of the Muskerry, on the east that of the United Hunt. To the west the country is not hunted at all. The

Duhallow is a bank country; pasture predominates; there are lesser proportions of plough, moor and wood land. There are small gorse coverts. The best centre is Mallow; meets are also accessible from Fermoy and Cork. (Near Bowen's Court, meets are held at Terry's Screens at the foot of the Ballyhouras, at the house itself or at crossroads down the valleys of the Farahy river or the Funcheon.)

Mr. de la Cour remained Master till 1849, when he was succeeded by Mr. Courtenay of Ballyedmond. When, in 1853, Lord Doneraile became Master he moved the hounds to Doneraile Court, where they remained till 1863 — in that year, upon Lord Doneraile's resignation, a Committee took over the Hunt. Lord Doneraile left the neighbourhood for some time: when he returned he set up a pack of his own (the " Lord Doneraile's hounds " of the *Diary*) — this raised, between his lordship and the Duhallow Hunt, the rather ticklish question of whose country was whose. Mr. G. S. Ware took over, as Master, from the Duhallow Committee. In 1876 (the year of the *Diary*) a Mr. Hare, as Master, kept the hounds at Cortigan; two years after this, under Lord Listowel, they were to be kennelled at Convamore. Mr. Bruce succeeded Lord Listowel; after him came, jointly, Captains Peacocke and Scobel, then Mr. Bagge. Mr. Norton Barry took over from Mr. Bagge in 1886, and moved the hounds to his residence, Castle Cor. Lord Listowel's son, Lord Ennismore, followed Mr. Norton Barry in 1893; three years later came Mr. Nigel Baring, who saw the Duhallows into this century. The Hunt's more recent history belongs to a later chapter than this.

All Robert's friends hunted — or rather, all his friendships had this basis of the hunting field. Jogging home at the end of a day his most frequent companion would be his ally and neighbour Mr. Montgomery of Killee — a house, in fact the only big house, just off the Bowen's Court-Mitchelstown road. Passing any known gate, on these rides home, Mr. Bowen and Mr. Montgomery would turn in, dismount and make inroads on the family tea-table. They came to take a low view of the teas provided at Mitchelstown Castle, where economy now ruled — the rareness of fruit in the Kingston barmbracks (spiced currant-and-raisin loaves, much eaten, buttered, in Ireland) became a byword with them.

One afternoon, however, Mr. Montgomery secured a slice of barmbrack in which at least a segment of fruit appeared. Whereupon he, with a gesture, held this slice up to show my grandfather. " *Vous avez raisong*," said Robert loudly, in authoritative County Cork French, to Lady Kingston's enervated surprise. Though I am sure that Robert made other jokes, this is the only one that has come down to me. It seems to bear out the theory that men are just great boys. It was with the great boy in Robert that his grown-up son Henry was to have to contend.

Another ally of Robert's was Mr. Harold Barry of Ballyvonare — son of that Mr. Harold Barry who had stood up to the Brunswickers. This Mr. Harold Barry, exceedingly popular, was not only a rider to hounds but a great whip — he drove a four-in-hand. He had even more children than Robert Bowen, and one day, a day never forgotten, he had the four horses harnessed tandem, put all his children in or on to the coach and, with some one loudly blowing a horn, drove at a spanking pace, with terrific dash, in at one gate of Bowen's Court, past the front of the house and away off down the other avenue. All the little Bowens burst from their lessons to the steps and windows to wave and cheer: all the little Harold Barrys waved and cheered from the coach.

Very great excitement was felt in the neighbourhood when it was learned that H.R.H. the Duke of Connaught was to come to Fermoy, commanding a battalion of the Rifle Brigade, and intended to hunt with the Duhallows. Gloom supervened, with the news that the Duke of Connaught had, on a visit to Convamore, been kicked by Lady Listowel's horse. (Convamore, that Victorian mansion over the Blackwater, with a view for whose equal you might search the world, was tremendously gay these times: on the rock the old castle flew the Listowel flag; the castle chapel, repanelled Gothic, became a dancing-room, and boating parties slipped down the river between Nagles Mountains and the Convamore woods.)

The injury, however, was either slight or bravely sustained: the Duke was quite soon about again. His first appearance at Bowen's Court was at a Duhallow meet in front of the house — and on this occasion, for the Bowen children, glory rose over what might have been lasting shame. The wagonette, with Miss Flavelle and the children, was driving out down the Lower Avenue (on its way, I suppose, to the covert to be drawn) when it almost converged with, and blocked the gate for, the Duke of Connaught — riding, well ahead of his equerry, through Farahy on his way up to the house. His Royal Highness, with smiling equability, reined back his horse to let the wagonette through. " Bow, children, bow! " in a fever cried Miss Flavelle — and their little chins ardently bumped down. ("It was the first time," says my Aunt Annie, "that I had ever bowed, but I found I could.") And the Duke raised his hat to Miss Flavelle and gave all of the children a royal smile. The wagonette rolled on, and he rode in at the gate.

Then, later on in that winter, there was the day when he came to lunch. There was to be a meet in the near neighbourhood and, when Bowen's Court got the equerry's intimation, a large and rather mixed lunch party had been already invited. In view (it is thought) of the fact that etiquette forbade him to eat in other company than his host's, H.R.H., most thoughtful, delayed his arrival. So the lunch party had been raced through its lunch and seen on its way by the just sufficiently not agitated Robert, the crumbs had been cleared away and the ladies — my grandmother and a Mrs. Norcott, who, having relatives in the Rifle Brigade, had been invited to stay on after the others — were in the drawing-room, before there were any signs of the royal presence at all. A selection of children sat around the drawing-room, tense. Had there been some mistake, some hitch — would He not, after all, come? . . . When the Duke did arrive, he was unobserved; he handed his horse to some one and " just wandered in," the family says. He was unheard on the steps, in the front hall. It was felt — after, when the royal day, being over, had time to expand its fullness for every one — that there must have been something homely about the Duke of Wellington's presence (his cast-iron bust) in the front hall: the Duke of Wellington had been the royal Duke's godfather. Passing the Duke of Wellington, the Duke of Connaught " wandered " through to the back hall, where he put down his gloves. Doing this, he was watched by two witnesses — that composed little boy, my Uncle Charlie, ambushed on the upper flight of the staircase, looked keenly down through the banisters on to the very top of the royal head, while, rooted in the back hall itself, stood the cook — of great size, from the West and therefore called " the Great Western." Immobilized by the presence of Royalty, the Great Western — who surely should, at this moment, have been dishing up the important lunch down below — was unable to speak, stir, even to bob. The Duke put down his gloves, took his bearings, then, unannounced, walked into the drawing-room.

Robert had married his wife for just such a moment as this. She rose, flushed slightly (" and," says one of her daughters, " looking very beautiful "), made her deep Court curtsey in her deep rustling dress as His Royal Highness crossed the carpet towards her. Mrs. Norcott, with the Rifle Brigade behind her, followed suit with her curtsey; the children bobbed to the floor.

The Great Western rallied and sent up lunch. The ladies stayed in the drawing-room, while Robert conducted H.R.H. into the dining-room. Robert sat at the head of the table; the Duke placed himself on his host's left hand, his back to the windows. The children were now permitted to file in, as mutely as though entering church; on the horse-hair sofa between two windows they sat themselves in a row, eyes glued to H.R.H.'s back. They marked only one hitch in the talk that they drank in — their father, advancing a decanter, said: " Sir, some of our native drink? " The Duke, glancing at the decanter, said: " Ah, potheen? " and Robert had to make clear, without abruptness, that potheen never entered his house — Irish whiskey had been what he had meant.

" All that afternoon," the children remember, " we kept meeting Him; He was in and out of the house." He asked their names and he shook their hands. The wagonette came round in front of the steps and the Duke, standing in the winter afternoon sunshine, watched the children pack in for their afternoon drive.

Robert's prosperity has the firm amber glow of a winter afternoon. It had been consolidated during that prostrate period after the Famine; it was never not, to a certain degree, threatened; it was being maintained by him with a virtuosity one is bound to admire. In the financial chaos of the mid-century many of his class had succumbed, and though privileges still existed, in principle, security was to become less. The horrors of 1847, the examination of evils that had led up to that year, had given reformers new impetus. Smith O'Brien's rebellion had been premature — but, as the country slowly recuperated, feeling drew strength and became active again: delay-action resentments started to operate. Democratic Ireland, with re-emergent or new leaders, once more took up the struggle; unsparing critics of the land tenure system, of the persistent evils left by the Settlement, were to be drawn, even, from Robert Bowen's class. And landlords must not hope to receive, even from England, the old moral warrant and unstinted support.

Ireland, unlike Robert, was not prosperous. In her population there had been a drop alarming enough to be taken into very anxious account; on top of the Famine death-roll, there had been, and was still being, a steady exodus to America — to

America to be outside the English rule, outside the power of landlords. The emigrants, the most vigorous of the people, carried with them into the New World a persistent bitterness, and were to foster and voice it there. At home taxation was heavy; after the Famine Ireland had been in debt to England for the millions advanced for relief. Gladstone's budget of 1853 remitted this debt, but in consideration of taxes to be imposed: these went steadily up. So Irish taxation, which up to the time of the Famine had been considerably lower than that of England, had increased, by 1861, by fifty-two per cent. This money had, largely, to go to meet Imperial expenditure; little of it was laid out in Ireland, which remained undeveloped. And, in this almost wholly rural country, the complete insecurity of the small farmers and peasants — liable to raised rents, to rack-renting, to instant evictions if their land were wanted or their rent in arrears — made in the weak for demoralization, in the stronger for a militant discontent. The Fenians came into existence, to work on this discontent, direct it and make it powerful.

In the Westminster Parliament, Irish members began to make themselves felt *en bloc*. After the General Election of 1852 more than fifty of them had pledged themselves to the policy of independent opposition; they not only had and used the means to obstruct (either because they did not approve or for strategic reasons) any measure, but, being not allied to either English party (and the two English parties being, at this time, almost equally balanced) they held a determining vote — and with this could bid for support for their own programme. This block of Irish members was the constitutional arm of Young Ireland: its first object was, at the outset, to get accepted the principle of the Tenant Right.

At the same time, however, in Ireland the Catholic Church showed a repressive attitude to reform and to the disaffection that seemed to go with it. Dr. (later Cardinal) Cullen, Roman Catholic Archbishop of Dublin, was a strong Ultramontane, smelling Mazzini everywhere. He reined in the younger clergy, put his embargo on meetings at which agitation possibly might arise, and did all he could to discredit the progressives in Parliament in the eyes of Catholics at home. He could do nothing, however, to check the violence of those factions in Ireland for whom the constitutional party were not working fast enough. Outrages multiplied; Whiteboyism was on the increase and took the law in its own hand — land clearances and evictions produced bloody reprisals that made, abroad, for further Irish ill fame.

James Stephens, with other leaders of 1848 who had fled to America and were now returned, founded in 1858 the Irish Republican Brotherhood, soon to be called the Fenians. This organization took on and made further use of much of the machinery and propaganda left by the Young Irelanders of ten years ago. The old momentum made itself felt; recruits in large numbers were sworn in. The oath committed the Fenians to allegiance " to the Irish Republic now virtually established," and to implicit obedience, " in all things not contrary to the law of God," to superior officers. Funds came from America. In all workings of the organization secrecy was at first closely observed; recruits were largely from cities, from the new class of workers, rather than from the peasants. The democratic Ireland O'Connell brought into being was strongly there in the Fenian ranks, but the spirit, now, had the coldness of a new age. In 1861 the Fenians made their first demonstration, in Dublin; in 1863 the movement became more open: its organ, *The Irish People,* appeared, to launch a campaign of violent criticism against the Irish working in Parliament. This paper not only drew on the Fenians the strongest denunciations of Cardinal Cullen, but brought the threat of the movement, and its dimensions, to the official eye. Arrests and searches were made by Dublin Castle; *The Irish People* was summarily suppressed. Stephens escaped, but a number of Fenian leaders, seized at the paper's office, were held and got heavy sentences. More sol-

diers from England strengthened the garrisons. The Fenians
waited till 1867 — there were then, in the counties of Kerry
and Tipperary and outside Dublin, outbreaks: nothing much
came of them. The Fenian organization in England made sympathetic sorties; blood was shed in the North of England and
there were some executions.

Gladstone, in power in England, felt a conciliatory gesture
might now be tried. He therefore disestablished the Church of
Ireland and made some of its property over to Maynooth. The
Presbyterians also got a bonus: the remainder was held over,
rather ambiguously, as a fund for general utility. Materially,
this undoing of Strafford's work was not of great profit to the
country in general. It did, however, remove one outstanding
landmark of the Ascendancy, and might appear to promise the
removal of others. It made Protestants, dislodged from their
State-religious position, decidedly more extreme, more evan-
gelical, and it undermined their political dominance. As a step
to reform in land tenure it was not important — only some few
tenants of glebe lands got a better position. As a sop to the
Fenians, already half outside the pale of their own Church,
it does seem, as one looks at it, rather strange.

Disestablishment was, as a *démarche*, followed up by Gladstone's Land Act of 1870. This was a failure; it contained
clauses not able, in practice, to be applied. It caused some confusion, provoked every one and struck at the root of no main
abuse.

The Gladstone administration, from 1868 onwards, showed,
with regard to Ireland, the Liberal defect: it ignored or mis-
construed Irish realities and worked on its own English good
ideas. It was hampered in showing its good intentions by the
need to suppress by stern legislation the violences of the Irish
home campaign. Dismayed by the chaos across the water, it was
loath to consult Irish opinion, so continued to work quite in the
dark. Its attempt, for instance, to promote Irish Universities was
resented as so much tampering. Disraeli's Government, on from

1874, also grappled with Irish education — less ambitiously and with more success.

In this Parliament, of from 1874 to 1880, there appeared for the first time a majority of Irish members returned with a definite pledge to demand self-government. Under the leadership of Isaac Butt this party modified the Repeal O'Connell had fought for to Home Rule. Home Rule — Ireland to have her own Parliament, but to keep a federal connection with the Empire and be still, by virtue of this, represented at Westminster — was, accordingly, put forward, though not at first with great force: it was still a newly-formulated idea. Some Liberals played with it. It was not, however, until the emergence of Joseph Biggar that the Irish Party fully made itself felt. Biggar, an impious Ulsterman, without regard for the sanctities of the House, evolved what had been random Irish obstructiveness into a very definite technique. By sheer clowning — deplored, be it said, by Butt — Biggar often could and did immobilize Parliament. And when, in 1876, the young Protestant squire James Stewart Parnell was elected member for Meath and joined the Party, he took on and adapted Biggar's methods, raising them from the plane of an exhibition to a fine-strung exasperation of English nerves. His knowledge of procedure was thorough; he knew how to exploit a point of order, and he could prolong or side-track any debate till it had reached the point of absurdity. There must have been many days in the harassed House when the Union with Ireland was regretted.

The divergence between the two Nationalist parties — one making towards parliamentary action, the other towards physical force — was by now declared. Inevitably, the two were antagonistic. Fenianism, however, had passed its best days, while the parliamentary party increased in power under the leadership of Parnell. Here was the first Irishman after O'Connell to move to the very centre of the Irish stage. Legend surrounded his real greatness: he showed the virtuosity Ireland loved and, behind this, iron abilities. When, in 1878, Parnell replaced Butt as President of the Home Rule organization of Great Britain, he was, effectively speaking, taking on from where O'Connell had left off.

Parnell recognized, and worked to remedy, the disabling split in Nationalist energy. The check to the Fenians and their present discredit made it possible that Irish popular feeling might be swung round to back the parliamentarians in their thrust for reform. Violence had shown itself so much waste: ordered pressure (the pressure used by O'Connell) could effect more, and must be exerted now. To secure Home Rule, to break the landlord's crippling hold on Ireland — these were the two main aims. Parnell set out to concentrate Irish will and to break down the Irish mistrust of constitutionalism.

Onward from 1875, agricultural prices in Ireland had been dropping: the land situation became still worse — rack-renting had been on the increase, tenants found it impossible to pay up and evictions multiplied. Michael Davitt came into the field — son of Mayo peasants who, evicted, had gone to Lancashire, he had worked in an English factory, lost an arm in machinery, been convicted for Fenianism in England and now, in 1877, was out of an English prison on ticket of leave, having served eight of a sentence of fifteen years. Davitt brought into the Irish struggle more *broadly* democratic ideas: believing that workers of Ireland and England could unite for the common good of their class he saw no issue as purely national. For some time he worked with the Fenian Devoy in America on Devoy's plan, christened " A New Departure," to unite all Ireland to secure land reform. Movement towards the land revolution started in Mayo — where people, displaced from elsewhere by evictions and clearances, were congested, starving. Two mass meetings, at Irishtown and at Westport, were inspired by Davitt and sponsored by Parnell. A peasant proprietary, still unheard of in England but already established in parts of the Continent — Belgium, France, Germany, even Russia — was held up as the revolutionary aim. For this Parnell went all out; in a succession of speeches he directed and rallied the people. That same year saw the Land League come into being: as its president Parnell went to America, to make the programme known and to raise funds. He there — though never accepting in its entirety the Fenian principle — made close contact with Davitt. The combined drive in America brought Land League funds in quickly — their first allocation, however, had to be for relief, for another famine was already threatening the West. The approach of the General Election of 1880 brought Parnell back in haste from America: his campaign amongst Irish electors was carried through at top speed — as its result, he brought with him into the House a formidable new party of Irishmen. These included John Dillon (who had worked with Parnell in America) and T. P. O'Connor, and these were to be joined, after bye-elections, by Redmond and T. M. Healy. The ability of the young men was outstanding: their aims were declared and their energy manifest. They carried obstructiveness a point further, combining, by a diabolic misuse, completely to jam parliamentary machinery. It was not only difficult to ignore their presence, it became dangerous to ignore their cause.

Complementary to the attack on Parliament was the mounting of agitation in Ireland. The Land League, well organized and with imposing funds, threatened the old order at every point: it was, in contradistinction to other movements, made effective by an excellent discipline. It had, moreover, begun to exercise a judiciary system of its own: it condemned crime, examined each case coldly and wielded against offending landlords the instrument of the "Boycott" — called after its first victim. A boycotted landlord found himself cut off, by interdiction, from all communications and all supplies. In cases where rents had been raised arbitrarily there were systematic refusals to pay rent at all. Tenants acting under the Land League's orders were compensated for any loss. Alarm spread rapidly through the landlords. "Sullen indignation" in tenants had been taken for granted: organized opposition was quite another thing. Alarm communicating itself to the authorities, the League was denounced as a criminal conspiracy. In England, exasperation ruled.

Parnell, who had only waited for this moment, was not slow to drive the point of the situation in. Since England found Ireland so vexing to govern, why not let Ireland govern herself? This crisis in Irish land trouble need not, then, be met by the Westminster Parliament. The class-war in Ireland — for such it had become — was inflamed by England's support of " the garrison." For the land trouble Parnell saw one remedy: he did *not* suggest confiscation; he suggested, rather, the buying out of the landlords at a price to be fixed by the State, then the setting up of the peasant proprietary. The very idea of compulsion was, however, enough to embitter the class that felt its title attacked — and Parnell, an Irish landlord himself, could only be seen as a renegade. Isaac Butt had had some support from those Anglo-Irish who still had in mind Grattan and 1782. But now the gentry were solid against Parnell.

The Liberal Government's aspiration was to keep all Irish trouble banked down. One bill, conciliatory in purpose (compensation for disturbance to be paid to evicted tenants) was, however, thrown out by the Lords. It remained to be faced that Ireland's virtual government was the Land League. Conciliation having miscarried, the law now had to assert itself: a series of prosecutions for conspiracy was embarked upon, and all aimed at the League. Against Parnell and the leading men in his party nothing specific could be proved, but Davitt's ticket of leave was cancelled: he was returned to gaol. This aroused fury throughout Ireland, where Davitt stood second to Parnell. Further on this, the debate on a bill for special powers with which to meet the trouble in Ireland was obstructed by the Irish at Westminster.

Such were the conditions that gave birth to Gladstone's Land Act of 1881. The Act had genius in its conception; it was, in principle, revolutionary: it appeared at once to strike at the basis of property and at property's moral prerogative. It was, also, the first marked step in England's retreat from whole-hearted support of the Settlement. But in its actual application the Act did not cut the intended ice. At the time, it produced confusion; it had, for all its apparent boldness, some inherent weaknesses of the half-measure, and its incomplete grasp of Irish realities made it, in its working, inequitable. It controlled rents, stopped arbitrary evictions and gave the tenant-occupier at least some degree of security. It bore with unforeseen heavi-ness on landlords, who with estates heavily charged got no re-mission of these charges to match enforced reduction of rents. Good landlords (of which there had been many) suffered with, and in some cases more than, those who had been the monsters all landlords appeared. To a very large proportion of cases the Act's application was so unclear that litigation became neces-sary — there ensued fatigue, dissatisfaction all round, expense. This, however, was for the present as far as Westminster could be hoped to go.

Parnell's mistrust of the Act was marked: he and his party refused to vote on it. He advised for Ireland a wary acceptance, with careful examination of test cases. Tenant Ireland, how-ever, was disposed to grasp at any ready relief, and Gladstone, who entertained high hopes of the Act, saw every reason why things should work out well *if* Parnell would only let the peo-ple alone. Parnell's attitude at this juncture was felt to be quite intolerable: he was accused of keeping Ireland in agitation and a warrant went out for his arrest. The arrest was followed by a round-up of " agitators " throughout the country, then by the suppression of the Land League (till now not more than de-nounced). Parnell's riposte to this was to issue a No-Rent mani-festo from gaol. With the restrictive control of the League gone, violence broke out again throughout Ireland: the Bad Times, with their chain of horrors, set in. Parnell's hold on the people had to be recognized; after a pourparler with the pris-oner Parnell was released from Kilmainham gaol to assist the

Government in re-establishing peace. On all that was hoped of this new alliance the Phoenix Park murders brutally interposed. Lord Frederick Cavendish, newly-arrived Chief Secretary for Ireland, and Mr. Burke, the Under Secretary, died on the knives of a secret society, the Invincibles, on the 6th of May, 1882. The brutality gave a terrible name to Ireland: the black spirit was seen to be the work of Parnell, and the entire constitutional movement received, from the implication, a setback from which it did not rally for two years. England, outraged, applied coercion: Ireland resisted and worse phases of the bitter trouble set it. High feeling in Ireland Parnell *had* inspired — it had been needed behind the Westminster fight — but violence he had, in every instance, opposed. In the dreadful two years after 1882 he seemed likely to see his hopes go to the wall, his work go for nothing. He did not lose his grip.

His grip, in fact, was so sure that he and his party were able, by an alliance with the Tories, to bring about the defeat of the Liberal Government on its budget, and Gladstone's resignation. Lord Salisbury came into power, and the Irish adherence to him was for some time marked: before the General Election of 1885 Parnell decided that the Irish vote in England was to support the Tories. In spite of this, the Liberals came back with a majority — though after the same Election there was an increase of Parnellites in the Irish ranks: 86 were Parnellites out of 103. This Nationalist majority, and its firmness, was enough to show Gladstone where Ireland stood. Gladstone declared for Home Rule, in face of strong opposition from both sides of the House.

In 1886 the first Home Rule Bill was rejected. The ensuing General Election put the repressive party into power again: renewed attempts at coercion in favour of Irish landlords made for worse agrarian trouble. The Pope, asked by the Government to denounce lawlessness, did so, but this only produced a disassociation of Parnellite Catholics from their reactionary Church. Straight on from the Bill's rejection the campaign for Home Rule continued, with its trumpet-call to democracy.

The spectacular failure of an attack on Parnell – the *Times'* printing of facsimile letters implicating Parnell in murder, the Commission, Pigott's collapse and confession of forgery – served to swing feeling in both countries, after intense excitement, strongly round to the Irish leader again, and his cause, which had become Gladstone's, gathered momentum. By-election results had been marking increasing support for Home Rule among the British electorate when, in 1890, O'Shea took divorce proceedings against Parnell. The case was not defended, and Parnell, with his party at first steady behind him, did not propose to flinch. The scandal broke. Nonconformist England set up the clamour, and this was, at the other side of the water, raised to a deafening pitch by the Catholic Church. Gladstone was pressed to withdraw support from Parnell. Asked by Gladstone to withdraw, Parnell refused: he faced the storm, but for him this was the end. The Irish party was split, and he saw desertions: his power to act for Ireland was gone. Gladstone continued the Home Rule fight. A second Bill fought its way through the House of Commons only to be thrown out by the Lords. Whereupon, Gladstone's resignation was followed by a Unionist dominance: though four-fifths of the Irish members remained Home Rulers they could do nothing against the block. At all immediate settlement of the Irish question was not part of the Tory policy – left in the air the Westminster Irish served not only to harry the Liberal conscience but, usefully, to keep that party divided. The Tory conscience was imperturbable.

Robert Cole Bowen signalized 1881 and the Land Act by having his portrait painted by an R.A. The portrait hangs on an end wall of the Bowen's Court dining-room, some way above the chair where he used to sit. Robert confronts all time, and the special threat of that year, with a glass-blue stare that shows pressure behind. He is now fifty-one; any touch of accessibility in the 1860 photograph has gone: the thin-lipped, brow-jutting energy of the young man of thirty has disappeared behind beard and full ruddy flesh. The untactile hands have thickened; at the base of his waistcoat they rest folded into a sort of bunch. Below his great father-beard, a beard forked like that of Moses, glints a seal hung from a fob. The pear-shaped outline — head sunk in beard and collar, elbows without angle — shows heavy ripeness. Robert sits before Mr. Brenan, the hired artist, in a tolerant lump.

While its master confronts the artist, Bowen's Court functions; while he sits without budging he has an ear for it. He has installed machinery; in the yard it is almost uninterruptedly humming — soon there will be the threshing; the machine crushes the oilcake for the fattening cattle whose heads are screwed into yokes low over the troughs, whose flanks must bulge till they press the sides of the stalls. The donkey treads round the wheel, driving the churn shaft. The winter turkeys are bought up, turned out among the stooks; hooves and heels in the stables send out the ring of cobbles. Carts and wains and wagons strain and lurch and rattle under the back avenue trees; iron field-gates swing open, oiled, between mortared posts. The farm buildings, the estate cottages now all have tarred roofs over curved struts; hedging, fencing runs taut over Robert's land. Four times a day, the imperious yard bell penetrates the demesne, ringing Robert's men to and from work. . . . The place now runs like a belt over a wheel; the driving power is being generated inside the Master's, at this moment, slumped and quiescent form.

To such a man, change could only look like attack. Robert was not a bad landlord. He was a business man, and in business, a realist. He was as sharp as a fox and as hard as iron — if the voluminous softness of his body should mislead you, look at the eyes. It is true, his leases were drawn up rigidly, and God help the tenant who fell behind with rent. (It is said that my grandmother in some cases interceded, or, where she knew intercession could only fail, used to wait on rent days, inside the glass

door to the passage, to slip the required sum, from her own
pocket, into some hand that came empty and damp with fear.
Robert never knew of such dealings — they were reported only
after her death and his. Robert's eldest daughter Sarah has also
told me — though I must say, before I can vouch for this, that
her memories were in all cases dramatic — that she used, as a
young girl of seventeen, to be sent by her father on an outside
car round the outlying farms to collect rent, and that when
hard cases so much softened her feelings that she could not
continue to press for what was due, she would face the exposed
drive home to her father not only numb with cold but " crying
with fear.") At the same time, to break tenants gratuitously
never had been, never was Robert's policy — he took the long
view. He expected to, and did, extract from his property, as
much from his own farms as from his tenants, the income on
which he had budgeted. What he touched, paid — and he did
not exact more. It no more pays to squeeze men than to
squeeze land. Interference in the order he had established
would have seemed to him a fatuity, first of all. The conflict,
however, could but declare itself; the pressure mounted — and
was to work in his brain. Robert, in the end, cracked — and the
reasons were multiple. Very much soon had to be pardoned,
and was pardoned. His children all say now, " He was not
himself."

HENRY VI

Henry VI, my father, reacted in every particular against his father Robert's success regime. First child of a propitious and not unworldly marriage, he showed from childhood a detachment from the usages of the world. Henry was courteous, deliberate, absent-minded, and clumsy in the use of his hands — in his relations with people he was not clumsy because of his fairness and charity. If he saw men as trees walking, he bowed to the trees. The energy he inherited from his father went almost wholly into his mental life; from Robert he also inherited the obstinacy that backboned his gentleness — but whereas Robert's obstinacy was a matter of passion, Henry's was a matter of principle. To be Robert Cole Bowen's eldest son was not easy, and Henry, by the design of his own nature, was the man least fitted to play that onerous part. Between a father and son who are equally egoists at least a conflict is possible, and conflict not only has its own queer satisfactions but makes some kind of relationship. But Henry was unegoistic; the " I " in him offered no attackable ground; he seldom opposed his father, but merely differed from him. There is no doubt that Robert, full-blooded and overbearing, affected the character of his eldest son — as, in different ways, he affected the characters of all the children he had. Robert's rule developed in Henry, young, the sense of solitary moral being. It worked on Henry's deep-down contrariness, and also gave him a lasting bent against horses, men servants, social discrimination, ideas about farming, display in any form.

Henry was more his mother's son than his father's: she and he matured as well as delighted in each other's society. Henry was always a great talker — he was unsuspicious; he assumed in every one a pure and eager love of truth for its own sake — but in his youth he used to talk most to her. For her part, the candid quickness of mind for which (allied to good manners) Robert had married her had been, perhaps, since marriage a little threatened by social claims, by Robert and by maternity, but by the growing Henry this was asked for again. Her interests widened with his. To me, later, he often spoke of her beauty — her wide, clear-featured face was less the mould than the window of the creature within. I think her memory must have contributed to the pleasure he always took in women's society, and to his respect for a woman's point of view. Perhaps it was not without some dread of trouble that she watched him grow up to be what he was. She must have known he would not make a country squire. The troubles she may have foreseen for him she, happily, did not live to see.

Complaisance and real family feeling made Henry do all he could to fit into Bowen's Court life. He rode — slackly, stoopingly, vaguely, less nervous than bored, deep in thought or looking about the country with pleased eyes: he could think as well on a horse as anywhere else, but he was always glad to see the last of the horse. (Once he was his own master, he never rode again.) With detached, almost avuncular kindness he went with his younger brothers and sisters on their be-governessed walks; he played croquet with them (as we see from the *Diary*) and made them run races up in the Pleasure Ground. He did once, by sheer reflex, kick out at his brother Charlie — the bright little boy plagued him when he was reading — and the kick happened to land in Charlie's stomach. "Poor little Charlie," my Aunt Sarah remembered, "cried his heart out:

children are very sensitive " — and Henry's penitence knew no bounds. Driving about the country with his father and mother he attended parties, cricket matches and the archery matches at which she shot so well. If his heart was not wholly in these pleasures, I doubt if he ever asked himself why. Like his much gayer forebear Henry III's, his love of society was contemplative. The constant comedies of his vagueness kept him from ever being a prig.

Henry was always tall: as a man he was six foot two. His joints seemed to articulate just by chance. In youth he had a great shock of springy red-gold hair; his eye-sockets and cheek-bones (Clarke characteristics) were prominent under his pale skin. His hands freckled quickly, and were like Robert's un-tactile, but no part of him was insensitive. He handled objects with anxious, often ineffectual care — he constantly dropped or lost things. His walk — with the stooping head — was digni-fiedly ungainly but (until his last years) amazingly tireless. His love of the country, his Ballyhoura country, was too deeply innate to be emotional — he had no contact with it through farming or sport, but all the same this was an informed love, for Henry knew about rocks and trees. To animals he showed courteous indifference — I have seen him plucking a kitten from his person as unconsciously as though it had been a burr, and he would apologize with humility if he kicked or trod upon an unseen dog. He told me that once, as a little boy, he did keep rabbits, and these he loved. But their end was sad — in that year of Henry's childhood there were alarming rumours in County Cork: neighbouring landlord families from the country round moved in to fortifiable Bowen's Court; sets of nurses and chil-dren, in rival parties, camped down the length of the Long Room, and soldiers from Buttevant packed the basement — they had been sent to defend the house. Once the alarm was over Henry, released, dashed out again to his rabbits — but the hutch was empty: the military, to whom one denied nothing, had been lusciously fed.

After his mother, Henry's great love was Bob, the brother next him in age. Bob stopped growing at six foot four; he was short-headed, a great rider, devoted to country life. All those contacts Henry missed, Bob enjoyed. In fact, only because of his lack of drive did Bob fall short of being Robert's ideal son: he decidedly was not ambitious; he liked life as it was. Even so, I believe that Robert, who liked good looks and gusto, had a sort of angry hankering after him. When Bob had failed twice, and looked like failing a third time, in his entrance examinations for Sandhurst, Robert threatened to put him into a bank in Mallow. That this might have been tough on the bank in Mallow does not seem to have occurred to either of them: what Bob did understand was that this would mean extinction — and at the third try he passed his army exam. Bob died, killed by a horse, as a fairly young officer, and there is something heroic about his photograph — of which, to judge by the number of reproductions, one must have hung in every Bowen's Court room. He has a broad forehead, short upper lip and sweet straight candid indolent eyes. He remains the image, this second short-lived Bowen, of what *the* Bowen of Bowen's Court might have been; his unborn sons and daughters seem to congest the place, and I wonder how often, in years that followed, this image recurred to Henry VI's mind.

Robert was, as we know, a tiger for education: from the time his unnerved children recited to him at dessert he never flagged in his wish that they should continue to learn. Henry made every use of his brain, and his father had cause to be proud of him. The five Bowen boys were schooled in Ireland, at St. Columba's College. This fine school under the Dublin mountains was called the Eton of Ireland, in days when that meant much. Stephen Gwynn writes in *The Columban:*

When I came to S.C.C. in the Autumn of 1876, Henry Bowen was somewhere near the head of the school. David Davenport, Warden Rice's nephew, was by far the best scholar, in the strict sense. But Henry Bowen, the tall, shambling, untidy youth of fifteen, and J. E. Galbraith, barely reaching to Bowen's elbow, were already serious runners-up. The others whom I remember as belonging to the same flight were W. E. Bunbury, head prefect, son of the Bishop of Limerick; his brother, V. T. Bunbury, W. Fry and Henry Irwin. These were the real leaders of the school; upstanding young men, good at games — and not just simply good at games. Both the Bunburys and Fry scored with high distinction and became generals. Irwin, who went to Canada as a missionary, was the finest athlete of the lot, and was always a fine human being.

But the brains of the school were with the other three. . . . Henry Bowen never, to my recollection, attempted either cricket or football, and he seems to me, looking back, to have lived a very solitary existence. He was far too unlike the average to be popular, and too gentle to be formidable for all his bigness. Small boys mobbed him, as jackdaws mob a heron. Even his younger brother Bob, who became a great friend of mine, was looked on as rather eccentric, and perhaps too gentle; none of us knew, for he never talked of himself, that he was already a bold rider to hounds in County Cork. But Henry had not this sportsmanship.

In short, though he grew up in a beautiful countryside, with all the means for country pleasures at his command, and though he was successful at his studies at a good school in one of its best periods, I cannot think he had a happy boyhood. Yet, when he and I met, as we did so often, past middle age, his talk would perpetually recur to school days, and always with affectionate memory. It is easy to love a place when things have gone well with you; but Henry Bowen, to the last years of his life, loved St. Columba's, where he had not been happy, and grudged nothing that he could do for it. He gave his time and his thought; but the loyalty of his devotion was even more shown in his constant turning back to little incidents of those old times, and to the boys and masters with whom he lived in them.

He left school a little before I did and went to Trinity where he distinguished himself; but I doubt if his success represented his real attainments. Passing examinations is largely a matter of agility, and, to begin with, he was handicapped by the physical clumsiness which made his handwriting slow and laborious. More than that, his mind was slow-moving; he had no power of improvization, and as a scholar he lacked quick perception for the niceties of language, and still more the imitative knack that often goes with it. He probably knew much more of what was written in the Latin and Greek classics than other men who could give a better suggestion of knowing Latin and Greek.

I share this view, that Henry VI was not happy when he was young. Yet for me to say so seems a sort of intrusion, for of feeling he seldom spoke to me. His attitude to himself was impersonal; in fact he hardly had an attitude to himself. He in no sense coveted life, and frustrated covetousness is, I suppose, at the root of most people's conscious unhappiness. Certainly, to hear him speak of his schooldays one would have supposed they had been idyllic. Admiration was a pleasure to him, and at St. Columba's he found much to admire. I suppose that, in regard to his early days, memory did for him what Proust calls the work of art — it either eliminated or fructified what had been painful, puzzling, futile or barren. He used to talk a great deal to me (especially when I was at school myself) about David Davenport and his eccentricities, about walks in the Dublin Mountains, about the Warden, Rice. And every one of these anecdotes he would prefix with an inward contented rumbling reminiscent laugh. I noticed that he spoke of no intimacies, no triumphs, no drama of any personal kind.

In fact, he was accustomed to distance and hardly felt it. At Bowen's Court in the holidays, at Youghal, at Camira, things must have been much the same — except that at home he enjoyed, in a sort of abstract manner, the dignity of the heir. He did not share Robert's love for Camira — here was to be one of the many thorns — nor the rest of his family's sentiment for the place. Camira was just one thing too much to cope with, and when his day came he sold it — badly, the others said. The great Cole revival (or call it the Ballymackey fantasy) promoted by Robert lapsed in Henry's day. Old King Cole to him was no more than a genealogical query, and the Agincourt ancestry a

genealogical fact. In his later days he strenuously opposed a
wish on the part of some of the family to distinguish themselves
as the *Cole Bowens* (with an inferred hyphen). It may have
been, even, some complex against the Cole cult that made him
so quick to be rid of Camira. At Kilbolane he never looked back
once; one lived a good deal better out of that area mined with
susceptibilities, loss and griefs. But he *had* a regard for our
Welsh descent, and this, as his one child, I was brought up to
share. Above all, Bowen's Court was the abiding thing in his
life — for Henry VI's feeling for Bowen's Court I can find no
word that he would have countenanced.

In 1881, when Henry was nineteen, he entered Trinity College auspiciously, as a scholar. But in this same year there occurred the tragedy that was to injure him: his mother died, and
he considered himself, or was aware that he was considered by
others, to be the cause of her death.

To mark Henry's leaving school and going to college Robert
sent his heir abroad to make the grand tour. So Henry carried
across the two Channels his classic-stored red head and his
County Cork French accent. *Where* he went, abroad, I am not
sure; he never spoke to me much of those early travels; I suppose that what followed darkened their memory. There was an
outbreak of smallpox in London, that summer, and Robert sent
abroad urgent messages warning Henry not to return that way.
These messages Henry either did not get or ignored — it would
have been hard, those days, to by-pass London on a return
journey from Dover to County Cork. Henry not only passed
through London but, I believe, stopped there two or three days.
My Aunt Sarah's version was that on the (English) Channel
crossing Henry's hat blew off into the sea, whereupon he bor-
rowed, from a fellow-passenger, what turned out to be an infected cap. At all events, Henry returned to Bowen's Court
with the smallpox upon him; he went down with it and was
desperately ill. His mother then did not hesitate; she nursed
him, allowing no one else into the room. Robert's decision was

simple also — as soon as Henry's smallpox became a fact Robert removed himself, the rest of the children and almost all of the servants post-haste to Youghal: there he stayed. In his flight showed his Famine-bred hatred of disaster, and that deathly death-dread behind his big façade. What he said of his wife Elizabeth's choosing the part she chose is not on record — those hours before his flight must have been clouded, frantic. This was the first of the contexts in which his children say of him, "He was not himself."

From the sickroom, Henry and his mother heard the wagon-ette, the carriage, the dogcart, the luggage-carts driven away. You could almost have said, a start for Camira. She, already deep in her quarantine, may have gone to an upper window to wave them off — if so, she saw for the last time, foreshortened, the blond heads of her children packed in the wagonette, and the winking silver hawk-buttons on the liveries as horse after horse in the cortège was whipped up. Through a house more silent than she had ever known it she returned quickly to Henry's side. It was August, with Robert's acres of harvest yellow and a heavy silence in the Bowen's Court trees. For fear she might carry infection on her she left the wine-and-oyster-hung marriage bed and used to rest, when Henry did not need her, in one of the rooms on the top floor. Later, when Henry was out of danger, she used, I am told, for hours together to walk up and down the Long Room. Like Henry III, she saw through the three north windows the Ballyhouras, veiled in rain or in light; through the south windows the trees on the mount-ing lawn. Her step, in that ballroom that had been never danced in, raised the same echoes as Henry III's. She approached the decisive day of her quarantine — I have wondered what passed through her mind: she was forty-five. The smallpox developed, as was to be expected, and my grandmother died of it. Only the convalescent Henry was with her — there was then an interval, quite alone, for Henry, before Robert returned for the funeral.

Sarah, the seventeen-year-old eldest daughter, began the first phase of her reign as Bowen's Court housekeeper. To Sarah the loss, and loss in just this way, of her mother was as much a moral as an emotional shock. Her first reign, though zealous, was to be very brief, for her father could not endure his wifeless state — in 1882, a year after Elizabeth's death, Robert married Elizabeth's cousin Georgina Mansergh, of Clifford, a house on the Blackwater. (Clifford, before the Mansergh occupation, had been the home of that Richard Martin, attorney, who had been Henry IV's ally, and whose reputation had been exhumed by the Bowens in the course of *Bowen v. Evans* of 1843.) Details of Robert's second, necessitous courtship are not known by me, and a veil I would not disturb hangs over the greater part of his second marriage. Georgina's position at Bowen's Court was a difficult one — with Elizabeth's elder children she could not hope to be welcome, and I gather that, though not in any way ill-meaning, she was rigid, and deficient in " heart " and tact. ("Black as crows " a cousin remembers the young Bowens, that year after their mother's death, " and with their blue eyes starting out of their heads.") The young people watched one another to see that no step towards Georgina was made, and to be for even an hour " in " with the stepmother was to be in bad odour with all the rest. It was not in the poor woman's power — had she wished to — to break this emotional strike. As for Robert, his nature darkened without cooling; disastrous mental changes proclaimed themselves, and he became incapable — if he had ever been capable — of an unspoilt relation with any one. It is agreed that, under the circumstances, Georgina did her best. She is now referred to as " poor Georgina." She was not young when she married, this was her first marriage, and she died in 1886.

At Trinity, Henry VI distinguished himself. He was Senior Moderator in Classics and Ethics, and University Student in 1883. He became Wray Prizeman and Berkeley Medalist. These distinctions extended his time at college, and he decided to read law. His intensive studies were carried on, as at school, in a solitary atmosphere: he made no close friends, joined no clubs or societies and, while beholding with kindness, made no attempt to enter University life. Trinity is not intrusive: his rights to himself were admitted and he was let alone. He shared rooms in Botany Bay — a set-back square, like in plan to but with less lovely façades than Peckwater, Christ Church, Oxford — with a County Cork neighbour, Dickie Oliver. Dickie Oliver later became a clergyman: meticulous neatness was his outstanding trait, and I have gathered (from Henry) that he found Henry a trial. Though Henry had no conscious aesthetic sense, architecture always affected him, and he loved Trinity's classic nobility — the great grey spaced-out façades that reflect humid Dublin light, the lawns that glow in summer, the pediments that heighten and harden under a bright sky. The students lived then, as now, with a simplicity that suited Henry's tastes — though this, also, had its embarrassments: he had to attempt to cook, and Dickie Oliver winced at sausages that, on their uncharred sides, remained indecently pink. In that sense in which he understood happiness, Henry was, I think, while at college completely happy. But in vacations at Bowen's Court, with his mother gone, there was that pain of a lacking intimacy, and his academic laurels meant much less now they could not be laid at beloved feet. He may have looked at the velvet-lined bookcase she had given him for his prizes at school. Elizabeth would have delighted in all he did. Robert, it is true, at the outset was proud of him — Henry followed the rule that one must excel. But pride gave place to misgivings, then to bitter mistrust. The break between the two natures appeared: the father cared for success, the son for accomplishment. Henry's prolonged pursuit of knowledge *qua* knowledge was not to the Bowen interest, in Robert's eyes. Henry, preoccupied student, continued to fail to show interest in the functional aspects of Bowen's Court. For some time, storm-threats increasingly darkened the home skies. The storm

broke when Henry announced he meant to have a profession —
he had decided, in fact, to become a barrister.

There ensued a contest between two equally strong wills —
one hot with feeling, one cold with mind. Robert felt — and in
this he was not unreasonable — that one cannot have two professions. Fate had selected Henry's profession for him: he was
to be Henry Cole Bowen of Bowen's Court, landowner, master
of two houses, administrator of two still quite large estates. And
Robert himself, remember, is to be honoured for the profes-
sionalism he had brought to just that life. To attempt to subju-
gate Bowen's Court and Camira to an ambition purely of the
brain seemed to Robert not only an error but a betrayal. And
the times — these eighteen-eighties — made the betrayal double:
landlordism, for landlords, was now a *cause*. By English reform
as well as by Irish feeling hereditary position had been assailed.
Henry by, at this juncture, turning from his position must have
appeared to slight it. He asked, for his faculties, an unheard-of
channel: he was not content to say, " I have, therefore I am."
The crisis was royal in miniature. And, the dreadful mixed up-
rush in Robert of passion and his own virtue was the stuff of
Shakespearean tragedy. His case, as I try to show, was up to a
point sound. But he could not support it soundly, for mono-
mania inundated all of his arguments.

Henry's case, I believe, was, that a man is not only bound to
use the best that he has but to put this to the best use for the
world. His decision, matured by years of lonely reflection, was
that the law was his calling, and he must follow it. The accident
of his birth as Robert's heir did not, and in Henry's view ought
not to, affect the decision. How far the ethical (as apart from
political) aspect of landlordism affected Henry I am not prepared to say. Though his years at Trinity had been the great
Parnell years he had not (as Stephen Gwynn remarks) appeared to concern himself with politics. He loved Bowen's
Court, was prepared to inherit it and hoped to serve it in every
way, but he would not pretend to himself or Robert that either

his interests or his duties ended with the estate. Briefly, Henry's argument was for free will, as against predestination. Behind this may have worked a profound revulsion against whatever Robert had been. Henry saw the estate structure, Robert's life-work, mortared together by Robert's egotism. He could but mistrust the profession, Robert's profession, that was at the same time so much a role.

The strong stone house, the frail-nerved family in it must have trembled during that bad time. Bowen's Court being en-tailed on the eldest son, Henry could not be disinherited. Robert, however, could and did do a good deal to hamper Henry's succession: in the will he drew up he disposed of what he was free to dispose of, and it would have been a tax on even Robert's genius to run Bowen's Court with any hopes of advan-tage on the means that Henry was to enjoy. (Make your pile at the Bar then, may have been Robert's taunt.) In fact, if not the destruction the headlong decline of Bowen's Court seems to have been implicit in Robert's will: in the dark in which he now increasingly dwelled he planned the destruction of his life's work. To-day, his fine iron field-gates rusting off their hinges, his metalled avenues grass-grown, his roofless farm-buildings, his " machines," that used to fill the yard with their humming, now with belts snapped, teeth rusting into the ground, make me feel a pang — on Robert's behalf. I think of the Giotto figure of *Anger*, the figure tearing, clawing its own breast. Robert had inherited fine timber, and he had planted more — the screens that shelter our fields. He determined Henry should not enjoy his trees, so wood after wood began to fall to the axe, till Henry took out an injunction to stop this.

In 1887 we read: " *Calls to the Bar — On Friday, the 22nd inst., before Baron Ashbourne, Lord High Chancellor of Ire-land, Henry Charles Cole Bowen, B.A., Sch. and Senior Mod-erator, University of Dublin, eldest son of Robert St. John Cole Bowen, M.A., J.P., of Bowen's Court in the county of Cork, and Camira, Nenagh. Proposed by Mr. Serjeant Hemphill.*"

In 1888 Robert, child of August, died just short of an August, on the 28th of July. His children put up, in Farahy church, a white marble memorial to their father and mother. Below the two names is written: *Here we have no abiding city, but we seek one to come.*

Henry and Sarah Bowen now ruled the house together — he went and came from Dublin, she was mostly at home. The positive side of Henry became urged to the fore: he put away his detachment so completely that the others spoke of him as " the Boss." As a child I heard my uncles and aunts, in familiar moments, address my father as " Boss," and was never clear how far this name was satiric, how far affectionate. I have said that my father's grandfather, Henry V, forced by inheritance out of romance to duty, embraced duty with a romantic zest. Henry VI, forced by the same fate in the same direction, brought to duty a concentration of intellect — though, with this, a great heart. His wise but unworldly view of the world made him dogmatic on matters of principle. His youth appeared largely in his intransigence. He wished most for those that he loved that they should do right, and was prepared to go far to see that the right was done. His brothers — large-limbed, affectionate, easy-going — fell in very equably with his main ideas, but these youths, already on their ways out into life, were not now for long stretches at Bowen's Court. The girls, more confined and more temperamental, tended to fidget under that young rule. They complained that they might not even choose their own trains — when they chose one train, Henry enjoined another — and that when they set out to drive up one avenue, Henry would come out and turn the horses round. That his interference was wholly benevolent did not make it less trying.

On paper, each of the Bowens was independent: that is to say, one merit of Robert's will was that each of his sons and daughters controlled either capital or equivalent property. But it took much to detach the brothers and sisters from the habit of centripetal Bowen's Court life.

Sarah balanced Henry on the feminine side — if these two did not always see eye to eye, they maintained to the rest of the family an unbroken front. She was a tall pale girl, full of feeling and dignity, modelled much like Henry about the face, and she did all she could to fill her mother's position. The tension at which she had grown up showed in her rather uncertain health, but Sarah's control was absolute: she had no time for " nerves." Feeling it right to effect economies, she ran the house calmly on (I am told) two servants: to fill gaps she was tireless in her activities. For, while she was Elizabeth's daughter in poise and kindness, she was very much Robert's in her regard for the grand, and she did not like economies to appear. Streams of advice and criticism came to her from vivacious Aunt Creagh at Mallow, and from the more distant, less vivacious but more dogmatic Aunt Disney at Abbeyleix; but Sarah, her chin at the proper level, continued to steer her considered course. Least selfish of women, Sarah's pride was vicarious: she took a very high view of the Bowens. Hyperconscientious, eager and sensitive, she suffered when she fell short in her own or the family's eyes. She said to me once, she had had no time to be young. But she was a person born to *se faire valoir*, and though, like Henry III, she lived and died in the provinces, she could raise to a high level her own world. Her personality mellowed as the years went on: I remember her stately and disciplined.

In their mother's mirrored bridal drawing-room, now faded, the four sisters kept such state as was possible for a group of unmarried girls a long way from anywhere. When the period of their mourning was over they drove in the carriage to pay and return calls. Only the coming and going of brothers and brothers' friends broke the green isolation of Bowen's Court. Sometimes officers came out from Fermoy, calling: then they sent invitation cards to the military balls. On the tense eve of

one of these balls Lizzie got stung by a wasp and her face
swelled, and Mary, whose whole future turned on the pleasure,
decided it would be "cruel" to go without her. Family sensi-
bility was, these days, at its height; even brothers, returning,
waded knee-deep in it — dominated who knows by what ghost,
the Bowens continued the world of the *Diary*. The sisters were
not natural countrywomen: they gave up riding, wore thin
shoes and were more familiar with the carriage-roads than the
fields. I think they liked flowers better than gardening — a
preference I have inherited. In the drawing-room stood Elizabeth's grand piano in its walnut veneer, also a harp, only heard
when one more string snapped; Robert had acquired at auc-
tions and had had placed in the hall not only a harmonium of
some power but a large-size organ with gilded pipes; in the
lobby decayed Eliza Wade's piano and in the Long Room a
mute spinet — however, the sisters were not musical; the harmonium and the drawing-room piano were only used for the
practice of Sunday hymns. Painting, embroidery, rather erratic
study were the chosen pursuits. Annie's studies were serious,
and she went to Oxford, to Lady Margaret Hall. Lizzie, very
tall, with her broad troubled white forehead, dark hair and
Brontëesque temperament made a break for Paris, to study art.
But she had sustained a shock while at school at Brighton and
was never quite free of nervous fears: in consequence, she
broke down — her canvases, ghostly with her endeavour, are
now stacked round the house.

The girls, most often Sarah or Mary, made visits to London
to stay with Aunt Sarah Clarke — the Miss Clarke who had refused Robert's umbrella. Unregretful, "interesting," well-to-
do, and with a warm heart for her sister's children, this aunt
was ideal. She took her nieces, one by one, abroad with her:
they returned to Bowen's Court from the Rhine or Italy with
sketch-books filled with castles and olive trees.

For the brothers life was much more straightforward: the

past does certainly seem to belong to men. Bob passed from
Sandhurst into the Essex Regiment: he was popular in the regiment; he seems to have exercised a passive, simple and rather
introverted charm. Charlie, the clever sociable dark-haired one,
went from Trinity College to Woolwich, then got his commission in the Royal Engineers. St. John and Mervyn, when home
from Trinity College, played cricket and flirted with the
young ladies they induced their sisters to ask to stay. I understand that for mornings together they used to sit on the steps
and simply flirt — an art lost now. As for cricket — they got
together a home eleven and levelled a ground in a field below
the garden, above the Farahy stream. The Bowen's Court
eleven — men on the place, near neighbours — played matches
all over the country, returns on their own ground. Home
matches ended with great festivity — jigs danced on the kitchen
table — and there were some famous " aways," for instance,
the three-day party at Castle Harrison, Charleville.

Such was the tenor of Bowen's Court life, the life of a republic of brothers and sisters, up to 1890, when Henry VI
married.

It may be remembered that after Aunt Disney's husband the
Rev. Brabazon Disney gave up the Farahy living, he hecame
curate to the Rev. the Hon. William Wingfield, fourth son of
the fourth Viscount Powerscourt, at Abbeyleix, Queen's
County. A faint previous connection may have existed, for Mr.
Wingfield's elder brother Edward, also in holy orders, had in
1819 married Louisa, third of the six daughters of the Hon.
George Jocelyn and of his wife Thomasine *née* Cole Bowen,
who had been the second daughter of our Henry III.

The Rev. William Wingfield, of Abbeyleix, had in 1830
married Elizabeth, daughter of the Rev. Thomas Kelly of
Kellyville. Mr. Kelly wrote hymns, of which all are, to me,
very moving. The two best known, I think, are " *We sing the
praise of Him Who died,*" and the evening, " *Through the day*

Thy love hath spared us," of which this is the second and last verse:

> *Pilgrims here on earth, and strangers,*
> *Dwelling in the midst of foes,*
> *Us and ours preserve from dangers;*
> *In Thine arms may we repose,*
> *And when life's sad day is past,*
> *Rest with Thee in heaven at last.*

Mr. Kelly's daughter Elizabeth (my great-grandmother) of whom a water-colour drawing exists, had the bloom of a rose: she is painted against a pink curtain. Her waist is said to have been no larger than the circumference of two oranges, and the blood of kings of Ireland flowed in her veins. She was, alas, consumptive. As Mrs. Wingfield she bore two sons and four daughters, of whom the eldest, Elizabeth Isabella, married Henry Fitz-George Colley in 1858.

Henry Colley's father, George Francis — formerly a commander in the Royal Navy, and resident, at the time of his son's marriage, at Ferney, Stillorgan, Co. Dublin — had been born a Pomeroy, being the third son of the fourth Viscount Harberton. He agreed to change his name to Colley in 1830, in order to inherit property. His maternal grandmother, wife of that Arthur Pomeroy who in 1783 became the first Lord Harberton, had been Mary, daughter and heiress of Henry Colley of Castle Carbery, Co. Kildare.

The Colleys are first heard of as Cowleys: Walter Cowley was Solicitor-general for Ireland in 1537, and was later, by patent dated 1548, appointed Surveyor-general of the kingdom. His son and heir, Sir Henry College of Castle Carbery, was a captain in the Elizabethan army. Sir Henry's son, Sir Henry Colley II, continued to be active in the Queen's service, and was succeeded by *his* son, Sir Henry III, who was in turn succeeded, in 1637, by his eldest son, Dudley Colley of Castle Carbery. Among this Dudley Colley's numerous children stand out two: his eldest son and heir, Henry Colley IV, and his eldest surviving daughter Elizabeth, who married Garrett Wesley (or Wellesley) of Dangan, Co. Meath.

Henry Colley IV left two sons, Henry V and Richard. Henry Colley V married Lady Mary Hamilton in 1719 and, dying early, left as his sole heiress a daughter, Mary — the Mary who in 1747 married a Pomeroy.

Meanwhile, Garrett Wesley of Dangan and his wife Elizabeth (daughter of Dudley Colley and sister of Henry Colley IV) had had two sons, William and Garrett. William died young and was succeeded by his brother Garrett, but Garrett's marriage was childless — therefore an heir was wanted for the considerable Dangan property. Garrett cast round, and is said to have offered the property to his near cousin John Wesley (*the* John Wesley) on condition that he give up preaching: these terms were refused. Garrett Wesley found himself better pleased by his first cousin Richard Colley (Henry Colley IV's second son) who was already making his way in the world: he proposed to make Richard his heir, on the condition that Richard assume the Wesley name and arms. This agreed to, Richard succeeded in 1728. He did not look back: in 1746 he was elevated to the peerage of Ireland under the title of Baron Mornington. His son Garrett was advanced to the dignities of Viscount Wellesley and Earl of Mornington. This first earl's third son, Arthur, became the first Duke of Wellington.

The senior line of Colleys having become, through the heiress Mary's marriage, merged in the Pomeroys, and the junior and only other line of Colleys having become the Wesleys, it was necessary to reclaim a Pomeroy younger son in order to continue the Colley name and identify this with the Carbery property. The foregoing paragraphs lead up to George Francis's change of surname in 1830. Carbery Castle itself, like the Coles' Ballymackey Castle, had by this time fallen to ruin, but George Francis, now bearing the name of his grandmother's family, enjoyed and later bequeathed to his heir

Henry Fitz-George the rents from the Carbery lands. Henry Fitz-George, having married Elizabeth Isabella Wingfield, lived during his father's lifetime at Lucan Lodge, Co. Dublin. At Lucan his ten children were born. The third of the six daughters, Florence, was my mother.

Mr. and Mrs. Disney, arriving at Abbeyleix some time in the course of the eighteen-seventies, formed the highest impression of the Wingfield family. Mr. Wingfield was now an elderly widower (Elizabeth *née* Kelly having died in 1856) with two unmarried daughters living at home. And his married daughter Mrs. Colley must have visited Abbeyleix as often as the distance from Lucan and growth of her family allowed. At all events, Aunt Disney *heard* enough of the Colleys to extend her good opinion to them. She never quite let the Colleys out of her view — they removed to Clontarf from Lucan: Aunt Disney's eye followed them. I do not know in what year she formulated the plan that her eldest Bowen's Court nephew, Henry Bowen, should visit the Colleys at Clontarf.

Mr. and Mrs. Colley left Lucan upon the death of his father — a move to a larger house had for some time been desired and now became possible. For a year they resided at Ferney, clearing up, then, having absorbed into their household not only heirlooms due to the eldest son but Henry Fitz-George's unmarried sister Lily, they disposed of Ferney and bought Mount Temple, Clontarf. They did well to abandon Ferney, which must have been, in all senses, a sunless house. Henry Fitz-George's childhood had not been happy: his mother (Frances, daughter of the Rev. Thomas Trench, Dean of Kildare) had been a Plymouth Sister, a woman of hatchet countenance and intransigent so-called religious gloom. So little kind, under her rule, had been Ferney that one of Henry Fitz-George's brothers, John, had fled abroad from it and disappeared. And the other brother, who as General Sir George Colley was to lose and die at Majuba Hill, told his wife he thanked nobody for his upbringing.

Mount Temple was certainly sunny. It is a large, mid-to-late Victorian house with gables, narrow but many windows and an ornate brick front, beautifully placed, with lawns going down in terraces over a wide view of Dublin Bay. Its downstairs rooms are spacious, good for family life. It stands, or stood when the Colleys acquired it, in a sufficient number of acres of land. Its nearness to Dublin was convenient in many ways.

The young Colleys' names were — Bessie (Elizabeth), Maud, Florence, George, Laura, Wingfield, Gerald, Constance, Gertrude and Edward. The girls had been educated by a Swiss governess and spoke French with a prepossessing confidence and German a little; they read a good deal, delighted in conversation, revered and copied great pictures, had a feeling for music (though perhaps not much knowledge of it) and a persuasive touch on piano-keys. In their love of the present, in their power of storing up memories, they were ruled by an innocent sensuousness. As a family they created their own society — the Colleys had a flair for family life. The sisters adored each other; the brothers were charming and funny, with a good deal of reserve — the emotional idiom of Mount Temple was perhaps rather more difficult for young men. The Colleys were good-looking, with vivid, expressive faces in which the features were rather strongly marked — through the family ran fine dark eyebrows and a tendency towards the Wellington nose. Their colouring was of the kind called Irish — brown hair with a gloss on it, big-pupilled grey-blue eyes and fresh, glowing skins. They were spontaneous in feeling, manner and thought — in speech their spontaneity was so striking as to be identified (rightly, I think) with wit. The desertion and decay of Carbery Castle worked out — at least for this generation — well: the Colleys were unlike most Anglo-Irish families in not being tied to or conditioned by any *place*. They combined to make Mount Temple their present idyllic world. The Colleys were not, like the young Bowens, inhibited by proud fine-strung place-bound nervousness. In the Bowen sense, they were not nervous at all, and the past to them was no more than a friendly myth. When Henry Bowen first came to Mount Temple, the warmth and the spontaneity must have charmed him most.

I have shown the young Bowens at Bowen's Court in the eighteen-eighties as being what one might call very motherless. The Colleys were the reverse. Mrs. Colley's temperament was dynamic. She was a very good woman with all those gifts through which wicked women most often succeed — she could enchant and affect people; her derision could reduce objects to dust and, with the authority of a delicious nature, she could be captious, arbitrary and sometimes, I am afraid, unfair — although her standards were of the highest and she could be also sincerely wise. Religious, happy and well-connected, she could afford to take an airy-derisive view of the world that lay outside Mount Temple gates. Denouncing the marriage-market, she refused to take her daughters into society: she considered it vulgar and ludicrous to " drag girls about." (If the Dublin seasons of those days really *were* as depicted in *A Drama in Muslin*, she would seem justified.) A young man wishing to marry a Miss Colley — or, in fact, even wishing to look at one — must be prepared himself to travel the whole way. Mrs. Colley (contrary to all modern theories) was more closely bound to her daughters than to her sons — the sons, though without defections in loyalty, were more outside the sphere of her influence. For instance, she saw no reason to deviate, in the bringing-up of her family, from the strictness in which both she and her husband had been brought up — cards, dancing and theatre-going had been alike forbidden, in their otherwise very unlike homes. (For her own part, she admitted to having suffered, as a young girl, on her visits to Powerscourt where these pleasures reigned. This youthful embarrassment, besides accounting for the break made with the heads of both families, may have set up in Elizabeth Isabella her satirical bias against the world.) So, at Mount Temple ball- and theatre-going were not permitted. But the sons — good-looking and popular and susceptible to the charms of the opposite sex — determined, while they continued to live at home, not to avoid these pleasures. Their goings-off in white ties were unostentatious, and they would announce at breakfast the next day that they had " been to a circus." No one pursued the matter.

Mrs. Colley could, as a mother, hardly be called *possessive*, because that implies some assertion or fear or wish. She was, rather, *possessing* — instinctively and almost without a check. Though her nature had not a touch of languor, though, in fact, she was vigour itself, with her children she was too wise ever to leave the role of one who *se laisse aimer*. Quick-minded and witty — in fact, clever — she was sturdily anti-intellectual: she denounced reading as a selfish and useless habit. " Whoever's is *this*? " she would say with ringing contempt, if she found a book in the downstairs part of the house. So her daughters read upstairs in their rooms. She could not be called snobbish — in so far as snobbishness shows any wish to advance oneself through one's friends — for beyond that rank to which she herself was born she felt that degrees of rank existed in fancy only. At the same time she was intransigent in any distinctions she chose to make: she would receive barristers, not solicitors — happily Henry Bowen was a barrister — she would countenance wine merchants (members of old wine families) but not brewers. The Church, the Army and (I suppose) the Navy were the only professions regarded as natural. Her husband's poet Trench cousin, at that time Archbishop of Dublin, was a little too High Church for her tastes; at the same time, the John Wesley connection was discredited by his Dissent. Though, inevitably, a Unionist in politics, my grandmother took a low view of Union Peers — not on the ground of their faulty patriotism but as their being people who had received bribes. Her own family, in this matter, were irreproachable — the Lord Powerscourt of that time is said to have shot from his bed of gout to kick downstairs the government agent who was offering him promotion in the Peerage and a sum down on condition that he support the Union. One Colley connection, a Trench, had, however, lapsed: Lord Ashtown did not stand well with the Colleys, though I do not know if he were aware of this. . . . In the long run, my grandmother Mrs. Colley was, simply, less naive and more accomplished in worldliness than my grandfather Robert Cole Bowen. She would have made circles round him, had the two ever met. She submitted the Bowens to minute examination before permitting Florence's engagement to Henry.

I think it says much for Mrs. Colley that she did not repress personality in her children but, rather, seemed to develop it. She must have been one of those women — in my experience more often *amoureuses* than mothers — who have the power to give an increased stature to anybody they like, love or are interested in. I doubt whether she understood her children — in fact, I believe she was shy of many of them — but she did, somehow, stimulate them. She insisted that they should have a quality. She detested " softness," and said so many times.

Mount Temple was, as may be inferred, a matriarchy. From the start I imagine that Elizabeth Isabella had shown more go than Henry Fitz-George. (In fact, I can form almost no view of my Colley grandfather's character.) For some time Henry Fitz-George had not been in good health, and not long after the move to Mount Temple he was attacked by an illness that kept him sad, silent and immobilized till he died. His state cast a shadow over the family, and also it accounted for a second shadow — the continuous presence of his sister Aunt Lily. Aunt Lily's means were sufficient, she could have lived elsewhere, but for years she sat in the midst of them at Mount Temple in the protracted hope that she might " help." She kept for her own use and drove round the roads a chubbed, pink-eyed white pony the family called " the Pig." I remember Aunt Lily herself as having a bleached but determined air, and she could command, I understand from her nieces, a particular kind of martyred obtrusiveness. If the Colleys were a little in love with each other, Aunt Lily certainly was not in love with them. Her presence acted as a restraint: they all tried hard, but . . . For instance, on Sunday afternoons Aunt Lily withdrew to her bedroom to study Hebrew. But Sunday afternoons were, also, the time set apart by her nieces for cracking toffee with pokers and shouting with mirth — they, rightly, felt happy when they had been to church — and this cracking and shouting took place in the back drawing-room, immediately under Aunt Lily's room.

Nothing stemmed Aunt Lily's desire to do right. Like the Bowens' Aunt Sarah Clarke, she took her nieces abroad — she not only chaperoned them but paid for them. She began, I believe, in rotation: the success of each trip could be judged by the nieces she took abroad again. Bessie had married young, so was out of it; strong-minded Maud was so very short with Aunt Lily that I doubt if Aunt Lily ever attempted her. Laura, who took with her gratitude, philosophy and a forgiving humour, was by far the greatest success. Handsome, spirited Constance was, like Maud, fierce with Aunt Lily; very pretty Gertrude, through no fault of her own, attracted Italians, and Florence, I am sorry to say, behaved like a fiend: she could not forgive Aunt Lily for spoiling Italy for her. From the city of Florence Florence stole out alone to find Mrs. Browning's grave, lay a bunch of white violets on it and meditate there for some hours — leaving Aunt Lily frantic.

Not only Aunt Lily found Florence difficult. There were clashes between Florence and her mother. To be a rebel in an unhappy home might be comparatively straightforward, but Florence was, rather, a misfit in surroundings recognized as idyllic. She found herself difficult. Her reflections and visions were punctuated by stormy naughtiness. She locked herself up and wept. About her bad behaviour, as about her good behaviour, there was something ecstatic and spiritual — she may have had the complex make-up of a saint. It took her years to acquire calmness, or to be on the plane of ordinary life. My own feeling is that Florence, in the heart of her family, suffered from some sort of claustrophobia — in a less special, more *terre-à-terre* atmosphere she might with much less fuss have toed the line for she had plenty of social sense. Had she, for instance, been told of and allowed to accept her Aunt Edith's invitation to London she might have been both chastened and understood, for Aunt Edith not only lived in an astringent world but knew many perceptive people, such as Henry James. (Aunt Edith was the widow of General Sir George Colley: after Majuba, desperately unhappy, she had spent some time at Mount Temple and had responded to the young Florence's ardent feeling for her. After that, Aunt Edith was granted apartments at Hampton Court, but, finding this beginning to pall, used to take small houses in London for the seasons — to, I am told, the annoyance of Queen Victoria. She wrote to Mrs. Colley asking that Florence might visit her, but Mrs. Colley, not feeling this would be for the best, suppressed the invitation and wrote back that Florence did not care to leave home. Aunt Edith, comprehensibly, lost all interest in Florence.)

Florence was liable to accesses — penitence, worship, love. By the sacrifices she asked of herself could be seen the strength with which she desired things. She might be maddening, but she was never " tiresome " — for one thing she was, in a sublime way, very funny; also, she had a flamelike quality; she was never ponderous or " intense," and play-acting was unknown to her. And from childhood she was always full of ideas, which made her the most perfect companion, though these ideas sometimes ended in trouble. Among her sisters Florence was a born leader: she always knew what to do next.

She went through all sorts of phases. For weeks together (when she was about eighteen) she refused to have a looking-glass in her bedroom — nuns did not have them, so why should she? Her appearance became so odd that at last her brothers complained. And then, allied to her love of reading was a quite

fanatical sense of wickedness: she was upstairs reading a book
in her bedroom when the book suddenly struck her as very
wicked (I do not know its name), so she plunged it into her
bedroom fire. The Mount Temple bedroom grates were small;
the book was large, so it did no more than roast and exude glue
— smells filled the house, the brothers mentioned the matter,
the sisters rushed to the spot. Up in Florence's bedroom she and
Laura used to study together, and read poetry, and besides this
they went in to classes in Dublin, rattling along the coast road
in a horse 'bus. Throughout these expeditions Florence insisted
on the strictest economy, so for lunch they bought some kind
of marine biscuit that so quickly tired the jaws and dried the
palate that it stifled appetite at low price. Crossing St. Stephen's
Green, the sisters proceeded to Alexandra College with these
biscuits inside their muffs. . . . Florence loved her cousins the
Miss Trenches, the Archbishop's daughters, and some of her
happiest days were spent at the Palace. With the Low Church
her experiences were less happy: she attended (I think in Clontarf) a prayer-meeting, in the course of which, without warning, any one not " saved " was invited to leave the room. No
one budged but Florence: she had to scramble for her umbrella
and wade out past eyes and knees. . . . Her first essays at
practical life were hardly more fortunate: my grandmother,
while withholding from her daughters facts about money, also
the so-called facts of life, believed that they ought to know
about housekeeping; so, in rotation, each Mount Temple
daughter kept house for a week. But when Florence's turn
came round she was taken off after three days, in response to a
general request. . . . Her feeling for clothes was sporadic, and
very personal: she and Laura (this was Florence's idea) made
for themselves dresses of scarlet butter-muslin that cost a penny
a yard, and in these and in white chip straw hats went to a
garden party at which they were much admired — but heavy
rain fell and the scarlet ran, over Florence and Laura, everything, every one.

She was lovely to look at, with a pointed and curved face over which expressions, like light from quick-running water, played. Her bronze hair (in the year when she met Henry) was swept up and coiled on the top of her head. Her eyes not only brightened but deepened in colour when she laughed or had any access of feeling. Her subtlety — for she could be disconcertingly subtle — was veiled by vagueness, or, if not vagueness, something gentler than nonchalance. Perhaps, from having been in the wrong, her vagueness was a sort of retreat. But also it established a quiet bay in which she and Henry met without alarm. I do not know how long it took Henry, how many visits, to detach Florence from the rest of her family. The evening they walked together in the Mount Temple fields he was already deeply in love. They came to a stream between high banks, with a plank lying beside it — the dexterous Colley brothers were accustomed, for any lady, to throw the plank crosswise so as to form a bridge. So Florence paused by the stream and, eyes upon the horizon, went into a sort of trance. The sense of something usual not happening recalled her to earth: " — Oh, Mr. Bowen," she said, " you just throw the plank across the stream." We know that Henry was clumsy: not without anxiety did he even put a book down on a desk. He told me that he had never prayed so hard as when he picked up that plank, with Florence there. God guiding it, the plank fell in position and Florence, unconscious, passed across.

She told one of her sisters that she loved him for his nobility and great mind. I imagine that there was no one to whom he could speak of his feeling for her. These two unusual people continued to love one another on the plane on which they had first met, a plane of innocence and nobility. With regard to the engagement, Mrs. Colley raised a number of objections that were entirely reasonable, and that had one by one to be overcome — Henry's newness in practice as a barrister, the undue size (given Henry's income) of Bowen's Court, the house's extreme isolation and the fact that it was occupied by his brothers and sisters. And there was the impression, hardest of all to combat, that the Bowens had an unhappy family history. However, all was arranged — with not much help from Florence, who signalized her engagement by a last burst of difficultness. She refused, for instance, to cope with her trousseau, so Mrs. Colley, in whom taste in the ordinary sense was lacking, went shopping alone. (Mrs. Colley, when her children were younger, had been used to go into Dublin and purchase bales of grey flannel: unrolling the length of these on the floor she would gaily cut out garments *à l'improviste*. When any one criticized this procedure, she replied that it did not matter what Colleys, *being* the Colleys, wore.) Florence, when all was assembled, cast one sick look at the trousseau and declared it to be unwearable. So what she did wear the year after her marriage I have no idea. The Colley brothers and sisters already valued Henry, who took all their teasing with a serious pleasure. One of the girls wrote to a cousin: " Florence is engaged to a young man with corn-coloured whiskers — Henry Bowen."

I have broken the rule I have tried, in this book, to keep — the rule of not leaving Bowen's Court for more than a page or two. Having had to go to Mount Temple to explain Florence, I have stayed there rather too long. Because the Colleys are as much my family as the Bowens, and because they themselves make such a study of memory (any Colley having the power to saturate one in the mood, colour and smell of the hour of which they choose to speak) I find it hard to be brief about them. However, the two families now converge, in the proper course of my narrative, with the state visit paid by Mrs. Colley and Laura to Bowen's Court when the Bowen-Colley engagement had been announced. Why Laura, not Florence? Because Henry, whose delicacy on behalf of Florence was extreme, felt that it would be hard on the bride-elect to " come down and be looked at." So Laura, as Florence's confidante, was chosen to prospect Bowen's Court, and to write home to Florence at Mount Temple lively descriptions of the future home.

Sarah Bowen, supported by her sisters, received the Colleys with dignity. The ordering of the house, for this occasion, must have fallen short of few of Robert's ideas. The bust of the Duke of Wellington, still on the hall sideboard, gave the Colleys a look. Laura, kind as she was observant, was touched to find that every chair in the drawing-room had been placed with great care over a threadbare patch. Mrs. Colley overbore any Bowen remoteness with charm, warmth and aplomb, and Laura and Annie made friends and used to read Milton together. It was agreed that Henry and Florence should not, for the first year or two of their marriage, occupy Bowen's Court, but only visit there. This should give the Miss Bowens time to look round — and Henry's profession would keep him much in town.

Henry Charles Cole Bowen married Florence Isabella Colley at Clontarf parish church on the tenth of April 1890. He was twenty-nine, she was twenty-four. On the honeymoon, which was spent at Roche's Hotel, Glengariff, Henry began to teach Florence Greek: to mark her good progress he gave her a Greek Testament and a gold watch. Then, the couple arrived at Bowen's Court, late one evening in spring. In the darkness outside the big gates there was a surge of people, a hum of voices — the bridal carriage was stopped. The tenants took the horses out of the shafts and themselves drew the carriage up the avenue. Florence, her eyes swimming, unable to speak, was seen in the flashes of lantern-light — she wore a long dark-red caped cloak, which has never been forgotten. They praised her beauty and wished her happiness. Ireland is a great country to die or be married in.

In the autumn of that year came the O'Shea divorce, inculpating Parnell. When in June 1891 Parnell married Mrs. O'Shea, Bishop O'Donnell of Raphoe gave it as his opinion that

" this news only capped the climax of brazened horrors." That
ill-seen marriage lasted less than six months: he died. The dis-
integration of the Parnell party, the apparent eclipse of Home
Rule has been told elsewhere. There was more than disintegra-
tion, there was demoralization — the country had suffered a
sexual shock. After the split between Parnellites and Anti-Parnellites, the Anti-Parnellites split again. In the years following
1890, recriminations, mobbings and faction-fights dragged Irish
hopes in the mud. " Ireland," said John Redmond, speaking of
those years, was " in a position of dis-union, squalid and hu-
miliating personal altercations and petty vanities." Idealistic
persons turned from the exhibition, and Unionism (if *this* were
to be Nationalism) acquired a stronger and stronger case. In
1892 Mr. Gladstone, as Prime Minister, introduced and got
through the Commons his second Home Rule Bill — but the
Lords flung it out by 419 to 41. Home Rule was now more
than an object for prejudice, it had begun to acquire a sort of
taint, and for the time being it sank the Liberal Party. The
Conservatives came in, looked over at Ireland and took a hand.

The hand was a kindly one. The Conservative object was to
present to Ireland a thought-out alternative to Home Rule, and
to interpose, in place of repression and exploitation, an administration that should be enlightened, benevolent, tactful and upright. English good intentions towards Ireland had, in the
Liberal view, best been made manifest by the espousal of Home
Rule: the Conservatives continued to make good intentions
manifest, but in another form. All round, concessions were
offered, complaints examined, reforms instituted and evils met.
The Conservative undertaking could not be seen as merely
propitiatory; the Government coupled fairness with dignity.
Conservative civilization in England being, in these years, at its
height, the civilization of Ireland became one aim. The Union,
though not to be broken, was no longer to chafe — gradually,
control of affairs in Ireland was to be handed over to Irishmen,
with England in a no longer purely possessive but senior, ad-

visory, kindly role. Already, in 1891, Mr. Balfour, as Chief
Secretary for Ireland, had established the Congested Districts
Board — " a body to which was entrusted the special charge
of districts where the population was greater than the resources
of the soil could support." This Board, towards whose work
Parliament voted sums, was, indeed, to mark a striking advance,
not so much in its achievements as in its constitution: on it
served, by Government nomination, not only Catholic clergy
but active Nationalists. And this was only the outset of the attempt to develop Ireland through Imperial expenditure. The
attempt came to have more than a moral backing; its object
was restitution, for this reason — in 1893 the Liberal Government had appointed a Commission, of English financial experts,
to inquire into the financial relations between England and Ireland. The Commission's Report, issued in 1896, found that
" the Act of Union had imposed upon Ireland a burden which,
as events showed, she was unable to bear." The Commission, in
fact, found — though it must be said that the finding was not,
in detail, unanimous — that Ireland had, since the Union, been
so grossly and steadily overtaxed that the arrears of overtaxa-
tion now amounted to three hundred millions. The issuing of
the Report created a situation that the Conservative Government had to, and did, face. The Commission, nothing if not
thoroughgoing, suggested an annual refund based on their figures, but to this Lord Salisbury's Government did not immediately see their way. The Irish members, naturally stimulated,
clamoured for money back in one or another form. The form
found was that the money should be remitted in a series of
grants for Irish development. This, however, was to become
merged in the immense project of Land Purchase — Liberal
project that the Conservatives took on. Briefly, the landlords
were to be bought out by the Government, and their former
tenants were to become proprietors by means of a series of
payments (or " annuities ") made to the Government over a
given number of years. The complexities of the transaction

were infinite; the search for all-round fairness demanded, and
got, the best brains of the time. There was not only fact to deal
with, there was feeling: the subject of land in Ireland is a mined
area. The machinery of Land Purchase came to be vested in the
Irish Land Commission Court. I know enough of the matter to
know it outside my province: to *Statutory Land Purchase in
Ireland* my father Henry VI devoted, in writing a book of that
title, sixteen of the later years of his life.

The *modus vivendi* should have been good enough. But there
is no doubt that by a number of Anglo-Irish landlords this
abrogation of their power, and by a Conservative Government,
was felt as a bitter blow. It was, " *Et tu, Brute!* " One felt in-
jured in spirit, if not in purse. As to the purse, the landlords
were compensated by the issue of Bonds backed by the Government, and landlords willing to sell received bonuses. But the
landlords were, or felt themselves, sacrificed to the hopes of
successful continuance of that very Union to which they had
looked to maintain their authority. Aubrey de Vere, poet-land-
lord, Catholic by conversion, expresses towards the close of his
Recollections the nobler side of the landlord point of view:

The gentlemen of Ireland have within the last few years received hard usage at the hands of many among their fellow-
Irishmen, who, during a long period previously, had felt, I will
not say professed, a strong attachment to them. They have received also during the same years of trial, from many of their
English friends in both houses of Parliament, a treatment different from that which they had expected. What proportion of
that property which they received from their ancestors and had
hoped to bequeath to their descendants will remain with them
we know not. It is only certain that their duties will remain.
Their first duty as Christians will be to allow no vindictive or
selfish interests to determine their course. Their highest duty to
Ireland will be to remain among their poor, no matter how
wronged or defamed, there or elsewhere, so long as they can
continue to benefit them, even with means so often reduced to
one half or less, and to resist the progress of that Jacobinism

from which Ireland has suffered so much. Their duty to both
countries will be to cement their union and make it become at
last, if possible, a union alike of hearts and of interests.

Onwards from 1889 Horace Plunkett had been working for
co-operation amongst the Irish farmers. Throughout the country he had continued to urge that, instead of hanging their
hopes on rent abatements, farmers should take a progressive line
of their own, co-operate, study the modern methods and secure
prosperity for themselves. By 1894 co-operative societies were
active enough to have formed a central union, the Irish Agricultural Organization Society. In the early eighteen-nineties,
after the *débâcle*, Home Rule appeared so unlikely as to be
counted out, and Horace Plunkett had won an Irish seat as a
Unionist. His endeavours to promote a prosperous Ireland
under conditions other than Home Rule could not, in some
quarters, be well seen. The " Anti-Parnellite " Nationalists
would have none of him, but John Redmond, now leader of the
" Parnellite " group, recognizing the value of his activities,
agreed to serve on Plunkett's Recess Committee of Irish members, to discuss Irish home questions of a non-party kind. Plunkett's movement pleased the Conservative Government, with
whose hopes for enlightened Irish development it fell in exactly. The outcome was the establishment of a special Department of Agriculture and Technical Instruction for Ireland:
to the Department went an impressive annual grant. The Act
that brought the Department into being was further important
in creating a new ministerial office, that of Vice-President of
the Department — its nominal President being the Chief Secretary. The Vice-President was to hold an Irish seat, and might
(unlike the Chief Secretary) be an Irishman. The Government's readiness to hand back departments of Ireland to Irishmen could be again inferred from the Local Government Act,
which, in 1899, set up all over Ireland, on the English model,
county and district councils. The Act's working was democratic: control of matters affected passed from the landlords'

into the people's hands. In the election of councillors party feeling could freely appear, so that, except in Ulster, the county and district councils, creations of a benevolent Unionism, were early compact with votaries of Home Rule.

As a whole, the Conservative experiment might be summarized as an attempt on the part of English gentlemen to treat the Irish as English gentlemen. Ironically, it was viewed on the Irish side of the water as either bribery or an admission of guilt. It did, however, confirm in their Unionism a number of thoughtful and patriotic Irishmen; it created among wide-minded people a class of Liberal-Unionists — of which Henry VI was one. For such men, reason supported and solid promise for Ireland accompanied this new phase of the English policy; one foresaw an Ireland adult and stabilized, and Union showed its ideal aspect, strength. And, for the ethical Irish Unionist, the divorce of Unionism from landlord interest made for clearness of conscience. Unionism, now, became rational: if one felt the shadowy presence of class-tradition, there was no thought of class-interest. Alike to Aubrey de Vere in his conception of duty, Henry VI differed on the question of (almost) divine right. The Ascendancy, if it were to remain an ascendancy, must now take its stand on morals and discipline. The disarray and impotence in the Home Rule party gave point to every doubt that one had felt of their cause.

The Parnell scandal, and the succeeding tragedy, had been far from the *bois dormants* of Mount Temple and Bowen's Court. These, like woods in the sunset, glowed in the golden close of the English nineteenth century. No unkind wind blew. The 'nineties, for Anglo-Ireland, were a decade of fine consciences and of a humour that was uncombative, mellow and disengaged. Protestantism became less bigotted: under the august guarantee of Italian art Madonnas appeared on the walls of Protestant homes; the Church of Ireland, for some time now disestablished, had produced some outstanding churchmen — such as Archbishop Trench, who had written sonnets in praise of the *Risorgimento*. Under the influence of a liberal Christian culture, the outlook on Europe widened. And the gentry, in their turn being disestablished, produced gentler men and women. The " well-dressed savage " was rarer. To be " rich " became vulgar; the grandness of Robert Cole Bowen's day gave place to a favoured originality — in fact, Anglo-Ireland, after this second step-down in power, entered upon its second romantic phase. In art there the great cult of Italy — though not, as in Henry III's day, of classical Italy. And one was Francophile: an idealized Frenchwoman, who never wore *new* clothes but was faultlessly poised, gloved, shod, became the model for ladies — her fading image is stamped on my memory. The Germans were liked as feeling and musical. Anglo-Ireland, in the course of her late flowering, looked for culture everywhere but inside her home shores. The Gaelic League seemed no more than a bizarre activity on the part of the son of a clergyman, Mr. Douglas Hyde.

The revival of Irish was *not* an Irish development in which the Conservative Government saw reason to interest itself — though it did not oppose it. Though for some time no penalties had attached to the speaking of Irish, advantage lay all on the other side, and since the Union the language had been in steady decline. This decline both O'Connell and the Roman Catholic clergy had, if not encouraged, done nothing to check. By halfway through the century, urban and more accessible Ireland was English-speaking: the remoter, still Irish-speaking districts had had a heavy mortality in the Famine, and had, since, been drained of their young people by the continuous exodus to America. Overlooked in the fierceness of other struggles, the language had been quietly dying out. Now, in these doldrums of the 'nineties, the call to save it came — and came from a study, not from any political platform. In 1893 the Gaelic League was founded by Douglas Hyde: it was, avowedly, nonpolitical, and the whole enterprise might have been academic. But, to an Ireland disappointed in politicians, low in stock of ideals, mocked by concessions that she did not desire and, in some views, did not deserve, and altogether half-killed by English kindness, " the thing became a trumpet." It rushed on the people that for Ireland to lose her language would be to lose her soul, her memory, that whole range of wordless associations that underlie some but not other words — in fact, to lose herself. Ireland for the Irish had been the politicians' promise, yet to be made good. *Irishness* for the Irish was the League's promise, subtler and more essential. The League proposed to save and bring back to active being not only the Irish language but its concomitants in the expression of national character — games, arts, industries. The most aggressive act on its blameless programme was the instigation of a " Buy Irish " campaign. But its whole trend was against anglicization: therefore, the League pursued its cultured way, through classes, exhibitions and Gaelic playing-fields, in a surround of enthusiasm that might have appeared sinister, for there was much behind it. The enthusiasm not only marked, by contrast, renewed contempt for Parliamentarian aims; it was Ireland's rejoinder, sufficiently pointed, to an attempt to make a second England of her. Ireland wished to reclaim her past and be *just herself*. The integrity of the Gaelic League was absolute: it was not intended to cover anything else. But its influence, at this juncture, could not but be dynamic: it not only inspired a literature and a theatre; it was to become the nursery of Sinn Fein.

Henry and Florence Bowen were a young married couple in Dublin in the 'nineties. She was intelligent, sensitive, curious, and on all subjects he had an open mind. But by the literary Dublin of the 'nineties they remained, as far as I know, untouched. If, at the parties that they attended — *conversazioni*, they were called — Florence met either Yeats or Æ., her mind must have been elsewhere, for they made no impression. She remained fixed on Browning and Italy. Henry is said to have been present when another (and very different) literary figure

was kicked down the stairs of a Dublin club for speaking dis-
respectfully of a lady, but this, as far as I know, is the nearest
approach he made to any Irish writer prominent in his day.
Emancipated by marriage, Florence went to dances — though,
having begun late, she told me, she never danced very well.
Also, she took to theatre-going — but, as a late-comer, she took
that view of the theatre now so freely denounced: she expected
of it something superb, stylish, altogether superior to the real.
So, it was to the Gaiety Theatre, not the Abbey Theatre, that
Florence inside her clouds of shetland and Henry in his flap-
ping overcoat bent their steps or directed their evening cab.
Henry — to become an ardent cinema-goer some years before
the movies became the thing — was a passive theatre-goer; also,
he drew the line at Opera, which, he said, was silly. So complete
was my parents' immunity from the Irish Revival that *I* only
heard of this for the first time when I was at school in England,
about 1916. Their dining out and their own entertaining were
either in Florence's circle or among Henry's legal and Trinity
College friends. The big Georgian drawing-rooms of the Dublin of that period were lit by gas made kind by pink glass
shades, and the extreme advance of the century showed in a few
Morris hangings and wallpapers.

At first, after their marriage, they lived in lodgings in one of
the streets off Fitzwilliam Square, and went down for Henry's
vacations to Bowen's Court, where they were in the position of
not quite guests. The situation with regard to Bowen's Court
was for some time kept static by almost excessive delicacy. But
there were blunt interpolations from Mrs. Colley, and finally
these prevailed: Henry's sisters decided to live their own lives,
and Sarah, by moving from Bowen's Court into a house in
Mitchelstown, formally handed over to Henry and Florence.
Sarah's choice of Mitchelstown as a home was dictated by her
attachment to Lady Kingston — her romantic love for her
mother had left its mark on her, so that all her life she was to
form friendships with older, rather august women. Lady King-

ston, after Lord Kingston's death, had married a cousin of Florence's, Mr. Willie Webber, but she retained her title. Sarah's
double-fronted house in King-square overlooked the approach
to the Castle gates; her back garden was shaded at evening by
the demesne trees, and at the foot of the garden were stables and
carriage-house: she thought of keeping a carriage, but did not.
In the house there were rooms for any of Sarah's sisters who
might care to continue to make their homes with her.

Florence loved Bowen's Court. Its large light strong plainness touched her sense of the noble, as Henry had. Free, now,
to move without trespassing upon feelings, she penetrated
every inch of the house. She exhumed from the basement and
had restored with care the original Bowen's Court furniture,
banished by Robert in favour of the more massive; and she had
the family portraits taken down in a row and cleaned Bowen
faces and jabots with raw potato. (It may have been at this time
that Jane Cole's little dog reappeared on her blue satin knee,
out of the grime of nearly two centuries.) Florence had no
great historical sense, and in her make-up she was so unaca-
demic that she could hardly be said to have, in the cold sense,
taste; she had, rather, a sort of genius for feeling that extended
even to things. All the same, it was not till the seventh year of
their marriage that she and Henry came on the family silver-
chest. The leisurely wooded walk to the garden, the rooks, the
lawns, the steps in the sun, the high ceilings indoors became
woven or melted into her happiness. Encouraged by her
younger brothers and Henry's younger brothers, she and
Henry gave a not large ball, to which were invited young ladies
and officers said to be so dashing that Mervyn Bowen and
Gerald Colley pinned up in the sitting-out places *Please Kiss
Quietly*. Florence and Henry thought this lovely but doubtful,
so I suppose they had the notices taken down.

Alas, with Henry's career to think of, they could not be always at Bowen's Court. So, having found lodgings unsatisfac-
tory, they began to look about for a Dublin home. They found

15 Herbert Place — one of a row of brown brick Georgian houses with high steps, facing across the canal with its pollarded trees. From across the canal, in those days, travelled the singing hum of a saw in a wood-yard. To furnish this new home without too much expenditure, they moved up some of the Bowen's Court furniture — this, in the following sad years, went with Florence to England, and is still in exile there, in my London house. And Bowen's Court, by this Dublin-ward trend of Henry's and Florence's, was to be deprived of much more than its furniture — for the first time since Henry III had moved his family in, a break came in the house's continuous human life. While Florence and Henry were in Dublin nobody lived at Bowen's Court, no one at all. For a grander house, country seat (or one country seat) of a peer these periodic desertions would be in the general plan. But Bowen's Court was, in essence, a family home: since 1776 it had been a symbolic hearth, a magnetic idea, the focus of generations of intense living. Now, the caretaker from Robert's outlying wing unshuttered the windows in the morning only to let light fall on to sheeted furniture. Fires were lit, but to warm nothing but air. No voices were heard in the surprised rooms, and, when the windows were left open, birds began to fly unalarmedly in and out. It may be said that Bowen's Court met and conquered the challenge of emptiness — but on the house the conquest has left its mark: it is to these first phases of emptiness that I trace the start of the house's strong *own* life. There were to be years of this; so much so that when I re-enter the house after an absence, I feel I must come to terms with something already there.

When they had been married for some years, Florence and Henry began to wonder why they did not have a child. Bowen's Court asked for an heir, who was to be called Robert. Every one else seemed to have children, and Florence, with an increasingly thoughtful eye, watched her County Cork friends and neighbours, her Dublin friends and even her much younger sister Gertrude (who had married her cousin Alberic Fiennes)

setting up families quite effortlessly. Perhaps she connected her
failure to have a child with her inefficacy — well-known since
the days of Mount Temple — in any form of practical life. She
engaged on impetuous, troubled talks — so that those who loved
her knew enough how she felt to share her triumph when,
nearly nine years after her marriage, she could announce that
Robert was on the way. Mrs. Gates, a Bowen's Court neighbour much in Florence's confidence, called at Herbert Place to
find Florence, elated and serious, on the drawing-room sofa,
with her Persian cat Tory (after Queen Victoria) curled up in
her skirts: she was eating her way through a large number of
raisins, which she had been told would be good for Robert and
her. She offered raisins to Mrs. Gates, whose existing family of
three children had been one of Florence's envies for some time,
and Mrs. Gates, though not just then in need of raisins, shared
in the feast. The cat Tory seldom quitted my mother, and is
said to have had some influence on the child. Henry's to-be
son Robert came to be *the* Robert, superseding his grandfather
in the right to that name. His arrival was late, so much so that,
greeting each other, people would say: " Any news of Robert
yet? " And in the exact sense he never arrived at all, for the
child who, at 15 Herbert Place, on the 7th of June, 1899, came
to very difficult birth was, after all, a girl — whom they christened Elizabeth. The name had Henry's mother and Florence's
mother and the whole range of Bowen tradition behind it. They
hoped to call me " Elizabeth " in full, but my tongue could not
get round that, so I became " Bitha." The birth was celebrated
at Bowen's Court by immense rejoicings; jigs were danced
on the kitchen table with still more solemn fervour than
after a cricket match, and no one, from the moment the sex
was announced, said a word against Elizabeth for not being
Robert.

My mother had no more children. About four years after my
birth the start of another set up a serious illness of which she
nearly died. And Henry wasted no more wishes on Robert: he

had, as I said, from his mother a high opinion of women, and the Bowens were not bound by the Salic law.

I arrived at Bowen's Court for the first time when I was about six weeks old. Late one July evening my mother, my nurse and I drove down the Upper Avenue in an inside car. Mrs. Gates had come down from Kildorrery to welcome us. Florence, advancing into the dark hall, turned up the oil lamp on the sideboard under the portraits: quickly she took the baby from the arms of the nurse and held it close to the lamp for her friend to see. Mrs. Gates raised her eyes from the baby's face to meet a look from Florence that she never forgot — an invitation into the heart of the moment, a tilted, tender, quizzical, deprecating and above all sublimely triumphant look. ". . .?" There was nothing to add.

By the time that I begin to remember, life had divided itself into winter and summer halves. Towards the end of May we came down to Bowen's Court; about half-way through October we returned to Dublin, leaving Bowen's Court to its winter sleep. My father could not be with us all through the summer, for he remained in Dublin for the Trinity Term. My birthdays were generally spent at Bowen's Court, but my fourth birthday had to be at Mount Temple, because at that time my mother was very ill. Mrs. Colley, driving in in a Clontarf cab for one of her Dublin days, had happened to call in at Herbert Place to find, without warning, Florence at death's door. Mrs. Colley's detestation of " softness " made her, as a rule, rather crisp with a sufferer (for instance, Laura developed consumption and had to be taken to London to see a specialist: while in London she had a bad hæmorrhage; Mrs. Colley, having rendered some sort of aid, said, " I'm afraid I can't stay with you now, dear; I have to go out and have my photograph taken "), but this *was* a shock to her, and she took the matter in hand. My grandmother was hard, first of all, on herself; she died, not long after Florence got better, of an illness that if admitted might have been cured.

I remember our Sunday tramrides out to Mount Temple from Herbert Place. Those first winters, we spent many Sundays there. The terraced lawns, the big double drawing-room and the enchanting persiflage of the uncles and aunts on me very early worked their spell: I remember my grandmother's decisive manner and animated face. On weekdays I wore a Robert-like, buttoned-up reefer coat, and was gratified by strangers calling me " Sonny," but on Sundays my sex proclaimed itself by the wearing of a white fuzzy muff, slung round my neck on a cord, a white coat and a white saucer-shaped hat with an ostrich feather peeping over the brim. With my grandmother's death Mount Temple came to an end: the house was sold and the Colleys scattered. My mother's brothers and sisters, for different reasons, gravitated to England or even further abroad. Only Aunt Maud, at that time occupied with the conversion of Jews in Dublin, and other interests, remained for some time in lodgings at the other side (from us) of the canal. And my mother's eldest and much-loved brother George settled in bachelor lodgings in Herbert Place, two or three doors away from No. 15. He had been left deaf by an illness when he was very young, but he lip-read and, quite apart from the lips, read character and sized up a situation with almost disconcerting exactitude. His great interest was motor cars; he kept the earliest kind, and I remember going for dreamlike drives with him. He came placidly in and out of No. 15, and he was to support my mother through the worst of her years.

As a mother my mother was far from vague; she had many ideas, but none of them foolish ones. She arranged for me to drink a good deal of milk, because she believed that children who drank tea early grew up rather runty, or like jockeys; she made me wear gloves, because Bowens got freckled hands; she did not let me learn to read till I was seven, because she perceived that Bowens overworked their brains. It was her great wish (survival, perhaps, of the expectations she had formed of Robert) that I should not be muffish. Though horses bored and alarmed her, and bored Henry, she insisted that I should learn to ride — on a sofa-broad white Iceland pony called Softnose — not long after I was able to stand, and, mortified by her own late start in dancing, she sent me to dancing-class at about that time. Determined that I should be with literate people, she dismissed my nurse for a governess when I was four years old. My first governess was not a great success: she was not very literate, looked like a Manet and found Bowen's Court *triste*. My mother insisted that I must not be shy; she considered shyness common and, still worse, dull; she detested children who " burrowed " when they were introduced. To counteract the effects of my being an only child she plunged me into the middle of young society. In Dublin, in County Cork I was seldom alone — or if I were I do not remember it. Her quest of ordinariness for me was quite successful: I was neither interesting nor dreamy, nor, except in the use of long words, original. She gave me — most important of all as a start in life — the radiant, confident feeling of being loved. But her behaviour with me was never fatuous; she tried very hard to be critical. She explained to me, with a belyingly hopeful look, that I would never be pretty, but that she hoped I would grow up to have a nice character.

In Dublin there were, of course, plenty of children, and in County Cork I was as social as Henry III. Most of the houses known in Henry III's day, and others new since his day, had put out children, and where there were no children we were kindly received. There were a great many parties. At Bowen's Court one used to jump on the steps with excitement as a vibration throughout the silent country developed into a rumble of carriage-wheels — the little So-and-Sos coming to tea. The governesses made friends, exchanged novels and taught each other to plait crêpe paper hats. They kept dry jerseys and changes of knickers for when each other's charges fell into the stream or river near which each big house was unerringly placed, and beside which we always wanted to play. And on summer Sunday mornings at Farahy church we had, in those days of King Edward, quite a parade — the little Olivers from Rockmills, the little Gateses from the other side of Kildorrery, myself and the little Johnsons from Lisnagorneen. The sun winked in through the trees and the south windows on to pewfuls of little girls in white muslin dresses and starched white muslin hats, and of little boys in sailor suits. Parents, grandmothers (there was " old Mrs. Oliver "), visitors, governesses, Protestant farmers and, packed at the back, the Protestant servants of all households, composed the rest of the congregation; the organ was played either by Mrs. Oliver or by Mrs. Gates, and we all sang loud, confident Protestant hymns. The rector loved all insects, and was said to encourage the ingress of wasps to church; he had a sharp sense of the sins of society, and sometimes he used to denounce us from the pulpit. The Olivers — I think in surviving protest against the shutting-down of their Rockmills church, of which nothing but spire and weatherfish now remained — always used to come in a little late, clattering booted over the grating in the aisle. After church we all trooped down to the Farahy gate, to watch the horses being unhitched from the gateposts and backed into the shafts of the wagonettes and the traps. . . . Like every one else's, my early summers were fine. My mother had a white India-muslin dress, on which the silk embroidery turned to parchment-yellow: from the hem a green rim never quite laundered out — the dress was always trailing over the grass. We used to have tea where my grandmother had had tea, in the spongy, shady corner of the big tennis lawn. She tried to drive the phaeton, but she did not drive well and my father thought the enterprise a mistake. I remember standing with her, in the sunset, at the end of one of the Bowen's Court fields: at the other end stood a horse, quietly eating, so she took my hand and said in her most controlled voice: " We won't be frightened, will we? "

At three I was taken to England to visit my Fiennes first cousins, and when I was six they visited Bowen's Court. When

I was five a little girl called Gerry, whose parents were in India, came to live with us for a year — she was very pretty indeed, with brown eyes and a cleft chin, and she was mad on horses. At Bowen's Court, she and I slept in the four-windowed bedroom over the drawing-room that had been my nursery from the first. On one pane of a window my name is written, with the diamond in my mother's big ring.

It was in the year Gerry was with us that the shadow I did not notice began to form. My mother had been right in her intuition that all Bowens, and Henry VI in particular, overtaxed their brains. Henry had left the Bar for the Land Commission: he became an examiner of titles in one of the most technical branches of the Court. The rhythm of his intellectual life changed, and became too much accelerated: under the attraction and excitement of his special subject, and under new conditions that did not suit him (the solitude and high pressure of an office after the chatty amenities of the Law Library) he consistently worked too hard, till, day and night, his work was never out of his mind. At the same time, he was prey to a private worry: owing to some misjudgement or inattention he had lost some of his capital — a sum that, in view of what were his father's finances, appears really pathetically small. Self-reproach, and a fear that my mother and I might suffer, pressed further upon his desperate tiredness. He was in the grip of a sort of prolonged, relentless *coup de trois heures:* he began to see the past as a burning pattern not of his own injuries but of his own mistakes. His childish isolation from the rest of the Bowens, the Calvinism of nursery teaching, his mother's death and its reason, his struggles against his father, followed by Robert's darkness of mind and death, the anxieties with which, as the young Boss, he had attempted to rule his younger brothers and sisters — pain from the past, sense of losing grip on the present and dread of the future all rushed in on him now. The illness that stole six years of Henry VI's life from him was called anaemia of the brain.

Much of the physical weakness was to be traced back to early days. I have described the cheerlessness of *that* Bowen's Court nursery: Robert's heir, like all the rest of his children, had been under-nourished. On top of this, he had overdrawn on himself by growing tall so quickly, thinking so hard — no attempt had been made to slack Henry down. When he had been promoted to Robert's dinner table, when he was at school, at college, it must have been always the same — he bolted his food absently, and he had not the temperament that makes for a good digestion. And on uncertain digestion followed uncertain sleep. As one instinctively seeks health he had always sought merriness, gentleness, simple things, but the apparent placidity of his own nature was deceptive. For marriage he had chosen a beautiful companion, some one who in his keeping had acquired a calm she did not by nature have — but not a capable soul who would mother him. He had been exposed, through no wish of Florence's, to more than the usual discomforts of a young *ménage:* as had already appeared at Mount Temple, she was not a born housekeeper. Henry had said once that he liked chops, so chops, in all stages of over and undercooking, appeared with affectionate regularity. In the first years of their marriage they had had some shocking cooks. There did finally come to them as a cook a Kerry girl, Margaret, who was an angel: through one of the worst phases of Henry's illness she was one of the few friends to whom he would listen, but her wise care and good cooking came too late. Henry, as a man in his early forties, needed much he did not get and did not consciously want. He was in no position to overwork, as he overworked from his start with the Land Commission.

My father and mother were accustomed to be together in long phases of happy absence of mind, punctuated by impetuous moments when they communicated to one another their thoughts. When she came down to earth, she could be very perceptive, but she was not observant in the ordinary way. I believe that for months, at the outset of his illness, she only found him more absent-minded than usual. She would have feared to hurt him by commenting on his increasing sombreness, or on the irritability to the point of violence that was so very unlike him. If his estrangement from her, that she could not understand, hurt her, it hurt too much for her to speak of it. For a long time she, who as a girl had been so stormy, went on flying her flag of serenity: she may have told herself that she was imagining things. The world saw what was the matter before she did. The dignity or detachment that lay behind her intimacies with people made it hard for friends to speak bluntly to her. Her mother was dead, her brothers and sisters, with the exception of George, scattered, and she was more alone than she really knew. But I think it must have been from something *somebody* said that she first realized the truth about Henry's state.

From her and me, from the safeness of Herbert Place with its canal reflections and friendly hum of the sawmill, from Bowen's Court and its people and the guests on the steps he was being drawn away. He saw these things in the distance and through black glass, till to see them became the most terrible thing of all. He wanted to be with me, because I was a child and his child. And with strangers he remained most like himself, because his habit of courtesy was stronger than any illness. He was at ease with my Uncle George, who used to come and take him for long walks, round the Dublin roads or along Sandymount strand.

Most of the summer of 1905 my mother, still hoping to fight this, stayed with my father at Herbert Place, while Gerry and I were at Bowen's Court with my second English governess, Miss B——. Miss B—— was pretty, with liquid brown eyes and fluffy hair; she adored my mother, as appears from her letters, and she took pride in holding the fort. We three lived in our corner of Bowen's Court, and carried on that sort of miniature drama that forms between two girl children and an emotional woman cut off from every one else. My mother would come to

us for two or three days on end, then go back to Dublin, and to
my mother in Dublin Miss B—— wrote constantly. The other
day I came on a batch of letters: I cannot help giving extracts
— they have so much the colour of that July.

*Sunday afternoon. The babes are resting, so I have a nice quiet
hour to send you heaps and heaps of thanks for your lovely little
presents! Such excitement and delight at breakfast here, I wish
you could have popped in and seen us, the children are charmed
with their silver things, Babe's face was a picture when she opened
Beauty's glass. The little brooch and your sweet thought I love,
I cannot put into words how much I value it, it will be one of my
greatest treasures, and when I go, will always remind me of one
I LOVE, and of Bowen's Court. Many thanks for the haberdash-
ery, such a neat little box full, its so interesting opening the different things, and then your nice letters to read, they keep me from
feeling too lonely, they all come in the morning, but Mike goes
every evening with the letters, and I always get the papers. What
a grand sight the Royal wedding must have been, I should love
to have seen it, I do love weddings, don't you. The thought of the
melancholy service to-day without music worried me last evening,
so I scribbled a hurried note to Mrs. Oliver, telling her Mrs. Gates
is still away, and asking her to kindly play for us, and wasn't it
kind of her, she did, and we had such a nice bright service and
full congregation, but the sermon was awful, he shouted at us,
and told us not to keep Sunday as a day of rest but a holy day,
and that all the high outward signs would not help us to reach
God. The clergyman Oliver was in church, perhaps he will preach
for us one Sunday, it would be a treat. Mr. Oliver told me he had
seen you yesterday for a few minutes, they asked me to take the
children over one day this week, but I refused because we are
out Monday, Tuesday and Friday, and I think the Olivers are to
be asked to the Luthers, so I thought it best to leave their visit till
next week. I know it's not far, but better for the babes not to have*

*too much at once, and they are so happy and well now. I want
to wash their heads Wednesday, I felt too limp on Saturday to
do them. It's fine to-day, but showery, we had to wait for a heavy
shower this morning and did not get to church till the end of the
first lesson. Our visitors did turn up yesterday, the same two, no
Miss Blackie, I wonder why she is always at home. They thought
us all looking the picture of health, Gerry especially — fancy, she
sang Twinkle Twinkle to them all alone and so nicely. I am SO
SORRY about Mr. Bowen, isn't it disappointing, when he seems
so much better and then goes back again. Dear Mrs. Bowen, don't
leave him till he is better. . . . . I must tell you, Bitha told me yesterday that I am uncommonly picturesque and would do for an
act. I can't think where she gets her words from. I'm sure she has
never heard me say anything about any one. . . . . Gerry has written to her mother to-day. I wonder if you could get Bitha a pair
of cheap doeskin gloves or something strong to wear in the garden,
she has quite worn out two prs. since we came. Never mind if you
can't get any, I can manage.*

*Thursday, 7.15. The babes are in bed, and now to finish my
letter to you. They have been so sweet and loving this evening, I
read Perseus to them for a little while, isn't it strange their love
for such a weird book, and then we went down to the drawing-
room for a dance and a romp before bed. Sarah Barry was polishing the hall, so we invited her in, and the babes gave her a little
entertainment, she was so delighted with them. I gave her your
message this morning, her first words when she saw me were enquiries for Mr. Bowen. How fond all the people are of you, dear
Mrs. Bowen, it is nice to see such respect and devotion. I think
they would do ANYTHING for either of you, to say nothing of
the wee one, and I am not surprised, I have never met kinder
friends than you and Mr. Bowen, and I am sure I never shall. We
were so hoping to send you some flowers to-morrow, but am
afraid all this rain to-night will spoil them. . . . . I saw Mrs. Han-*

lan last evening, and she said, " Oh Miss, you are much better look-
ing than when I saw you before," I suppose she meant that I look
much stronger, did she?

Tuesday afternoon. It's such a close wet afternoon we couldn't
go to Mrs. Hoare's, I think we must be going to have thunder. I
am hoping it will clear for us to get a walk after tea. The babes
are drawing, they have been very busy playing dollies hospital. I
have written to Miss Luther and I must send a line to Mrs.
Hoare. I hope you had a comfy journey? I'm afraid you'll find
Dublin very hot and stuffy, but I hope we shall have you back
with us again soon, and I shall much hope for better news of Mr.
Bowen. Rogers asked me please to tell the Master that the smoke
he saw this morning did NOT come from the study, but from the
laundry fire. Bitha has just told me to send you twenty-two kisses
for yourself, and twenty-two for Mr. Bowen! She's so funny, she
told me to say Mr. Bowen not Daddy.

Thursday morning in the garden, 11 o/c. You must please excuse
pencil, I am writing in the garden, and the babes are playing in
their little house, it's a very warm morning, but dull. I had a p.c.
from Mrs. Luther saying to-day would be quite convenient, so
we're off at 2.30. I am so much looking forward to to-morrow
and hoping it will be fine, what an ideal place for a house Annes-
grove is. I am SO glad you think Mr. Bowen better, I do trust the
good nights may continue and so give the poor tired brain rest.
What an anxious time this is for you, dear Mrs. Bowen. I am so
glad that I am able to help you and that you feel perfectly happy
leaving your precious wee one in my charge. It makes just all the
difference working for those who REALLY appreciate you. . . .
The babes are now sitting on the seat beside me, having their
lunch, with oh such black faces! And a plague of flies all round
us. . . . Dear Mrs. Bowen, I LOVE my jacket, and shouldn't like
another one half so much. I put it on last evening, it looks sweet,
and such a lovely collar. . . . It seems it's an Irish holiday to-day,
but Rogers came for his orders this morning and is willing to drive

us, so that's all right, but I didn't know it when I fixed to go out
to-day. . . . I hope you will enjoy the duck and peas, with the
sweet roses in the centre of the table. My snuggery is so sweet,
just full of honeysuckle. I love my postcard, it reminds me of the
babes. I heard them whispering to each other yesterday " Isn't
she horrid when she's cross, but a darling when she's like this." I
think I had just promised to read Jungle Jinks to them.

If Florence had been alone in her first unawareness of
Henry's condition, she was not alone when the trouble broke.
The Herbert Place friends stood round her: I have found many
letters that have a very true ring. Later, these friends could keep
in touch with my father, when the doctors ordered husband
and wife apart. The loyalty, at this juncture, of Henry's brothers could have been a model to the generations before. Bob was
dead — his accident with the horse had been part of the wave
of Henry's disasters — and St. John and Mervyn were now
abroad: they could do no more than write to Florence from
there. But Charlie was with his regiment in England, and it was
he who took charge when Henry had been persuaded to cross
the sea and put himself under a doctor's care. Of the sisters,
Mary was quickest to understand the difficulties of Henry's
wife's position. Charlie helped out Florence in matters of
money — as, steadily, did her own brother George. She had,
as we know, at Mount Temple learned nothing (had, in fact,
been deterred from learning) about the management of money
affairs, and though she received on her marriage her share of
the Colley inheritance, Henry had always looked after this for
her, along with everything else. Practical life, and in its grim-
mest form, now confronted her for the first time. Shorn of
Henry's professional earnings, she had to administer Bowen's
Court, meet the expenses of illness, provide for herself and me.
For some time Henry kept the name of control, and, money-
anxiety being one cause of his illness, to ask him for funds was
very distressful to her. She had never been extravagant, and

now she practised devoted economy, but she had to find out, by trial and error, just how far money would and would not go. Her and my subsequent wanderings about England were punctuated by crises that I remember well, crises she met with a sort of rueful philosophy, and that ended with interventions by Uncle George.

That winter of 1905–6 my mother hoped I would notice nothing, and I did not notice much. My father returned from England to Herbert Place, and, soon after, Gerry left us and went back to her mother. My father's excitability became extreme: he constantly wished to be with me, and to take me for walks. My campaign of not noticing was assisted by the accentuated calm cheerfulness of Uncle George, and of Aunt Laura, who reappeared in Dublin. It was in the course of that winter (though I did not know it) that my mother was for the first time told by the doctors that she and I must leave Henry, for his good. So she and I and Miss B— sailed for England, to stay with my Fiennes cousins. It was at their house, at Ealing, that Miss B— left us — I fancy that we could no longer afford her, or possibly her emotion became trying to my mother's controlled, anti-emotional state — and there were tears and embracements on all sides. Our round of visits in England prolonged itself; June, time for Bowen's Court, came; we were still over the sea, and we celebrated my seventh birthday in Suffolk. I was exceedingly anxious to go home.

Later on in that summer of 1906 my mother and I did return to Bowen's Court, but I remember finding, that summer, for the first time, that a desired place could seem to have lost life. There was added to me my third governess, a sharp, composed little Welshwoman, Miss M—. She had formerly been with titled English pupils, in, apparently, large Elizabethan homes; she therefore made short work of the mere county, and it was from her dispassionate lips that I heard, with distinct shock, that Bowen's Court was rather an ugly house. " Though of course you love it," she said, " as it is your home." She considered it might look better covered with ivy, and she and I used to poke about in the area to see if there were nascent ivy down there. But still no home, in Miss M——'s view, was complete without gables, mullions, galleries and groined halls. Looking back, it appears to me that Miss M—— must have been still more expensive than Miss B——, and I can only suppose that my mother indulged in her because the relations in England said I was running wild. She de-snugged Miss B——'s snuggery of last summer and made it into a schoolroom, and the very first morning after her arrival she called me in from the yard, sat me squarely down at a table and announced that, with my mother's approval, she was now about to teach me to read. The sense of approaching initiation was tense and, somehow, embarrassing: with burning cheeks I watched Miss M—— open the reader, wondering however she would begin. Like a witch she slowly tapped with her pencil along the impregnable lines of print. Gone, from that morning, were the honeysuckle and languors of Miss B——, and those enchanted readings-aloud of *Perseus* and *Jungle Jinks*. To this day print smells to me of metal and ink, and throws a lonely coldness over my senses: I would very very much rather be read out to than read to myself.

That winter my mother and I, with Miss M—— attached, made a last attempt to return to my father in Dublin. Those few months made it clear that, for his own sake, he must fight his illness alone — he did never cease to fight it, and in the end won. Late one night, after a day of alarms, I was got out of bed by Miss M——; a cab came round and she and I drove through the dark to Killiney, where my mother's cousins the Vernons took us in. I had left Herbert Place forever, without knowing. Later my mother joined us, then she and I and Miss M—— again went over to England — this time, to live. No Bowen child had ever yet lived in England: I was the first to make the experiment. After some travels we gravitated to Folkstone: Cousin Isobel Trench (the Archbishop's daughter-in-law) and her family lived there. So Kent was my England, for several years. That

first spring, Miss M—— and I went our morning walks on the
Leas, strong salt winds never ceasing to blow. I liked the height
of the Leas, and on the first clear morning I saw with excitement the coast of France. All that could be done was done to
make me think of England not as exile but as a new kind of
treat. My mother and I now left the sheltered orbit of our relatives' houses and adventured in English friends of our own.
Miss M—— left us after some months at Folkstone — too expensive again, I suppose — to be succeeded by nineteen-year-old,
almond-eyed Miss ——, who wore her soft hair in a Geisha
roll. My mother found the English very kind but impertinent;
she said she liked them best when they were a little sad. For my
part, I liked the bustling *newness* of England, and also, perhaps
because I was Robert's granddaughter, I was susceptible to its
air of success. I liked the dressy clothes, the hotels and villas
that looked like models just taken out of a box, the knick-
knacky shops, the unthoughtful speed of the streets. Also, in
Ireland our trouble had gathered round us a pity that became,
at my age, rather oppressive and something in the nature of an
ordeal, so that to be in a place where almost nobody knew us
was a distinct relief. England became for me, when I was seven,
the image of every kind of immunity. The tradesmen's eyes,
the houses themselves, looked *safe*. So much so that now, when
I hear bombs fall on England, or see rubble that used to be a
safe house, something inside me says " *Even here?* "

As that spring of 1907 gave place to summer, Folkstone became dazzling with new paint and awnings, and parasols moved
up and down the Leas. Caesar's Camp — yellow-green, bald,
chalk-gashed, very unlike a hill in Ireland — disappeared in a
veil of heat; military bugles from the heights of Shorncliffe
sounded clearly across the blue, dry air, and poppies appeared
in the fields outside the town. I let these things enclose me; I do
not remember thinking of Bowen's Court. The senses enter
deeply into love of a place, and the senses are unfaithful, easily
won away. Also, perhaps children are sterner than grown-up

people in their refusal to suffer, in their refusal, even, to feel at all.

The right-and-tightness of Folkstone, that I liked, soon, however, began to oppress my mother. Horse *char-à-bancs* plied up and down the coast road to Hythe; one afternoon we got into one of these, and the result was my mother's falling in love with Hythe. So we moved out there, into a furnished house. She and I, who had been anxious in Georgian rooms, together developed a personal love of villas — villas with white balconies, bow-windows so rotund that they stuck out like towers, steps up the garden, rustic arbours and Dorothy Perkins roses bright in the sea glare. In those Kent-coast years we lived in many such villas, and each move from one to another, though made for the best reasons, was attended, as I remember, with great expense. Nothing so vain as whim directed my mother's movements, but series of inspirations did dominate her. She had lived in a world in which meanness did not exist, and when any new arrangement had to be made she took people freely into her confidence; a sort of ideal glow surrounded all her transactions, and it says much for the people with whom she dealt that her confidence was seldom abused. From time to time came her lonely journeys to Ireland, while I stayed behind with Miss H——. It was decided, beyond question, that Herbert Place would have to be given up: my father could no longer remain there. So the Herbert Place furniture crossed the sea to Hythe, and with or just after it our Irish cook Margaret, to make us feel more at home. A number of Henry III's chairs, tables, wine-coolers and gentleman's wardrobes were settled into a villa called Oak Bank — to be later moved to a Folkstone flat (to make my day-schooling easier), to Erin Cottage at Lyminge, then back to Hythe again.

Possibly it was the arrival of the furniture that made me go through, with regard to England, a rather more haughty phase. I became increasingly proud of my Irish origin, and was determined to make it felt. But there were manners and manners of doing this. My Trench cousins, handsome young girls with black hair, resolutely paraded the Leas at Folkstone in blowing-about Celtic robes of scarlet or green, with Tara brooches clamped to their shoulders. I failed to connect this dress with Ireland, and the Trenches' conspicuousness embarrassed me — especially when they swept down on my school crocodile. Even my mother said, a shade tartly, that no Trenches were ever so Irish as all *that*. The Trenches continued to inundate us with green booklets with shamrocks on the outside: my resist-ance to propaganda became extreme, and when my cousins spoke to me of Cuchulain I countered with Perseus and Her-cules. But the songbook they gave us had a greater success: alone with my mother by her piano I sang *Let Erin Remember*, *The Harp that Once*, *The Wearing of the Green*, and *Come Back to Erin* most often of all. Apart from this, my sense of nationality showed itself — as too often with Irish people in England — in a tendency to show off; this was counterposed by my wish to out-English the English by being impassibly fashionable and correct. I made ill-chosen generalizations, such as " in England there are no mountains," and when at my Folk-stone day-school I got over my shyness, which was prolonged by my having a bad stammer, I became truculent and was in-clined to bully. That first suggestion (to soften sadness) that England was on the whole rather a treat made me egocentric and prone to quarrel with anything English that did not go my way. My aunts, on their visits to Hythe, commented on my increasing bumptiousness, and my mother did everything that she could.

So, the lives of Henry VI's wife and his child went on, year after year, a long way away from him. In the dark of his illness the separation cannot have been easy for him to understand, though the doctor's edict, told to him, remained firm. The best of his years and all his manly inheritance must have seemed to be taken away. At Herbert Place he had stayed with the chairs and tables and the familiar, through-everything smiling faces of the two servants Margaret and Annie, that were his link back with the happy years in the house. At Bowen's Court, hurriedly opened for his visits, he found waiting, round the uncertain fires, nothing but the unhappiness of his ancestors, as the terrible vision of his illness contracted the Bowen history into the Bowen doom. Through the empty rooms and on the land round them may have echoed ghostly tormented steps. In 1903, two years before the start of his illness, the Swansea barrister Mr. Llenfer Thomas had sent him that extract from Baxter's *World of Spirits* with the story of Colonel Bowen, Henry I. "*Bowen immured himself in a small Castle . . . he oft rose in the Night, and talked as if some were talking with him.*" When I saw my father when he was well again, he treated our Welsh ghost story as an excellent joke. But on one page of the copy, which I hold, Henry VI has traced, I do not know in which year, his direct descent from the Welshman Henry I. . . . Henry VI's sister Sarah, whose immovable calmness was built up over an early sense of disaster, was much with him, and he liked to stay at her Mitchelstown house. For some time, a friendly couple, Major and Mrs. M——, took charge of Bowen's Court and made a home for Henry inside his own home; they had one child, a little boy whom Henry liked to be with. At times he was under treatment — once again in England, when he came to join us for a Christmas at Hythe. Attempts were made to build up at least his physical health. Treatments did much but did not do everything for him: in the end he was saved by his friends and his own powers — to which his friends, men whose stature he had admired, best knew how to appeal. Intellect, humanity, good manners remained through Henry's darkest hours alight: the very impersonality of his friendships kept them, at this time when all emotion was toxic, disinfected and pure. Men who had been dear to Henry and Florence were untiring in their visits to him, and with them there the darkness round him cleared: from the level of their conversation, his natural level, Henry began less and less to descend. Also, as he had been attacked through the finest part of his nature — early-developed sense of responsibility, devotion to whatever he undertook — he was saved through its strongest part — his will. He meant to return, and did. In Henry VI appeared the whole force of the Bowen will, unimpaired by the Bowen weakness of self-regard. Whatever torments my father knew, he never knew the torments of egotism. Accustomed to being more alone than he knew, he fought his illness impersonally, and was, so, enabled to pass the turning-point. My father was pronounced better, then much better: before I was twelve years old he was well again. He could come back to us — or we could go back to him.

But my mother and I did not return to Ireland to live. Life is so much a matter of minutiae that large changes cannot be made at once. Our complete family life renewed itself in the series of visits my father made to Hythe: between these visits he stayed in Dublin, where he was resuming practice as a barrister. The move back to Ireland of ourselves and the furniture was always, always discussed, but remained always ahead. Explicitly, there was the question of my schooling. Also, at Hythe my mother had found an ideal happiness that she, by now, identified with the place: I think our troubles had bruised her feeling for Ireland, and that she dreaded making a new start there to an extent she did not admit but that my father perceived. But there was another factor I did not know of, and this was the tragic determining one: just before my father's complete recovery my mother herself had begun to be very ill. She had cancer. The first of her operations was kept a mystery from me, and after it she seemed to be well again. How and when this second blow to his marriage was made known to my father I do not know. At first there may have seemed to be some hope — but no future was to be built upon. The sense of impermanence sifted through to me and made me enjoy our present with an intensity too conscious to be natural in a child. As for my father, his patience ruled everything, when he was back with us. In front of me my mother and he talked plans — plans they came to know to be fictions, in the temporal sense. But these two people were held, most of all, together by their very strong sense of eternity. The two last late summers in Kent were happy: he pleased her by his good opinion of Hythe; he adapted his frame and his habits, with masculine humbleness, to the very feminine world of our little house. He and I watched a great deal of cricket, making pilgrimages by train to Canterbury to see Woolley bat: he ate sponge cakes and I ate ices in cafés in the shady Canterbury streets. At Hythe we went for long walks along the sea wall: the stoop of his tall figure was now pronounced. As some new idea entered Henry VI's head a phase of silence interrupted our talks. He tolerated my singing of Irish songs, till one day when he said frankly that that was enough. But he liked to hear Florence play the piano, so in the evenings she did. Or else, he read aloud to us — one of the books was *Emma* — in the long bright twilights of the seaside.

In the early summer of 1912 my mother and I went over to Bowen's Court. That spring in England had been under a shadow; my mother's sister Constance had died of consumption at Folkstone on the return from a winter in Switzerland, and her beloved youngest brother Eddie had gone down on the *Titanic*. He had spent with us the last Sunday before he sailed: he was my favourite uncle because he was the funniest, and when the *Titanic* news came I could only remember him balancing the brim of his bowler hat on the tip of his crooked nose with the upward expression of a performing seal. So, the *Titanic* disaster was the first black crack across the surface of *exterior* things. But the return to Bowen's Court seemed to promise everything. For five years my mother and I had not been there — except for one flying trip, on a fortnight's excursion ticket, in the summer of 1908, when it had rained the whole time and the house felt bemused and cold. This time it was to be a real, triumphant return.

It was. June sun baked the steps and streamed in at the win-

dows; the bare floors gave off their familiar smell. On my
thirteenth birthday I woke up early and ran barefoot all over
the house: already the windows were standing open, and the
air was fresh with mosses and woods and lawns. Until my
father joined us from Dublin my mother and I were alone:
sleeping in her room with the blue Morris paper, at nights we
heard herons utter their lost-soul cry. We had walked round
the place, through the screens, to see all the people; and I saw,
with amazement, grown-up tears. Our neighbours came driving
over, some now in motor cars: I and the other children were
now taller, and shy, and when we went down through the
woods to fish for minnows we found one side of our island in
the Farahy stream washed away by a succession of winter
floods. Gerry's and my secret tunnels were overgrown, but
Miss Pretty's garden was just as ever; in the walled garden, each
side of the new-raked paths, lolled the damp red peonies. She
and I were busy opening up all the rooms, for, as always here,
we were to have visitors: Uncle George Colley and his wife
were coming to stay, bringing their two young children No-
reen and Dudley. They came: in my grandmother's drawing-
room my aunt and my mother sat with their heads together, or
else they walked round the garden and made plans. I was re-
lieved to see life go on just as before. There were now no horses
at Bowen's Court, but Uncle George had come in his motor
car, and in this we drove at unknown speed to Rockmills,
Annes Grove, Mitchelstown Castle and the Clonodfoy that
used to be Castle Oliver.

That early summer was only imperfect in the matter of time:
before July we were all going away. My mother was to go into
a Dublin nursing home for another " rest cure " — her operation at Folkstone had also been called that. So she and I walked
through the boundary woods and through Farahy on a second
round of visits; this time to say goodbye. There were old people
who had stood at the gates to greet her that night she arrived
as a bride, in her red cloak. Something made me look closely

into their faces as they said: " God bring you back to us soon."
The day she and my father left for Dublin was very wet, and
gusts shook the Bowen's Court trees. (I was to stay and motor
back with the Colleys.) Henry and Florence, like all Bowens,
were to travel by train from Mallow: Uncle George's car, with
my mother waving, drove off up the Upper Avenue through
the rain. When, leaving the steps, I returned to the library, I
could see from its look that my mother would not come back.
Indomitable loneliness once more reigned; the weather reflected itself in the glass bookcases of what appeared to be a
finally empty room. My grandfather Robert's billiard table
now blocked the library: I got out the faded billiard balls and
pelted them rapidly up and down.

My mother did not die in Dublin. After the operation, she
moved out, to convalesce, to Uncle George's house at Rathgar.
It was a fine, hot July, and she and Henry used to sit for hours
talking under a tree on the lawn. When she seemed well again,
she travelled back to Hythe, where her sister Laura took
charge. But in August, when my father and I joined her, her
illness took a new phase that brought almost continuous pain.
The french window of her bedroom stood open on to the bal-
cony, looking straight at the sea; in the evenings and on into the
nights candles threw light on to the peacock-blue walls. When
not in pain, she said she was happier than she had ever been in
her life. She died near the end of September 1912, and was
buried in Saltwood churchyard, just inland from Hythe. She
had never liked the Bowen family vault: my father had promised her she should not lie there.

After that I went, as my mother had wished, to live with my
Aunt Laura at Harpenden: Aunt Laura was keeping house for
her brother Wingfield, who was curate-in-charge at St. John's
church. My father returned alone to his work in Dublin: he
used to come to Harpenden for his holidays. In the August of
1913 he accompanied me and my uncle and aunt abroad. Our
destination was Switzerland, but on the way we stopped a night

in Brussels, a night in Cologne. Doubled into a *fiacre*, with his
back to the horse, Henry VI looked around him with grave
pleasure as we drove, sight-seeing, round these foreign towns.
This was, I think, his first trip to the Continent since that grand
tour from which he brought smallpox home. It was my first
and last view of pre-war Europe, but in the inscrutable haughti-
ness of adolescence I refused to look twice at anything. We
travelled some way by a Rhine steamer, and Henry, with puck-
ered, half-seeing eyes, watched the Lorelei heights his sisters
had sketched slide past. At one jetty, when sunset melted
everything, German schoolboys trooped off the steamer, singing. My grown-up companions said this was beautiful, but I
stayed hostile to the emotion that made those children sing.

The outbreak of the 1914 War came, for Ireland, like an
earthquake-shock to a theatre inside which the drama grows
unbearably tense. It may be too much to say that the German
march into Belgium averted an interior war in Ireland — but
everything looked that way. Summer of 1914 had been dreaded
as Ireland's zero hour. Now, the internal tension did not snap,
but it slackened. The distraction came only just in time — ten
days before August 4th, a company of English soldiers stationed in Dublin had been mobbed, hooted and pelted on their
march back into the city from the direction of Howth. Acting
on orders from Dublin Castle they had seized arms, just landed,
from the National Volunteers — and the seizure had not been
made without violence. Now, hemmed·in by the mob in a
narrow street, and infected by the nervous fever everywhere,
some of the rear rank of the soldiers turned and fired, wound-
ing thirty people and killing three. And this on the apparent
eve of Home Rule, under a friendly Liberal government. For
it had *not* been, this time, against England that the National
Volunteers of the south of Ireland were attempting to arm.
Batchelor's Walk and its bloodshed seems a far cry from the

soporific Ireland of the late 'nineties. How had things changed so much?

The Boer War, 1899, had had the effect of uniting the Irish parliamentarian party, split by Parnell's fall. Parnellites and Anti-Parnellites not only felt an equal sympathy for the Boers, as a small people struggling against a great power, but, more, rose to voice their sympathy in the House. The reunited Party took as its Chairman Mr. Redmond — though Parnellites were in the minority. Reunion, improved morale and pro-Boer feeling did much to put the Party back on the map where its electorate was concerned: with the Irish at home the parliamentarian Irish regained much of the prestige lost since the Parnell split. Once more, something was hoped of them.

This come-back was, to an extent, countered by Arthur Griffith's paper, *The United Irishman*, founded in 1899. The paper continued to express opposition to the accepted leaders at Westminster, and to suggest that Ireland should disregard Parliament, cease to send members there and, instead, concentrate her powers upon her own affairs. Mr. Griffith pressed, in his columns, for a restitution of the Dublin Parliament of 1782, with some constitutional changes towards a fuller autonomy. Things should, in fact, go steadily on from the point where Grattan, defeated, had left off. In 1906 *The United Irishman* changed its name to *Sinn Fein*. Griffith was opposed to physical force: he preached nonpayment of taxes, boycott of British goods and organized passive resistance to British rule. He stopped some way short of the Fenian extremists' demand for an Irish Republic — to be obtained, if necessary, *by* force. But Griffith and the Fenians were alike in seeing the Westminster Nationalists as committed to ineffective methods and, anyhow, too moderate in their aims.

Extremists in the opposite direction were represented by the Irish Tories, hot with grievance against the Conservative government's " rotten, sickly policy of conciliation." At Westminster, these found their spokesman in Sir Edward Carson, who did not cease to rise to denounce "betrayals." Among these Irish Tories, out to obstruct Land Purchase, Mr. George Wyndham, on his appointment in 1900 as Chief Secretary, was to find implacable foes. For, in Mr. Wyndham the coming Ireland found an avowed friend. At a Land Conference, planned and indefatigably promoted by a young Galway squire, Captain Shawe Taylor, a few — too few — progressive Irish landlords met the tenants' party, under Redmond and others, with the object of arriving at some agreement by which Land Purchase could become (at least reasonably) fair to all. The report the Conference drew up was adopted by Mr. Wyndham for his Bill of 1903. Encouraged by having reached this *modus vivendi*, Mr. Wyndham's supporters among the advanced landlords urged him to further measures for Irish peace. Further control by Ireland of Irish administration — a control, in fact, so nearly complete as to amount to modified Home Rule — was, as " Devolution," fairly freely discussed. This was the moment for Wyndham's enemies: they succeeded in so falsifying his position with the Conservative party that he resigned the Chief Secretaryship.

There had been changes in England, and, at the close of 1905, a General Election swept the Tories from power. The new House of Commons met with a large majority in favour of Home Rule. However, the Liberal leaders, for tactical reasons connected with their campaign against Protection, were pledged not to introduce a Home Rule Bill: they were able, only, to lend themselves to a sort of variation of Devolution — a Bill to establish an Irish Council, whose powers, severely limited, should not affect legislation or finance. Mr. Redmond's position was rendered difficult; hoping to gain at least something he entered into discussion of this Bill. But he insisted the matter should be referred to a Convention in Dublin — upon whose strong protest the Bill was dropped, leaving Redmond compromised (in the home view) for nothing. So, onwards to

1910, the Liberal government contented itself, if not Ireland, with a continuance of the Tory policy of propitiatory benefits. An Act established the National University, with colleges in Dublin, Galway and Cork, and this was followed by the — for England very expensive — Old Age Pensions Act. In Ireland the aged poor existed in larger numbers than had been reckoned on. And the same expensive misfit of English rule for Ireland became evident in the workings of the Insurance Act. By 1910, for the first time since the Union, more money was being spent by England in and on Ireland than the Irish revenues brought in. In England this was soon felt by the taxpayer, and the wish to continue to govern, and pay for, Ireland became restricted to the English governing class — elsewhere, it had never been very strong. The at one time recalcitrant South Africa had, in 1907, been granted Dominion status, and the success of this concession — in spite of Tory misgivings — went to better the outlook on Home Rule.

The apparently impassable obstacle to Home Rule was the House of Lords, stronghold of governing feeling. The power of veto vested in the hereditary house was, up to this time, unlimited, and, however strong the majority in the Commons, the Lords were to be relied on to, automatically, throw out any measure against the Union. Redmond recognized this when, in 1909, he ranged his party behind the Liberals in the constitutional struggle against the Lords, occasioned by the Lords' rejection of the Lloyd George budget. The largeness of the issue called for a General Election, but the General Election did not change the face of things. King Edward VII's death heightened the crisis: a conference failed. By 1911 the revolutionaries had won through — the Parliament Act was carried, which declared that if the House of Commons carried a Bill in three successive sessions, the right of the Lords to reject it should cease with the third passing. It was in the conditions created by this change that the 1912 Home Rule Bill was introduced.

Materially, this third Home Rule Bill differed only a little from its predecessors. Some ties of the Union were to remain. The Imperial Parliament, for instance, was to keep control of all naval and military matters, also the right of fixing and of collecting customs and excise. Major matters, such as the Crown, and war or peace, were excluded from Ireland's right to legislate. And the police — representing authority — were, by the terms of the third Bill, to remain in England's pay, and, implicitly, under her control for six years after Home Rule should take effect. In order that Ireland should vote on Imperial matters, outside the scope of a Dublin parliament, the Bill proposed that some Irish members should continue to come to Westminster. In order that these should not affect too much the course of purely British legislature, their number was to be limited to forty. The Bill showed a wide gap — widest in fiscal arrangements — between the position offered to Ireland and that already accorded to the Dominions. Also, in several essentials there was to be no return to the pre-Union constitution of 1782. Subordination was still to be felt: this would not be Grattan's " co-equal " parliament.

Mild as this Bill might appear to be, it was too much for Ulster. Or, should it be said that at this point exploitation of Ulster feeling by the extreme Tories, still sore from the Parliament Act defeat, began? At any rate, the most virulent opposition to the Liberal-sponsored Home Rule Bill came in Ulster's name. Ulster clung with fervour to English rule, and charges of disloyalty to the loyalists were sent pelting across the House. That fatal principle of separation — still damaging to us — was foreshadowed. There *did* maintain this difference between North and South: in Ulster, the Protestant Ascendancy was a living fact; in Munster, Leinster and Connaught it had become, within the last fifty years, a ghost only. And Protestant Ascendancy knew that its backbone was English rule.

Mr. Bonar Law, the leader of the Tory party in England, declared that, so far as his personal feeling went, he would support Ulster's resistance to any lengths. Sir Edward Carson was soon able to state that arrangements were being completed to make Home Rule (for Ulster) "absolutely impossible." "We will shortly challenge the Government," said Sir Edward, "to interfere with us if they dare." In Ulster itself, the summer weather only brought trouble: a Catholic Sunday School picnic broke up a Protestant Sunday School picnic with some slight damage to little Protestants, and this incident, faithfully publicized, caused a lock-out of thousands of Catholics from Belfast works. It is possible that if Ulster had not been so precipitate, the deficiencies of the Home Rule Bill, *qua* Home Rule, might have been more visible to the south. As things were, the Bill was in Dublin supported with a reciprocal heat: at an open air meeting that packed the length of O'Connell Street even extremists spoke in support of it. "Let us unite," said Pearse (who fell in 1916), "and win a good Act from the British. I think it can be done." Constitutional methods, urged by the Party leaders, were adhered to with unusual calm. Any rough-house was to be left to Ulster.

In this atmosphere, after protracted halts, the Bill passed its last stage in the House of Commons by a majority of 110, to be, inevitably, defeated by ten to one in the Lords. The Government must now, to overcome the veto, remain in office to carry the Bill again through the Commons sessions of 1913 and 1914. As an invitation to members to think again, Ulster, since some time openly drilling, in 1913 began to arm. These bands were called Covenanters. Some arms were intercepted, but none by force, and no steps were taken against the prominent people to whom, in many cases, guns were consigned. Ulster — a situation puzzling to me at the time — could be watched all but officially mobilizing against the England she said she loved so well. County families did their bit by passing the dinner dishes to one another while butlers helped chauffeurs bury in flowerbeds arms run from beaches in the family car. The piscine face of Sir Edward Carson and the traffic-stop sign of the Red Hand dominated every one's mental view. And the intimidation began to work. In the House, more than one Liberal statesman moved the exclusion of Ulster from Home Rule.

This mobilization of Ulster could not fail — was it intended to fail? — to provoke the South. There, Labour trouble came to a head in a great strike, called in Dublin by Mr. Larkin at the end of August 1913; the strike took six months to starve itself out, and ended with nothing settled, bitterness in the air. But it gave birth to the South's first answer to Carson, the " Citizen Army." This, though it stood first for the rights of Labour, became incorporated in the Volunteer Force — initiated, in the course of November, in response to a call from the Vice-President of the Gaelic League. Among the thousands who were enrolled, some were constitutionalists, others not. The avowed object of the Volunteer Force was to give Redmond the means to enforce Home Rule. These Volunteers of the South were *not* overlooked: the Government issued a proclamation prohibiting the importation of arms. The South could not fail to note that arms continued to enter Ulster freely. Redmond, in close consultation throughout that autumn with Mr. Dillon, Mr. Devlin and Mr. T. P. O'Connor, expressed no view, at this stage, on the Volunteers. At the beginning of 1914, with the temperature thus steadily rising, Mr. Asquith, for the necessary third time, introduced the Home Rule Bill. With the introduction came the offer of a *modus vivendi* — that any county in Ulster should have the power to vote itself out of Home Rule for six years more. Redmond's disposition to accept this found no favour in his own Party's ranks. Any inter-Nationalist crisis that might have followed was stopped by Ulster's rejection of the offer — Ulster would not hear of the time-limit, and Redmond would not yield an inch on it.

So the Government reluctantly faced the issue that Ulster seemed determined to force. Troops from the Curragh were ordered to move north. Taking this to mean action against the " loyalists," a general and fifty officers resigned. In the commotion that followed this virtual mutiny, the Secretary of

State for War and the military heads of the War Office supported the Curragh by resignation. Mr. Asquith kept this in hand by himself taking charge of the War Office. Stimulated, however, by what seemed general approval, the Ulster Volunteers seized two ports, took in a continuous run of arms, suppressed the police and other officials and placed Ulster under their own command. Tory support for Ulster did not lessen, and Redmond had no alternative but to sanction the Volunteers of the South — now called the Irish Volunteers — and call for further enlistment in their ranks. The response was, naturally, immediate. But these Volunteers remained unarmed.

Control of the Irish Volunteers was not easy. The alternative, for Ireland at this crisis, between the constitutionalism Redmond was vowed to and the force the North invited by every act was latent, and had to be recognized. From the control committee formed by Redmond, eight extremist members withdrew. The impunity of the northern gun-running, under Carson's aegis, all through that heated summer of 1914, had its result in the South on the 26th of July. A plan to land arms at Howth came to be known of, the Government took the action it had not taken elsewhere; the British troops, intercepting, clashed with the Volunteers, then, marching back through a strung-up and hostile Dublin, let off their guns in Batchelor's Walk.

On August 3rd the German march into Belgium and the British ultimatum to Germany were announced in the House. Mr. Redmond, instantly acting, offered the Volunteers to defend Ireland, leaving British troops there free for service elsewhere. He stated his belief that, to defend Ireland, the Ulster and Irish Volunteers would unite. And his own people did not give him the lie. But to defend Ireland one must be armed. And Lord Kitchener, as it was to turn out, was not willing either to arm or to recognize the willingness of the Irish Volunteers. " Is it too much to hope," Redmond had said, " that out of this situation a result may spring, which will be good, not merely for the

Empire, but for the future welfare and integrity of the Irish
nation? " How far, for how many decades the terrible situation
was to prolong and renew itself was not foreseen then. Must
an undivided Ireland be always a shadow? Must anything else
be always too much to hope?

At the beginning of August 1914 Henry VI and I were at
Bowen's Court. My cousin Audrey Fiennes was staying with
us, and Aunt Sarah had come over from Mitchelstown, for that
summer holiday, to keep house. She reassumed her born role
with dignity. To signalize my beginning to grow up, or to
comfort me on this return to the house, my father had had several rooms redecorated: my former nursery was now a stylish
bedroom with light-grey walls and a lilac frieze. August having
opened in heavy rain, my cousin and I spent the time indoors,
constructing furniture for the dollshouse out of matchboxes
and scraps of silk. I remember no concern but the dollshouse,
also, the hope that the weather might clear up in time for the
Mitchelstown Castle garden party, to be held on August 5th.
Also, what hat was I to wear? What my father thought about I
do not know: in breaks of the rain he walked up and down the
avenues, hands behind his back, sometimes pausing to look re-
flectively at the house. Or, he talked to his sister Sarah — their
voices pitched much on the same note, their very alike faces
turned to each other. News in those days travelled slowly to
Ireland: I do not even remember the word War.

August 4th passed: in the course of it the rain stopped.
August 5th was a white-grey, lean, gritty day, with the trees
dark. The newspaper did not come. A wind rose, and, as about
eleven o'clock that morning we drove down the avenue in the
large pony trap — the only conveyance Bowen's Court now
had: but for the pony the carriage-stables were empty — my
cousin and I held on the hats we had elected to wear. We were
to go round by Rockmills, pick up the youngest Oliver — a girl,
but christened Silver after her ancestor — then on to Mitchels-

town, where we were to eat lunch at Aunt Sarah's house in King-square. Aunt Sarah remained at Bowen's Court: her friend Lady Kingston was now dead, and she did not care for Castle parties without her.

At Rockmills my father — whose manner, I do remember, had been growing graver with every minute — stopped the pony and went into the post office. There was a minute to wait, with the pony stamping, before I again saw him framed in the low dark door. He cleared his throat and said: " England has declared war on Germany." Getting back into the trap he added: " I suppose it could not be helped." All I could say was: " Then can't we go to the garden party? " . . . We picked up Silver Oliver and drove on to Mitchelstown — Henry, with his whole mind, courteously answering a rattle of questions from us girls. If at ten or twelve I had been precocious, at fifteen I was virtually idiotic. The bye-roads had dried in the wind and were glaring white; the War already gave them an unreal look.

That afternoon we walked up the Castle avenue, greeted by the gusty sound of a band. The hosts of the party were the late Lady Kingston's second husband Mr. Willie Webber, and his companion Miss Minnie Fairholme. They were not young, and, owing to the extreme draughtiness everywhere, they received their guests indoors, at the far end of Big George's gallery. In virtue of this being a garden party, and of the fact that it was not actually raining, pressure was put on the guests to proceed outside — people only covertly made incursions into the chain of brocade saloons. Wind raced round the Castle terraces, naked under the Galtees; grit blew into the ices; the band clung with some trouble to its exposed place. The tremendous news certainly made that party, which might have been rather flat. Almost every one said they wondered if they really ought to have come, but they *had* come — rightly: this was a time to gather. This was an assemblage of Anglo-Irish people from all over north-east County Cork, from the counties of Limerick, Waterford, Tipperary. For miles round, each isolated big house

had disgorged its talker, this first day of the war. The tension
of months, of years – outlying tension of Europe, inner tension of Ireland – broke in a spate of words. Braced against the
gale from the mountains, licking dust from their lips, these
were the unmartialled loyalists of the South. Not a family had
not put out, like Bowen's Court, its generations of military
brothers – tablets in Protestant churches recorded deaths in
remote battles; swords hung in halls. If the Anglo-Irish live on
and for a myth, for that myth they constantly shed their blood.
So, on this August 1914 day of grandeur and gravity, the Ascendancy rallied, renewed itself. The lack – it was marked –
of one element at that party made us feel the immediate sternness of war: the officers from Kilworth, Fermoy and Buttevant
had other things to do with the afternoon. They were already
under orders, we heard. We few young people got together in
groups – would the War prevent out return to England, to
school? My father's overcoat blew about; his head rose above
the crowds on the terrace. I heard several people say, " Let us
ask Mr. Bowen." I have, now, some notion what he may have
been asked. For through the grown-up talkers ran and recurred
one question – Will *this* having happened stop Home Rule?

It was an afternoon when the simplest person begins to anticipate memory – this Mitchelstown garden party, it was
agreed, would remain in every one's memory as historic. It was,
also, a more final scene than we knew. Ten years hence, it was
all to seem like a dream – and the Castle itself would be a few
bleached stumps on the plateau. To-day, the terraces are oblit-
erated, and grass grows where the saloons were. Many of those
guests, those vehement talkers, would be scattered, houseless,
sonless, or themselves dead. That war – or call it now that first
phase of war – was to go far before it had done with us. After
1918 came the war in Ireland, with the burning down of many
of the big houses – some already futureless, for they had lost
their heirs. For Ireland, between 1918 and 1939, " peace " contracted into a shorter space than people in England realize –

in fact, perhaps one does not say of Ireland that war began
again, but that war resumed. North of the Galtees, south of the
Galtees, familiar military movement was to announce itself;
and that landscape, known to so many generals, was soon
mapped for other campaigns. Once more the old positions were
fought for; once more, bridges were blown up; limestone valley walls rang with the old echoes, and flames were making
people run through the night when, in their beds in the peaceful darkness of England, people dreamed that war would not
occur again.

Even in the little area I have covered, the few miles of country between the Galtees and the Blackwater, even in the little
society — Anglo-Irish settler society — whose evolution, being
also that of the Bowens, I have tried to describe, the events and
plans and passions of the years between 1914 and 1941 would
make a book that should be as long again as the book that I have
written by now. In the life of what we call the new Ireland —
but is Ireland ever new? — the lives of my own people become
a little thing; from 1914 they begin to be merged, already, into
a chapter of different history. So, on the terrace of Big George's
castle, I shall say goodbye to the society that he once so very
fittingly led, and which, perhaps, in idea he continued to dominate — say goodbye at the start of one war that War as we
now know it encloses in its immense To-day. The unseen descent of the sun behind the clouds sharpens the bleak light; the
band, having throbbed out God Save the King, packs up its
wind-torn music and goes home. From different points of the
terrace, most of the landscape of which I have written is to be
seen. So from here I say goodbye to the landscape too — for
this book only, not for myself.

Henry VI, returning to Dublin, soon joined the Four Courts
division of the Veteran Corps — equivalent of the Home Guard
to-day. Like his and my ancestor Henry III, he began to be
military late in life. Never, I think, made splendid by uniform

the Veterans gravely marched and drilled. My father's difficulty in knowing which was his right hand, which his left,
made drill a matter of nervousness for him, but upon this, as
upon everything he attempted, he bent every faculty. In April
1916 he was with me in England when the news of the Easter
Rising in Dublin came. The Veterans, returning to Dublin
after a route march, had been fired on (or had, at least, marched
into some zone of fire) and one of my father's friends had been
killed. His distress at being out of his own country, at such a
juncture, was very great: he caught the next boat back, and
somehow got into Dublin, to take part in what might be going
on. Hard upon this return to Dublin came the affair of our
cousin, Captain Bowen Colthurst, whose distracted mother,
Cousin Georgina, forthwith arrived at my father's flat. Henry,
being a lawyer, was taken by his family to know all — but his
specialization in Land Purchase hardly qualified him to deal
with this fevered and ghastly breach of the rules of war. He did
what he could to calm Cousin Georgina, in a position he thoroughly deprecated, and assisted her to find other advice. In
the uneasy silence that followed the Dublin fighting, he continued to work at his great book, *Statutory Land Purchase in
Ireland*. His flat was at the top of a Georgian house, 19 Upper
Merrion Street. He went every day to the Law Library, which
provided him, amongst everything else, with very congenial
society. Mr. Maurice Heally's description of the Law Library,
in *The Old Munster Circuit*, describes, with a knowledge that
Henry's daughter lacks, the background of Henry's happiest
days. By this time, his hair, thick, springy and glossy as ever,
was pure white. He walked the streets of Dublin, his overcoat
blowing back, with a forward pitch — head forward in rapid
thoughtfulness, not dispiritedly. Cigarette ash, and often cake-
crumbs — for, like Doctor Johnson, he liked cake — tended to
settle in the waistcoat-wrinkles of his dark-grey, rather baggy
suits. His face, of which the skin remained very smooth, and
of which the frame became increasingly noble, had one fine

system of wrinkles for thought, another for amusement: pre-occupation was there in it almost always, but happy preoccupation as much as grave. On Sunday afternoons, or on summer evenings, he would take the tram out of Dublin to visit friends. He liked reading shockers, he bought many magazines, and, long before cinema-going went up in the world, he had become a cinema-goer.

When my father visited Bowen's Court, he took the manuscript of the Land Purchase book, its attendant papers and any books he required to the country with him in a gladstone bag. His sister Sarah came over to keep house, and I joined the two of them there for my summer holidays.

In Dublin, my father kept in touch with Trinity College, and in still closer touch with St. Columba's, his old school. The Gwynns were his great friends, who had run through those early days, Edward Gwynn was one who had kept closest to him in his illness. Old Doctor Gwynn's house, at Clontarf, was one at which my father felt very much at home, and, in the summer of 1918, he became engaged to Mary, the younger sister of Stephen and Edward and of the other Gwynns. They were married in the September of that year. The Merrion Street flat, skied above floors of offices, became very much less bleak under Mary's touch: slowly, at the opposite side of the street, the impressive light stone structure that is now the Government Buildings rose. Meanwhile, in Dublin and in the country, Ireland's bitter struggle for Ireland entered on a new phase. Between the armed Irish and the British troops in the country, reprisals and counter-reprisals — tragic policy — raged. Fire followed shootings, then fires fires. In the same spring night in 1921, three Anglo-Irish houses in our immediate neighbourhood — Rockmills, Ballywalter, Convamore — were burnt by the Irish. The British riposted by burning, still nearer Bowen's Court, the farms of putative Sinn Feiners — some of whom had been our family's friends. What now? From the start, Henry VI had watched this pointless fatal campaign more

with moral distress than with fear of loss. He now wrote to me
— I was in Italy — telling me what was latest. " I am afraid," he
said, " that, as things are now, there can only be one other development. You must be prepared for the next news, and be
brave. I will write at once." I read his letter beside Lake Como,
and, looking at the blue water, taught myself to imagine
Bowen's Court in flames. Perhaps that moment disinfected the
future: realities of war I have seen since have been frightful;
none of them have taken me by surprise.

It did not, after all, happen. When the tide turned, Bowen's
Court stayed untouched. I have been told, and have reason to
credit, that a determining protest against the burning of Henry
VI's house was raised by one of those very neighbours of ours
whose own farm had been burned by the military. I cannot go
into this — many men who had been liked as well as my father
lost their houses by fire, in those years. My father had the reputation of being a just, as well as a gentle, man. While he had
made no secret of his political principles, he accorded his neighbours an equal right to their own. At any rate, Bowen's Court
stood, and the kind inherited tie between us and our country
was not broken.

In 1921 came the Treaty, to be followed by the disintegra-
tion of Civil War — the dissentients to the Treaty, Republicans,
in arms against the Free Staters who had accepted it. Across the
area of the Munster fighting the Blackwater drew a dividing
line. At each side, the country was full of opposed men. Sys-
tematically, withdrawing troops burned the strong stone barracks built for the British military, left by the British when the
Treaty was signed. The Fermoy barracks, almost a little city on
the hill north of the town, were gutted to the shell that they
are now. On the heights of Kilworth, across the country at
Buttevant, other military buildings shared their fate. And the
war impinged on the country's organic life: the town of Mallow, already damaged in the fighting against the British, once
more burgeoned with fires; the railway station, the Dublin-

Cork main line bridges were destroyed. Republican forces, moving west across County Cork in the summer of 1922, established themselves in Mitchelstown Castle, decided not to defend it, burned the castle the evening they moved out. Bowen's Court lay next on the route west: seventy Republicans occupied it. Another detachment swung round and occupied Annes Grove, in its strategic position on the Awbeg.

Rumours of the Republicans' movements preceded them: at Bowen's Court the guests were not unexpected, and could not — given the Mitchelstown precedent — be welcome. My father and Mary were in Dublin, but those in charge of the house had already done what they could by the time the Republicans marched up the avenue. The family portraits — the Henry Bowens II, III and IV, the former Miss Cole, the former Miss Prittie, Robert and his wife the former Miss Clarke (whose own home, Graiguenoe, in County Tipperary, was to be burned that summer) — left the house in a hurry, for the first time, for a sojourn in a cottage at the end of the woods. Other valuables followed them. The Republicans came in to meet cautious faces, emptied cabinets, bare walls. They lost no time in mining the lower avenue — the mines are said to be still there, but, as my father said, no doubt damp got into them soon. They also made preparations to blow the house up, in case of surprise attack. Vital wires connecting with these mines came through a corner of the library wall, the corner where the wireless now stands.

Having done this, and seen that is was good, they rested. If the house had never had more numerous, it had also never had quieter visitors. Even prejudice allows it that they behaved like lambs. The young men — they were mostly very young men — were very tired. The bedding was gone from the few beds; the leaders lay on the springs, the others lay on the floor — there was much floor, for the house had now many empty rooms. Outside the rows of windows, the summer of 1922 droned on — and evidently the summer glare was too strong, for soon many

windows were shuttered up. When the men woke up, they read.
They were great readers, and especially were they attracted by
the works of Kipling: a complete set of these, in flexible scarlet
leather, with gilt elephants' heads, had been given to Mary, and
were available. Once a day, the men rose from their floors and
beds and went out through the country on reconnaissance.

On the third day — or was it the fourth? — they as usual left
the house, with what intentions, this time, I do not know.
Hardly had they departed when my Aunt Sarah, already sufficiently vexed by a series of circumstances, drove down the
Upper Avenue, from the direction of Mallow, on an outside
car. She had been staying in Cork, and had planned to return
to Mitchelstown in the usual manner, via Knocklong — a station
on the Dublin side of Mallow. Aunt Sarah's train (she says)
was well on to Mallow bridge when it started to back off it: the
bridge was in flames. The passengers all had to get out, and the
Mallow car-men, who were at the spot in dozens, did not fail
to profit by the occasion. Rather than gratify her car-man by a
drive the whole way from Mallow to Mitchelstown, Aunt
Sarah had decided to stop at Bowen's Court, spend the night
there, borrow the pony trap and proceed to Mitchelstown next
day. She was, therefore, in her own words, put out to find
Bowen's Court shuttered up and the front door barred. Her
battering and her tugs at the bell produced, after an interval
that displeased her, only an inch of the face of the caretaker,
Mrs. Conroy, inserted in a cautious crack of the door. Mrs.
Conroy lost no time in telling Aunt Sarah that the Republicans
were in it, and that she had better fly.

Aunt Sarah replied that that was nonsense: this was her
brother's house. She demanded that the leader of the Republicans be sent to report to her at once. Mrs. Conroy replied that
this was impossible, the Republicans being at present out. Aunt
Sarah, entering with her usual firmness, replied that in that case
she would wait. Having ordered that her room should be got
ready, she made an inspection of the house. She did not, she

admits, find things in a bad state: propriety seemed to have governed everyone's habits. Nothing had been "commandeered" but the keys — and in some cases the locks — of all the presses, and, though this only appeared later, a pair of leather gaiters of Henry VI's. Aunt Sarah went round picking up the volumes of Kipling that lay face down on the floors or beside the beds. She then sat down to consider, to the last phrase, exactly what she should say to the Republicans.

But they never came back. For what reason, and where they went next, I do not know, and suppose that I never shall. Aunt Sarah remained convinced that they had got wind of her presence, and that either timidity or, better, the "nice feeling" she did not cease to attribute to Irishmen deterred them from return. A mattress and bedding having been found for her, she slept well that night, then moved on according to plan.

The Civil War gave place to at least a surface of peace — a surface beneath which, in the exhausted country, many people were not anxious to probe. I was in London, intending to be a journalist — which at that time seemed to me the least self-exposing way of beginning to be a writer. I lived in Westminster, with that Aunt Edith whom, years ago, my mother had loved so much, and with whom she had not been allowed by her mother to go and stay. In the summer of 1923 I married Alan Cameron, and Henry VI and Mary came over for the wedding, which was in Northamptonshire, at my uncle Wingfield Colley's church. Alan worked in England, so in England we lived. My father was still at the Bar, so he and Mary kept to the flat in Dublin: for all his vacations they went to Bowen's Court, and Alan and I used to join them there.

Sixteen years of my father's concentration and energy went into his book on *Statutory Land Purchase*. His life grew to centre very much round it. At Bowen's Court, while Mary worked in the garden, which became a real garden under her hand, he, in a sea of papers, would write at the table in the library window, beside the wall still torn by the Republicans' wires, the gladstone bag open beside him on the floor. When he wanted to break he would walk, now rather slowly, through the woods to the garden, smoking a cigarette, to see what Mary was doing. One time, he missed her, among all the apple trees; she left the garden, locking the door behind her, and he remained placidly, locked in. The work my father put into the book had, as things turned out, to be its own reward — but I know enough about work to know that is possible, and enough about him to know he did not complain. He did not complain — but there was an irony that one saw for him, that he must have seen for himself. Briefly, the changes brought about in our Irish constitution, after the Treaty, put the former system of Land Purchase out of effect. So, before Henry VI's long book, carried out on the scale of a standard work of reference, had so much as gone to the publishers, it had become, in the phrase he preferred to use, " a work of historic interest only." It could no longer have a functional part in law. *Statutory Land Purchase in Ireland* came out — at, as things were, some expense to Henry. It was worth that: it is a monument — not only to him but to the wills and the intellects of two countries that gave their best to the settlement of a bitter question — a question that had a moral issue behind.

In 1928, my father retired from the Bar. He and Mary both wanted to live at Bowen's Court — to live there fully, properly, all the time. So, at this late age he took up, in a diminished form, the life that his father Robert had once so proudly projected for his heir — the life of the County Cork gentleman, master of Bowen's Court. It may be said that this life, the life not sufficient for Henry in his youth, had stayed on the steps of Bowen's Court, waiting for him. But, does vacuum fill the life one has not chosen to live? It seems to me sometimes that Robert's bitter anger must have brooded over this late attempt. The new life began well. Henry renewed his interest in the plantations — the farm was out of our hands, which was just as well. He talked to his neighbours — in Farahy, in the remaining houses round — he walked, he read by the fire. One of his great pleasures was seeing his brother Mervyn, who had come home from Ceylon and bought a house near Fermoy. But the rains were heavy, the days long, the winters long — and Henry was not a country man. He missed the Rockmills Olivers, his oldest friends as well as his nearest neighbours, who had been burnt out and not come back. I imagine that he missed Dublin, too — the talk, the go of the streets that he had used to watch with half-seeing eyes, the encounters at the street corners, the cinemas, the tea shops in which he used to sit — always, from some inherited landlord instinct, with his back placed firmly against a wall. The most steady, the most self-sufficient nature depends, more than it knows, on its few chosen stimuli. Lassitude settled down on him — and, more profoundly, reaction, after his book was gone. On top of this, he was fretted by money worries. All Mary's courage came into the battle against mood, circumstance and heredity. But his physical health gave way — and that let back, in the early spring of 1930, the illness of mind that had troubled him years ago.

My father left Bowen's Court, to see doctors in Dublin. He did not want to go, his nature clung to the place and to his will to live nowhere but there now, but we persuaded him to: it was worth trying. Everything was tried, but the doctors finally said, it is no good, it will not be for much longer, let him be where he wants. So, one evening, late in April, Henry VI, with his nurse and Mary, came home. The nurse, who since the car turned in at the Bowen's Court gates had become, in Henry's feeling, a guest, liked everything; she praised the trees on the avenue and exclaimed at the size of the house in the spring dusk. Henry hoped the nurse would enjoy her stay. When they had had supper, he took up a pair of candles and showed this new friend all over the house. Raising the candles before each portrait, he introduced her to the Henry Bowens, and Robert, and he was not to be contented till she had got each name, and each relationship, right. After that he was tired, and went to bed.

The week of May 1930 before my father died was more beautiful than any May I remember. The sun shone all day; the trees glittered with their new leaves, and the back avenue Robert's carts used to travel was an aisle of laburnum. Stephen Gwynn was among those who, in the house, were waiting to say goodbye to Henry: in the evenings he and I used to go for walks — coming back we would see transparent shadow fill the hollow in which Bowen's Court stands. Death, for whose coming we waited at every moment, seemed then almost visible to the eye. Henry lay in the Blue Room, the room at the head of the stairs in which his mother had nursed his smallpox when he was young. I used to sit with him: I was sewing some gold stuff — when the sun came in and caught it, it caught his eye. " That's pretty, what is it? " he said to me once or twice. But then his stream of anxious, tormented, lonely and self-upraiding talk, that had checked for only a moment, would go on. The nurse was better with him: " Nonsense, Mr. Bowen," she used to say — as one person of reason to another. Quite often, after that he would go to sleep. One afternoon, about five o'clock, his talk weakened out; his look of trouble dissipated a little, and some minutes after that he died. When he was dead, I went upstairs to the Long Room, where I walked up and down. The day now seemed endless, outside time. Like all the Bowens whose dates are known, I had inherited before I was thirty-one.

The day of his funeral was as fine as all the other days of that week: in fact, it seemed to blaze even more brightly. The steps glared, and the glare struck into the hall where the coffin stood, awaiting the bearers, among tulips and peonies from the garden. Then we, with Henry VI, moved out on to the steps, and David Barry asked me to give the sign. A great sea of people, so many hundreds of people that it looked like a dream, people from all over the country, from the most remote mountainy places, stood on the gravel and on the lower avenue, their eyes fixed on the house. When I gave the sign and the coffin went down the steps, the sea moved, at first in silence, ahead of, around, behind us. Henry VI was to be carried all the way to the church: the coffin soon left the original bearers' shoulders for other shoulders, then other shoulders again. I saw it move ahead of me, like a boat, in those perpetual transits that were made without a jolt or a jar. The crowd would just part, to let my husband and me keep our places close to my father, then it came round us, with friendly closeness, again. The people, now naturally talking, because in Ireland death makes no false or inhuman hush, swept over the grass alongside the avenue, pressing down almost to the verge of the woods. When we came to the churchyard, the service was read there, so that the friends who were Catholics should not be left waiting outside the doors — an inhospitality that would have been Henry VI's first. He was buried not in the vault but in a piece of ground that had been consecrated only a little before: the wall backs on one of his own screens.

AFTERWORD

So, Henry VI died, and I as his only child inherited Bowen's Court. I was the first woman heir; already I had changed my father's name for my husband's. We had no children.

We continued, onward from 1930, to live for the greater part of the time in England, where Alan Cameron worked and we had a home—first at the edge of Oxford and then in London. Not until 1952 was there any question (that was to say, any possibility) of our taking up a continuous life at Bowen's Court. Nonetheless, since the place had become mine it became familiar to me at every time of year: hitherto, I had known it in summer only. Till 1939, when the war came, I was in the way of crossing the sea to Bowen's Court, known to be waiting there. When Alan could he came with me; sometimes I went alone. Existence there, though in fact it was discontinuous, did not seem so: each time one came back, it was as though one had not been away. I was surprised, I remember, when one of our visitors from England spoke of Bowen's Court (commendingly) as "a holiday house." It was never that. It was, however, designed for people, and there were many there.

World War II, while it lasted, put a stop to our coming-and-going. After 1945, that began again. Friends from England and America, as well as from other parts of Ireland, came to stay with us. And, as a family house, Bowen's Court was made happy by the presence of our relations, members of Alan's family and of mine. It became part of the memories of many children. August and September were the most sociable months, but in spring and early summer, and sometimes also around Christmas, there were people in most of the rooms too.

In anything like summer, we used to sit out on the steps in the sun, walk in the demesne or the country round, drive to Bridgetown to swim in the Blackwater or to Youghal to swim in the sea. In wet weather we played deck tennis or french cricket up in the Long Room. In the evenings we played *vingt-et-un* at Henry IV's card tables in the library, or paper games in the half-ring of chairs round the fire. Superficially, my way of living at Bowen's Court, either alone or in company, could not have been more unlike, in idea and manner, that of my grandfather Robert. It was less reflective and diligent than Henry V's, less racy than Henry IV's, less ample than Henry III's. But the house stamped its character on all ways of living: the same fundamental ran through them all.

One year I stayed on at Bowen's Court through the late autumn: for the first time I saw the last of the leaves hang glistening, here and there, in the transparent woods or flittering on the slopes of the avenues. The rooks subsided after their harvest flights; in the gale season one or two gulls, blown inland, circled over the lawns. I heard the woods roaring, and, like pistol shots, the cracking of boughs. For years the house had been empty at this season.

At Christmas itself—and there were many Christmases— I remember no storms. All winds dropped then: a miraculous quiet rose from the land. When we came back from walking, at an hour when it would have been dark in England, the white mid-winter twilight was still reflected in the many windows. We had a cycle of mild Christmases—the moss up the trees was emerald, the hollies and laurels sticky with light; lambs had been born already; sun-pink mountains glowed behind the demesne. On one such Christmas morning we were able to sit on the steps, waiting for aunts and uncles, remaining children of Robert, to come to dinner. Only for Christmas dinner, eaten at midday, did I re-open my grandfather's dining-room.

Christmases, later, became colder: for one we had a thin fall of snow. Or, the lawns were tufted and crisp with hoar-frost; the sun rose tawny, the moon curdled through low-lying, frosty mists. That change of temperature was no more than a return to the rule of the past—when, I am told, Bowen's Court Christmases always were very cold. It had been a mistake to think that my own rule was to see in a new era of weather.

At that season, the family house made felt the authority of its long tradition. It also embraced those of the country round. Every Christmas Eve I lit the Christmas candle, gift of a neighbour in Farahy. Very tall and thick, of green, pink or yellow wax, the candle was planned to burn until Twelfth Night. Wreathed at its base with holly, on to whose berries the wax dropped, it stood on a folded card-table at the north end of the library—here was once Eliza Wade's room. In the cottages of Farahy and Kildorrery the fellows of that candle were alight. Here, the room was so high that any light faded before it reached the ceiling. In the silence you heard the sound of the fire; the underneath of Robert's white marble mantelpiece and its two supporting pillars were flushed. When the library shutters had been shut for the night and the dark heavy curtains drawn over them, mist, starlight or a cloud-thickened darkness lay forgotten outside the chilling panes. In the shadow cast up by the mantelpiece stood vases of holly, and Christmas cards. Footsteps of people taking the shortcut through the demesne were heard, now and then, under the windows.

Outside that room, the house. Darkness succeeded daylight in the naked windows of the staircase and lobby: we burned no lights here. The shaft of the staircase was faintly warmed by vibrations up from the hall stove. Under the portrait of Henry IV the stove sent out through its mica a square dull glow—thanks to its presence, the hall portraits were now no longer filmed over by winter damp; they were now only dimmed by their own age. In the deserted drawingroom, which in my grandmother's day used to be the focus of Christmas, the black iron bars across the shutters revealed themselves to any momentary light: that same light travelled into the deep of mirrors framing perspectives of empty room. Yes, life had shifted—but not lost intensity.

The empty parts of the house, piled up in the winter darkness, palpably and powerfully existed. I was not conscious of the lives of the dead there. It may be that, like so many writers, I have not much imagination to spare. But the unconsciousness—the unknowingness, the passivity—in which so much of those finished lives had been passed did somehow reach and enter my own. What runs on most through a family living in one place is a continuous, semi-physical dream. Above this dream-level successive lives show their tips, their little conscious formations of will and thought. With the end of each generation, the lives that submerged here were absorbed again. With each death, the air of the place had thickened: it had been added to. The dead do not need to visit Bowen's Court rooms—as I said, we had no ghosts in that house—because they already permeated them. Their extinct senses were present in lights and forms. The land outside Bowen's Court windows left prints on my ancestors' eyes that looked out: perhaps their eyes left, also, prints on the scene? If so, those prints were part of the scene to me.

I accepted the ignorance, set up by time and death, that divided my ancestors' conscious lives from mine. In the writing of this book, sheer information would not have taken me

very much of the way—only a little displaced by my re-
searches, the greater part of that ignorance still remains: it is
natural. So, I have made the frame of this family history from
hearsay and some certain retrieved facts. Inside this frame, I
have written about the Bowens out of what I do know but
do not know why I know. Intuitions that I cannot challenge
have moved me to colour their outlines in.

Though I have stressed, in writing about the Bowens, the
recurrent factor of the family will, it is the involuntary, or
spontaneous, aspect of their behaviour that interests me most.
Having looked back at them steadily, I begin to notice, if I
cannot define, the pattern they unconsciously went to make.
And I can see that that pattern has its relation to the outside
more definite pattern of history.

The Bowens' relation to history was an unconscious one. I
can only suggest a compulsion they did not know of by a
series of breaks, contrasts and juxtapositions—in short, by
interleaving the family story with passages from the history
of Ireland. My family, though notably "unhistoric," had their
part in a drama outside themselves. Their assertions, their
compliances, their refusals as men and women went, year by
year, generation by generation, to give history direction, as
well as colour and stuff. Each of the family, in their different
manners, were more than their time's products; they were its
agents.

I may seem to have made use of history to illustrate the
Bowens rather than the Bowens to illustrate history. Inevitably, I have stressed such outside events as may make the
Bowen story, since the coming to Ireland, more comprehensi-
ble and significant. But I have tried not to wrest from their
larger contexts events relevant to the moral plan of this book.

In my re-writing of history, a considerable naivety may appear. In the course of my reading for *Bowen's Court*, I have
learnt a good deal that I did not know. I am, evidently, not a
historian, and it seemed to me more honest to leave my re-

actions to history their first freshness, rather than to attempt
to evaluate. Conclusions have been suggested rather than
drawn. I cannot tell to how many of my readers the past—this
particular past of Anglo-Ireland—will be as new as much of
it was to me, or to how many it is familiar already. My tran-
scripts of history have, at least, been drawn from source beyond reproach: I have relied upon no authority who did not
place fact above passion or interest. The stretches of the past I
have had to cover have been, on the whole, painful: my family
got their position and drew their power from a situation that
shows an inherent wrong. In the grip of that situation, England and Ireland each turned to the other a closed, harsh, distorted face—a face that, in each case, their lovers would
hardly know. With the Treaty, with which I virtually close
my book, a new hopeful phase started: I believe in its
promise. But we cannot afford to have ghosts on this clearing
scene. I wish not to drag up the past but to help lay it. A past
that Ireland still too much dwells on is still by England not
enough recognized. But also, acts of good will, and good intentions that did or did not miscarry, have not been allowed
by Ireland to stand to the English score. . . . For my part, it
has been necessary for me to embed my family story in at
least some account of the growth of "the Protestant nation,"
and of the events that marked stages or declines in this growth.
I have done my best to make the account fair.

I began to write *Bowen's Court* in the early summer of
1939. The first two chapters were, thus, completed before the
outbreak of World War II. When, for instance, I wrote about
ruins in County Cork there were as yet few ruins in England
other than those preserved in fences and lawns. I do not know
how much, after that September of 1939, the colour of my
narration may have altered. The values with which I set out
—my own values—did, at least to my own feeling, remain
constant: they were accentuated rather than changed by war.

The war-time urgency of the present, its relentless daily challenge, seemed to communicate itself to one's view of the past, until, to the most private act or decision, there attached one's sense of its part in some campaign. Those days, either everything mattered or nothing mattered. The past—private just as much as historic—seemed to me, therefore, to matter more than ever: it acquired meaning; it lost false mystery. In the savage and austere light of a burning world, details leaped out with significance. Nothing that ever happened, nothing that was ever even willed, planned or envisaged, could seem irrelevant. War is not an accident: it is an outcome. One cannot look back too far to ask, of what?

Inevitably, the ideas and emotions that were present in my initial plan of this book were challenged and sharpened by the succeeding war years in which the writing went on. I was writing (as though it were everlasting) about a home during a time when all homes were threatened and hundreds of thousands of them were being wiped out. I was taking the attachment of people to places as being generic to human life, at a time when the attachment was to be dreaded as a possible source of too much pain. During a time when individual destinies, the hopes and fears of the living, had to count for so little, I pursued through what might seem their tenuousness and their futility the hopes and fears of the long-ago dead. I was writing about self-centred people while all faces looked outward upon the world. But all that—that disparity or contrast between the time I was writing in and my subject—only so acted upon my subject as to make it, for me, the more important. I tried to make it *my* means to approach truth.

Possibly, the judgements of war-time affected my view of my family? These unhistoric figures are made historic by the fact that, as I show, they once lived. So, I examine them as we now re-examine historic figures. I have stressed as dominant in the Bowens factors I saw as dominant in the world I wrote in —for instance, subjection to fantasy and infatuation with the idea of power. While I was studying fantasy in the Bowens, we saw how it had impassioned race after race. Fantasy is toxic: the private cruelty and the world war both have their start in the heated brain. Showing fantasy, in one form or another, do its unhappy work in the lives of my ancestors, I was conscious at almost every moment of nightmarish big analogies everywhere. Also, the idea of the idea of power governed my analysis of the Bowens and of the means *they* took—these being, in some cases, emotional—to enforce themselves on their world. I showed, if only in the family sphere, people's conflicting wishes for domination. That few Bowens looked beyond Bowen's Court makes the place a fair microcosm, a representative if miniature theatre. Sketching in the society of which the Bowens were part, and the operations behind that society, I extended the conflict by one ring more: again, its isolation, what might be called its outlandishness, makes Anglo-Irish society microcosmic. For these people—my family and their associates—the idea of power was mostly vested in property (property having been acquired by use or misuse of power in the first place). One may say that while property lasted the dangerous power-idea stayed, like a sword in its scabbard, fairly safely at rest. At least, property gave my people and people like them the means to exercise power in a direct, concrete and therefore limited way. I have shown how their natures shifted direction—or the nature of the *débordement* that occurred—when property could no longer be guaranteed. Without putting up any plea for property— unnecessary, for it is unlikely to be abolished—I submit that the power-loving temperament is more dangerous when it either prefers or is forced to operate in what is materially a void. We have everything to dread from the dispossessed. In the area of ideas we see more menacing dominations than the landlord exercised over land. The outsize will is not necessarily an evil: it is a phenomenon. It must have its outsize outlet, its big task. If the right scope is not offered it, it must seize the wrong. We should be able to harness this driving force. Not the will itself but its wastefulness is the dangerous thing.

Yes, the preoccupations of war-time may have caused me to see Bowens in a peculiar or too much intensified light. Some of their characteristics, here, may be overdrawn. They were in most ways, I take it, fairly ordinary Anglo-Irish country gentry. I have done my best to come at, then to transmit to paper, a detached picture of them. In the main, I do not feel that they require defence—you, on the other hand, may consider them indefensible. Having obtained their position through an injustice, they enjoyed that position through privilege. But, while they wasted no breath in deprecating an injustice it would not have been to their interest to set right, they did not abuse their privilege—on the whole. They honoured, if they did not justify, their own class, its traditions, its rule of life. If they formed a too-grand idea of themselves, they did at least exert themselves to live up to this: even vanity involves one kind of discipline. If their difficulties were of their own making, they combatted these with an energy I must praise. They found no facile solutions; they were not guilty of cant. Isolation, egotism and, on the whole, lack of culture made in them for an independence one has to notice because it becomes, in these days, rare. Independence was the first quality of a class now, I am told, becoming extinct. I recognize that a class, like a breed of animals, *is* due to lapse or become extinct should it fail to adapt itself to changing conditions—climate alters, the feeding-grounds disappear. The gentry, as a class, may or may not prove able to make adaptations; that is one of the many things we must wait to see. To my mind, they are tougher than they appear. To live as though living gave them no trouble has been the first imperative of their make-up: to do this has taken a virtuosity into which courage enters more than has been allowed. In the last issue, they have lived at their own expense.

Bowen's Court, in that December of 1941 in which this

book was finished, still stood in its particular island of quiet-
ness, in the south of an island country not at war. Only the
wireless in the library conducted the world's urgency to the
place. Wave after wave of war news broke upon the quiet air
of the room and, in the daytime when the windows were open,
passed out on to the sunny or overcast lawns. Here was a
negative calm—or at least, the absence of any immediate
physical threat. Yet, at the body of this house threats did
strike—and in a sense they were never gone from the air. The
air here had absorbed, in its very stillness, apprehensions general to mankind. It was always with some qualification—most
often with that of an almost undue joy—that one beheld, at
Bowen's Court, the picture of peace. Looking, for instance,
across the country from the steps in the evening, one thought:
"*Can* pain and danger exist?" But one did think that. Why?
The scene was a crystal in which, while one was looking, a
shadow formed.

Yes, there was the picture of peace—in the house, in the
country round. Like all pictures, it did not quite correspond
with any reality. Or, you might have called the country a
magic mirror, reflecting something that could not really exist.
That illusion—peace at its most ecstatic—I held to, to sustain
me throughout war. I suppose that everyone, fighting or just
enduring, carried within him one private image, one peaceful
scene. Mine was Bowen's Court. War made me that image
out of a house built of anxious history.

And so great and calming was the authority of the light and
quiet round Bowen's Court that it survived war-time. And it
did more than that, it survived the house. It remains with me
now that the house has gone.

The house, having played its part, has come to an end. It
will not, after all, celebrate its two hundredth birthday—of
that, it has fallen short by some thirteen years. The shallow
hollow of land, under the mountains, on which Bowen's Court

stood is again empty. Not one hewn stone left on another on the fresh-growing grass. Green covers all traces of the foundations. Today, so far as the eye can see, there might never have been a house there.

One cannot say that the space is empty. More, it is as it was —with no house there. How did this come to be?

It was not foreseen. Early in 1952, upon my husband's retirement from work, he and I left London, to live at Bowen's Court. This was the life we had always promised ourselves. We brought back with us furniture which, originally Bowen's Court's, had been absent long—first in Dublin, afterwards in England: travelled tables and chairs were reunited with those which had never known anything but County Cork. The house, after its many stretches of patient emptiness, of returns only to be followed by departures, looked like, now, entering upon a new phase of habitation—full and continuous habitation, such as it had been built for. It made us welcome. This homecoming was like no holiday visit. In spite of the cold of a bitter January, all promised well. We had the spring of that year, and the early summer. But then one night, that August, Alan Cameron died in his sleep.

I, remaining at Bowen's Court, tried to carry on the place, and the life which went with it there, alone. Already I could envisage no other home. I should, I thought, be able to maintain the place somehow. Had not others done so before me? But I was unable to.

For seven years I tried to do what was impossible. I was loth to realise how impossible it was. Costs rose: I had not enough money, and I had to face the fact that there never would be enough. Anxiety, the more deep for being repressed, increasingly slowed down my power to write, and it was upon my earnings, and those only, that Bowen's Court had by now come to depend. (Does not the economic back-history of the Bowens, as shown in this book, the quarrels, the lost law-suits, the father-and-son conflicts, the spasms of *folie de grandeur*, account for that?) Matters reached a crisis. By 1959 it had become inevitable that I should sell Bowen's Court.

The buyer was a County Cork man, a neighbour. He already was farming tracts of land, and had the means wherewith to develop mine, and horses to put in the stables. It cheered me also to think that his handsome children would soon be running about the rooms—for it was, I believe, his honest intention, when first he bought the place from me, to inhabit the house. But in the end he did not find that practicable, and who is to blame him? He thought at one time, I understand, of compromising by taking off the top storey (I am glad he did not). Finally, he decided that there was nothing for it but to demolish the house entirely. So that was done.

It was a clean end. Bowen's Court never lived to be a ruin.

Loss has not been entire. When I think of Bowen's Court, there it is. And when others who knew it think of it, there it is, also. You will understand that I am more than ever glad that I wrote this book, and that I am grateful to Alfred and Blanche Knopf, who, having inspired the book in the first place, now are bringing it back into print again. Knowing, as you now do, that the house is no longer there, you may wonder why I have left my opening chapter, the room-to-room description of Bowen's Court, in the present tense. I can only say that *I* saw no reason to transpose it into the past. There is a sort of perpetuity about livingness, and it is part of the character of Bowen's Court to be, in sometimes its silent way, very much alive.

Old Headington, Oxford, 1963

BOWENS' FAMILY TREE

SIMPLIFIED FAMILY TREE OF THE BOWENS FROM THE TIME OF THEIR COMING TO IRELAND

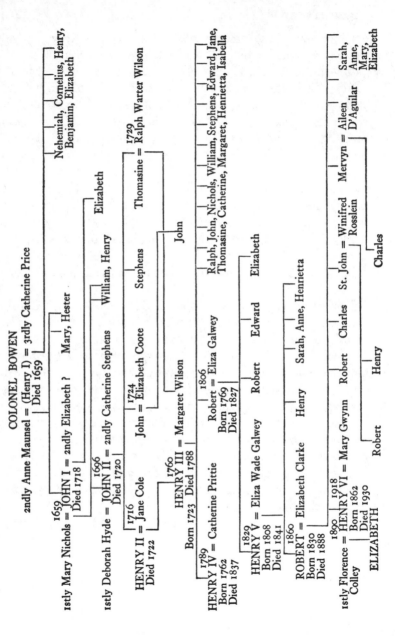